Pueblo's Finest

and Pueblo's Bloody Worst

John P. Ercul

Published by Pueblo County Historical Society
203 West B Street, Pueblo, Colorado 81003

Printed in the United States of America

Contents

Foreword...i

Acknowledgments v

About the Author..ix

Introduction..xi

Chapter 1: Wild West Days... 1

Chapter 2: Growth & Scandals 17

Chapter 3: Motorization & The Flood 47

Chapter 4: The Black Hand 71

Chapter 5: Lynching 91

Chapter 6: Chief Grady..111

Chapter 7: Axe Murders 127

Chapter 8: Trials & Speculation 153

Chapter 9: The Cistern 171

Chapter 10: Grady's Final Years................................... 185

Chapter 11: The Harper Years 205

Chapter 12: More Crimes of the '60s and A New Chief 235

Chapter 13: The Burglary Scandal...............................257

Chapter 14: The Willoughby Years...............................281

Chapter 15: The Transition... 303

Chapter 16: The Silva Years..325

Chapter 17: The Archuleta Years.................................. 361

Chapter 18: The Billings Era 375

Chapter 19: Recent Years 411

FOREWORD

By James W. Billings, Jr.
Pueblo Police Chief 1998 - 2011

Policing is one of the most exciting careers in the world and every police department can boast of interesting events and a history that could fill a book. However, many of those intriguing stories are lost with the passage of time as those who lived and experienced the myriads of unique and momentous events have, themselves, passed on with little or no documentation of what happened in days gone by.

John P. Ercul, who served as deputy police chief, the second in command of the department for over 20 years, and who retired in 2011, has done a remarkable job of capturing the exciting history and true flavor of the memorable events of the Pueblo, Colorado, Police Department from the agency's inception in the late 1800s to modern times.

John served as a dedicated member of the force for over 41 years, beginning at age 22, and advancing rapidly through the ranks under eight police chiefs, and serving as commander for two other officers who became chiefs after his retirement. He is a graduate of the prestigious FBI National Academy and the FBI Law Specialist School, both in Quantico, Virginia, and several other renowned law enforcement training schools worldwide. His talents and accomplishments are truly remarkable. He is the most qualified person I know who could take on this endeavor of capturing and telling the history of our hometown police department. He has given us a rich and insightful understanding of the people and events that shaped the department throughout the years, as well as many true accounts of some of the most egregious and disturbing crimes that ever shocked the consciousness of local citizens.

At some point in his career, John Ercul worked in every division of the Pueblo Police Department (PPD). He excelled in every position and left his mark wherever he served. Among his many different assignments was being named the agency's first press officer (public information officer) by Chief Bud Willoughby during a time of tremendous change for the department. Later, John wrote the Emergency Dispatch Procedural Manual and co-authored a new department manual in the 1980s. He created and designed numerous police yearbooks throughout his career, beginning with the first ever for Pueblo in 1986; highlighting the men and women of the department along with recounting significant historical events which, in retrospect, was a precursor to this book.

He designed the new shield and shoulder patches which are proudly worn on the officers' uniforms to this day. He also designed police vehicle markings for the cruisers and special purpose vehicles unique to the PPD, and he created, scripted and coordinated the annual Police Awards Banquet every year for more than a decade. His model for that distinguished event is still being used today.

It is noteworthy that John has served as a homicide detective, the commander of the department's SWAT Team and the deputy chief in charge of narcotics, vice and special investigations. He was the department's lead officer for VIP protection details for several U.S. presidents, presidential candidates and other important visitors to Pueblo. In retirement, he continues to make fascinating presentations about major crimes and historic police personnel and incidents to community groups in and around Pueblo and southeastern Colorado. And he has served for many years on the board of directors of the Pueblo County Historical Society, including three terms as president of that organization.

John has earned the titles of army veteran, artist, illustrator, author, actor, playwright, director, animal lover, organizer, tactician, strategist, lecturer and historian. There are stories to tell behind each of those titles, but the title he most highly deserves is that of "mentor." He has mentored more officers than anyone I know of in the history of the department, and he continues to do so to the present, 12 years after retiring from the PPD.

Early in my career, John became my mentor, and he has continued to be my mentor and my friend. He helped me and many others aspire to achieve a level of success we otherwise could not have accomplished without his guidance and support. He knows more about the Pueblo Police Department and its history through personal research, relationships and recollections from his own experience than anyone I know.

I am honored and humbled to have been included in this book that covers so much history, including the story of my grandfather's time as a Pueblo police officer from 1926 until 1947 when he was shot in the back while walking the beat. I am familiar with some of the stories which John has written, but I could never have told them as accurately, completely or as interestingly as John has done. This book is a treasure for anyone who loves history, policing, or true crime stories, or who just enjoys curling up with an outstanding, fun, fascinating, and at times, spine-tingling book!

James W. Billings, Jr.
Pueblo, Colorado,
October 2023

ACKNOWLEDGMENTS

It's hard to know where to begin—I received so much help in this endeavor from so many people that I know I will miss someone who is truly deserving of being recognized. I suppose the first I should mention is my fantastic editor, Tom Perkins. Without his constant prodding and ever diligent oversight of my written work I'm not sure this book could have ever been completed. Tom is a true professional. How he managed to stay focused on my efforts while simultaneously editing the *Pueblo Lore*, the monthly historical magazine of the Pueblo County Historical Society, and other society publications, I will never know. Tom, you are the best.

Similarly, I was fortunate enough to have been afforded the very best team of proofreaders I could have imagined. All accomplished historians, they sought out every error in my work, every misplaced comma, every misspelled word and every assertion of fact they believed needed shoring up with additional research. Their tenacity slowed me down at times, but their collective efforts ensured this book emerged as historically accurate and free of inevitable errors as possible. Those who served as proofreaders included Judy McGinnis, Peggy Willcox, Jack Ward, Marilyn Rhoades, Larry Green, Patricia Crump, Garrett Jett, Jerry Miller and Peg Walker. I think a few others may have been handed a few pages for their comments concerning their specific areas of knowledge and expertise, and for that, and for every other member of the Pueblo County Historical Society who offered critical input, I thank you.

Pueblo's Finest and Pueblo's Bloody Worst

I would be remiss if I didn't mention my friend, the late Chuck Green. Chuck took me under his wing when I began writing for the *Pueblo Lore*. As a former editor of the *Denver Post*, and a renowned columnist whose writings for that newspaper and others received national attention for over three decades, Chuck became my writing mentor and my friend. Without his early tutelage and encouragement, I don't think I could have taken on the task of writing this book.

I must also acknowledge my many friends whom I frequently corralled and forced to listen as I read excerpts of this book to them, which allowed me the opportunity to read aloud my own work to see if it made sense and sounded good to me, and to get their feedback. I did get several suggestions from those friends that became incorporated in my work. They also gave me the support and encouragement I needed to keep pressing on.

Those friends include my wonderful lady friend Helen Kneib and my buddies Joe Gregorich, Catie Gregorich, Mike and Josh Ragulsky, Kurt Thalhamer, Jacqui Thalhamer, Ryan Massmann, former Pueblo Police Chief Ruben Archuleta, retired Assistant Chief Sam Vecchiarelli of the Lakeside, Colorado, Police Department, Denver police detective and author Daril Cinquanta (who went through the process of writing his own exciting book, *The Blue Chameleon*, about his years on the Denver Police Department), retired Pueblo Police Chief Robert O. Silva for his recollections about many of the stories from the 1960s through the 1980s and retired Chief Jim Billings who graciously provided the very complimentary and humbling foreword for this book. Thank you all for standing with me and lending me your unconditional friendship and support.

Thanks to the Edward Broadhead Library—the library of the Pueblo County Historical Society with its massive photo collection—the Pueblo Library District, retired Pueblo police historian Deputy Chief Ron Gravatt and current Pueblo police historian Peg Powell who both shared research, stories and photos with me.

And a special thanks to the men and women of the Pueblo Police Department, past and present, many of whom provided me their own take on crimes they investigated, including people, places and situations they encountered during their careers, and for suggestions they felt should be included in this book. I thank you all from the bottom of my heart.

John P. Ercul
October 2023

For Ike

ABOUT THE AUTHOR

John and Ike

John P. Ercul, a three-term past president of the Pueblo County Historical Society, retired as Deputy Chief of the Pueblo Police Department in 2011. During his almost 42-year law enforcement career, John served in virtually every capacity with the department. He has a degree in English and Mass Communications from Southern Colorado State College (now Colorado State University Pueblo) and is a graduate of the FBI National Academy, the FBI Law Specialist School and the DEA Drug Unit Commanders Academy in Quantico, Virginia. He also attended the University of Colorado Law Enforcement Executive Program and the Trinity University Drug Training and Resource Center in Texas.

He has had extensive training in police tactics—he served as commander of Pueblo's SWAT Team for over 21 years. John was also a military police investigator during his short career in the U.S. Army at Fort Carson. He is past president of the Pueblo Zoological Society doing business as the Pueblo Zoo, past vice president of PAWS for Life, the Pueblo Animal Welfare Society—Pueblo's only no-kill animal shelter—and has served on the board of directors of the Bessemer Historical Society, the Pueblo Family YMCA, the Pueblo Child Advocacy Center, the PCC Vocational Advisory Board, The Southeastern Colorado Heritage Center and Pueblo Heritage Museum, the Impossible Players Community Theater and the Damon Runyon Repertory Theater Company, for which he wrote and directed a play—*The Viper Strikes Quickly*, which is an audience participation murder mystery.

He is also a current member and two-term past president of the Pueblo Optimist Club and a current board member of the Pueblo County Historical Society and a writer for the society's *Pueblo Lore* monthly magazine. He continues to live in Pueblo, Colorado, with his beloved dog Ike, to whom this book is dedicated.

INTRODUCTION

The City of Pueblo is not much different from any American City. It boasts the amenities of other cities its size; an outstanding arts center, museums, very fine though small zoo, numerous parks and recreational opportunities, an excellent library and lots of good food.

The city's signature dish is the Pueblo Slopper; an open-faced hamburger with anywhere from two to nine burger patties topped with Pueblo's spicy red chile or even spicier green chile. Pueblo green chile is generally made with Pueblo peppers grown in the fields east of the city and featured at the annual Chile and Frijole Festival in the downtown area. That festival is attended by thousands of hungry people from throughout the state and beyond, anxious to purchase bushels of the hot and tasty delights.

The Colorado State Fair, Lake Pueblo State Park, the Pueblo Riverwalk and the Center for American Values also bring tourists to the city. The Center for American Values highlights the recipients of the Medal of Honor—the country's highest award for heroism. Four Medal of Honor recipients came from Pueblo.

There are many good things about Pueblo. Unfortunately, there is also crime, gang activity and a history of corruption dating back to the turn of the last century. If one only looks at statistics, they would be led to believe that Pueblo is unsafe, being overrun by violent and predatory criminals.

The fact is the criminal activity is generally confined to three small areas of the city. Most Puebloans know where those areas are, and they avoid them. The rest of the city is statistically as safe as any city Pueblo's size.

Pueblo has a very fine and proud police department, though from time to time in its history it did experience some corruption and weak upper-level management that allowed that corruption to prosper. However, honest members of the department always overcame corrupt influences and were successful in setting the agency back on a recognized course of excellence.

I served with the Pueblo Police Department from January 4, 1970, until June 30, 2011, when I retired. I lived through the corruption of the early 1970s, which began in the mid-1960s. I saw firsthand what can happen when a department loses the respect and the confidence of citizens. I can't even count the times I made a traffic stop and the driver would make an angry comment about corrupt or crooked cops.

I was too young, too new, too inexperienced and too naive to realize what was going on before my very eyes. I was therefore shocked when the corrupt officers, one of whom was my first training officer, began to fall. But I was very proud of those who worked diligently to root out the corruption and restore what had been a good department reputation. Men like Bob Silva, Bill Hurley, Bob Simon, John Koncilja, Edson Lutes and Ben Crossno became my heroes and my role models. Bob Silva and Bob Simon eventually would become police chiefs and good friends of mine. Though Bob Simon and the others have since passed, I still have coffee with Bob Silva a couple of mornings a week. Out of respect I still call him "Chief."

As I weaved my way through over 40 years of service, I learned so much about the history of the department. Much of it through the spoken lore of older officers who lived and worked through the "old days." I was fascinated by some of the stories about former officers, previous incidents and infamous local crimes. I began taking notes about some of the stories because I enjoyed driving by and looking at the scenes of what remained of those locations about which I had heard.

In 2019 I was asked by members of the Pueblo County Historical Society if I could write a magazine article about the history of the department. I said "No–there's too much history to crowd into a magazine article; even a long one." It was then suggested I could write a series of articles. After demurring for a few months, I finally agreed to pen several articles which would run in the society's historical magazine, the *Pueblo Lore*. I had no idea how many articles it would take to cover the almost 150 years of department history, but I set out to give my writing assignment a try.

I started where most historians begin—doing research. I knew the department was formed in the "cowboy" days, but I had no idea how many of the legends of the Old West I would encounter in that research. I learned of men like Bat Masterson, Wyatt Earp, Doc Holliday, wars, gun fights and murders of early town marshals—the precursors of our modern police officers. I was intrigued and fascinated by what I found.

As I continued, I discovered more about early lynchings, tragic accidents that led to the deaths of police officers and how those accidents were the result of a lack of training we would today consider routine. And I learned about investigative techniques that would today be forbidden by policy, if not illegal.

I also discovered that there existed in the early days of the last century, an element of organized crime in Pueblo that was directly connected to criminal enterprises active in New York and Chicago. Shotgun and machine-gun slayings on the streets of Pueblo were not unusual up through the 1930s, and names like Al Capone, Salvatore Maranzano, and in later years, the Smaldone family all figured prominently in Pueblo's crime history.

Pueblo has also been mentioned in the history of well-known gangsters John Dillinger and Bonnie and Clyde. Bank robber and killer Charlie "Pretty Boy" Floyd was actually jailed in Pueblo in 1929 before he was elevated by J. Edgar Hoover to the dubious position of Public Enemy Number One. His photograph, taken in the Pueblo city jail, led to his being identified, tracked down and killed by federal agents and local police in an Ohio cornfield in 1934.

And in later years, I found many gruesome and terrifying murders, many of which I had heard about, but of which I did not know the details. As my research moved forward, I finally realized what a monumental task I had undertaken. There were so many crimes I had to pick and choose from for inclusion in this book.

As my writing drew to a close, I found it might be advantageous for my readers if I would include a chronological listing of Pueblo's police chiefs and FBI Academy graduates as I frequently referred to them in the text. I also have included a list of Pueblo heroes: the officers who have given their lives in the line of duty.

The chiefs are as follows:

Police Chief	Dates Served
H. P. Wooten	May 1886 – 1887
W. H. Haskel	April 1887 – 1888
Andrew Royal	1888 – 1890
Andy Groom	1890 – 1893
Samuel A. Abbey	1893 – April 1894
Joseph Loor	April 1894 – 1897
Robert Griffin	1897 – 1900

W. F. McCafferty . . . . 1900 – 1902

H. M. Schoup . . . . 1902 – 1904

W. F. McCafferty (2nd administration) . . . . . . 1904 – 1910

Cornelius Sullivan . . . . 1910 – 1911

Charles Yund . . . . 1911 – 1912

Denny McDermott . . . . 1912 – 1913

Joseph M. Daly . . . . 1913 – 1922

Tom Johnson . . . . 1922 – 1922

J. Arthur Grady . . . . 1922 – 1952

(longest serving chief – 30 years)

Roy F. Harper . . . . 1952 – 1967

Robert L. Mayber . . . . 1967 – 1973

Elbert L. "Bud" Willoughby . . . . 1973 – 1977

Robert O. Silva . . . . 1977 – 1992

Robert E. Simon . . . . 1992 – 1992

W. A. "Bill" Young . . . . 1992 – 1995

Ruben E. Archuleta . . . . 1995 – 1999

Ronald A. Gravatt . . . . 1999 – 1999

James W. Billings . . . . 1999 – 2011

Luis Velez . . . . 2011 – 2017

Troy Davenport . . . . 2017 – 2021

Steven "Chris" Noeller . . . . 2021 – present

FBI National Academy Graduates

Graduate	Session and Date	
Roy F. Harper	52nd session	11-20-1953
Jack E. Stiffler	54th session	11-19-1954
William T. Hurley	68th session	11-8-1961
Robert E. Simon	98th session	9-12-1974
Robert O. Silva	102nd session	9-25-1975
John Koncilja, Jr.	107th session	12-16-1976
Ruben E. Archuleta	114th session	9-22-1978
John P. Ercul	127th session	2-11-1981
Ralph L. Smith	138th session	9-14-1984
James W. Billings	151st session	12-18-1987
Eddie C. Rhodes	164th session	3-22-1991
Steven P. Samek	181st session	6-23-1995
Richard T. Lipich.	189th session	6-20-1997
Richard Goddard.	197th session	6-25-1999
Lloyd J. Smart	206th session	9-7-2001
Michael Bennett	214th session	9-5-2003
Andrew McLachlan	224th session	3-6-2006
Troy Davenport.	233rd session	6-9-2008
Jeff Bodmer.	247th session	12-19-2011
Kenny J. Rider	250th session	9-21-2012
Eric A. Bravo	269th session	9-9-2017
James V. Martin	283rd session	7-11-2022

Note: Some department sources list Robert L. Mayber as the first attendee of the National Academy from Pueblo, Attending the 49th session in 1952. His name, however, does not appear on official FBI lists of graduates. Rumor has it that the FBI removed his name from their files due to the corruption scandal of the 1970s. My feeling is that he did attend the academy but was deemed by the FBI to be an embarrassment due to the corruption that occurred during his administration, though he may not have been complicit.

Pueblo Officers Who Died in the Line of Duty

Patrolman Alvin Phippenney – *End of Watch: Monday, June 30, 1879.   Cause: Felonious assault – gunfire.*

Marshal Casper Zweifel – *End of Watch: Friday, July 25, 1884. Cause: Felonious assault – stabbed.*

Police Officer Moses Lovern – *End of Watch: Monday, May 11, 1891.   Cause: Gunfire (accidental).*

Police Officer Silas Marts – *End of Watch: Wednesday, October 7, 1903.   Cause: Felonious assault – gunfire.*

Police Officer Elwin Slater – *End of Watch: Thursday, October 8, 1903.   Cause: Gunfire (accidental).*

Police Officer William Shellman – *End of Watch: Sunday, August 12, 1906.   Cause: Weather related (lightning strike).*

Police Officer Frederick Barner – *End of Watch: Sunday, March 21, 1909.   Cause: Felonious assault – gunfire.*

Detective Sergeant John Dunleavy – *End of Watch: Wednesday., July 21, 1909.   Cause: Felonious assault – gunfire.*

Patrolman Thomas Evans – *End of Watch: Saturday, September 13, 1919.   Cause: Felonious assault – gunfire.*

Patrolman Addison O. Hinsdale – *End of Watch: Monday, October 4, 1920.   Cause: Gunfire (accidental).*

Patrolman Elmer A. Trout – *End of Watch: Monday, September 23, 1935. Cause: Criminal assault – beating.*

Corporal Thomas P. Hansom – *End of Watch: Saturday, December 29, 1973.   Cause: Felonious assault – gunfire.*

Police Officer Nicholas Karl Heine – *End of Watch: Saturday, June 21, 2008.   Cause: Exertion (heart attack).*

So, there you have it. A history of a police department that spans several decades (Pueblo's Finest) and a history of some of the fascinating crimes handled by that department over the years (Pueblo's Bloody Worst). I hope readers enjoy my trek through history and come away with an enhanced appreciation of the challenges faced by American law enforcement, and particularly the Pueblo, Colorado, Police Department.

John P. Ercul
January 2024

WILD WEST DAYS

It was a drama that played out hundreds of times in saloons and "variety halls" in towns throughout the "Wild West." A group of rowdy cowboys, fresh from a grueling roundup of open-range cattle, was letting off steam in a local watering hole when things got out of control. Someone usually died when that happened.

The Pueblo incident occurred on a sweltering Monday afternoon, June 30, 1879, in the notorious Arkansas Hall Saloon at 305 North Santa Fe Avenue. A band of range-weary cowboys were drinking and carousing in the saloon when a few minor skirmishes with some of the locals ensued.

One of those locals was a drunk and quarrelsome farmer named John Baxter, who lived on the Steele Ranch located about ten miles north of Pueblo on Fountain Creek. Baxter, a large man with a reputation for being a troublemaker, was taunting the bartender, calling him names and picking fights with other patrons in the establishment. Word of the disturbance was soon conveyed to town policeman Alvin Phippenney, who was patrolling on foot in the area.

Officer Phippenney quickly went to the saloon and attempted to quell the unrest, which, within a brief time, had grown increasingly violent. According to a *Colorado Weekly Chieftain* article published the following day, Officer Phippenney "clinched" with Baxter, who by that time was waving around a large revolver. The bartender heard one shot fired at that point and several men, including the officer and Baxter, scrambled into the street where four more shots were fired. The two combatants then stumbled back into the tavern where a final shot was heard as the bar crowd pushed its way toward the door to flee the saloon.

As the smoke cleared, Officer Phippenney stumbled forward, fell to his knees, then toppled over to the floor beside the bar. A pistol ball had passed through his back just below his shoulder blade and he was bleeding profusely. Baxter suffered a bullet wound that penetrated his stomach. He cursed loudly as he sank into semi-consciousness and fell to the floor close to the prostrate Phippenney. Obviously in excruciating pain, Baxter began mumbling incoherently as a combination of saliva and blood issued from his mouth.

Doctors Courtright and Owen, whose practices were nearby, were immediately summoned. They worked for several minutes on the injured men, but quickly determined that Phippenney's wound was so severe there was nothing they could do to save him. He died on the dusty saloon floor within 15 minutes.

Police Officer Bilby, a close friend of Phippenney's, also responded to the incident. When he bent down to ask his friend who had shot him, Phippenney replied that Baxter and another man had done the deed. He then gasped, clinched Bilby's hand tightly for just a moment, then released his grip and silently passed away.

Baxter, however, was in a critical state and the doctors also determined there was little they could do for him. He was taken to a drug store across the street from the saloon and then to another building in the area where his condition continued to decline. He was unable to answer questions or make any statements about the incident.

Though there was some talk of organizing a lynching party among the raucous crowd, mostly inebriated men who packed the streets in the area, nothing transpired. The crowd dissipated by nightfall, the bar reopened as though nothing had happened, and Baxter died the following morning.

Three other men who had been identified as having been involved in the fracas were arrested and subjected to intense questioning. No one, however, admitted to involvement in the deadly conflict, nor could anyone say who had fired the fatal shot. Baxter's weapon and others were inspected, and it was determined that the pistol ball that killed the young policeman was too small to have come from Baxter's gun or the others looked at, so the crime went unsolved, and Town Policeman Alvin Phippenney became the first Pueblo police officer (at the time called a deputy town marshal) to be killed in the line of duty.

An unhappy side note to the tragic incident was that Phippenney was due to be married in the late afternoon of the very day he was killed. His fiancée was dressing in preparation for the wedding ceremony when word of his demise was delivered to her. She screamed, then collapsed into the arms of her mother.

The Pueblo Police Department was barely three years old when Alvin Phippenney became a member in 1876. From the time Pueblo was incorporated as a town under Colorado Territorial laws on March 22, 1870, law enforcement duties were managed by a succession of town marshals. A forerunner of a fully staffed police force was created in 1873 when the thriving community became a city of the legally defined second class. The force was further organized into an actual department of city government in April 1880, a few years after territorial laws were abandoned, and Pueblo became a second-class city (a city with a population of more than 10,000 and less than 20,000 people) under the laws of the State of Colorado.

In those days, two other communities or "towns," existed adjacent to the new Town of South Pueblo established in 1873, was a fairly large community beginning at the Arkansas River (site of today's Riverwalk), and extending south over the bluffs to today's Orman Avenue. Central Pueblo established in 1882 was a small community located just north of the current Riverwalk. It stretched just over a block and a half to today's City Center Drive. In 1882, the City of Pueblo extended from that point to what is now Ninth Street. In 1882 Pueblo's city limits were extended beyond 9th street to encompass the 1872 courthouse on 10th Street and the future site of the 1878 Centennial High School on 11th Street. The State Insane Asylum (today's Colorado Mental Health Institute) remained outside the city limits.

Each of those towns had their own governments and their own law enforcement by town marshals, mostly unskilled and unemployed or transient men chosen by local mayors because of their size and perceived toughness.

Royal Gorge Railroad War

Not long before Officer Phippenney struggled to the death with Baxter in the Arkansas Hall Saloon, a separate violent incident was brewing in the railroad yards in South Pueblo. For several weeks, a conflict between two major railroad companies was gaining momentum throughout Colorado. Shootings, some of which were deadly, had occurred in Colorado Springs and in the Cucharas Valley in southern Colorado. The issue that sparked the violence was a question of which of two railroads would have the right-of-way through the Arkansas River canyon, particularly through the steep canyon area we today call the Royal Gorge, where the canyon walls constrict tightly against the river to make rail bed construction difficult.

The Denver & Rio Grande Railroad had laid track through the canyon west of the gorge, then called the Grand Canyon of the Arkansas, and its corporate officers felt they had thus earned the right to the route through the gorge. The Atchison, Topeka & Santa Fe Railroad, however, had moved quickly to begin construction of a line through the gorge, leaving no room for a D&RG track. Both companies were anxious to gain what was shaping up as a very lucrative commercial route between Pueblo and other cities east of the gorge, to the town of Leadville near the Continental Divide where silver had just been discovered.

Community leaders of the two Pueblos (Central Pueblo was not yet in existence) were fearful of what an all-out war would mean for both towns. They were hoping for a compromise that would allow both companies to share tracks through the gorge, but neither company seemed willing to enter into any such agreement. A contract allowing the Santa Fe Company to lease the Denver & Rio Grande access was abruptly canceled by the D&RG corporation and that action increased the anger of Santa Fe management.

The question of which company should prevail had subsequently gone to the U.S. Supreme Court and everyone was awaiting a decision. Neither company, however, was satisfied with waiting for a legal resolution and both were spoiling for a fight. Pueblo, the largest city with railroad interests close to the eastern approach to the gorge, became the center point of imminent armed hostilities.

Acting quickly in anticipation of the "war," the Santa Fe Railroad hired the noted one-time sheriff of Dodge City, Kansas, William Barclay "Bat" Masterson to defend Santa Fe property in Pueblo. That property included the large D&RG

roundhouse that was being leased by the Santa Fe corporation. Through his many law enforcement and political contacts in Kansas, Masterson secured an appointment as a deputy United States marshal, then rounded up a collection of well-known western gunfighters and headed for Pueblo. He set up field operations in the Santa Fe railroad depot in South Pueblo, then fortified the large roundhouse in the town's sprawling rail yard. Working with Masterson was his close friend, the much-feared dentist John H. "Doc" Holliday.

W. B. "Bat" Masterson   *Dr. J. H. "Doc" Holliday*

Holliday was renowned as a fearless gunfighter and close confidant of both Masterson and Dodge City Marshal Wyatt Earp. A trained, educated and apparently very competent dentist, Holliday was generally considered a debonair and sophisticated gentleman—except when he was drinking, or when someone riled him. When that happened, he turned into a quarrelsome and violent "pistoleer" with a quick temper and a reputation for being fast at drawing his weapon and deadly accurate with his shots. Even the toughest of the western tough guys avoided him at all costs.

Holliday and Masterson assembled a troop of about 50 well-known gunslingers which included several occasional lawmen and more frequent outlaws. Mysterious Dave Mather, Dirty Dave Rudabaugh and Big Ben Thompson were three of them. Rudabaugh was an especially feared gunman, train robber and merciless killer who had once been a member of Billy the Kid's gang in New Mexico. He had escaped prosecution for his many crimes by betraying his own companions and testifying against them in court for what some said were the very crimes he himself had committed.

Ben Thompson and Dave Mather both had reputations as gunmen with quick triggers, and both would go on to become frontier lawmen in some of the Old West's roughest towns. One of Thompson's earliest friends was the infamous John Wesley Hardin, known during his lifetime as the cruelest and craziest outlaw in the West due to his murder of an estimated 25 men. Thompson once used Hardin as a pawn in a rather outrageous plot to assassinate Abilene, Kansas, Town Marshal William Butler "Wild Bill" Hickok. When confronted by the cool and self-confident Hickok, Hardin backed down and when ordered to do so, meekly handed over his guns to the marshal. He allegedly then told Thompson, "If you think Wild Bill needs killed—you kill him yourself." Thompson wisely never confronted Hickok, and both men eventually left Abilene. Such was the reputation of the steely-eyed and dangerous Wild Bill Hickok.

Because of the presence of many very well-known and extremely intimidating gunmen assembling in town, local law enforcement personnel from Pueblo and South Pueblo were apprehensive, if not downright fearful of the impending hostilities playing out in their jurisdictions. Some active-duty officers pledged their allegiance to the Santa Fe side, which they felt was legitimized by the leadership of a famous United States marshal. Others sided with the D&RG personnel who were led by Pat Desmond, who had just been named constable of South Pueblo. Pueblo Sheriff Price and other deputies worked alongside Desmond a few years earlier when he served as a Pueblo deputy sheriff, and they admired him. All, however, were extremely nervous about their instructions to remain as neutral as possible and merely enforce the law. They all knew that would be virtually impossible in the face of the superior forces, firepower and steadfast determination of men on both sides.

Pat Desmond was a one-time friend of Bat Masterson who had collaborated with him as a deputy in Dodge City before moving on to Pueblo. He had recently been hired by the founder and co-owner of the Denver & Rio Grande Railroad, William Jackson Palmer, as a private security operative to represent Palmer's interests in the anticipated railroad war. That appointment sealed his allegiance to the Denver and Rio Grande, even though he had been installed as constable of South Pueblo in April 1879. His coinciding positions pitted Desmond against his former friend Bat Masterson.

Desmond knew Pueblo well, and he instructed his stable of "operators," many former or active South Pueblo deputy town marshals and deputy county sheriffs, to march on the Federal Armory in Pueblo and take possession of a cannon stored there. To their surprise, Masterson had already secured the cannon and had it installed at the old Santa Fe depot adjacent to the roundhouse. The cannon was loaded with a form of grapeshot and aimed directly at the D&RG forces. That weapon—if it existed, since I was unable to verify it in early newspaper records—and the cadre of feared gunfighters gave the Santa Fe defenders a slight advantage should a shooting war break out.

Break out it did on the morning of June 12, 1879, when Pueblo County Sheriff Henley Price, along with Constable Desmond and several men, stormed the Santa Fe depot. They forced the doors of the telegraph office, routed the Santa Fe personnel there and retook the cannon. Masterson's men stationed at the depot abandoned the property and fled out the windows at the back of the building as several shots were fired. One of Masterson's men, Harry Jenkins of Dodge City, Kansas, suffered a gunshot wound to the back from which he later died. Another had at least one tooth knocked out. It is unknown if Santa Fe personnel fired any shots as they fled the telegraph office. Cut off from any communication with Santa

Fe management, the fleeing Santa Fe defenders rushed to the nearby roundhouse to fortify it against the sheriff's forces that were hot on their trail.

Sources differ as to what actually happened that day at the roundhouse. Respected railroad historian Larry Green has studied the Rio Grande Railroad War extensively for more than 40 years. He has unearthed strong evidence that Masterson was in Cañon City that fateful day. Bat reportedly left Ben Thompson in charge of Pueblo operations when he rode out toward Cañon City to oversee Santa Fe activities there.

Sheriff Price and Constable Desmond led a force of deputies, all armed with six-shooters, many inebriated and all bolstered by their "victory" at the telegraph office, toward the roundhouse. There they encountered Big Ben Thompson who claimed he was in charge of the Santa Fe defenders. Thompson was arrested by the sheriff's force without a struggle. Those inside the roundhouse were marched out peacefully. No shots were fired during the confrontation, and Sheriff Price ceded possession of the roundhouse to General Palmer's aggressors at that time. The end of the Pueblo roundhouse skirmish, however, would not be the last Pueblo heard from Bat Masterson or Doc Holliday. A famous Arizona gunfight would send both men back to Pueblo.

Gunfight at the OK Corral

A little over a year later in October of 1881, Wyatt Earp, perhaps the West's most famous lawman, left Dodge City to assist his brother Virgil who was the town marshal in the growing but still untamed town of Tombstone, Arizona. Wyatt asked his friend Doc Holliday to join him, and to back him up should he and Virgil have problems with a criminal gang of rustlers, stage robbers and general "bad men" who were running wild through the town. The gang was known throughout the area as "the cowboys" and their leader was believed to be a bully named Ike Clanton.

Clanton and the Earp brothers clashed several times without incident over a period of time, but their conflict came to a violent head on the afternoon of Wednesday, October 26, 1881, when Wyatt Earp, his brothers Virgil and Morgan Earp and Doc Holliday faced off against Ike Clanton, his brother Billy, outlaws Tom and Frank McLaury, their friend Wes Fuller and a reckless 22-year-old gunslinger named Billy Clayborne. The gunfight, which ensued when Billy Clanton drew a pistol, lasted only about 30 seconds, but it went down in history as the legendary "Gunfight at the O.K. Corral," the most famous of the Old West shootouts.

Virgil and Morgan Earp were slightly wounded, and Doc Holliday was grazed by a bullet but suffered only a minor scratch on his hip. Tom and Frank McLaury and Billy Clanton were killed. Ike Clanton, Wes Fuller and Billy Clayborne fled when the shooting started and remained unscathed. Even though Virgil Earp was the duly elected town marshal, and his brothers and Doc Holliday were sworn deputies, Cochise County Sheriff Johnny Behan took the side of the cowboys, a politically inspired decision based on the heavily Democratic affiliation of those in power in the town. When Ike Clanton swore out a murder charge against the Earp brothers and Holliday, Behan told Wyatt he would have to arrest him. Wyatt stared into the sheriff's eyes for a few seconds, then gruffly informed Behan he would not submit to arrest. Behan did not press the matter any further—at least not then.

Meanwhile, Wyatt and Doc stayed close by the side of the fallen Virgil as he recovered from his wounds. Within the week, the strong willed and resilient Virgil Earp sufficiently recovered to resume his duties as town marshal. He then secured an appointment of deputy U.S. marshal for his brother Wyatt who vowed to clear the territory of the criminal cowboys.

A little over two weeks after the O.K. Corral battle, a would-be assassin fired through a hotel window, striking Virgil. He was seriously injured by a slug that permanently disabled his right arm. Then, on March 18, 1882, Morgan Earp was ambushed and killed by an unseen assassin. The murder of Morgan Earp would set into motion a series of events that would take Doc Holliday back to a place he was familiar with— Pueblo, Colorado.

Wyatt was enraged by the attacks on his brothers and with the help of his ever-faithful friend Doc Holliday, organized a vigorous hunt for those remaining "cowboys" he was sure had perpetrated the killing of Morgan and the maiming of Virgil. As a federal marshal, he appointed a posse consisting of his two other brothers, Warren and James Earp and friends Sherman McMaster, Jack Johnson, Charles Smith, Dan Tipton, John Vermillion and Doc Holliday. The posse rode out in what became known as the "Earp Vendetta Ride." Two days later in Tucson, Frank Stillwell, the first of the cowboys they encountered, was chased down and killed by Earp's posse.

When his body was found the next morning, the Tucson Justice of the Peace swore out warrants for Wyatt, Doc and the federal posse men for what he called the "extra-judicial" murder of Stillwell. When word of the active warrants reached Tombstone, Sheriff Johnny Behan attempted to arrest members of the vendetta ride who had returned to Tombstone to freshen up, but they brushed past him, ignoring his attempts and rode out again to rejoin the hunt for the remaining outlaws. Over the next few weeks, posse members found and killed three additional members of the cowboy gang—Curly Bill Brocius, Florentino Cruz and Johnny Barnes.

Sheriff Behan then organized a posse to pursue the Earp vendetta riders. Although they did locate and arrest a few of the vendetta posse men, they never were able to find Wyatt Earp, who, along with Doc Holliday and other vendetta riders, left Arizona Territory. Word was that they headed east to Albuquerque, then split up with Wyatt going to Dodge City and Doc Holliday and Dan Tipton both heading to Pueblo.

Holliday was comfortable in Pueblo and he remained in town for several days, frequenting the taverns and gambling halls in the downtown area and generally relaxing. He had notified local authorities of his presence when he arrived in Pueblo, and informed them of the outside warrant, but insisted the warrant was no good outside Arizona territory. Aware of the O.K. Corral shootings and subsequent vendetta killings, but not wanting a direct conflict with the dangerous and volatile Holliday, Pueblo officers ignored Holliday's presence and did not act to enforce the warrant.

One evening, as he left a variety theater on Union Avenue, he was approached by someone he later described as a "strange little man." The man introduced himself as Perry Mallon and said he wanted to thank Doc for once saving his life in Santa Fe. Holliday responded that he had never been to Santa Fe and had never seen Mallon before. He attempted to brush past Mallon, but the pesky little man persisted, following Holliday and telling him he had recently spoken to Josh Stillwell, brother of Frank Stillwell, and he warned Doc that Josh was out to kill him. He then assumed a threatening manner and told Holliday to say nothing of their encounter or he himself would kill Doc. Mallon then dropped his trousers to show Doc some scars which he claimed were from gunshot wounds. Angered, but considering Mallon to merely be a "nutcase," Doc just laughed, shoved the weird little man aside and continued on his way.

A few days later, Holliday left Pueblo and headed for Denver to attend some widely advertised horse races. On the train en route to Denver he ran into his friend Bat Masterson, who was also headed to the races. He spent the day with Masterson, but that evening, as he approached his hotel, he was accosted by three men. He recognized the smaller of the men as Perry Mallon, the strange man who had confronted him in Pueblo. Mallon pointed two pistols at Holliday and announced, "I have you now, Holliday, throw up your hands." The other two men were Denver deputy sheriffs and they quickly seized the unarmed Holliday and whisked him off to jail. Mallon trailed behind still brandishing his pistols and yelling loudly that Holliday had killed his partner. Once at the jail, Mallon continued to point his weapons at Doc. Doc finally told him, "Oh, you can drop those guns, I am not armed, and no one is trying to get away from you."

Mallon had told the sheriff's officers that a warrant existed for Doc's arrest for murder, and as deputies furiously attempted to confirm the existence and validity of such a warrant, Holliday insisted that his friend Bat Masterson be contacted. Masterson arrived early the next morning in the company of a prominent Denver attorney, and they pressed for a writ of habeas corpus to allow Doc to be released from custody.

A local judge scheduled a hearing on the writ later that week and Doc remained in jail. Realizing that a delay in getting Doc released would work against him and could result in his extradition to Arizona and most likely, his murder, Masterson contacted Marshal Jameson of Pueblo who swore out a warrant against Doc for a larceny connected to a con game a week earlier in Pueblo. The warrant was delivered to Denver authorities that very day.

Masterson knew, probably due to consultations with the attorney, that Colorado law held that warrants issued by Colorado authorities took precedence over out-of-state warrants. After much legal maneuvering over several days, mostly against arguments that an out-of-state warrant for a capital offense should supersede a Colorado warrant for a minor offense, Colorado Governor Pitkin ordered the extradition order from Arizona quashed and directed that Doc Holliday be taken back to Pueblo to answer for the theft charge.

Once back in Pueblo, Holliday, in the company of Bat Masterson, posted a $300 bond for the trumped-up charge of petty larceny and was released from custody. He forfeited his bond by failing to appear and left Pueblo 10 days later a free man. He bounced around several towns between Kansas and Colorado over the next few years, occasionally in the company of his close friend Wyatt Earp, usually supporting himself by gambling.

Suffering from tuberculosis (then called consumption) for many years, Doc Holliday's health began to rapidly decline. He returned to Colorado one last time in 1885. He spent his final two years in gambling halls in Denver, Pueblo, Silverton and Leadville.

While in Leadville he became involved in an argument over his alleged refusal to pay a five-dollar gambling debt. The disagreement led to Doc shooting his adversary in the arm. He was charged with attempted murder and spent several weeks in jail before being acquitted in court. He then left Leadville and returned to Denver where he continued gambling. He was eventually arrested and charged with vagrancy. As gamblers were considered to have no visible means of support, he was briefly jailed, then escorted by officers to the train depot where he was unceremoniously sent back to Leadville.

Doc wintered there through the end of 1886 and early 1887. The tuberculosis was quickly taking its toll on him, and he apparently knew the end was approaching. Always the fighter, Doc sought any and every way to prolong his life. Hearing that the hot mineral baths in Glenwood Springs, Colorado, had curative properties, he caught the Carson stage to Glenwood to see if the hot springs mineral waters there would help alleviate his discomfort. Unfortunately, they didn't, and Doctor John H. Holliday died of consumption there on November 8, 1887. His last words were reported to have been "This is funny," likely referring to his long-time belief that he would die with his boots on in a gun battle, not wasting away in his bare feet in a bed.

Doc's friend Bat Masterson spent a lot of time in Pueblo through the years. He reportedly served a short stint as a deputy South Pueblo marshal, though it cannot be confirmed. He did serve as Ford County sheriff in Dodge City, Kansas, and in 1881 he was appointed city marshal of Trinidad, Colorado, where he served for just over a year. He then spent the next 20 years moving from town to town in Colorado, serving in law enforcement capacities, and frequently visiting Pueblo where he had made some close friends.

1902 found him in New York City working as a sports-writer and columnist for the *New York Morning Telegraph*. He wrote with pen and ink, eschewing the typewriter. Suffering from a severe chest cold on Tuesday, October 25, 1921, Bat Masterson sat in his Manhattan office penning a column that was to appear in print that Thursday. A colleague, concerned about Bat's congestion, looked in on him and asked how he was feeling. Without looking up, Bat replied, "All right." Those were apparently the last words he ever spoke. When others checked on him later in the day, they found him slumped over his desk. At age 67, Bat Masterson, one of the last of the flamboyant "Old West" gunfighters and lawmen, had died from a massive heart attack.

Bat Masterson in later years. He had made many friends in Pueblo and visited Pueblo often during his days as a gambler, gunman, and lawman.

GROWTH & SCANDALS

Casper Zweifel was just as proud of his shiny new badge as he could be. He had just two days earlier been appointed the city marshal of Central Pueblo, the small independent community between the towns of Pueblo and South Pueblo. He was having the time of his life walking the short beat on North Union Avenue on the oppressively hot Friday evening of July 25, 1884. As he popped into the taverns that evening, he was cordially greeted by bartenders and customers alike. It seemed everyone knew him and liked him. He was very comfortable in his new role, and he was sure he could handle the job well, even though he had no previous law enforcement experience.

Zweifel was a native of Switzerland, but he had been in the United States for many years. Prior to settling in Colorado, he had served with distinction in the Union army during the Civil War. It was said he had experience in Missouri and Kansas fighting the Jesse James gang and other criminal bands of rebels that were plundering homes and communities of people opposed to the Confederate cause. He had landed in Pueblo in 1880 and briefly held several jobs in Central Pueblo.

He and his wife lived in a rooming house at Second and Court streets in the town of Pueblo. Immediately prior to his marshal appointment, he had been employed as manager of a popular social gathering and entertainment spot in Central Pueblo known as Turner Hall. That job was how he became so well known in the neighborhood.

The day he assumed duty as town marshal, he was told by several businessmen that someone had been passing counterfeit coins in the area. He responded that he would do his best to identify and apprehend the scoundrel since he was committed to "making war" on the more desperate class of offenders rather than merely rousting drunks and "weak women."

The evening after his appointment he was actively searching for the suspect, asking bartenders and owners if they had any idea who had been passing the illicit coins, but no one seemed to have seen the culprit who did so. Several people, however, gave Marshal Zweifel a description of a smaller, well dressed and quiet young man who was seen in many of the establishments where counterfeit coins had been inconspicuously passed. He began looking for that man.

Simultaneously, W.S. Henderson, owner of the Bella Union Saloon on South Union Avenue, was told by his bartender that a young man had just passed a phony one-dollar coin to him. He pointed out the small, well-groomed man who was just leaving the tavern. Henderson followed the man to the street where he encountered Marshal Zweifel. Henderson told the marshal what had happened and pointed out the man who was then walking quickly up the street. He and Zweifel ran to confront the suspect.

When they approached the man, Henderson told him he would not press charges if the man paid for the beer he had obtained with the phony coin, but Zweifel said he needed the man to come with him to answer to complaints that he had passed numerous counterfeit coins to businesspeople during the past few days. The man told Zweifel to "go to hell" and tried to run. Zweifel grabbed him, and in the ensuing struggle the man, who was much shorter than the six-foot tall marshal, apparently pulled a knife from his pocket and rapidly thrust it twice into the officer's groin.

One of the small stab wounds had severed Zweifel's femoral artery causing profuse bleeding. The man ran as both Zweifel and Henderson drew revolvers, and in Old West fashion, began firing at the fleeing suspect as they chased after him. As they rounded a corner into a dark alley adjacent to the ruins of the recently burned Tivoli theater, Marshal Zweifel slowed, staggered, then fell hard into the dirt. A wide trail of blood led from the site of the stabbing to the spot where the policeman fell. He likely had not realized the severity of his injuries when he began running after the desperado.

Henderson immediately stopped his pursuit to assist the obviously critically injured officer, and the man, still running as fast as he could, disappeared into the darkness. Though several shots had been fired at the fleeing felon, he apparently had not been hit.

Henderson, and several others who had been roused by the sound of the gunfire, lifted Zweifel and carried him to the nearby Bessemer Exchange Saloon. They laid him across a table and did their best to stop the bleeding, but before a doctor could be summoned, Casper Zweifel died. It was later found that he had almost completely bled out in the minute or so it took to chase his killer into the dark alley where he then collapsed. The bloody knife was recovered by Henderson at the point where the murderer had discarded it. Marshal

Zweifel had become the second Pueblo officer to be killed in the line of duty.

An aggressive manhunt for the killer was quickly organized by law enforcement personnel from Pueblo, South Pueblo and the Pueblo County Sheriff's office, along with a constantly growing mob of very irate and heavily armed citizens. Reported sightings of the wanted party were quickly checked out by bands of angry citizens, but their efforts all hit brick walls.

After about fifteen minutes of searching, it was reported to Deputy Sheriff Kelly that a man matching the general description of the suspect was heading west beside the Arkansas River toward Cañon City. Fearing a lynching, should the mass of enraged townsmen rush to capture the man, Deputy Kelly grabbed Henderson and the pair set out on horseback to hunt for the fugitive.

Moving at top speed to make up time, Kelly and Henderson traced the fugitive as far as Rock Canyon where they dismounted and sent their horses back to town. They continued their search on foot along the Santa Fe Coal Branch north of the river for several miles. Past Rock Canyon they spotted a man on the riverbank and started toward him. Although some distance away when they saw the man, Henderson was pretty sure it was the party for whom they were looking. As they approached him, the man ran, then jumped into the Arkansas river and swam across to the north bank. Not to be outdone, Kelly and Henderson also jumped into the river and swam or waded across.

As the man, soaked to the bone, again began running, the lawmen noticed the locomotive of a gravel train stopped on nearby tracks. They jumped in as if in a scene from a western movie and resumed the chase. As the engine gained speed and the pursuers were about to overtake the criminal, he again leapt into the Arkansas and began swimming toward the opposite side of the river. Kelly and Henderson abandoned the locomotive and jumped back into the river.

The chase resumed along the D&RG tracks on the south side of the river. As they neared the running man, he again leapt into the river and swam to the north bank. Kelly and Henderson followed. The foot chase continued north of the river for about a mile when the man entered the water a third time and swam back toward the south bank.

The pursuers again jumped in the river to swim across, but when they got into rough waters Henderson hit a stump and went under. Kelly stopped to assist the drowning Henderson by pulling him from the rushing water. By the time the men made it to shore, the subject of their chase had disappeared into the night. Still on foot the two battered and mud-covered men made their way back to Pueblo dismayed by their failure to apprehend their prey.

An article in the *Colorado Chieftain* that week would state many Puebloans found Kelly's account of the pursuit "unbelievable." It seemed the story of the suspect and the pursuers swimming the Arkansas River so many times was laughable. Deputy Kelly, however, would continue to stand by his account of the chase.

Though many rumors spread through the Pueblos, some saying the murderer had been caught, no arrest was ever made. Numerous suspects were detained south and west of Pueblo, but none turned out to be the killer.

Though Denver and a few other cities reported counterfeiting crimes similar to those that touched off the brutal murder of Casper Zweifel, and every agency in the region had been notified of the Pueblo incident, all agreed to assist in the search for the killer. Hopes were raised locally when the arrest of a counterfeiter was made in Denver. Those hopes were dashed when it was revealed the arrested party was not the one who had committed the Pueblo crime.

A man named John Carp reportedly confessed to authorities in Arkansas in January 1885 that it was he who committed the murder. He was doing time in an Arkansas prison at the time and the Pueblo Sheriff said he would be returned to Pueblo for trial when he completed his Arkansas sentence in November of that year. If that ever happened, no record of it could be found. The Casper Zweifel murder officially remains unsolved.

Consolidation

It took another two years before consolidation of the three towns became a political reality, and in 1886 the City of Pueblo, as we now know it, was born. With consolidation came the formation of a larger and a more modern police department. Local citizen D. P. Wooton, a former Pueblo city marshal, was appointed Pueblo's first police chief by newly elected Mayor Delos Holden.

In those early years, every new mayor appointed a new police chief, each with the authority to retain or fire existing officers. Accordingly, the staffing of the Pueblo Police Department was constantly changing. As Doc Holliday was attempting to wash away the discomfort of slowly dying of consumption in the therapeutic mineral waters of Glenwood Springs, the Pueblo Police Department was busy hiring and dismissing officers at the whim of local politics.

In 1887 H. Haskel was appointed by newly elected Mayor Charles Henkel to succeed Wooton as police chief. That same year a newcomer to Pueblo named Edward O'Kelley applied for and was hired as one of the newly constituted city's police officers. Though he was held in high esteem by his fellow officers, O'Kelley's irascible nature made him unpopular with many citizens. O'Kelley was from Missouri. Rumors abounded that he had ridden with, or at least been associated with the infamous Jesse James gang and the notorious Younger Brothers, to whom it was said he was related. He had migrated to Colorado after the 1882 assassination of Jesse James by a gang turncoat named Bob Ford. O'Kelley held several odd jobs before settling in Pueblo.

As with many, he did not last long with the Pueblo Police Department and soon left to seek his fortune on Colorado's western slope, serving briefly as a city marshal in the town of

Bachelor, Colorado, (today a ghost town) and then settling in as a Hinsdale County deputy sheriff in Lake City.

Former Pueblo Police Officer Ed O'Kelley. He killed the man who killed Jesse James.

In 1892, O'Kelley was running a saloon in Creede, Colorado, when he heard that Bob Ford was opening a tent saloon not far from his own business. On June 8, 1892, Ed O'Kelley, carrying a shotgun, walked into Bob Ford's establishment. Ford's back was to him as he entered, and in a determined monotone, he called to Ford saying, "Hello, Bob, ole boy." As Ford turned to see who was addressing him, O'Kelley fired, hitting Ford in the neck, peppering him with buckshot and killing him instantly.

O'Kelley was arrested, tried, and convicted of the wanton murder of Bob Ford, for which he received a life sentence at the territorial prison in Cañon City. He served only nine years before being released due to an undisclosed medical condition.

O'Kelley found himself down and out in Oklahoma City on January 13, 1904, when he spotted Police Officer Joe Burnett walking his beat. He went up to the officer, called him some names and picked a fight with him. The two men grappled as O'Kelley drew a pistol and attempted to shoot Burnett. The startled officer grabbed O'Kelley's weapon as O'Kelley fired several rounds, none of which struck Burnett. After firing his last round, O'Kelley, still in the grasp of the officer, began scratching and biting, eventually biting off chunks of both of Burnett's ears. The fierce fight lasted for 15 minutes and attracted quite a crowd. Not one of the good citizens of Oklahoma City went to the aid of their officer. Finally, the exhausted Burnett was able to get his hand free and grab his own gun. He began blasting away at O'Kelley, shooting him in the leg and then in the head. That was the end of the former Pueblo police officer who had killed the man who killed Jesse James.

Between 1884, when Marshal Casper Zweifel was murdered, and 1920, eight additional Pueblo officers died or were killed in the line of duty—four by felonious assault, one by an act of nature and three by accidental gunfire. On Monday, May 11, 1891, the third officer to die on duty, Moses Lovern, walked into the Bucket of Blood saloon on Union Avenue and attempted to adjust his gun belt. He removed his service revolver from its holster and placed it on a slanted display case. The gun started to slide from the case, and as Officer Lovern grabbed it, it went off. The bullet struck Officer Lovern, killing him. It is unknown exactly how the revolver discharged, but it was assumed that when the officer grabbed the weapon, his finger or thumb connected with the trigger, causing the gun to fire. Several witnesses maintained the incident was strictly an accident.

Bessemer Annexed

The town of Bessemer, which ran adjacent to the south boundary of former South Pueblo, had been a separate community that grew around the ever-expanding steel interests of General William Palmer. Formed as several companies, created to secure the natural resources necessary to produce iron and steel in 1872, General Palmer's steel production subsidiaries consolidated in 1880 to form the Colorado Coal and Iron Company. That corporation included the new steel-making plant in Bessemer and the company's mining interests near Walsenburg that supported the plant. The company would ultimately become the largest employer in Colorado.

In 1880 a housing community and several businesses

were established to augment the needs of the mill and its employees sprung up around the facility. The community was christened the town of Bessemer. It was named after Sir Henry Bessemer, a British engineer credited with developing a relatively inexpensive process for the mass production of steel. The town of Bessemer quickly formed its own government, its own fire-fighting organization and its own law enforcement agency that mirrored the marshal system of its three Pueblo neighbors.

It was nearing the end of S.A. Abbey's tenure as Pueblo police chief in early 1894 when residents of Bessemer began reflecting on the financial benefit of joining the larger and better-established city of Pueblo. It was another eight months until the residents of Pueblo and Bessemer voted to annex the town of Bessemer into the city. That 1894 annexation resulted in the Pueblo force being increased to 30 officers and Joseph Loor becoming the new police chief.

Chief Joseph Loor

When J.B. Orman became mayor in 1897, he appointed Charles R. "Bob" Griffin as police chief. With the backing of the mayor, Griffin acted quickly to modernize the growing department. A student of contemporary police administration, Chief Griffin created the rank of police captain, initiating the first position between that of chief and what we today call "police officer," but what was then known as "patrolman." (The rank of patrolman lasted until the early 1990s when the more inclusive, less sexist designation of patrol officer was adopted.)

A burly and respected veteran officer named John Bell was appointed as Pueblo's first police captain. He served as head of the department during evening hours and at other times when the chief was not readily available. Two sergeants were also appointed to serve as detectives and as station supervisors, completing Griffin's reorganization of the department. Chief Griffin served until mid-1900 when William F. McCafferty was chosen as the new chief.

PUEBLO POLICE DEPARTMENT— *February 1900*

Front row: *Jailer J. W. Callaway, E. P. Thurston, Charles Venuto, John Fitzgerald, Chief C. R. "Bob" Griffin, John Peterson, Captain John Bell, F. O. Forsee, H. Sanders (who would resign before this photo was published), and Nick Badovinac.* **Middle row:** *M. B. Davis, J. T. O'Brien, Ed Worth, Charles Shaffer, Charles Fawcett, R. H. Thomas, G. W. Smith, J. E. McPheeters, and William Green (who would be killed in the line of duty in 1918).* **Top row:** *Jailer Matt McCabe, James Ragland (mounted officer), Sergeant W. C. Porter, George Morris, G. W. Reasoner (mounted officer), Dennis McDermott (who would be named chief in 1912), Sergeant W. F. Bradley, Joe Stanko, and J. H. Shepard.*

Dr. H.M. Shoup became chief in 1902 and served through 1904. At that time, the department consisted of some forty men, and one woman. The woman functioned as jail matron, fixing meals for the inmates of City Jail and managing all issues relating to females brought into police custody.

The first woman to be employed as police matron was Olga Kretschmer. She served through the administrations of five chiefs until 1912. Pueblo had police matrons working from that time until the mid-1980s when the city jail was closed and the need for matrons was eliminated.

Police Matron Olga Kretschmer. Note the star worn on her blouse.

Double Death

The Palace Drug Store, located in the Central Block Building at 2nd and Main streets was a well-known downtown pharmacy and its proprietor, Dr. C.O. Rice, was known by almost all of Pueblo's officers. On the night of October 7, 1903, Dr. Rice brandished a .45 caliber revolver and drove several of his customers out of the store. He had been drinking and had become angered that some of his "customers" were hanging around the store without making a purchase. Those who had been expelled from the establishment fled in anger to the police station some four blocks away to complain.

Officer Silas Martz was sent to the store to deal with the intoxicated doctor, whom he knew personally. Feeling he could reason with Dr. Rice, Officer Martz entered the pharmacy and told the doctor to put the gun away and calm down. When the doctor refused, Martz told him he was going to put him in jail until he sobered up. Rice then raised his revolver and shot the officer in the throat. Officer Martz fell to the floor just inside the store and began gagging and spitting up blood. Other officers responded, but, fearing the drunken and irrational doctor, hesitated to make an entry. A crowd gathered, and many began jeering at the officers, calling them cowards, and daring them to go into the store to rescue their fallen comrade. After a few minutes, Officer Elwin Slater said he would go in and pull his friend to safety. He started to draw his revolver as he rushed through the front door, ducking an anticipated shot coming in his direction. As he swept to the right, his arm struck the door frame and his gun discharged. The bullet passed through his holster and struck him in the thigh.

At about the same time Officer Slater entered the front door of the pharmacy, Detective F. Rubichaud, along with Assistant Fire Chiefs John Campbell and William Davenport, made their way into the basement of the building to find the doctor passed out from alcohol consumption. Rice opened his eyes as they searched him. Campbell spoke first trying to ensure Rice remained calm. "Doctor, I want to get you out of here, I'm your friend," he said. Davenport then told the doctor, "There are fifteen hundred people outside wanting to lynch you." Fearing the crowd would forcibly take the doctor from them, they took Rice through the basement and up to the side entrance to the Central Block. He was delivered to a group of officers brandishing revolvers who loaded him into a patrol wagon and removed him from the scene.

Officer Martz died at the scene and Officer Slater passed away at St. Mary's Hospital the following day surrounded by his family. He refused to believe he had shot himself and told other officers he had been shot by someone in the crowd gathered in front of the store. A careful examination of his weapon and holster by Chief Shoup and Mayor Brown, however, proved conclusively that the gun was fired before it had completely cleared Slater's holster. That meant he had his finger on the trigger as he jerked the revolver from the holster.

Officers Martz and Slater were given a double funeral, and both were laid to rest at Riverview, now Roselawn Cemetery. Doctor Rice, charged with first degree murder, pleaded insanity and on December 31, 1903, was found not guilty by reason of insanity. Though the verdict was unusual, it was not unexpected as several physicians had been brought in to testify. They all said they felt Rice was temporarily insane due to excessive alcohol consumption. When the verdict was read, a score of supporters in the courtroom went forward to congratulate him. He and his wife, arm in arm, then walked out of the courthouse. Police officers in attendance, though, were dumbfounded and angered by the decision.

Chief Shoup served through the end of 1904. During the last days of his administration a major weather-related disaster struck the Pueblo area, causing an "all-hands-on-deck" response from department personnel.

Eden Train Wreck

Chaos caused by acts of nature, serious accidents and other tragedies not resulting from criminal activity have always required major expenditures of time and resources from law enforcement agencies. On the early evening of Sunday, August 7, 1904, the southbound Number 11 Missouri Pacific Flyer crashed into an arroyo about 12 miles north of Pueblo during a heavy rainstorm. The train was carrying a minimum of 125 people, and it was later confirmed that at least 96 were killed. Because the conductor's manifest was lost in the wreckage, no exact number of people on the train could be determined.

As the train approached the arroyo (today known as Porter Draw), a huge wall of water fed by a massive rainstorm northwest of the city came rushing, carrying a dislodged county road bridge toward the trestle bridge over the draw about a mile north of Eden station. As the engine crossed the bridge, debris and swiftly moving water took out the bridge causing the engine to fall to its side and slide backward into the water. The forward part of the train was sheared off, breaking the coupling of the last two cars.

It was reported that a quick-thinking porter in the Pullman car, Melville Sales, quickly threw the emergency air brake stopping the Pullman and dining cars and saving them from going head-first into the maelstrom below the bridge. The forward four feet of the Pullman car was left dangling precariously over the edge of what remained of the bridge as the 17 terrified passengers hurriedly alighted from the rear of the car. Many of the survivors of those cars began the difficult hike through the blinding rain back to Pinon Station about two and a half miles north of the crash site. The first emergency call to Pueblo came from that location.

A call immediately went out to every doctor in town requesting assistance. Most of the city's physicians, particularly surgeons, quickly reported to the train depot, and a rescue train was on its way to the accident site within the hour. At eleven o'clock that night, a second train with emergency supplies and a number of police officers was also en route. The exact number of officers dispatched to the wreck site was not reported, but Chief Shoup and 25 officers were on scene by morning. All city police officers were eventually involved in the search for survivors and the identification of those killed.

The chair car (lounger), the smoking car and the baggage car had all plummeted into the torrent with the ill-fated engine and coal car. The chair car was washed a half mile down Fountain creek and was covered with mud. The smoker and baggage car were not initially found as they had been carried over a mile down the creek and were practically buried by the mud, sand, sludge and debris. The amount of mud made the search for the ill-fated passengers difficult.

By morning the waters had subsided, but the front few feet of the Pullman car remained hanging over the arroyo. Note the deep mud, sand and debris in the once dry, 15-foot-deep gully. Many bodies were buried in that sludge.

Many bodies were carried the quarter of a mile to Fountain Creek, and then into the city several miles to the south. Bodies were found in the waters of the Fountain several days after the wreck. Some had washed all the way to the confluence of Fountain Creek and the Arkansas river near the center of Pueblo and were discovered days later miles east of the city. In terms of lives lost, the Eden train tragedy was the worst train disaster in the United States up to that time.

The train was en route from Denver to the World's Fair in St. Louis, Missouri. It is thought that as many as a dozen potential fair goers boarded at various stops south of Denver with the expectation of buying tickets on board the train, but never got to do so. At any rate, the Eden train wreck remains one of the worst disasters ever to strike the Pueblo area and was a major test of Pueblo's readiness to handle such situations.

After Chief Shoup's retirement, William McCafferty, who had served as chief in 1902 and 1903, was again appointed chief in 1905, his second shot at the job. He remained in that position until late 1909. While he was adjusting to his second administration, another tragic accident, also the result of an act of nature, claimed yet another Pueblo police officer.

Lightning Strikes Officer

Officer William Shellman died as the result of an electrical storm in 1906. While patrolling his beat in the Bessemer area on horseback, Officer Shellman was struck by lightning and knocked from his horse. He received what he initially thought were minor injuries. While relaxing at his home later that evening, however, his condition worsened and three days later his family admitted him to St. Mary's Hospital where he sadly died from the effects of the lightning strike.

Officer Shellman had been much loved by citizens in the Bessemer neighborhood, particularly the children to whom he always spoke kindly and let them pet his horse. His funeral, which was conducted in his home in the 1400 block of East Evans, was one of the largest seen in Pueblo up to that time. The floral offerings were so numerous that an extra wagon was pressed into service to carry them.

Between the years of 1908 and 1910, scandals and errant officer behavior rocked the department and eroded much of the public trust earlier chiefs had worked hard to instill. On Saturday night, October 10, 1908, Officer James Williams shot and seriously injured an 18-year-old girl with whom he had become infatuated. Williams had allegedly been bothering the girl, Claudia Broemser, for days. He was on duty and in uniform when he went to the home of Emma Tolle where Broemser was employed to confront her. When she rebuffed him, he pulled his service revolver and shot her. The bullet passed through her shoulder and took her to the floor. The injury was serious, but not life-threatening.

When police arrived a short time later, they found Williams in what was described as a drunken stupor lying on the floor at the feet of the girl he had shot. As Chief McCafferty bent over the obviously inebriated officer, Williams said he had aimed at her heart, and it was not his fault he didn't kill her. McCafferty immediately plucked Williams's badge from the breast of his jacket.

During the investigation of the incident, it was revealed that many officers knew of Williams's propensity to become intoxicated on duty. He had on several occasions lost control of himself when drinking, once having created such a disturbance at the Mineral Palace where a dance was in progress that police were called. When officers attempted to quiet him, he left the venue, but shortly thereafter officers were summoned to deal with him again. He had apparently waded into Fountain Creek and up to his knees in mud and water, begun firing shots into the air.

Residents in the vicinity were so alarmed by the gunfire that nearly a dozen calls were sent to the central police station. Several officers reportedly responded and "rescued" the floundering officer from the muddy waters.

Chief McCafferty maintained he had never been told of Williams's previous behavior. He apparently took no action against any of the department personnel who knew of the erratic behavior and on-duty drinking by Williams but had said nothing about it. According to the *Pueblo Chieftain*, Williams's actions, particularly the shooting of the Broemser girl, was "one of the primary subjects of conversation on the streets" in the days following the incident. The *Chieftain* further reported that his fellow officers complained loudly after the shooting that he had disgraced the entire department.

Williams pleaded not guilty by reason of insanity to the charge of attempted murder. It was shown in court that Williams suffered from epilepsy and that his mind was unbalanced by a "too free use of intoxicants." He was sent to the State Hospital (then called the Colorado State Insane Asylum) for treatment.

Deadly Foot Beat

On Sunday evening, March 21, 1909, Chief McCafferty was required to oversee the investigation of the shooting death of another respected officer killed while detaining three residential burglary suspects in downtown Pueblo. Patrolman Frederick H. Barner was brutally murdered by one of the three who produced a gun and shot him at point blank range at the corner of 10th and Main Streets while Officer Barner was attempting to attract a police patrol wagon to transport his prisoners to the station for investigation.

When Barner went to work that afternoon, he was given the description of three men, one wearing a large, brimmed hat, possibly a sombrero, who had been seen prowling homes in the area of North Grand Avenue. He was further told that several homes in that area had been burglarized. As he walked his beat on north Main and Court Streets, he observed three men who matched the description of the suspects. He approached them and asked them to accompany him the block or so to Main Street where he was certain he could attract the patrol wagon working that area.

At least three people were witnesses to the shooting, but due to their distance from the crime scene none said they could describe or identify the man who pulled the trigger. All concurred that the shooter was a tall man, at least taller than the other two men Officer Barner had in custody, and they all described him as wearing a dark-colored sombrero. The witnesses said the three men ran east from the scene toward the railroad tracks that ran alongside Fountain Creek approximately where the Pueblo freeway is now located.

Upon receiving word of the killing, Chief McCafferty ordered all officers to duty and initiated a dragnet, or comprehensive search of the area toward which the three men had run. A black sombrero was quickly found on the street a block or so southeast of the crime scene, leading officers to believe the men were making their way to the south. And they began focusing their search on areas in that direction.

About four hours after the murder, officers noticed a tall man of Hispanic descent walking toward the east at 4th Street and Santa Fe Avenue. The man was wearing a small hat, which the *Chieftain* described as a "soft crusher" type cap when officers confronted him. When asked if he had shot the officer, the man, Felice Martinez, vehemently denied being involved. The hat Martinez was wearing was inspected and it was found to be too small to properly fit him. The larger sombrero found earlier was then brought to the scene and it fit Martinez perfectly, though he denied the hat was his. He was in possession of a .38 caliber revolver with an empty chamber when he was contacted, which indicated that one shot had been fired from the weapon. Martinez was then arrested.

Martinez denied being in the company of anyone else that evening and stuck to that story even though he was subjected to what the newspaper said were hours of close questioning. The evidence gathered by police seemed to conclusively link Martinez to the shooting, but evidence to the contrary was soon to come forward.

By the time Martinez was put on trial on June 10, 1909, less than three months after his arrest, Chief McCafferty had abruptly "retired" and a new chief, C.C. Sullivan was appointed to take his place. It was McCafferty's testimony, though, that became a focal point in the prosecution of Martinez.

Martinez was represented by attorneys Joseph Dye and D.M. Campbell, who argued that though much of the evidence introduced against Martinez was compelling, a whole lot more was weak and wavering. For instance, the revolver in Martinez's possession when he was arrested was inspected by a firearms expert, Jack Shepard, at the request of Chief McCafferty. Shepard testified that the bullet that killed Barner could not have been fired by Martinez's revolver. When asked to produce in court the bullet that did kill the officer, former Chief McCafferty testified that he had "lost" it.

Further, a man named Clarence Hagerman testified that he knew Martinez by sight, having seen him in the Derby saloon on the night of the murder and that Martinez was wearing a black sombrero type hat, but it was much smaller than the one found near the crime scene. Another defense witness, Angelo Froney, testified that he had been "back and forth" between the Derby Saloon and the Pleasure Saloon—both on West 1st Street—about the same time the murder was committed, and he had seen Martinez in the Derby. He said Martinez was eating some noodles and was playing a guitar.

Another witness, David Ortiz, a bartender at the Pleasure Saloon, testified that the night Barner was killed, Martinez had been in that saloon playing a guitar and singing for about 20 to 30 minutes prior to nine o'clock when someone entered the saloon and announced that a police officer had just been shot.

The case went to the jury on June 12th and as expected, the jurors were unable to reach a verdict. A second trial was ordered to begin on October 5. After hearing essentially the same evidence as the first jury, the second jury also failed to reach a verdict.

On October 9th, District Attorney J.W. Davidson entered a writ of *Nolle Prosequi*, an entry into the records of the court that the prosecution will proceed no further with the case. With that, the case against Martinez was dismissed and he was freed from custody. To the chagrin of the officers who worked so diligently on the case, the killing of Officer Barner became another unsolved murder of a Pueblo police officer.

Though the testimony of more than one witness placing Martinez elsewhere at the time of the shooting were factors in the hung juries, the critical issue listed by members of both juries that led to their inability to reach verdicts was their collective disbelief that Chief McCafferty could have lost or misplaced such a critical piece of evidence as the bullet that killed Officer Barner. It seems the jurors believed the chief was withholding evidence, contrary to his personal belief of the guilt of Felice Martinez.

The Sweat Box

Within days of the Barner killing, Chief McCafferty was subjected to considerable public criticism and official scrutiny after several former prisoners came forward and complained loudly about their treatment by officers when they were in police custody. Many others testified that during their district court trials the chief's office was a virtual "sweat box" used to force incriminating statements from them during interrogations. The *Pueblo Chieftain* reported that "prisoner after prisoner" claimed that statements had been "wrung from them by threats and downright assaults upon their persons."

Local attorneys protested that the situation usually involved the word of several officers against the word of a single prisoner and juries were in the habit of discrediting the word of a prisoner unless it was corroborated by direct physical evidence. Officers, they said, were adept at seeing that no such evidence existed.

The district court, bolstered by the petitions of several defense attorneys, called for an investigation into the matter. Numerous officers were questioned. All denied that physical tactics were employed but acknowledged that threats were sometimes used against recalcitrant subjects to "clarify" statements they had given. When questioned about such tactics on the stand, several officers said they felt the use of such threats was "perfectly proper" in order to obtain statements from witnesses when the case is not clear. Under oath Chief McCafferty steadfastly denied that interrogations that had taken place in his office even remotely resembled the use of a sweat box, a tactic which would subject a prisoner to non-stop questioning by a succession of three or four officers over long periods of time with little or no food or water provided. The tactic was said to wear down the will of the subject until they would say just about anything to make the unrelenting process stop.

The *Pueblo Chieftain* seemed to agree with the police denials, reporting that the complaints came about because of the "overwrought imagination" of attorneys playing upon a small amount of evidence to support their guilty client's complaints. Nothing came of the investigation into police misconduct, but Chief McCafferty very soon cleaned out his desk and departed.

In a surprise move on April 15, 1909, shortly after Chief McCafferty's "retirement," incoming Mayor A.L. Fugard announced that his friend, Cornelius C. Sullivan, an unknown in local political circles, would be the new Pueblo police chief. Sullivan was a contractor who had been employed at the Turkey Creek stone quarries. He had previously been a downtown restaurateur and had done a lot of work for the Colorado Fuel and Iron Company, but he had no law enforcement experience. Mayor Fugard was impressed by Sullivan's perceived intelligence. He felt he could quickly learn the specifics of the job and did not need prior job experience to serve as an administrator. The mayor also thought an outsider would not be tainted by the alleged corruption plaguing the department.

Just A Short Walk Home

On the night of Wednesday, July 21, 1909, just four months after the murder of Officer Barner and three months following the appointment of Chief Sullivan, another Pueblo officer fell to assassins' bullets. The murder of the officer many considered the best detective on the force enraged Chief Sullivan. Addressing reporters of the local newspaper at the scene of the crime, he publicly promised to have the assassins under arrest by noon that very day. It was, of course, a promise he couldn't or wouldn't keep—or maybe he did.

Detective Sergeant John W. Dunleavy, along with fellow detectives Joe Daly and Colombo Delliquadri, had made their rounds checking trouble spots in the downtown area and found things to be quiet. Dunleavy then took his leave of the other two, stating he was going to Bessemer to accompany his daughter, Edith, home from the CF&I main office building where she worked as a telephone operator. He rode the streetcar to Bay State and East Evans Avenue, then walked the block or so to pick up his daughter.

Dunleavy and Edith chatted and laughed gleefully as they walked together toward their home at 1544 Pine. A few minutes before 11 o'clock, as they passed between the Colorado

Supply Store and the Steelworks YMCA at Canal and Evans Avenue, two men stepped out of the shadows. Both men made some extremely vulgar and insulting remarks to young Edith, which were likely to incite Dunleavy and draw him away from Edith and toward them so he could be killed. When the men made the nasty comments, Dunleavy pulled his daughter behind him and stepped forward to confront them. Though Dunleavy was short in stature, he was feisty and unafraid of mixing it up with bullies.

But these two were more than bullies, they were cold-blooded and heartless killers. Before Dunleavy could challenge them, both men pushed guns forward and began shooting. Dunleavy stumbled backward against a telegraph pole. As Edith screamed, Dunleavy jerked his own revolver from its holster and began firing at the fleeing criminals. He fired four shots but may not have hit his targets—at least no one reported to a hospital with gunshot wounds immediately following the incident.

Edith Dunleavy went to her severely injured father and cradled him in her arms. He looked up at her plaintively and whispered, "Get an officer, quickly, I need to give a description of them." She screamed again to attract attention, then looked back at her father; "Get Yund...Yund" he continued, referring to his boss, Captain Charles Yund. Aroused by the gunfire and Edith's screams, the stableman at the Colorado Supply store came running. He assisted Dunleavy to the stable where he helped him into a chair to await an ambulance. Dunleavy, accompanied by his daughter, was soon rushed to Minnequa Hospital (later St. Mary-Corwin Hospital). He was in an extremely critical condition and those who attended him knew he wouldn't make it. He died four days later.

Chief Sullivan also responded to the scene. He was visibly distraught and when asked by a newspaper reporter for a comment, he went on a tirade. "Dunleavy was literally shot down without warning . . . I will catch those that shot him . . . They cannot escape and will pay the penalty for this horrible crime . . . I pledge my word that they will be caught with the least possible delay . . . I will have them by noon . . . They will pay for this contemptible crime."

Sullivan's well-intentioned comments came from his heart and perfectly reflected the sentiments of the department's rank and file. Unfortunately, as the investigation of the crime pressed forward without the expected rapid solution, the public's confidence in the chief waned. That decline in public trust and support would, within the year, work against him as he would be forced to fight a losing battle for his reputation, his career and ultimately his life.

Knowing that Detective Sergeant Dunleavy had been very active and successful in combating violations of gambling and liquor laws occurring in the Bessemer area, officers began focusing their investigative efforts on ethnic and family crime groups known to be operating in that neighborhood. Dunleavy's daughter was initially unable—by virtue of the traumatic experience of seeing her father shot down right in front of her—to remember details of the incident. Within hours, however, she regained her composure enough to discuss her experience with investigators.

She revealed that her father had received several menacing letters that threatened his life if he didn't "let up on arresting people out his way." She said her dad merely laughed at the threats, wadded up the letters and threw them away. She also told officers that because of their general appearance and vocal accents, she thought the shooters were "Austrians." That information tallied with what the officers already knew about Dunleavy's recent investigations. Acting on that information, Chief Sullivan moved quickly to fulfill his promise to have the scoundrels in custody without delay.

Relying upon the information developed by his team of detectives, Chief Sullivan personally rounded up and jailed three individuals whose names had emerged as likely suspects. Steve Chanak, owner of an Austrian boarding house, had been arrested by Dunleavy and Delliquadri about six weeks earlier. He had been fined $100 for selling beer without a license.

Word on the street was that he had loudly threatened the two officers, even offering his customers free beer if those cops died. Initially unable to locate Chanak, Sullivan himself found the man hiding in a barn in the Bessemer neighborhood.

Two of Chanak's associates, Joe Bubich and John Bedenikovich, were also arrested. All three were "sweated" (1909 term for the use of "enhanced interrogation" techniques) but no confessions were forthcoming. The three were taken under guard to Minnequa Hospital and paraded before Detective Dunleavy and his daughter. The detective, weak and barely conscious, was unable to identify either of the men as his attacker and Edith flatly stated none of the three were her father's shooters.

Undeterred, Chief Sullivan caused the arrest of ten additional suspects. Mike English, Steve Johnac, Mike Papewick, Andy Marek, Mike Bunnelich, John Moglish, Mike Guch, John Hando, Morris Pichart and Ed Hanes—all members of the Bessemer immigrant community, particularly the Austrian settlement. All were detained and questioned. None of the Mikes or Johns, or any of the others for that matter, could be connected to the crime.

Still not to be deterred, Chief Sullivan placed eight more men believed to be of Austrian lineage under arrest. John Kyakas, Albert Tayne, Bodie Chonick, Eli Leonovich, Steve Rochich, George Limlich, Pete Melovich and Henry Stronovich were likewise sweated and as the paper said, "put through the degree." Like the others, none could be identified as one of the shooters or connected with the crime in any way. Frustrated by the failure to identify a perpetrator or solve the dastardly crime, Sullivan publicly said, "I'll get the men who shot Dunleavy if I have to rake the entire state with a fine-tooth comb."

He was encouraged the following day when police interrogators reported that "many clews [sic]" (today we spell it clues) were learned in the sweating of Matt, Mark, Joe, and another Matt, whose last name was Nicksich. The four Austrians, all of whom matched the description of those who shot Dunleavy, had been arrested in the Vineland area. When presented to Edith Dunleavy for her inspection, she stated the one named Joe looked a lot like one of the shooters—but she could not be sure. She was sure the others were not involved.

The next morning the press reported that "there are rumors of partial confessions and sure-thing identifications, but the truth is that the case is seemingly as much a mystery as ever." It went on to say, "it may be . . . that Chief Sullivan has under arrest the men who shot Dunleavy down, but not one positive bit of evidence has so far been unearthed that would warrant a conviction."

With that, the case went cold, much to the disappointment of Chief Sullivan. He and others continued to believe he had located Dunleavy's killers very early in the investigation just as he said he would do. He just couldn't prove it.

Mayor Fugard, also dismayed by the lack of success in the Dunleavy case, stated publicly he had extreme confidence in Sullivan and felt he had served the citizens of Pueblo admirably. Within months, however, Police Chief Cornelius C. Sullivan would become the poster boy in what was the most egregious scandal involving local law enforcement up to that time.

Brothel Scandal

Sullivan and three detectives, one of whom was the aforementioned Colombo Delliquadri, had allegedly visited what the newspaper described as three "houses of assignation" (today we call them brothels). And in a state of intoxication, Sullivan reportedly fired several shots at a local barber who was a patron in one of the establishments. Sullivan and the other officers claimed they were not intoxicated, that no shots were fired, and they were hunting for crooks when they visited the houses of ill repute. Evidence uncovered by a special city council investigation, however, reportedly did not support their stories. Though the mayor was unwavering in his support of Sullivan, city council was not.

At the height of the controversy, Pueblo County Undersheriff Warren Hill complained that he had gone to city jail to get a county prisoner being held there. Hill said he entered the chief's office and asked, "Do you have anything for me?" He said Sullivan replied, "No, and I never will have," and then told him to get out of the office. Hill said he told Sullivan he was there in the official discharge of his duties and Sullivan then told him to leave or he would shoot him. According to Hill, Sullivan then moved to draw his gun. Hill said he tried to leave but was grabbed by Sullivan and physically thrown out of the office.

Sullivan's account of the event differed, placing the blame on Hill's flippant attitude and his well-known dislike of Sullivan. He said he merely told Hill to transact his business in the outer office, not interrupt affairs in the chief's office. Five officers who had witnessed the incident vehemently supported Chief Sullivan's account of the confrontation.

After a lot of discussion and some legal maneuvering between the mayor and city council, the city council won. The officers, Chief Sullivan, Detectives Miller, Delliquadri, and Shurtz, were all requested to resign or retire from their positions with the department. Miller and Shurtz resigned protesting their innocence, while Delliquadri, also claiming he had done nothing wrong, left the department to accept an appointment as a deputy sheriff for Pueblo County.

Prior to the current scandal, Delliquadri had been considered one of the city's best detectives. He was known as a fervent opponent of organized criminal activity, particularly the type that had led to the murder of his partner and friend John Dunleavy. He had also worked hand in hand with sheriff's deputies on numerous multi-jurisdictional investigations and had many friends in the sheriff's office. Upon his expulsion from the police department, he was enthusiastically accepted as a member of the sheriff's office.

Mayor Fugard was pressured by city councilmen into accepting a voluntary resignation from Sullivan and appointing another police chief. He asked his friend Sullivan to resign to prevent further negative publicity that could affect his own position as mayor and Sullivan reluctantly complied. The mayor named Captain Charles Yund interim chief. Yund was well liked by local officials and his appointment was uncontested by the city council.

Sullivan protested vigorously, claiming he and his fellow officers were the victims of politics and the machinations of an organization of local criminals that wanted him and his best detectives eliminated so they could continue their unlawful activities uninterrupted. He alleged that members of the sheriff's office were particularly corrupt, which led to the "spurious" complaints by Undersheriff Hill. He said he had had numerous disagreements with Hill about the lack of enforcement of laws relating to organized criminal activities just outside the eastern city limits. Unfortunately for him, he had no proof to support his allegations and little support from local businesspeople.

Chief Cornelius C. Sullivan

Sullivan left Pueblo shortly after his ouster from the police force and settled in Denver a broken and embittered man. His family said he brooded over the unfortunate events which occurred while he was Pueblo's chief. His depression intensified as did financial worries fueled by attorney fees and his lack of meaningful employment. On May 22, 1912, Cornelius

C. Sullivan penned a short note apologizing to his family. He then put a revolver to his head and committed suicide in his Denver bedroom.

His remains were returned to Pueblo where an escort of 14 Pueblo police officers was detailed to attend his funeral. Though over two years had elapsed, many Pueblo officers still expressed the belief that Sullivan and the others had been the victims of corrupt city and county officials, and innocent of any wrongdoing in the scandal that rocked Pueblo in late 1910.

MOTORIZATION & THE FLOOD

Charles Yund, a former sheriff from Laramie, Wyoming, a former Wyoming state senator, a Pueblo police officer for five years, and the most recent police captain under Chief Sullivan, was appointed chief in 1910 when Sullivan left the force. Yund had been extremely popular among the street officers and the detectives he supervised as captain. They trusted him and looked up to him as a boss who understood their needs, eagerly worked alongside them, and supported them when they needed it. He was considered a dynamic leader and a role model.

The first year of his progressive and no-nonsense administration saw the advent of motorized patrol in Pueblo. That year two automobiles were purchased for use by a special emergency squad. The squad, one of Yund's forward-thinking ideas, was an elite team of officers who were kept ever ready to respond to special police problems anywhere in the community. The following year, motorcycles and bicycles were added to the department inventory. Two more automobiles were added to the police fleet in 1913. However, the foot patrol remained supreme in the business districts of Pueblo until well after World War I.

Motorcycle officers Joseph Winterbottom (left) and Charles Baty in front of the Vail Hotel with the new police motorcycles.

Chief Yund served less than two years when a new commission form of government went into effect, and the newly appointed Commissioner of Public Safety Thomas D. Donnelly appointed Denny McDermott to the post of chief. That selection ended the almost yearly shift of appointees based on the pleasure of a mayor and the political party in power at City Hall.

Chief Charles Yund
Chief from 1910 through 1912.

Chief Dennis McDermott
Chief from 1912 to 1913.

Chief McDermott, also a well-liked and respected leader, made many improvements to the department. He improved the motorized capability of the department and strengthened the investigative functions by requiring officers to secure major crime scenes for inspection by detectives. Up until 1912, many officers failed to recognize the need to control access to scenes until all evidence could be recorded in a manner conducive to presentation in court.

Chief McDermott further recognized that the ability to communicate with station personnel in real time would speed the delivery of critical services to the beat officer and advance officer safety in the field. The chief was aware of the tremendous success of what were called "call boxes" in many of the country's larger cities, and he pushed Commissioner Donnelly to back the expansion of a call box system for Pueblo.

Pueblo Police Call Boxes

The Gamewell Company of Newton, Massachusetts, began manufacturing fire alarm boxes and police call boxes in the 1880s. Pueblo experimented with a rudimentary call box system beginning in 1908 with the installation of boxes along Main Street. At Chief McDermott's direction police call boxes, or signal boxes as he called them, began being installed in all business districts of Pueblo by 1912.

Call boxes were designed to provide a means of communication between patrol officers and foot-beat officers on their rounds and the desk sergeant or station officer at police headquarters. The patrol and beat officers would carry a key that would open the outer door of the metal box, allowing the officer access to a lever inside. By "pulling the box" (turning the lever inside the box) the officer could telegraph a location code to the station. By sending the message one, two, or three times, the officer could inform the station officer that he was "okay" and "on his beat," or he could request a patrol wagon to respond to the box, or he could request an ambulance. When the code was sent, a device at the police station would tap out a series of punches on a reel-to-reel tape that would identify the number of the box, and the desk officer would respond accordingly.

If the desk officer had a message for the beat or patrol car officer, he would push a button that would turn on a red light atop the call box. When he saw the red light, the officer would contact the station officer for the information. A red light was also located in the glassed-in portion of the dome above city hall. When that light was illuminated, officers in the downtown area would go to the station for the information.

Sometime prior to 1920, telephones, which allowed direct verbal communication between the beat officer and the desk sergeant, were added to the call boxes in Pueblo. If an officer made an arrest on his beat, he would take his prisoner to the nearest call box and ask for a wagon (or, later, a police car) to respond to pick up the prisoner. In the days prior to hand-held police radios, the call box was the beat officer's only means of communicating with his station. Up through the mid-1970s, officers patrolling areas of Pueblo on foot were required to "pull the box" in their patrol districts once an hour, between ten minutes before the hour to ten minutes after the hour, so the desk sergeant could be assured the officer was still "on his beat" and "okay."

Officer Max Graf using police call box #93 at the corner of Northern and Evans in the mid-1950s. Shortly after this photo was taken, he was seriously injured while trying to arrest a mentally unstable man in the Bessemer area. The man wrestled Officer Graf's night stick away from him and beat him severely until bystanders came to his aid.

By the late 1970s, the foot beats were discontinued except for special functions. The boxes were then modified to allow the general public access to the phone inside, thus enabling citizens to communicate directly and quickly with police headquarters to report emergencies or in-progress crimes. As Pueblo has a high Mexican American population, signs stenciled to the sides of the boxes gave user instructions in both English and Spanish. With the advent of more efficient phone systems and cell phones, the public call boxes became obsolete. They were phased out of service and removed in the mid-1980s.

Chief McDermott also made special use of one of the police motorcycles when he created a traffic officer, whose sole duty was to enforce speed laws. Up to that time there was no enforcement of offenses relating to vehicle operation. A local citizen named J. M. Killin whose son had been struck by a speeding motorist addressed council, and stated he held the city morally responsible for the injury because of the failure of city officials to enforce speed ordinances. Even today, we say, "the squeaky wheel gets the grease," and Chief McDermott was forced to grease the department's enforcement of traffic laws, thus creating the forerunner of our modern traffic division.

Motorized police vehicles continued to increase in popularity over the next decade, particularly for traffic enforcement. Mounted officers and officers on foot, however, continued to be used for crowd control and other specialized purposes.

Mounted Officer Max Stein and his horse. This photo was taken during the McDermott administration, circa 1912. Mounted officers were very popular with the public, especially with children. Max Stein was the grandfather of Marvin Stein, one of Pueblo's prominent civic leaders and a founder of PEDCO (The Pueblo Economic Development Corporation) and other community organizations in the late 1900s and early 2000s.

As his health declined, Chief McDermott decided to retire. He served as chief through the end of 1912. Joseph M. Daly took the helm of the department in January 1913. Chief Daly quickly made several changes to assignments in the organization, first promoting Desk Sergeant J. Arthur Grady to the position of city detective. It was a position Daly had held before being named chief. Patrolman Charles Colvin was simultaneously promoted to station sergeant.

Even before his promotion to the top position was certified by city council, Daly outlined the work he felt needed to be done to improve the agency. He soon tasked Detective Grady with the major responsibility of getting his agenda accomplished. Daly directed that the department work to eliminate prostitution and close the "red light district," and to eliminate gambling and after hours and Sunday liquor sales. He announced that all of Grady's detective work would be confined to those three objectives.

Seven days after assuming his new position, Grady moved against a gambling house in the Bessemer neighborhood where three men were arrested, and much gambling paraphernalia was confiscated. The men were fined $100 in municipal court the next day. Chief Daly informed the press that afternoon that he intended to "drive out all fake clubs and places established and incorporated merely for gambling purposes." His efforts were concentrated in the Bessemer area where his friend, Detective Dunleavy, had been murdered while engaged in investigations of the same nature three years earlier.

Additional motorized vehicles were added to the police fleet during McDermott's and Daly's administrations, including a prisoner transport vehicle that could double as an ambulance. That type of vehicle was widely known at the time by two slang terms, both of which might be offensive to some people today.

One term was the "Black Maria." According to Boston police lore, Maria was a very large African American woman known to be able to defeat almost any male opponent in a fight. When early Boston police officers were confronted by an extremely tough prisoner, they would call for a patrol wagon by saying, "Send Black Maria." The other term used to identify the vehicle, was the paddy wagon. As "paddy" was, to some, a derogatory name for a person of Irish descent, that term referred to the unjust and discriminatory belief that Irishmen were drunks and troublemakers who were frequently police "customers," and the wagon was needed to transport them to jail.

Both terms were widely used by the general public in the early 20th century, but most people were unaware of the origins of the names. The slang terms had mostly passed from the public consciousness by the late 1900s, but some still refer to prisoner transport vehicles as paddy wagons.

Gordon, Green, and Hinsdale Incidents

About 12:30 in the morning on March 9, 1918, Police Officer Maurice Gordon was patrolling his beat in the Bessemer neighborhood when he was told by a woman that a "foreigner" was causing a disturbance in the rooming house above Bergerman Brothers clothing store at Northern and Evans. Officer Gordon duly went to investigate, but as he climbed the stairs to the room indicated by the woman, he was instantly fired upon.

The bullet struck the young officer in the abdomen, penetrated his body, and lodged in his clothing. It was later found when he was undressed for surgery at St. Mary's Hospital. Gordon fell back against the wall when he was hit. As he drew his weapon the suspect fled down the stairs and out the door. Gordon attempted to return fire at the fleeing felon, but when the hammer of his weapon fell, the cartridge failed to fire. It was a common problem with ammunition of the day.

Knowing he had suffered a critical injury from which he could die, he struggled to get down the stairs and into the street from where he could attract someone to help him. Fortunately, the other cartridges in his revolver worked, because once outside he was able to fire his weapon four times, which brought a crowd of late-night revelers to his aid.

Word was sent to police headquarters and Night Captain Jack Sinclair, along with Officers O'Leary, Swearingen, Weiner and others rushed to the scene. Though a thorough search of the Bessemer environs was made, no suspect was ever arrested, and the case soon went cold due to lack of information that could identify the culprit.

Doctors Johnson, Keeney and Kidwell were not optimistic about Officer Gordon's chances of surviving the operation they deemed necessary, and they gave that grave news to the officers who gathered at the hospital to be with their injured comrade. Gordon, however, was tougher than everyone thought, and he pulled through.

Former police Detective William W. Green did not fare that well less than seven months after Gordon's shooting. He was viciously shot and killed by an escaping prisoner.

Bill Green was leading the good life. He had retired from the Pueblo Police Department in early 1918 after more than 25 years, many of those as a detective and a partner of Charles Baty, one of Pueblo's most respected officers. The team of detectives had worked together on Pueblo's most egregious crimes up to the time of his retirement. He was looking forward to spending more quality time with family and friends. To make a few extra bucks, he took on a part-time job as a jail attendant, or "turnkey," for the Pueblo County Sheriff's Office.

One of the prisoners being held at that time at county jail was 23-year-old Clifford Sprouls. A Pueblo native, Sprouls had just been convicted of burglary and sentenced to four years in prison. He was awaiting transfer to the state penitentiary and his wife, Mattie, had been granted permission to visit him. He had asked her to bring him a change of clothing and a small basket of snacks. She arrived at the jail about 2:45 in the afternoon, Tuesday, October 15, 1918, and was admitted by turnkey Green. He escorted her to a room in the office area, where he inspected the basket she was carrying. Finding nothing suspicious, he brought Sprouls down from his cell to meet with Mattie.

Another prisoner, John Renegar, who had also been brought out to meet with his wife, later stated that as soon as the two prisoners' wives had been let out of the building after the meeting with their husbands, he and Sprouls were being taken back to their respective cells by Green. He went on to say that Sprouls suddenly turned and struck at Green, knocking him backwards, then pushed a revolver forward and shot him. He said it happened so quickly that he could not say for sure exactly how it happened, but he did see one shot fired, and he heard a second shot as he ducked for cover. He claimed Sprouls then reached for the cell door, grabbed the keys, and ran down the stairs.

Renegar and a jail trustee then carried Green to a cot and attempted to make him comfortable. He said Green tried to say something but immediately lost consciousness. Renegar and the trustee remained with Green until he died moments later.

Another turnkey, Joe Vetere, stated he had just come on duty to relieve Green. He said he had just let the two women out of the building's main entrance when he heard the shots upstairs. He said he ran to see what had happened, and he saw Sprouls at the base of the stairs with a gun in one hand and the cell keys in the other. The desperate man pointed the gun at Vetere and forced him to open the jail's large steel exterior door. He then ran out the door. Vetere had to go to the office to retrieve a gun from a locked cabinet before giving chase.

After arming himself, he ran out and saw Sprouls running down an alley to the east of the building. He said he fired several shots, but apparently did not hit his target. As he ran after Sprouls, he passed Mattie Sprouls standing on the corner, and he said she asked what had happened.

Police and sheriff deputies conducted a massive manhunt and found Sprouls hiding in a barn at the rear of a house between Blake and Conley streets. He had covered himself with loose hay, and nearly evaded his captors. But as searchers began to withdraw from the barn, Sheriff Britt stepped through the haystack, and stumbled on Sprouls. His quest for freedom had taken him less than six blocks.

It had been assumed from the beginning that Mattie Sprouls had provided the gun used in the murder, but she vehemently denied it—at least at first. After several days of intense questioning, though, she finally told the sheriff how she had smuggled the revolver into the jail. She said she had the gun secreted in a bag of peanuts in the basket of clothing and other snacks. When she was taken to the reception room in the jail, she knew the basket would be searched, so she took the bag of peanuts out and sat with the peanuts in her lap. The gun was hidden by the peanut bag and partially covered by the folds of her dress while Green checked the basket for weapons or contraband.

She said Green then brought her husband in for a brief visit, and he watched as she handed Sprouls the basket. Before leaving, she leaned forward to kiss her husband, and, out of the sight of the officer, she slipped the bag of peanuts, along with the gun, to him. Both Clifford and Mattie Sprouls were charged with the first degree murder of retired Pueblo police detective and county jail turnkey William Green.

Partially because William Green had been so well known and respected as a detective with the police department, and, we assume, partially because the couple who stood charged with his murder were of African American heritage, Sheriff Britt feared the possibility of an attempt at a lynching. He therefore had the pair surreptitiously taken to Colorado Springs and secretly incarcerated there to await official proceedings in Pueblo.

The sheriff's intuition proved correct. That evening an angry crowd of about 75 people appeared at the jail and demanded that Sprouls be handed over to them. Turnkey Bradley, in charge of the jail at the time, told them Sprouls was not there. But the crowd persisted, growing meaner and more insistent by the minute. The quick-thinking Bradley finally informed the apparent leaders of the mob that they could appoint a committee to enter the jail to see for themselves that their quarry was not there. This was done, and upon being informed of the committee's findings, the disappointed mob disbanded.

During the Sprouls trial, the defense argued that Sprouls had actually received the gun several days before the murder from another prisoner, Phillip Blanda, who was allegedly planning a jail break. Mattie retracted her confession, saying it had been forced from her by a protracted and intimidating interrogation by the sheriff. Though the allegation was never proven, the jury, likely confused about where the gun had come from, found Mattie Sprouls not guilty. She immediately left Pueblo and faded into obscurity. Clifford Sprouls was found guilty of felony murder, at the time an element of first degree murder, and sentenced to death by hanging. He later received a reprieve and spent the rest of his life in prison.

A very tragic incident that occurred at the western approach to the Northern Avenue viaduct on Sunday, October 3, 1920, left one officer dead, and another without a job. The officers had both been recently appointed to positions with the department, and neither had yet been issued their uniform. They were thus assigned to foot patrol duties in the Bessemer area in plain clothes. Neither had been afforded any training or instruction in what was expected of them, nor had they been given any directions regarding how to conduct themselves while working on the street in plain clothes.

At about 6:30 that evening, a car being driven by one Halley Butcher was moving westbound on Northern Avenue approaching the bridge over the D&RG railroad tracks (same bridge that now crosses Interstate 25). Another car, driven by Scott Reed, came from Elm Street and turned to the east, into the westbound lane of the bridge approach. Reed then apparently realized his mistake. He tried to swerve to the right toward the eastbound lane, but it was too late—he struck the Butcher car almost head-on.

Officers Addison O. Hinsdale and Charles Meyers both witnessed the crash, and ran to the scene, apparently from different directions. At that time, Reed backed his car from the wreckage and attempted to drive away from the accident. Seeing this, Officer Meyers drew his service revolver and fired three shots at the tires of the Reed vehicle to disable and stop it. One of his bullets struck Officer Hinsdale in the stomach. As Hinsdale doubled up and fell, Reed hurriedly drove his battered vehicle from the scene and headed eastbound over the crest of the bridge.

Butcher, not realizing it was police officers who were involved and fearing that the injured man was a victim of an attempted murder by a gang of criminals, picked up the stricken Hinsdale and rushed him to St. Mary's Hospital. Others called the police, who arrived to find Officer Meyers shaken up and confused. When he was asked what happened, he told a great big lie. He said Hinsdale had been hit by a shot fired from a nearby rooming house. When detectives arrived and questioned him, they very quickly discredited Meyers's account of the incident. Chief Daly also responded to the call. After being briefed about the situation he immediately took Meyers's badge and gun and placed him under "permanent suspension." Today we would say he was "fired on the spot."

Scott Reed was tracked down within the hour. He stated he was just trying to free his car from the mangled Butcher vehicle when he heard the gunfire. He claimed he thought it was Butcher, the driver of the car he hit, who was shooting at him, so he drove away as quickly as he could. He was later fined $300 in City Court for reckless driving.

Hinsdale lingered in his hospital room for two days before dying from his wound. At one point, doctors thought he would survive, but complications set in, and he rapidly went downhill. He was only 21 years old and had been on the force for just two weeks when he was killed.

No criminal charges were filed against Meyers, as it was determined the incident was "just an accident." Though he was terminated from his job, the question of why he was shooting at a moving vehicle for a mere traffic offense, how he happened to kill another officer, and why he lied about the incident, apparently were not addressed by the courts.

The 1921 Pueblo Flood

Pueblo was the second largest city in Colorado in 1920. Only Denver exceeded it in size and complexity. It was also the main industrial and commercial center in southern Colorado. Steel and steel products manufactured at the Pueblo Plant of the Colorado Fuel and Iron Company, the largest steel production plant west of the Mississippi River, were shipped throughout the country and abroad. Additionally, Pueblo was widely considered the largest and most productive smelting center for silver, gold, copper, lead and zinc in the United States, even though smelting had declined steadily since 1905. By 1920 only two smelters were left in Pueblo.

The city was also a major railroad hub. Dozens of freight trains and numerous passenger trains ran daily through the large Walker Rail Yard between Main Street and Plum Street and onward to the D&RGW Yard behind the Union Depot to the west. The foundations of the long-gone D&RG roundhouse (remember Bat Masterson's defense of the roundhouse) can still be seen just to the east of the Main Street bridge in what was at that time the Walker Yard.

The Arkansas River channel ran adjacent to the rail yards where the Historic Arkansas Riverwalk of Pueblo is located today. A smaller Missouri Pacific rail yard bordered the river channel just east of Santa Fe Avenue and the Atchison Topeka and Santa Fe/Colorado Southern yard ran west of Elizabeth through the area known as Peppersauce Bottoms.

Being situated at the confluence of Fountain Creek and the mighty Arkansas River, Pueblo had plenty of life-giving water. Unfortunately, the river occasionally grew angry and overflowed, causing minor flood damage in the downtown area, and in the rail yards.

A major flood, dumping over three feet of water into the streets of downtown Pueblo, had occurred in May of 1894. That flood caused serious damage and forced city administrators to modify the river channel and to increase the height of the levees lining the river through the city. Those modifications kept the river at bay for just over 27 years, but the inevitable happened on June 3, 1921.

On Thursday afternoon, June 2, a raging rain and hailstorm west of the city dumped several inches of water into the Arkansas. The storm then moved into the city, causing considerable damage to trees, shrubs and some smaller structures. The Pueblo pjolice were called upon to rescue several stranded motorists on Santa Fe Avenue where tree branches, leaves, mud and debris blocked drains and caused the street to flood.

By five o'clock that evening the rain had subsided, but at one o'clock the next morning a warning call came into the police station reporting that exceptionally heavy rains west and north of town had caused the Arkansas to rise to a dangerous level. Within a few hours with no letup in the storm, it became apparent to some that Pueblo was in for a major flood.

Around 7 p.m. on Friday, June 3, 1921, the police department, assisted by the sheriff's office and Pueblo Fire Department, was dispatched to the low-lying areas of town to spread the alarm that flood waters were coming fast. Some listened, and out of an abundance of caution, abandoned their homes to relocate to higher ground with just the few personal items they could carry. Many people living in those areas, however, did not heed the warnings and stayed in their homes, likely believing the levees would hold and flood waters would not rise to a dangerous level.

Regardless of their stubborn refusal to believe in the magnitude of the oncoming flood, the waters did rise. Within the hour the deluge had topped the existing levees and poured about eighteen feet of water through the lower lying neighborhoods and into downtown streets. Union Avenue, South Main Street, and the Grove were hit especially hard.

Seeing a wall of water rushing toward the city's electrical generating plant and thinking the cold water hitting the large generators would cause an explosion, the facility foreman threw the switch that shut down the generators. The entire city was thus plunged into darkness at 8:45 that evening.

The railroad yards were hit particularly hard. More than 2,000 boxcars and other railroad cars from area rail yards were tossed, turned and floated away by the raging waters. Many were carried into city streets, crashing into buildings, and in some cases, bringing structures completely down.

Downtown stables were completely wiped out when the first wave of water topped the levees and rose into downtown Pueblo. Horses were seldom seen in the downtown area after the flood.

Livestock from cattle cars and horses from livery stables drowned, their carcasses carried into the streets and stacked up against debris. Rafts of burning lumber and other debris smashed into buildings, igniting them and causing major structure fires that firefighters could not reach.

Chief Daly led the department through the disaster as best he could. Hampered by a lack of communication with field units, street officers found it virtually impossible to function as a coordinated force. Though cut off from their fellow officers by the weather and the flooding waters, officers worked independently to rescue trapped or stranded people, provide first aid where needed and assisted citizens to places of relative safety. As flood waters receded over the following few days, officers, many of whom had worked 72 or more hours straight, were able to reach their command component for further instructions.

On June 5th, two days after the initial deluge, Governor Oliver Shoup declared martial law in Pueblo. He placed Lieutenant Colonel Newlon in charge of all law enforcement activity in the city. That action allowed many Pueblo officers to take a break to catch some sleep. In most cases that break was short-lived as the officers returned to duty as quickly as possible to assist with recovery and clean-up functions. Those operations continued for several weeks as Pueblo did its best to recover from the worst disaster in the city's history. When all was said and done, it was believed more than 500 people died in the flood, and an estimated 25 million dollars in damage was done.

One of the main concerns in the aftermath of the disaster was looting. Guardsmen and Colorado Rangers were stationed throughout the devastated area with orders to check the credentials of everyone entering or moving about the cordoned off locations and to be on the lookout for looters and others taking advantage of the disaster to commit thefts or other crimes.

The sheriff issued Springfield rifles and ammunition to several American Legion volunteers to facilitate dealing with looters and other criminals thought to be roaming the streets. Though stripped of their law enforcement responsibilities by the martial law edict, Pueblo police did participate in patrols to protect the many citizens who volunteered to help clean things up and restore a degree of order to the stricken city.

A Colorado Ranger on horseback patrolling the area of 2nd and Main streets where a railroad box car carried by flood waters, had crashed into and destroyed the corner of Pryor's Furniture Store, exposing the interior of the building to potential looters. The Chieftain, *however, reported a lack of looting as the Rangers had orders to "Shoot all looters on sight." No looters were, in fact, shot.*

Many stories of personal tragedy, heroism, life and death came out of the great Pueblo Flood of 1921. The disaster changed Pueblo forever. Many businesses were completely wiped out, never to reopen. Fortunes were lost, never to be regained. Families were torn apart, never to reunite. But Puebloans are resilient. Damaged buildings were razed or rebuilt. New businesses opened, the infrastructure was repaired or altered, and Pueblo people pulled together to rebuild their city and their lives. In the years immediately following the flood, the Arkansas River channel was moved to its present location below the south side bluffs and massive levees were built to contain the "mad river." Many lives, however, had been irreparably changed by the devastating effects of the flood waters and by the horrible images witnessed by flood survivors.

The Withers Tragedy

Just before midnight on June 6th, Pueblo Water Commissioner Ernest E. Withers, along with his 17-year-old son, Granville—known to family and friends as Vollie—went to the offices of the Pueblo Water Works at 4th and Grand. Withers wanted to check on the pumping equipment to see what damage had been done by the flood. He found that the power outage had caused the pumping equipment to shut down but that employees were on scene and working hard to rectify the situation and get Pueblo's water flowing again.

As there was nothing he could do to assist the workers, Withers, along with Vollie, left the 4th Street facility and headed for their home in the 2300 block of West Street. Withers drove north on Grand with Vollie by his side. As their vehicle entered the 700 block of North Grand, Vollie heard someone shout, "Halt." He later said he told his dad he "better slow up." Withers then stepped on the brake and as the car came to a stop, Vollie heard a very loud gunshot fired from outside the vehicle. His father then slumped over Vollie's shoulder and the car rolled forward. Vollie said he grabbed the wheel but couldn't stop the car from striking another vehicle ahead of them. Choking back some tears, Vollie closed his eyes, shook his head, and said, "then I looked down and Dad was dead."

A bullet had struck Withers in the side of the head and blew out the entire top of his skull, showering the inside of the car and poor Vollie, with blood and brain matter. Vollie's screams brought several guardsmen and a few neighbors running to the scene. They found Vollie hysterical, and the body of Ernie Withers hanging partially out of the open left side door of the car. Vollie Withers was immediately taken to the nearby home of a citizen who had heard the shot, the automobile collision and resulting screams of the young man and ran to assist. Oddly, one of the guardsmen who responded to the scene was Vollie's older brother, 18-year-old Newton W. Withers. He too was devastated by what he saw. He sunk to the pavement in tears and had to be removed from the scene.

Commanding officers and supervisors of the guards working that evening quickly rushed to the location, along with other emergency personnel. As talk at the scene seemed to indicate a belief that a guardsman had fired the fatal shot, Captain H. O. Nichols ordered the weapons and ammunition of each guard inspected. He also had every cartridge issued to every man counted, and he reported that every cartridge was found unused.

As Vollie had declared that the shot came immediately after he had heard the command to halt, Captain Nichols checked the position of every guardsman in the area. He reportedly determined there had been no guard patrol near 8th and Grand when the shooting occurred.

Ernest E. Withers was laid to rest at Roselawn Cemetery on June 9th following a funeral service at the family home. The same day, Assistant District Attorney Langdon reported that "the trend of opinion from those of us who are inquiring into the affair is decidedly toward an accidental shooting." He further said, "If there was murderous intent, that intent was not directed towards Mr. Withers."

On June 10th, the results of the inquiry were made public when J. Will Johnson, chairman of a hastily convened board of inquiry, said the bullet that killed Ernest Withers was fired from a Springfield rifle in the hands of a volunteer. He stated the man who fired the weapon was known to authorities, and he had made a voluntary statement to the board. It was revealed that the bullet first struck the stone pavement adjacent to the street, then ricocheted upward through the Withers car and hit Withers in the head.

The adjutant general of the National Guard stated a military hearing would be conducted, but the identity of the errant individual would not be released to the public. Case closed.

Vollie Withers, whose real name was Granville, went on to become a prominent motion picture actor under the name Grant Withers. He was a handsome and popular leading man who starred in over two hundred films, many alongside his friend and mentor, John Wayne.

Withers was in many westerns and war movies, including *The Yellow Rose of Texas, The Fighting Seabees, Fort Apache,* and *My Darling Clementine.* He also had a recurring role of Police Captain Bill Street in the Monogram Pictures film series *Mr. Wong,* which starred Boris Karloff as the intrepid detective.

Handsome motion picture star Grant Withers.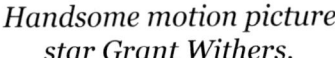

Withers was married five times, once very briefly to film star Loretta Young. John Wayne was his best man at his fifth wedding to actress Estelita Rodriguez in 1953 but that marriage, like the others, was an unhappy one. It ended in divorce in 1955. His closest friends said Withers was a very morose man who never seemed able to find contentment or true happiness.

Despondent because of continuing bouts of disabling depression, increasing obesity and failing health, Granville "Vollie" Withers committed suicide by overdosing on barbiturates on March 27, 1959, in his Hollywood apartment. He left a note that read in part, "Please forgive me . . . I was so unhappy. It's better this way." He was only 54 years old. Withers is interred at Forest Lawn Memorial Park in Glendale, California.

Martial Law Rescinded

Total responsibility for law enforcement activity was returned to the Pueblo Police Department on July 1, 1921, when the martial law edict was rescinded, and Colorado Rangers were withdrawn. Two Pueblo newspapers, the *Pueblo Opinion*, and the *Pueblo Indicator* both cheered that development in editorials. Both papers had been critical of the Rangers' heavy-handed enforcement of traffic and curfew regulations and their reportedly rude and disrespectful attitude toward citizens. The papers were also quite critical of Lt. Colonel Newlon, the National Guard officer in charge when the city was placed under martial law and of General Hamrock, commander of the Colorado Rangers, for their wide-ranging and unpopular proclamations issued unilaterally without consultation or inclusion of local authorities. They were also critical of the evident inexperience of many of the guardsmen.

The U.S. Army, however, particularly the Corps of Engineers, was praised by the press. Their efforts were vital to the clean-up and restoration of the city. They would depart Pueblo by August 15th. The help of the federal troops, local firefighters, sheriff's deputies, and public works employees, especially those under control of City Commissioner Mike Studzinski were publicly recognized by a grateful community.

Clean-up in the aftermath of the flood was an arduous task for everyone involved. It took several months.

Studzinski was a former state representative who was instrumental in bringing the Colorado State Fair to Pueblo. He also served as a Pueblo city councilman and county undersheriff. At the time of the flood, he was City Commissioner of Public Safety and Streets, the commission that included the police department. He was a hands-on commissioner highly respected by Pueblo officers.

Chief Daly's Performance Recognized

Police Chief Daly was also praised for his leadership during the flood. His officers performed admirably despite the lack of the resources we would today take for granted. The number of lives saved by police officers during the flood and recovery operations is not known but was probably many.

Daly also distinguished himself by assuring every inquiry sent to the police department from concerned people regarding the welfare of local citizens and visitors was answered. He realized the anguish of those who were unable to contact friends and relatives in Pueblo in the aftermath of the flood, and he vowed to assist them in their search for information.

Accounts of the Pueblo flood made big headlines printed on the front pages of newspapers throughout the country. Those articles caused worried relatives and friends of local people and travelers believed to be in the area to attempt to contact them to verify they were all right. Because phone and telegraph lines in Pueblo were down for several days following the flood and mail delivery service was overburdened and slow, many of the inquiries did not find their way to the intended person, so they went unanswered.

Several hundred—maybe several thousand—inquiries from throughout the United States, and a few from other countries, were then sent to local authorities. All requested assistance in finding loved ones who had not responded in a timely manner. The Red Cross, Colorado Rangers, National Guard, the Knights of Columbus, local hospitals, the fire department, schools and other community organizations all received inquiries. Hundreds of them were received by the police department. Most of those still exist in department archives, along with the telegraphed replies sent back to the senders. Each of the replies were "signed" by Chief Daly, though many may have been signed by others, indicating Chief Daly as signer. At that time, all correspondence from the department was sent over the signature of the department head.

Each inquiry generated a search of lists of those hospitalized or killed during the flood. If the names of those inquired about were not on a list, a police response to the address of the person asked about was made. If no information was uncovered, an investigation was initiated to attempt to contact the "missing" person. Chief Daly then personally notified the concerned relative or friend of the result of the department's investigation.

Photocopies of several of those inquiries, along with the official response, are included in the excellent book *Mad River—A Commemoration of the 100th Anniversary of the Great Pueblo Flood of 1921* (2021) published by, and available through the Pueblo County Historical Society.

Joseph M. Daly—
Chief of Police from 1913
through the end of 1921.

It is interesting to note that of the hundreds of inquiries processed by the police department, fewer than 20 of the replies that still exist (some have stuck together, crumbled or deteriorated to the point of being unreadable) contain information that the person inquired about was not located or had died in the flood.

Chief Joseph M. Daly served for nine years, an incredibly long term for a police chief up to that time. He retired at the end of 1921 after leading the police efforts in the aftermath of the flood. He was succeeded by Tom Johnson. Johnson served only a few months before being replaced by Daly's friend and trusted assistant, Chief of Detectives J. Art1hur Grady, in 1922.

THE BLACK HAND

By the turn of the twentieth century, Pueblo was beginning to be perceived as a melting pot of various ethnicities, driven by the diversity of immigrants attracted to jobs offered by the developing steel mill, smelters and area mines. Those immigrants consisted mostly of people from Italy, Austria, central and southern Europe, Greece and Mexico. Italian and Sicilian immigrants made up a huge population of those who came to Pueblo for work and a better life, but with them came some of the criminal element from the "old country" from which they were also attempting to flee. The Black Hand was one of those elements.

The Black Hand was an extortion racket practiced by both organized and unorganized criminal gangs that formed in Italy as early as the mid-1700s. The feared Camorra and the Sicilian Mafia, highly organized criminal enterprises operating throughout Italy, were both known to practice the black hand method of extorting money from their fellow countrymen. Freelance criminals also employed the lucrative practice. Victims would receive a letter demanding a certain sum of money or face death. The letters were frequently decorated with crude drawings of daggers dripping blood, skulls or hearts pierced with arrows or other menacing figures and "signed" with a drawing of a black handprint. Recipients of those letters knew, or believed, that the ones who ignored the terrifying threats were frequently assaulted, murdered or had their homes or businesses destroyed. They were justifiably terrified when they received such a letter.

The secret society of the Black Hand made its way to America in the late 1890s and early 1900s with the wave of Italian and Sicilian immigrants entering the country. The criminal Black Handers established their nefarious operations wherever they found conglomerations of immigrants, particularly those of a lower economic and educational status. They knew those individuals would be the most susceptible to their threats, less likely to go to law enforcement for help and too frightened to try to defend themselves using violence against their oppressors.

The first reports of Black Hand activity in Pueblo appeared in 1908 and 1909 and continued for a dozen or more years. Many immigrants, fearful of the government and of the police because of brutal governmental practices, corruption and police apathy or outright bias in their homeland, did not report the receipt of Black Hand threats. Many paid the money demanded and remained silent. Pueblo immigrants who did report Black Hand threats to police were often viciously assaulted. Some were even murdered.

In March of 1909, Pueblo police and sheriff's deputies laid in wait for the suspects who had sent a threatening letter to one

Tony Centenni demanding $2,000. The money was to be left at a specific place on the outskirts of town, or Centenni and his family would all be killed. Two men showed up in the night to retrieve the money and when officers attempted to move in for an arrest, the men opened fire. Officers returned fire, and during the furious gun battle one of the suspected Black Handers, Sam Falconi, was killed. The second man fled and was not caught. Due to the darkness and the distance involved, he could not be recognized or identified by any of the officers.

Appeals to the Italian community for information about Falconi's companion went unanswered as fear seemed to grip several segments of the city. Astonishingly, rather than receiving thanks for assisting the victims of Black Hand threats, the police received angry and loud criticism from leaders of the Italian and Sicilian neighborhoods for the shooting of Falconi, even though no individual officer admitted shooting the man, nor could any of their firearms be connected to the bullet that struck Falconi.

Testimony of several officers at the coroner's inquest held two days after the gunfight differed from the initial reports of the incident. Three of the sheriff's deputies involved testified that officers were quite some distance from the suspects when shooting broke out. They stated they were never closer than five hundred yards from Falconi when he dropped from the bullet wound. The deputy first to the fallen man was questioned, and he stated he inspected the dead man's pistol and found the weapon had not been fired, leaving the impression that only the unknown man with Falconi at the time had engaged the officers in the firefight. Since that man had fled and was not captured, his gun could not be inspected.

It was conjectured that in the excitement of the moment, Falconi's cohort may have accidentally misdirected a bullet and struck Falconi. The jury ruled that even if the man were to be apprehended, there would be insufficient evidence to convict him of a crime as he would have most likely disposed of the firearm. The search for the fugitive was discontinued at that point, and his identity was never discovered by law enforcement.

The verdict of the coroner's jury was that Falconi was shot to death by a person or persons unknown, and that he was engaged in the commission of a felony and resisting arrest at the time of his death. No further investigative action was suggested, and none transpired.

After the refusal of a priest to officiate at the funeral for a Black Hand agent, and because no cemetery keeper in Pueblo would allow the remains of such a loathsome criminal to be interred within their respective boundaries, Falconi's remains laid in limbo for several days. His family and a large segment of the Sicilian colony in Pueblo were upset and vocally angered by the proposition that he could not be given a proper Christian burial. City leaders, attempting to quell unrest, acted quickly to assuage discontent in the immigrant community.

After consideration of the growing restlessness in the community, and unsure of what to do with Falconi's corpse, a statement was issued by the coroner's office that Falconi's body had been taken to Philadelphia for interment. A burial permit was then issued under a fictitious name. The director of Mountain View Cemetery was told the deceased delivered to his facility was a young man from Kansas who had no living relatives. Falconi was buried at Mountain View under the fictitious name.

In another case, Pueblo citizen Michael A. Rossi, who resided in the 200 block of Santa Fe Avenue, packed up his family and left the city within an hour of receiving the following letter in January 1911:

> *"Tonight, at midnight bring me $2,000 at Salt Creek and be careful. Do not mistake and tell police because it will be worse for you because our gang is a large one and will make pieces of you and your family....If you don't bring the money, I will dig out your heart and, with my rifle I will shoot you and your children, and I will drink your blood."*

The illicit letter was signed with a black-inked outline

of a large hand with hand-drawn claw-like fingernails with representations of dripping blood. Rossi left the letter behind when he abandoned his home and fled from Pueblo. Rossi's friends discovered the letter and delivered it to Police Chief Yund. The chief immediately dispatched officers to the Salt Creek area, but as usual, no one showed up to claim a dummy packet, supposedly of money, delivered by undercover officers. The criminals most likely suspected that Rossi had notified law enforcement before he hurriedly left Pueblo, and a police trap had likely been laid for them.

Rossi had been employed by the Pueblo Smelter and had a full-time job, but so severe was his fear of the Black Hand, that he sacrificed everything he had, in his mind to protect his life and his family. Yund reported the next day that everyone he knew who had received threatening letters and subsequently notified police, had quickly left Pueblo forever. Yund further stated it was unknown how many victims had received the letters and paid the demanded money, nor was it known how many had been murdered for failing to follow the instructions in the letters they received. Several unsolved killings of immigrants had occurred for no apparent reason during the previous two years.

Near the end of 1911, grocer Martino Turano elected to stay in town after he received a Black Hand letter demanding a sum of money. He ignored the demand and took no action to defend his property. A few nights later, unknown parties placed dynamite against the door of his store at 910 Currie Street. The resulting explosion blew the front of the building away, heavily damaging the structure but causing no injuries to the Turano family who resided in quarters at the rear of the store. Turano refused to cooperate with the police investigation due to his fear of a repetition of such an act. It is assumed he then met the Black Hander's demand, as he suffered no further assault or property damage—at least none that he reported.

Members of the Italian community, still distrustful of the police, slowly began taking matters into their own hands.

By the end of 1912, two suspected Black Handers had been assassinated, or nearly so, by potential victims of extortion. One Sam Pagano, suspected of being a ruthless Black Hander, had been shot down inside the steel mill near the open hearth. As he was not employed at the mill, it was assumed he had gone there to collect money from a potential victim. No one, of course, admitted to having seen what happened though several steelworkers were in the area. No one was ever arrested.

The second extortionist was struck down with a meat cleaver wielded by a downtown grocer, Frank Bacino, whom the criminal had allegedly visited with the intention of collecting $2,000 of extortion money. The Black Hander, identified as John Falletta, barely survived the meat cleaver attack. Bacino's actions were determined to be in self-defense, as Falletta was found to be armed and threatening the grocer's life when the incident occurred. Police Chief Daly reported that the severely injured man was suspected of being the head of a Black Hand gang that had been terrorizing the local Italian colony for years.

It was later reported by people who knew Falletta, that Falletta and Bacino had been known to each other and had worked together before a falling out occurred over an unpaid loan, which had nothing to do with a Black Hand threat. That information, however, was contested by both Bacino and Falletta, along with others in the community, and nothing of the sort was ever proven by police investigation.

Additional Shootings Occur

A 24-year-old Italian immigrant, Rosario Napoli, who had recently arrived in Pueblo with his family, got up early on the morning of Monday, March 13, 1916. He hurriedly dressed, ate a quick breakfast and right at 5:30 a.m. left his home at 826 Elm Street for the 20-minute walk to his place of employment at the Minnequa steel plant.

As he stepped from his front door, he was hit by a fusillade of gunfire. At least four bullets struck the young man while others perforated the exterior of his home.

Numerous witnesses heard the shots fired and many ran to their front porches to see two men run to the intersection of Elm and Summit Avenue, turn onto Summit and disappear into the early morning twilight. No one could identify or describe the fleeing men or give investigators any information about them. After being shot, Napoli stumbled back into his house and his mother, Antonia Ballona, assisted him to the front bedroom.

Police were summoned and officers found the severely injured man in bed. Though in a very critical condition, he was alert and strong enough to walk to the police patrol wagon. He was taken by police to St. Mary's Hospital where it was determined he could not be saved. Night Police Captain Jack Sinclair interviewed Napoli in an attempt to get a dying declaration identifying the shooters, but Napoli claimed he did not know his assailants, nor could he provide a description of them. He declared he had no enemies and could not shed any light on a motive for the attack. He died within hours without revealing any information of value to the investigation.

Police Chief Daly commented to reporters that he was sure the shooting was the result of a resurgence of Black Hand activity after having been quiet for a year. Napoli's mother said her son had no enemies she knew of and had no idea who would want to shoot him. With no one willing to provide any worthwhile information and an absence of hard evidence, the murder of Napoli went cold.

A very similar murder occurred within two blocks of the Napoli home a little over a year later on September 12, 1917. Twenty-one-year-old Nick Parrino was shot in an ambush at 6:00 that morning when he stepped from the front door of his house at 905 East Abriendo. Like Napoli, he was on his way to work at the steel mill when he was shot from ambush by two men who had laid in wait for him behind a neighbor's fence. He fell to the ground with five shotgun pellets in his chest as the two men fled. His wife, who witnessed the attack, pulled his prostrate body back into the house before calling police.

Parrino was rushed to St. Mary's Hospital where physicians declared that his death was imminent within hours. He stated to investigating officers that he did not know his attackers and had no idea why he would be targeted for murder. He said he had never received threats or Black Hand letters and he had never had any problems with anyone.

His wife, however, had quite a different story to tell. She said she recognized the shooters who were known to her as Tony Scala and Tony Savoca. She also said her husband had received Black Hand letters demanding money, but he had paid no attention to them. A milkman making deliveries in the next block also reported seeing men he knew as Scala and Savoca running from the scene of the crime. With this information, the district attorney filed charges of first degree murder against Scala and Savoca and the manhunt for them was underway.

It was discovered by police that two men matching the descriptions of the wanted parties had boarded a train in Pueblo headed for Los Angeles by way of Albuquerque and Gallup, New Mexico. Convinced that the wanted men were the ones on the train, Chief Daly telegraphed Albuquerque, Gallup, and Winslow, Arizona authorities. Albuquerque police responded that the train had already departed from that location, but Gallup police had set up to intercept them when the train arrived there. They shortly sent a telegram back stating the men were in custody.

A Pueblo deputy sheriff was dispatched to Gallup to get the arrested parties and return them to Pueblo. When he arrived in Gallup and began questioning the arrestees, it became apparent that, though they perfectly matched the descriptions of the wanted men, they were not Scala and Savoca and had no connection with the crime. They were released with an apology and the deputy returned to Pueblo alone.

On Monday, October 15, Pueblo police and sheriff's officers were surprised and baffled when Scala and Savoca walked into Deputy Sheriff Colombo Dellaquadri's home at 108 Summit Avenue and surrendered to him. They had been hidden by friends in several different neighborhood homes since the day of the shooting. Knowing they had been identified and were being sought, and realizing they would eventually be captured, they had arranged to retain well-known Pueblo attorney Thomas Hoffmire to represent them. After a conference with their attorney at Dellaquadri's home, they were taken to county jail. From that point on, acting on the advice of their lawyer, they both refused to say anything else to the police. Legal maneuverings in the case continued for several years. No record of Scala and Savoca going to trial was found. Parrino's murder is still listed as unsolved.

Black Hand activity continued for another couple of years in Pueblo, but subsided when victims, bolstered by the arrests of many of their tormentors, slowly began reporting crimes and cooperating with police. As freelance Black Hand societies began to disappear, some in the Italian and Sicilian communities banded together, partially to make money and partially to protect themselves from opposing factions that still existed and posed a perceived threat to them.

Many formed their own organized groups around criminal activity such as gambling, loan sharking and bootlegging. Those groups, sometimes called clans or crews, associated themselves with an organized crime operation known as the Mafia that was prominent in New Orleans, New York City and other large eastern cities. They called themselves La Cosa Nostra, though the name was not then known to the general public.

Black Hand to Mafia

The Mafia had come over to the United States in the late 1800s from Sicily and by 1890 had established itself in cities with larger Sicilian and Italian populations. Though Black Hand extortion rackets were often a part of the activities of the early Mafia, and some still associate the name "Black Hand" with the American Mafia, most of the Black Hand gangs operating in the country, and certainly the ones in Pueblo, were initially independent from the Mafia's domination of American organized crime. Black Hand crimes, however, had not completely disappeared from Pueblo by 1919 when an entire family fell victim to what was believed to be Black Hand reprisal for the family patriarch's failure to acquiesce to criminal threats.

Dominic Pusateri, his wife and four young children had attended a wedding reception at a gathering hall in Bessemer. They took a cab to the area of 1st Street (City Center Drive) and Santa Fe Avenue, then set off on foot for their home on Tenderfoot Hill (Goat Hill). As they walked up 1st Street toward home, they were accosted by an unknown assassin who fired about 10 shots at them. Pusateri and his wife were killed instantly and one of the children, 12-year-old Angelina, was injured when a bullet struck her in the knee. Her nine-year-old brother and her seven-year-old sister were uninjured, as was the family's newborn baby found under the body of Mrs. Pusateri. She had been carrying the child when she was hit by gunfire, and her body covered the baby when she fell. None of the children could shed any light on who had fired upon them and the crime, like many others at the time, went unsolved.

Incentives to Immigrate

Attracted by the rich and fertile farmland east of Pueblo and by the jobs offered by the Colorado Coal and Iron Company, the smelters and the mines located throughout southeastern Colorado that provided much of the resources needed for the production of steel in Pueblo, immigrants from Sicily—many from the town of Lucca Sicula located in Sicily's Agrigento region—flooded into Colorado. As with generations before them, many were fleeing the danger they faced due to the repression by the corrupt government in their homeland, abject poverty, lack of schools, famine and forced military conscription.

Once in the United States, the Sicilian and Italian immigrants found life more difficult than they had anticipated as their assimilation into American society was not easy. Many found it hard to support their families because of racism and the discrimination against immigrants by potential employers, school districts and other organizations. Lack of education and inability to speak English, also drove immigrants to band together, often isolating themselves from the rest of their communities.

In the larger cities, the Italian immigrants settled into lower economic and densely populated local areas that became known as "Little Italy." In Pueblo they settled into the neighborhood adjacent to the large Pueblo Smelter known as Tenderfoot, or Goat Hill, so named because many of the inhabitants kept goats. That area became known as the "Italian Colony." Many took up farming in that area, while others moved into east Pueblo County and began developing larger and more lucrative farms. Sugar beets were a favorite crop in the Vineland and Avondale communities as well as the Goat Hill neighborhood and the sweet wine produced from that crop was highly valued by the immigrant colonies.

When Colorado enacted a prohibition law in 1916— four years ahead of Federal Prohibition—Pueblo Sicilians were outraged. Many asked "how could the government outlaw such an important and ingrained part of our culture and heritage as wine making?" Prohibition however, offered an opportunity for the farmers to begin illegally producing the same wine for which they had become known before what they considered the anti-immigrant prohibition law was passed. The Colorado prohibition law was perceived to have made criminals out of ordinary law-abiding citizens, most of whom were of Italian/Sicilian heritage; at least that's what the local moonshiners believed. The Colorado law, however, ensured that Colorado bootleggers were strategically way ahead of the Mafia-controlled operations in the rest of the country that only began embracing the illegal alcohol business when the 18th Amendment, passed in 1919, prohibited the production and sale of liquor, but not the drinking of liquor. The Volstead Act was passed in 1920. It gave the federal government the power to investigate and prosecute the persons who made and sold the alcohol.

As the country's thirst for intoxicating beverages increased, Pueblo bootleggers, already operating very lucrative local businesses, began working with outside elements to import illicit alcoholic products from elsewhere. They also formed alliances with Mafia organizations nationwide to export the sweet Pueblo wine and whiskey products to other places in the country. Local police, used to dealing with local problems, were loath to admit the obviously growing presence of the Mafia in Pueblo. They found their local resources insufficient to properly address the type of criminal activity beginning to take place.

Though the Pueblo police did establish a "booze squad" to enforce liquor code violations, they were ineffective in penetrating far enough into the various criminal organizations operating in the city to identify the heads of the operations, or the supporting outside interests. In November 1916, the presence of a large, organized bootlegging operation in the Pueblo area was revealed when a special investigator for the state, C.E. Burkhart, announced that an "automobile truck" had recently been pressed into service between Raton and Pueblo for the purpose of bringing in massive quantities of illegal alcohol.

Police, concurring with the investigator's findings, said that "until recently, Pueblo officers had the bootlegging situation well in hand." They then added the rather contradictory statement that "many who were selling liquor were not arrested because of the lack of proper evidence to secure a conviction." Officers acknowledged that the use of a truck to bring in liquor and the influx of an organized crime, or Mafia element, would give them "another major problem" for which they were woefully unprepared to combat.

As the Mafia gained strength in Colorado, particularly in Pueblo and Denver and primarily involving moonshine crimes, rivalries between bootlegging families frequently led to violence. Murders, shootings and serious assaults fueled by the competition for the dollars generated by bootlegging, gambling, loan-sharking and other crimes, began to become commonplace in southern Colorado. By 1920, two Mafia families, the Carlinos (Pete and Sam) and the Dannas (also Pete and Sam, along with Tony and John), were engaged in an all-out war over control of organized crime, particularly moonshining, in the Pueblo area. A lot of the mayhem was played out regularly on the streets of downtown Pueblo, much to the chagrin of Pueblo police.

Pueblo Chief J. M. Daly (in cap and overcoat) and Detective Charles Baty (holding whiskey bottle) supervise the loading of several barrels of moonshine seized from local Mafia bootleggers in a 1920 raid.

Pellegrino Scaglia, also known as Antonio (Tony) Viola, was a friend of the Carlino family and he distributed the Carlino brothers' illegal liquor through his grocery store and pool hall at 904 Elm Street. That operation was in direct competition with Frank Bacino's grocery and soft drink parlor in downtown Pueblo. Bacino's store was the main sales outlet for the Danna family's illicit booze.

Around 11 o'clock in the morning of May 6, 1922, Scaglia, in the company of his four-year-old daughter, Anna Marie, and nine-year-old Frank Cordero, son of a reputed cousin of the Carlinos, was operating a horse-drawn grocery wagon westbound in the 200 block of East Mesa Avenue in front of St. Mary's Church. Suddenly, a Dodge touring car with Colorado plates, later determined to be a stolen car, pulled alongside the wagon.

Several shotgun blasts erupted from the vehicle. Both Scaglia and the Cordero boy were struck by numerous pellets. The young boy was thrown from the wagon and one of the wagon's wheels rolled over his head crushing it. It was determined at autopsy that he was dead from the gunfire before the wheel smashed his head. Scaglia was killed instantly. His body fell backward over his young daughter, shielding her from gunfire. She was found under her father, covered with his blood and severely traumatized, but otherwise uninjured. A bystander nearly a block away was also struck by buckshot, but his wounds were minor.

Police investigators discovered a loaded revolver under the seat of Scaglia's cart, but Scaglia did not have a chance to reach for it when the shooting started. Pueblo police knew Scaglia and were aware that he had a history of violence, having once been arrested for murder in New York City, though he beat that rap.

Author Sam Carlino, grandson of Pete Carlino, recently revealed in his excellent book *Colorado's Carlino Brothers—A Bootlegging Empire* that the murder of Scaglia was an unsanctioned hit (not authorized by the Mafia higher-ups) on the man considered the head of the Pueblo Mafia. So significant was the death of Scaglia, that it warranted a meeting of the eastern Mafia capos (bosses) to "adjudicate" it—Mafia style. The hit on Scaglia had also solidified the rift between the two Pueblo factions, the Carlinos and the Dannas that had been brewing for some time. The shooters were never identified, and no arrests were made, but many more murders bloodied the streets of Pueblo in the years to come.

Grandson Sam Carlino's exhaustive research into his family's history further revealed incontrovertible evidence that a definite connection had existed for years between his family, the Chicago "outfit" headed by Al Capone and a vicious New York Mafia family headed by Salvatore Maranzano. Sam's grandfather, Pete Carlino, had met several times with Maranzano, ostensibly to discuss details of the relationship between Pueblo's criminal empire and the leadership of the New York Mafia.

Interestingly, at least four, possibly many more Maranzano sympathizers and Maranzano himself, would be murdered on the same day on September 10, 1931, when Charles "Lucky" Luciano and other younger and disgruntled Mafiosi, moved to eliminate the "old guard" and reconfigure the Mafia to create a national crime syndicate. Pete Carlino was one of those killed that day. Pueblo police had received an anonymous call telling them they could find Pete's body southwest of town on Siloam Road, then a little used country lane. He had been "taken for a one-way ride"—Mafia parlance for being driven to his execution.

About eight months after Scaglia's killing in 1922, John Mulay, a known associate of the Carlino family and owner of the American Pool Hall, stepped out of a streetcar at Mesa and Evans avenues in the Bessemer neighborhood. With him was his 16-year-old son. As the pair stepped up to the sidewalk, a touring car pulled alongside and someone inside the vehicle opened fire with a sawed-off, double-barreled shotgun. Mulay's son was able to escape unscathed by running down an alley. Mulay also ran, but as buckshot had penetrated his heart and lungs, he only made it a quarter block before dropping dead in the street. Once again, police were given no information that could identify the shooter, or the vehicle involved.

Three months later, Carl Mulay, brother of the murdered John, was sitting in a car with Vincenzo Urso, a Denver area thug who had been hired as a bodyguard for Carl. Another vehicle pulled alongside the car they occupied and, before Urso could pull his gun, several shots were fired into their car. Carl sped away but his car floundered with a flat tire. He abandoned the vehicle and ran to safety, but Urso died instantaneously from multiple buckshot wounds.

Reacting to citizen outrage at the number of Black Hand or Mafia shootings in the city and relying upon information provided by witnesses to the Urso killing, Pueblo police quickly arrested two members of the Danna gang, James Giarratano and Joe Piscopo. However, after hearing conflicting testimony from 16 witnesses, a coroner's jury concluded they could not indict anyone. Giarratano and Piscopo left the courtroom unindicted and free men.

On September 10, 1923, the feud between the Dannas and the Carlinos reached its zenith east of Pueblo at the Baxter Road bridge over the Arkansas River. Apparently, a northbound car containing Charlie Carlino, his bodyguard Dominic Ingo and as many as four unknown associates passed the southbound vehicle containing Danna brothers John and Pete along with their bodyguard, Carlo Valenti. As they passed one another they recognized their opponents and pulled off at the ends of the bridge. The Carlino faction at the north end of the bridge opened fire on the Danna vehicle which had stopped at the south end. The ensuing gunfight lasted for more than two hours.

When the Dannas ran low on ammunition, Pete drove their bullet-riddled car away to his nearby home in Vineland. He called Frank Bacino in Pueblo and told him to bring reinforcements and more guns and ammo, and he loaded up additional ammunition himself. He returned to the bridge to find the firefight still in progress. When Bacino and friends arrived (some say as many as eleven gunmen were involved) the Carlino faction, realizing they were out-gunned, fled to the river bottoms but continued firing.

Charlie Carlino and Dominic Ingo were both killed in the battle. When Ingo fell, the remaining members of the Carlino crew hurriedly drove away toward Pueblo while the Danna group headed back toward their Vineland ranch. Though the gunfight began about 9:30 a.m., it was not until afternoon that the sheriff's office was notified.

A cursory on-scene investigation followed. The questioning of those involved was punctuated by vociferous accusations and denials, along with conflicting accounts of what had happened. The sheriff arrested Pete and John Danna and Carlo Valenti for the murders of Charlie Carlino and Dominic Ingo. No one from the Carlino faction was arrested or charged.

At trial, the Dannas plead not guilty, acknowledging that they had indeed killed Carlino and Ingo, but saying it was done in self defense. Their attorney regaled the jury with a passionate claim that the Carlino faction had initiated the firefight and the Dannas were merely protecting themselves from an unwarranted attack. The jury could not reach a decision and the case ended in a hung jury. The Dannas were released on bond pending the scheduling of a new trial in the year of 1924. The case was never reopened and the Dannas remained free.

Pete Carlino (left) and brother Sam Carlino

The Carlino/Danna feud continued for several years. On May 14, 1926, Tony and Pete Danna were shot down in front of the Monte Carlo Pool Hall on North Union Avenue in downtown Pueblo at 1:30 in the afternoon. They had just alighted from a vehicle parked at the curb with their brother, Sam, relaxing in the back seat. As the bullets started to fly from two passing cars, Sam Danna slid out of his vehicle and pulled a pistol. Before he could begin firing at the attackers as they sped away, he was tackled by a bystander. The man heard the shots fired and observed Danna with a gun. He thought he was grabbing the aggressor and preventing a murder in progress. The man slammed Sam to the sidewalk right next to where Sam's brothers lay severely injured and dying at the doorway of the pool hall.

Though police always launched comprehensive investigations into acts of violence, they were usually stymied by the failure of participants to cooperate. Observance to "Omertà," the Mafia code of silence, meant no one would talk to legally established authority about underworld affairs. In most cases, even though perpetrators of crime were known to the police, there was little officers could do when witnesses suddenly forgot what they had seen. Even the victims of violent crime almost always refused to identify or testify against their attackers. An old saying in law enforcement is: "You can't just wish someone into jail—you have to have evidence." Without witness and victim cooperation, and little to no physical evidence implicating a particular individual in the commission of a crime, there is little or no probable cause to support an arrest.

The shooting of Tony and Pete Danna, however, turned out to be an uncharacteristic exception to the rule of silence. Defying Omertà, both dying brothers gave detailed deathbed testimony identifying Sam and Pete Carlino and three of their associates as being responsible for the shooting. Deathbed testimony is considered an exception to "hearsay" evidence provided it is given following an announcement to the dying party that they have no chance of surviving, and that the dying party acknowledges that they know they are going to die.

The testimony of the dying Danna brothers caused Pueblo police to begin a massive manhunt for the five alleged killers. Huge rewards were offered by Colorado's governor and Pueblo County officials for the arrest of the five.

Fearing one of their own men might be tempted by the substantial reward and betray them, Pete Carlino and two associates surrendered to the Pueblo sheriff on August 22, 1926. Sam and the other wanted party remained at large.

During the November 1926 trial of Pete Carlino, the last of the Danna brothers, Sam, testified that he had seen both Carlinos fire the shots that killed his brothers. Further, Tony and Pete Danna's dying declarations were presented in nail-biting clarity in court. Though police and prosecutors thought they had an airtight case against Carlino, the jury, after seven votes, returned a verdict of not guilty. Astonishingly, they claimed the prosecution had presented insufficient evidence to warrant a guilty verdict. Pete Carlino and his two henchmen, Carl Mulay and Pete LaRocca, hugged each other and walked out of the courthouse together joking and laughing.

Following the trial, the Carlinos intensified their bootlegging business in Pueblo and Southern Colorado with seeming impunity. In 1927 they expanded their operation into the Denver area and formed strong alliances with Denver mobsters. Many more murders occurred in the following years as the Mafia gained strength throughout Colorado.

On May 6, 1930, Sam Danna, the last of the once powerful Danna Mafia crew, was lured to a downtown Pueblo alley, most likely by someone he trusted. His fear of being "rubbed out" by rival gangsters following the murders of his brothers was so intense that he rarely ventured far from his fortified Vineland home. When he did, he was usually heavily armed and in the presence of a bodyguard or close friend. In the nearly four years since the audacious daytime murders of his brothers, he had fallen victim to two attempts on his life.

One of those attempts was a machine gun attack that caught him off guard and came close to killing him as he operated his beet puller in the field next to his home.

Police suspected that he went with an unknown "friend" to that fateful meeting in the downtown alley to discuss ways and means of exacting revenge against the Carlino faction he deemed responsible for those attempts on his life. He was armed with his .45 automatic pistol and a short shotgun when he stepped into the alley.

His blood-stained body was found in that alley a short time later. Three shotgun blasts delivered at close range into the center of his back brought a dubious end to the vendetta between the Carlino family and the Danna family. It was thought he was killed with his own shotgun. Sam Danna's murder was never solved.

The end of the Carlino/Danna war and the departure of the Carlino family to Denver did not end Mafia activity in Pueblo. Frequently referred to on the streets as "Little Chicago," because the Mafia influence was so well known by citizens, Pueblo continued to be Colorado's most important Mafia stronghold through the 1970s and '80s.

LYNCHING

Lynching, or the extrajudicial and illegal mob murder of those known to or merely thought to have committed serious crimes, were not as common before the turn of the last century in Colorado as many people believe. Most instances of lynching during that time were motivated by crimes committed in localities that had little to no formal law enforcement presence to deal with law breakers or bring perpetrators to justice. Most lynchings seem to have been brought about by the commission of financial crimes, like cattle rustling or horse stealing, or by extremely heinous crimes that shocked the consciousness of otherwise law-abiding citizens, even though the tendency today is to think of lynchings of that era as being motivated strictly by racial animus.

Though many believe that lynching crimes were committed mostly in the southern states, Colorado saw its share of the dreadful occurrences. Records indicate that at least 160 people were lynched in Colorado in the 60 years between 1859 and 1919—a terrible statistic but actually a low number considering the thousands of suspects brought before legitimate courts of justice.

Almost all those subjected to the violent illegal executions of that era, mostly hangings, were Caucasian. Research had indicated that of the 160 lynchings, 19 of the victims were of Hispanic ethnicity and seven were African Americans.

Even after so-called frontier justice was replaced by the establishment of organized law enforcement, lynching was occasionally accepted by otherwise responsible citizens as a means of dealing with crimes that outraged public sentiment.

Though the following story has nothing to do with Pueblo, or the Pueblo Police Department, I chose to include it in this book for the following reasons: First, I believe it exposes the very worst of mob mentality and second, I believe it points out a shameful failure of early organized law enforcement in our state to intervene in an obvious act of wanton murder. It shocked me to learn that this sickening incident occurred in Colorado.

The Preston Porter Tragedy

On November 16, 1900, a fifteen-year-old African American boy named Preston John Porter was tied to a rail used as a stake in Limon, Colorado, soaked in kerosene, set afire, and burned alive. Some few in the mob cheered as he screamed, "Oh my God, let me go, oh my God," but news reporters that were present claimed the majority of the crowd witnessing the event stood grim faced, stoic and quiet, not uttering a word as they watched the poor boy burn to death. He had been accused of the murder of a 12-year-old white girl, Louise Frost, in Limon just days before the horrific lynching.

News reports of the time indicated there was some initial cause for suspecting young Preston of committing the crime, and some evidence, though circumstantial, led Louise's family to believe he was guilty. A number of townspeople fanned out to search the area for clues after the girl's ravaged body was found. When coworkers of the Porter boy reported that he had left work early that day, some of the searchers went to the bunkhouse where he had been staying and found him scrubbing some of his clothes. A later search uncovered a pair of his shoes with nails in the heel that matched footprints in the dirt around the girl's body and marks on her battered head.

When it was revealed that Preston Porter and his brother had both been convicted of assault in Kansas prior to moving to Colorado, and Preston had been recently released from a Kansas reformatory where he has served time for a nonfatal attack on a young girl, the suspicions of local citizens began to focus on the new-to-town African American teenager.

Preston Porter and his family, originally from Kansas, had just arrived in Limon where his father had obtained a job with the railroad. When the Frost girl was found murdered and "outraged," a term used at the time to mean "raped," Preston, his father, and brothers left Limon for Denver. They were likely fearful of being accused of the crime, either because the father was afraid of racial persecution, or possibly because he thought his son might be guilty of the crime. Their flight, however, made angry Limon citizens certain the family's action was an indication of the youth's guilt.

The Porter family was arrested when they arrived in Denver. They were placed in the Denver jail to undergo "questioning." That questioning lasted for four days. A Denver newspaper reported on that fourth day that Preston had confessed to the heinous killing. Preston later retracted his confession saying it was extracted from him by torture and by threats to lynch his father.

When arrested, Porter's father admitted to Denver authorities that they were planning on going back to Kansas and had shipped some of their clothing ahead of them. When the clothing was retrieved and inspected, two items belonging to Preston were found to have blood stains on them. In addition, it was reported by the Denver press that when he confessed, Preston had provided information only the killer of little Louise Frost could have known—like where he had discarded Louise's pocketbook. Two officers sent to Limon from Denver, found the pocketbook exactly where Preston said it would be.

After Preston's arrest there were demonstrations and riots during which angry crowds threatened to take over the Denver jail and lynch the boy. Colorado Governor Charles Thomas, a former Confederate military officer and avowed racist, said, "If Porter is lynched there'd be one less Negro." His unfortunate comment appears to have been the only instance of racial animosity that surfaced in the case. He claimed he would do nothing to keep Preston in Denver where he would be relatively safe.

Denver Police Chief Farley and Logan County Sheriff Freeman agreed that Porter should remain in the Denver jail until direct evidence of guilt could be found, but they relented when the Denver DA said he would authorize Preston's release to Limon authorities due to the threat of a lynching in Denver. Initially all three were skeptical of Porter's guilt but after the bloody clothes were found Freeman said Porter must be transported back to the county where the crime occurred to stand trial. Farley concurred. The decision to take Porter back to Limon and his assured murder thus appears to be more than just a failure of law enforcement to protect the young man, but a political miscarriage of justice as well.

The state's death penalty had been discontinued four years earlier when Puebloan Alva Adams was governor. Many people were outraged that the death penalty was not available to deal with such a horrid crime as that of which Preston Porter was accused. Rather than hysterical irrationality, reports of the time commented on the highly organized and unemotional actions of those awaiting Preston's return from Denver. They had planned the extra-judicial execution.

Preston Porter was taken by train back to Limon where the angry mob, which included the murdered girl's father, was waiting. The grief-stricken father, Robert Frost, was "allowed" by the mob to select the method of execution. He chose fire, and it was he who lit the fire that consumed the boy. Preston had no chance of escaping the mob's horrible vigilante violence.

A hearing was conducted in Denver about the lynching. At least two news reporters who attended the hearing claimed they had photographs that could identify several members of the mob that murdered Porter. Their testimony, however, was ignored. The official inquest returned a finding that Preston Porter had been murdered by a person or persons unknown, but that Preston Porter was most likely guilty of the murder of the Frost girl. There appears to have been no evidence that the lynching was ever motivated by race, but only by a conglomeration of circumstantial evidence that convinced a majority of the citizens of Limon that Preston was indeed guilty.

The discontinuance of capital punishment in the state was cited by members of the lynch mob as the reason for carrying out the execution. They reportedly stated that if the state would not provide the appropriate form of justice, it was their duty to do so. It wasn't until the following year (1901) that the state legislature, along with Governor James Orman of Pueblo, reinstated capital punishment in Colorado.

Pueblo was not immune to such displays of brutal anarchy in the years following the turn of the last century. News accounts of several crimes against women, children or well-known or respected citizens in those years were replete with reports of threats to lynch the supposed perpetrator and authorities having to "spirit away" prisoners to keep them from becoming victims of mob violence. As we have seen, a large crowd attempted to force their way into Pueblo County jail in 1918 to get the suspect who murdered turnkey William Green during a jail break. They were thwarted only by the foresight of Sheriff Britt who ordered the suspect removed to an out-of-county facility. His action most likely saved the prisoner from the vilest of mob "justice."

Calvin Kimblern Incident

Calvin Kimblern and his wife Hattie were an African American couple hired in late April 1900 by the Reverend Alvin Fries just six months prior to the Preston Porter tragedy. They were needed to work in the Fries Home for Orphans. The home, located at 2812 4th Avenue on the then northern outskirts of Pueblo, had taken in 17 orphans who were being cared for by the reverend and his wife. The *Chieftain* reported that by 1919 the facility had grown to 50 or 60 children housed in three houses in the 2800 block of 3rd and 4th avenues so that additional help was needed to care for the children.

Kimblern was recruited to be the cook and Hattie was to serve as a nurse for the younger children. She soon became very popular with the youngsters under her care, who affectionately called her "Aunt Hattie," and apparently confided to her many of their worries, concerns, and fears.

On Sunday evening, May 20th, Kimblern and Hattie became involved in a loud and violent argument that awoke several of the youthful inmates of the home. An eight-year-old girl, Christina Carter, would later tell Pueblo Police officers that she heard Kimblern yelling at his wife, and then she heard two gunshots. She said she awoke to find Kimblern and Hattie in the room where she and several other young girls had been sleeping.

Carter said Kimblern appeared to be very angry at two of the girls, 13-year-old Ethel Straussen and 11-year-old Jessie Skaggs. He reportedly told the girls he was going to "punish them for telling lies about him." He then raised a revolver and shot Ethel, injuring her badly. As Ethel screamed and cried out, he turned the gun on little Jessie, and shot her to death. According to Christina, he then shot Ethel again, killing her. At that point he may have shot his wife. He then fled from the home. Hattie Kimblern, having been wounded by two gunshots, ran from the scene to a neighbor's home and called for police, then went to the aid of the children who were all awake and hysterical.

A huge manhunt was organized in the area, but Kimblern could not be found. Hattie told the officers she had confronted her husband because the girls told her they wished Kimblern would leave her. She said he flew into a rage and he pulled a revolver and shot her twice and also shot the two girls who he said had been "telling lies" about him. She was not critically injured. A subsequent autopsy on the two young murder victims revealed they had both suffered previous sexual "indignities," but Hattie said nothing to the officers about the girls being molested.

Pueblo officers, fearing correctly that Kimblern had fled town, sent telegraph messages to all area law enforcement agencies advising of the horrendous crime and giving a description of the wanted man. One of those messages went to Denver, where Hattie said she and her husband had once lived.

On Wednesday afternoon, May 23, Denver Police Officers Gregory and Connor walked into a Larimer Street tavern in downtown Denver and noted a man of African American descent calmly sitting alone at a table brooding and imbibing in alcohol. Since he fit the description of the wanted murder suspect from Pueblo, they approached him and asked his name. He immediately gave his correct name and confessed to killing the two girls saying he was in a rage when he did it.

He was placed under arrest, and Pueblo officials were notified that their wanted party was in custody. Arrangements were quickly made for two Pueblo officers, Chief Griffin and Sheriff Beamon, to go to Denver to transport Kimblern back to Pueblo by train. On the train, Kimblern initially refused to discuss the incident but finally admitted to both sexually molesting the girls and shooting them to death.

It was decided to keep the arrest and subsequent transport to Pueblo secret. So great was the anger of a growing mob of local citizens outraged by the murder of children that local authorities feared an attempt to lynch the suspect if it became known he had been captured and was being returned to Pueblo. It didn't take long, however, before the information leaked out, and mobs of enraged Puebloans marched on Pueblo's four railroad depots waiting for the return of the man. Several members of the mob, estimated by the *Chieftain* at 2,000 people—other papers inflated the number to anywhere from 3,000 to 5,000—mostly men and boys, rode north of town on horseback. They began stopping trains, boarding them, and searching for their quarry.

The train bearing Kimblern apparently made it through the roving mob, but upon arriving at the 8th Street Depot, then located just south of where the current railroad line passes under the 8th Street bridge, the mob attacked. Several Pueblo police officers detailed to meet the chief, the sheriff and their prisoner, were overpowered and held while the mob placed a rope around Kimblern's ankles and drug him to the corner of 8th and Santa Fe. As they crossed several train tracks on the way, Kimblern's head bounced each time it struck a rail.

A rope was then tied around his neck, and he was hoisted toward the top of a telegraph pole. The rope slipped, however, sending him to the ground. He was again hoisted to the top of the pole, but the rope slipped a second time and he again fell to the pavement. A "newspaper boy" then shimmied up the pole, looped the rope over a cross beam, and again the battered, bloody and likely unconscious Kimblern was hoisted up the pole where he was hung by his neck. The *Chieftain* reported a doctor examined him after the second fall from the pole and pronounced him dead. He possibly was dead from head injuries before being hoisted up the pole the first time.

Some reports indicated members of the crowd began shooting at the corpse as it hung from the pole. The *Chieftain*, however, said no shots were fired. The crowd dispersed quickly after the brutal lynching, leaving five or six officers, some bruised and battered by the mob, to cut the body down. No one involved in the slaying was ever identified or prosecuted for the terrible crime.

Upon being told what had happened, Hattie Kimblern went into hiding, frightened that she would somehow be accused of involvement in the murders and dealt with in a manner similar to that of her husband. The Fries orphanage was soon closed, and the remaining children were dispersed to other local orphans homes. The Reverend Fries quickly left Pueblo—basically run out of town by angry citizens who claimed the orphanage was a virtual "hell hole." The obvious question we might ask in retrospect is, had the children been murdered by a white man would the mob have been so outraged as to organize such a violent illegal execution?

William McAllister, a black man, later reported he and about 10 other black men had witnessed or participated in Kimblern's hanging. He told the *Chieftain* he was certain the same fate would have befallen anyone of any race accused of such an awful crime. McAllister, like the citizens of Limon in the later Preston Porter case, stated he and others condoned the lynching because the state had abolished capital punishment.

The lynching of Calvin Kimblern was the first of two very disturbing extrajudicial mob murders that shamed Colorado in 1900. The Preston Porter tragedy was the second. Unlike in the Porter case in Limon, Pueblo officers apparently tried in vain to prevent the lynching in their jurisdiction. Officers were successful several years later in thwarting a lynching in the Lewis Smith case.

Lewis Smith Case

Lewis Smith, an African American soldier, had been lodged in Pueblo city jail on December 17, 1917, pending trial for the sexual assault of a disabled Pueblo girl named Caroline Pelc. The Pelc girl had been waylaid in an alley off C Street in the Grove, a part of downtown Pueblo then considered the Austrian colony. She was forcibly raped and beaten by a man she described as a "Negro soldier." Two men had reported seeing an African American man emerging from the alley on foot shortly after the attack. Others told police they had seen a Black man enter a house in the neighborhood. The house they pointed out was found to be Smith's home. They later identified Smith as the man they had seen. Their identification resulted in suspicion focusing on Smith as the perpetrator of the sexual assault.

Smith had denied his guilt, but the investigation had revealed several inconsistencies in his protestations, and he had fled the city, likely afraid of the rapidly gathering mob in front of his Grove home. After a review of the evidence, word was sent out that Smith was considered the primary suspect and was wanted by the police to answer further questions. He was tracked down and arrested by Detective J. Arthur Grady and Officer Tom Johnson west of Pueblo near the Swallows cemetery and returned to city jail.

He had only been in jail for a few hours when word reached the Austrian community in the Grove where the Pelc girl also lived, and the crime had occurred. A crowd of about 75 agitated men and boys of Austrian heritage began noisily assembling in the Grove neighborhood.

By nine o'clock that evening, the angry crowd began marching the short distance to police headquarters to demand that Smith be released to them, presumably to exact their own form of justice. Simultaneously, a call was received at the police station reporting a "riot with shots fired" on Schley Street near the Bessemer steel mill. Police Captain Jack Sinclair took several officers and headed south to Bessemer, leaving only two officers at the station where the jail was located. Hardly had Captain Sinclair, along with Officers Baty, Walton and McDonald left the building, when the station officers, Sergeant Colvin and Officer Tylor, were confronted by a crowd that pushed its way into the station lobby. The mob, shouting horrible racial epithets and, threatening the officers, demanded that Smith be turned over to them.

Thinking quickly, Sergeant Colvin addressed the mob saying the accused had been taken away earlier in the evening and was incarcerated in another town. Though many members of the mob were not satisfied and moved to force their way into the jail, they did not notice that Sergeant Colvin had pushed several buttons on his desk. The buttons illuminated the red lights located on call boxes at other strategic locations throughout the city notifying beat officers of problems at the station.

As the crowd began to force the large iron door to the cellblock, six additional officers arrived. Captain Sinclair and the officers with him also rushed back to their headquarters. Captain Sinclair bolstered Sergeant Colvin's statement to the apparent leader of the mob that the prisoner was no longer there, and he further informed the men that any attempt at violence would be met with whatever degree of force was necessary to stop it.

The crowd, still disgruntled and unsure whether the officers were lying about the prisoner's presence, began to disperse, passing in a relatively orderly manner out the station's front door, but still muttering offensively about the African American suspect. As the last man left, Captain Sinclair secured the door and called out additional officers to stand guard over the facility.

Several angry men assembled in the alley behind the police station. As additional officers and a group of supportive citizens arrived, the angry men left the area after firing several shots into the air as a parting "salute." When the crowd was gone and it was deemed safe to do so, Lewis Smith, who had been in the jail the whole time, was bundled into a car and rushed to Colorado Springs for safekeeping.

Two nights later, on December 19, 1917, a second attempt was made to lynch the prisoner who enraged members of the crowd had convinced themselves had been returned to Pueblo. The second mob was accompanied by the girl allegedly assaulted by Smith. Members of this mob were better organized, better armed, and more determined. This time, officers opened up the jail and allowed representatives of the mob, including Caroline Pelc, to enter and assure themselves Smith was not there. The girl reportedly looked into every cell to see for herself that the man who viciously assaulted her was not there.

The following day Smith was secretly returned to Pueblo for arraignment. He was taken from the train depot to the county courthouse in disguise and ushered in through the little-used west door off Court Street. The arraignment process only took about ten minutes, following which he was rapidly whisked away by car back to the train depot, and on to the jail in Colorado Springs.

Interestingly, Pueblo detectives, working with the commander of the local troop of the state national guard and local Commissioner of Public Safety J. Knox Burton, assembled a group of uniformed African American soldiers and lined them up for inspection. Lewis Smith was included in the group. Caroline Pelc was brought in and allowed to pass before the soldiers. She was even given time to closely inspect each one, including Smith. She then stated the man who attacked her was not in the lineup. Burton later addressed a gathering mob outside the courthouse, saying Smith was not the man who assaulted Pelc.

As further evidence regarding Smith's movements on the night of the crime tended to contradict assumptions made during the initial investigation, it began to appear Smith just might be innocent. Two witnesses had stated they had seen a "Negro" soldier leave the alley about the time the crime occurred, but they were unable to identify Smith. Smith, however, readily admitted walking through the alley on his way home from the Bessemer neighborhood that night. He said he went straight to his house and did not see the Pelc girl or anyone else in the vicinity. As there were several African American soldiers in Pueblo during the week, questions were raised whether it was Smith or someone else who had been seen by witnesses.

Officers, along with a national guard attorney, walked the route Smith said he had taken from a tavern in Bessemer where he was known to have been on the evening in question. They discovered the time it took to walk from the tavern to his home coincided with what Smith had claimed. If that were the case, Smith would have had little or no time to commit the type of assault reported by Pelc. Still, the district attorney, convinced Smith was guilty, pressed on with a vigorous prosecution. Detectives who worked on the investigation from the beginning also felt they had the right guy, even though the case against him was growing weaker by the day. There was no record to indicate Smith was ever tried in a court of law.

Murder Of Patrolman Jeff Evans

Pueblo Police Patrolman Jeff Evans was a diligent and aggressive officer who was feared by the criminal element that lived or worked on his beat. His patrol beat covered the rough and dangerous part of downtown that bordered the Atchison Topeka and Santa Fe railroad yards next to what is now Midtown Shopping Center. That area was primarily a business district, as it is now, but several private homes were nestled in its environs near the tracks. The Arkansas River channel flowed near the southern border of Evans's beat in 1919.

The railroad yards, where itinerant hobos frequently alighted from passing freight trains to prey on the mostly quiet and law-abiding citizens living in the area, was the dangerous part of his territory. On more than one occasion, he had been required to use force to effect the arrest of a thief or other miscreant. Though over 60 years old, he was both admired and feared by citizens living on his beat because of the speed with which he could draw his revolver and shoot if necessary. A few months earlier, Evans had arrested two young men for a robbery in the neighborhood. When one of the men turned a gun toward him, Evans rapidly drew his revolver and shot the offender, seriously wounding him.

Claude and Maude Hudson, who resided at 508 West Second Street, were sitting on their porch enjoying the cool early morning of Saturday, September 13, 1919. They heard a shot fired between their house and the one next door to the west. Claude Hudson ran to see what had happened. As he rounded the corner to the neighbor's home, he saw Officer Evans lying on the ground on his back with two men Hudson described as "Mexicans" standing over him. Hudson saw one of the "Mexicans" fire a shot directly into the prostrate officer. He said both men then ran from the scene toward the railroad yard. Hudson immediately notified police. He remained by the side of the stricken officer until a contingent of policemen lead by Captain Jack Sinclair arrived. The officers found Evans dead. He was lying on his back with his revolver on the ground beside his body.

Hudson told investigators he had seen the shooters before the killing and thought they lived in the neighborhood or worked for the railroad in the rail yard near his home. He further stated he could identify both the man who shot the officer and the man's companion, if he were to see them again.

Sheriff Thomas, along with Undersheriff Slagle, Deputy Delliquadri and Police Officers Grady, Baty, Miller, O'Leary and Johnson made a thorough search of the Colorado and Kansas Railroad Station in the southwest quadrant of the Irving Place development near the Colorado Insane Asylum. A thorough search was also made of the buildings, roundhouse, train cars and shops in the rail yard between Peppersauce Bottoms and Irving Place. When they entered a Colorado-Kansas Railway passenger coach used daily for transports to and from Stone City, 25 miles northwest of Pueblo, they found three Hispanic men inside.

The officers took the three to the Hudson home, where both Hudson and his wife positively identified one of the

Popular Pueblo Police Officer Jeff Evans—murdered on Friday, September 13, 1919.

men as being involved in the shooting, but they said the other two were not involved. The single suspect was quickly whisked away to city jail and the officers resumed their search of the rail line north of the yard. Officer Miller again checked the passenger car where the first suspect had been located and found another man asleep inside. The man had a revolver by his side and forty rounds of ammunition in this pocket. Miller took that man back to the Hudson home where both Claude and Maude Hudson positively identified him as the second man involved in the shooting.

With both suspects safely in custody, officers began reconstructing the chain of events leading up to the murder of Officer Evans. A more intensive interview with the Hudsons revealed that they had seen the men earlier in the day and that both were drunk and raving about "cleaning out the white people in the neighborhood." Hudson, apparently remembering more than he originally did, told the officers that he saw Officer Evans enter the alley between his home and that of his neighbors. He watched as Evans approached and spoke to the smaller of the men and then the larger man struck Evans in the jaw. As Evans reeled from the blow, the smaller man pulled a gun and shot him. When he fell, the smaller man shot him a second time. The Hudsons both claimed to be certain about their identifications of the two men when police brought them to their home.

The men, Jose Gonzales and Salvatore Ortez were confined in a single cell with other prisoners at city jail pending further investigation. Gonzales was the man identified as the smaller of the two—the one who had pulled the trigger after Ortez had struck the blow that dazed Evans. That evening the newspaper ran a front-page story about the murder of Officer Evans and the arrest and incarceration of two "Mexicans" for the terrible crime.

About 9:30 that night, a mob variously estimated at from 100 to 1,000 forcibly took the two accused men from their jail cell, rushed them by automobile to the West Fourth Street bridge and hanged them from the bridge girders during a driving rainstorm. The battered bodies of the men were discovered by police about 45 minutes later. They were hanging by their necks below the bridge girders.

According to a *Pueblo Chieftain* article the next day, the leaders of the mob resorted to a strategy to get police officers "off their guard" so they could abduct the two prisoners. That strategy was to report a riot on Schley Street in the Bessemer neighborhood to cause the police to rush from the station, leaving it unprotected. Wasn't the exact strategy, right down to the location of the supposed "riot," used just two years earlier to accomplish the same goal in the Smith case? But Smith was not accused of killing a popular policeman revered by other officers.

Regardless, Captain Jack Sinclair took a wagonload of officers to Bessemer, leaving only Desk Sergeant Garfield McCafferty and City Health Officer Jim Byrnes at the station/jail. Apparently, Captain Sinclair did not recognize the riot call as a ruse as he rushed to empty the station of officers. After all, he had been confronted with the same situation before as he was the commanding officer who handled the Lewis Smith case discussed earlier. A police response would of course be required to address a reported riot situation with the implied risk of injury or death to innocent persons. All calls for service, especially reports of an emergency nature, necessitate rapid and appropriate police presence. But did the captain not consider the risk of a lynching of high-profile prisoners being held in his jail? He had encountered exactly that just two years earlier.

Captain Sinclair, along with Chief Daly, later stated they "had been given no intimation of what was going to happen or they would have removed the prisoners to out-of-town facilities or had irresistible protection at hand." The *Pueblo Chieftain*, however, reported the day after the murder of Officer Evans that "rumors and subtle hints were fluttering about the city from the time *Chieftain* carriers made their rounds early that morning until the "Mexicans" were actually hung." Apparently, no one told the chief and the captain about those rumors.

The abduction of the two suspects was accomplished not only by luring officers away from the jail by a false report of a riot, but also by waylaying the officer walking the beat that included the police station. Moments before the mob moved on the jail, Officer Pezoldt was approached by two men as he rounded the corner by the new city hall (across the street from the old city hall where the jail was located). The men, both wearing cloth masks over the lower parts of their faces, pointed guns at Pezoldt, and ordered him to surrender his firearm. They took the cartridges from his revolver, returned the empty gun to him, and told him to "beat it." He ran around the corner back to where he had started and did not go near the police station until after the prisoners had been taken.

Almost a half hour before the storming of the city jail, the streetlights in the downtown neighborhood surrounding police headquarters temporarily went out. Officer Pezoldt could not identify the men who accosted him because it was very dark without the streetlights. The outage occurred at about the same time as the false call reporting the riot on Schley Street. It is unknown if the streetlights just went out at such an inopportune time, or whether the blackout was orchestrated by members of the lynch mob. Rumors began floating around that the darkening of the downtown area was a part of the plan for accomplishing the lynching. But as the lights came back on before the mob entered the jail, that theory was officially discarded.

It also began raining about the same time the jail was entered, but no one blamed the rainstorm on the lynch mob. Rain continued for over an hour, becoming a downpour not long after the men were forcibly taken. It was raining heavily when the men, who appeared to have been beaten and had likely been rendered unconscious before they were linked together by a single rope tightened around their necks, were tossed over the bridge railings. The later autopsy indicated the men had died from strangulation, not from a broken neck resulting from the drop from the bridge.

When news of the lynching reached Colorado Governor Shoup, he promised to have the matter investigated. "Such action as this cannot but be deplored," he announced. "I will use all the powers at my command to run down the mob leaders and see that they are adequately punished." Sheriff Thomas also joined the bandwagon saying he would join the governor to "ferret out and punish to the full extent of the law the leaders of the vigilance committee that hung the two Mexicans last night."

Special Consul for the Mexican government A. J. Ortiz also weighed in, condemning the lynching of his countrymen as barbaric. When a newsman reported that Señor Ortiz implied that Pueblo police officers colluded with the vigilantes in the murder of the two suspects, Ortiz was quick to deny the charge, saying the news service did not quote him correctly. He even sent a telegram to Chief Daly saying he never made such a charge against the Pueblo Police Department.

Though an investigation was conducted, no members of the "mob" that lynched the two alleged killers were ever identified or charged. Though initial reports stated the "mob" numbered between 100 and 1,000, testimony by Sergeant McCafferty and Health Officer Byrnes indicated the group that entered the jail numbered less than 25. McCafferty said members of the mob had gathered behind the station out of his sight. The first he was aware that the prisoners were in danger was when a man appeared at the open window behind his desk and pointed a gun at him. The man ordered him and Byrnes to "raise their hands," which they did. He said he did not have time to press the buttons to light the red signal lights to summon help. He did that only after the mob had left the area with the unconscious victims.

With McCafferty held at gunpoint, the mob entered the office, disarmed the sergeant and demanded that Byrnes open the cellblock. Byrnes obtained the keys from McCafferty and under threat of death unlocked the doors to the cellblock. Byrnes said the vigilantes then went into the cells, found the two accused men, battered them unconscious, carried them out to a waiting car and sped away. Neither McCafferty, Byrnes, nor Pezoldt could identify any member of the lynch mob, saying they all had handkerchief-type masks over their faces, and hats pulled down over their eyes. They reportedly also spoke in whispers so their voices could not be identified.

Byrnes and McCafferty also testified that all, or nearly all the mob members, were armed with large revolvers. Byrnes objected to the group of men being characterized as a "mob," saying the small group was too organized and too much in control to be considered a "mob." He said their actions appeared to have been rehearsed and were very deliberate. He felt the individual members of the group knew each other and appeared to be following a well-thought-out plan.

At least two cars were used to take the prisoners from the jail to the West Fourth Street bridge (Sergeant McCafferty later said he heard the engines of the "machines" used). The press did not report any effort to obtain a description of the cars. Statistics indicated 6.7 million Ford automobiles, or one for every fifteen persons in America were on the streets by the end of 1919. Still, a good description and possibly an identification of the cars used could have revealed the identity of at least one member of the mob. With the increased number of privately-owned vehicles at that time, I wonder if the police, or anyone else, even thought to pursue a vehicle description or question who might own such a car as those used in the abduction. I can't imagine they didn't at least think about it. Perhaps they found no one who would admit to having seen the vehicles. On top of the problems of identifying cars, most people were inside, away from the downpour. It would be very difficult to find a witness who could describe the cars.

After hearing testimony from the Hudsons, and from several officers, a coroner's jury concluded that Ortez and Gonzales were guilty of the murder of Officer Evans. They were, however, unable to uncover even a single clue as to who lynched them. Chief Daly testified before the hearing officer that both Ortez and Gonzales had confessed to him that they had killed Officer Evans. Gonzales reportedly said he struck the officer in the face, causing him to stagger backwards. Ortez then shot him before he was able to draw his weapon—though Evans's gun was found lying at his side. He must have at least "cleared leather" before being shot.

Gonzales said both he and Ortez were intoxicated at the time, and both had been arguing with a woman before the officer entered the alley and confronted them. He further said his memory of what happened was fuzzy due to being drunk. The two may have feared they would be arrested by Officer Evans for possession of alcohol—which at the time was illegal—and the argument with the woman would likely be interpreted as disturbing the peace or perpetrating a physical assault.

The killing of Ortez and Gonzales was the last recorded act of lynching in Pueblo's history. A few additional cases did require Pueblo officers to take measures to thwart attempts to take prisoners from them—but never again was a "criminal mob" successful in doing so.

CHAPTER 6

CHIEF GRADY

The two men were desperate. They knew that if they were caught by the angry mob, which had gathered to assist police officers on a manhunt, they stood a good chance of being severely battered, or maybe even killed. They huddled together behind some hastily gathered piles of loose hay in the dark loft above a ramshackle barn. It was adjacent to the railroad tracks bordering Fountain Creek near the part of downtown Pueblo known as Tenderfoot Hill, or as most local people referred to it, Goat Hill since many people living there kept goats.

It was a cold winter evening in 1916, and the men, both hardened and ruthless bank robbers, had a short time earlier murdered Special Agent William Langdon of the Santa Fe Railroad who had approached them, and a group of hoboes trespassing on railroad property. Fearing the agent would recognize them as wanted men, they both drew guns and cruelly shot him dead before fleeing into the darkness.

They had not counted on the rapidity of the response by Pueblo police, or of the growing mob of angry locals determined to assist the officers in their quest for the guilty parties. Frightened of being overtaken, they hurriedly took refuge in the loft of the dilapidated barn not far from the scene of their crime.

Things seemed to be going well for them and they began to relax a bit. Four or five times in the past hour, officers or "posse" members had stuck their heads up through the opening to their darkened hiding place and scrutinized the interior of the cluttered loft without finding them. Perhaps, they thought they would luck out and avoid detection until the search party left the area and they could make a getaway. They may have breathed a little easier as they heard their pursuers moving along the tracks away from the barn, apparently satisfied that their quarry had left the area.

Then, suddenly, they heard voices in the barn below them. Hushing each other and flattening themselves against the floor in the darkest corner of the loft, they waited for what they must have hoped would be the final attempt of officers to find them at that location. Surely, they would not be discovered in this fifth or sixth attempt. They held their breaths as an officer climbed the short boards nailed to the wall to form a makeshift ladder to the loft and they did not move a muscle as the officer, Tom McGovern, stuck his head into the loft and scanned the interior. When he withdrew and they heard him tell his partner that the loft was clear, they likely breathed a sigh of relief, but then they heard the second officer say he was not satisfied, and they stiffened in silence as the second officer climbed up to the loft. That officer then pulled himself into the loft and played his flashlight across the interior. When the beam of light caught the hiding men, they knew it was all over for them. They had already hidden their pistols and ammunition in the barn's manger, thus preventing them from engaging the officer in a firefight as a last-ditch effort to escape.

The two killers, Joe Kitterman and Lige Higgins, had just been captured by a very brave and tenacious detective for the Pueblo Police Department named J. Arthur Grady. Since his appointment to the police department in 1905, under the administration of Chief W. F. McCafferty, Grady had gained a reputation among his fellow officers for having a sort of sixth sense regarding crime and criminals. The arrest of Kitterman and Higgins was just one example of the successes he had had in capturing wanted felons and solving many of Pueblo's most egregious crimes.

From the time of his initial appointment, Grady had served in almost every position in the department, including patrolman, jailer, desk sergeant and detective. He had risen quickly through the ranks to become the department's most renowned investigator. On his own as desk sergeant, he began the practice of photographing every prisoner brought into police custody. So impressed by this was Chief Daly that he appointed Grady the official department photographer and placed him in charge of all departmental records. With Daly's blessing, Grady then established the Bertillon system for the department to assist in identifying criminals. Though fingerprinting had all but replaced the Bertillon system which focused on a generally reliable but inconsistent science called anthropometry, the "pseudoscience" was still used into the late teens to assist in identifying arrested and wanted persons. Anthropometry, as Grady pointed out, was only inconsistent due to human error in applying it, which caused irregularities in obtaining accurate measurements and false identifications. Grady used the system to buttress other evidence, including fingerprints, to reach conclusions during an investigation.

The Bertillon system was named after famous French criminologist Alfonse Bertillon who invented the technique in

1879. Predating fingerprinting, it was a method of measuring and describing individuals based on a set of biological characteristics, such as standing height, sitting height, length of trunk, head, arms, and legs, the distance between fingertips when the arms and hands were outstretched, and others. The system had been used for many years by larger city agencies but was rarely seen in smaller city and county departments.

Though the system was nearing the end of its widespread use by American law enforcement to identify individual criminals, certain techniques, such as camera positioning when photographing crime scenes from above remained an accepted practice well into the 1920s. Grady, having studied the system for years, obtained a Bertillon table, a table used for positioning certain body parts so they could be properly measured and photographed. That table was converted to a fingerprinting table in the city jail in the mid-1920s. It still exists and is kept by the department as a historic artifact.

The Newman Murder

Grady was also known as a tough and persistent interrogator who had elicited confessions from suspects in several high-profile murder cases. One of those cases was the horrendous bludgeoning murder of popular jeweler Max Newman during a daylight armed robbery of his downtown jewelry store and pawn shop in April 1914.

Max Newman had a small but prosperous jewelry store next to the popular Colonial Theater in the 200 block of N. Union Avenue. He was known as an honest and fair entrepreneur who always had a smile for passersby and customers alike. When two men walked into his store, pointed a gun at him and demanded he raise his hands, he quickly did so. He watched compliantly as the men lowered the weapon and snatched up loose jewelry from display cases, but when they started toward the heavily stocked safe, Newman leaped ahead of them to the safe door and slammed it shut.

Enraged by Newman's act, both men began beating him unmercifully. The older man struck repeatedly and violently with the butt of his revolver until Newman was near death. The men then scooped up the valuables displayed in the shop's window and shoved them into a sack. They also took a revolver Newman kept in the store for self-defense and fled. Max Newman lingered until death took him on May 28, 1914.

The two men, Lemma Grose, a notorious ex-convict who had a history of escaping from prisons and George McDonald, Grose's 22-year-old companion from Scotland, ran from the scene, finally finding themselves at the Colorado State Fair grounds. They hid in a horse stall at the fair grounds for several hours, unsure whether anyone was hot on their trail. Eventually, assuring themselves that they had made a clean getaway, they slowly walked from the fairgrounds, made their way back downtown and caught a train to Denver.

Grose and McDonald stayed for just a few days in Denver, then hopped an outbound train. They were unaware that the train was headed south, back to Pueblo. When they alighted in the Pueblo rail yards near 4th and Elizabeth, they became concerned that they would be found with Newman's gun and the one used in the murderous assault on the jeweler. Unsure of what to do, they stashed one of the weapons in a switchman's hut. They then went to eat breakfast at a nearby café and pawned another gun to the restaurateur for their food.

Fortunately, but not for them, they were later spotted loitering in the rail yards by two Pueblo police officers and taken into custody. While they were serving their jail sentences for the city's "loitering ordinance" violation, a railroad switchman discovered the gun hidden in the switch house and turned it in to police.

Detective Grady, who had made it a point to examine every gun taken into police custody, checked on the gun turned in by the railroad man. He found it to be a Spanish made weapon sporting what appeared to be a new handle. Knowing that a broken piece of a handle from a Spanish made weapon resembling a Colt revolver had been found at the Newman store—apparently broken when Newman was struck with it—Detective Grady had the broken piece brought to him from the evidence room.

At about that time, the café owner who had received the gun for a meal for the two men he described as hoboes brought that weapon to the station to see if it was stolen. Grady did some checking and found that, though it had not been reported stolen, a local hardware firm had sold that weapon to Max Newman. He realized that he had the assailants of the unfortunate jeweler but wanted to shore up his case against them with a confession.

After days of intense grilling, McDonald broke and gave Grady a full confession. He agreed to turn state's evidence and testify against Grose at his trial believing that he would be given executive clemency and extradited to his native Scotland. Lemma Grose was convicted of robbery and murder and sentenced to life in prison.

Grady Named Police Chief

Chief J. Arthur Grady

So successful had Grady been as chief of detectives, everyone on the department knew he would someday become chief of police. That day came on July 3, 1922, when Grady was given the provisional appointment as police chief. The provisional term was dropped and he was certified as police chief on January 3, 1923. When he received the provisional appointment, Pueblo was recovering from the 1921 flood that had devastated a major portion of the downtown area and forced many rapid changes in both the political and business climate of the city.

That political turmoil meant the police department would be required to completely reorganize to meet the challenges of the day, and Grady proved to be a capable administrator. He was to serve as chief of police until 1952, making him the longest-serving chief (30 years) and one of the longest serving officers (47 years) in the department's history.

Though beginning his service as provisional chief, Grady retained his post as head of the detective unit. In that position, he personally solved two other very high-profile crimes. The first one was the vicious murder of an Alamosa mail clerk during the robbery of a mail shipment that netted the perpetrator Liberty bonds, cash and a large diamond. That sensational crime had occurred in Alamosa, about 120 miles southwest of Pueblo, on February 18, 1922.

On June 1, four months after the heist and murder, a downtown Pueblo pawn shop operator, suspicious of a man attempting to pawn a large and expensive diamond, called police to tip them that the man was on his way to another pawn shop. A police officer hurried to the second shop, took the proprietor's place behind the counter. When the 31 year-old Denver & Rio Grande railroad brakeman, Thomas Raish, handed him the diamond, the officer arrested him and he was taken to headquarters along with the diamond. He apparently had a good story about how he came into possession of the diamond and an alibi for the time the crime was committed, because the officers, satisfied he had nothing to do with the dastardly act, released him. He immediately headed to the railroad yards.

Grady, who had spent the morning in court testifying in another murder case, returned to the station that afternoon. Hearing other officers talking about the diamond Raish had attempted to pawn, Grady realized they had failed to thoroughly investigate the matter—at least not to his satisfaction. He then called the chief special agent of the Santa Fe Railroad, William McCafferty (yes, the same William McCafferty who had once been Pueblo's police chief). He asked that Raish be detained before he left town.

Raish and his diamond were brought to Grady's office where Grady confronted him with some apparent inconsistencies in what he told the other officers. He also checked on the diamond and found that it perfectly matched the description of one taken in the robbery. After seven days of questioning, Raish admitted to having committed the robbery and killing the mail clerk whom he believed had recognized him.

Liberty bonds and cash taken in the robbery were found by officers in Raish's garage in Alamosa. They had been concealed in a five-foot-long piece of pipe with a plug at each end. Raish pled guilty to avoid the death penalty and received a life sentence in federal prison.

The second case personally overseen by Grady after being appointed chief, was one that had shocked Pueblo citizens and caused excitement and fear in the local legal community. It was the cold-blooded murder of district attorney, justice of the peace and practicing attorney J.H.H. Low at his office in the downtown Thatcher Building on April 15, 1924. Detectives had looked at every case recently handled by Low but were unable to connect anyone with the crime. Grady focused on one particular case, that of John Bargfrede, who had been sued for divorce by his wife. She had been represented by Low, who won a hefty settlement for her. Grady noted that Bargfrede appeared very angry about his wife's success in securing from him alimony and payment of legal fees to Low.

Though Bargfrede, a dairy rancher and former army officer, appeared to have a solid alibi for the time of the crime and appeared very confident in his ability to escape detection. Grady suspected he had fudged on his account of his whereabouts and activities. He had Bargfrede brought to his office, where, under Grady's relentless questioning, Bargfrede confessed to having gone to Low's office, shot him, and returned to his ranch before anyone noticed him gone. He was convicted of murder and sentenced to 20 to 30 years in prison.

Killing of Officer Trout

Officer Elmer Trout was patrolling his beat on foot during the early evening hours of Saturday, February 22, 1930. His attention was attracted by a boisterous crowd of approximately 15 or 16 Italians in front of Benfatti's Pool Hall at 320 North Union Avenue. Members of the group were using profanity and loudly insulting passersby.

Trout ordered the group to disperse and move along, when several members of the group attacked him, knocking him to the sidewalk. He attempted to fight back, but quickly became overwhelmed by several young men who began beating and kicking him. He was able to draw and fire his revolver one time but was disabled and unable to fire a second shot. His one shot pierced the fatty portion of 22 year-old Angelo Martino's leg. Office Trout was then rendered unconscious and cut several times on his face and head, presumably by a knife. The crowd dispersed before other officers arrived. Officer Trout was rushed to St. Mary's Hospital by police. He was admitted in critical condition.

He was later able to identify Joseph Farbo and Sam Frankmore, both 18, as being members of the crowd that attacked him but he could not say they had personally struck or cut him. Both were immediately arrested. Within a few days, 16 youths and one 58-year-old man were taken into custody for the attack on the officer. Due to conflicting witness accounts concerning who did what and who was merely an observer, no one could be proven to have caused Trout's injuries. Four of the men were found guilty in municipal court of causing a riot. Three were fined up to a hundred dollars, and one, Gaetano Buccambuso, 58, was sentenced to six months in county jail as being the ringleader of what was then being referred to as a "gang."

Apparently not realizing the seriousness of Officer Trout's injuries, the rest of the suspected participants of the attack were released for lack of evidence. Officer Trout returned to work but complications of the injuries he received in the beating forced him to take a medical retirement in July 1934. On September 23, 1935, he died from what doctors said were severe complications of the deadly attack. His name is currently listed on the The National Law Enforcement Officers Memorial in Washington, D.C. as having been feloniously killed in the performance of his duty.

Also in 1930, Chief Grady announced the state's first police school due to open in Boulder, Colorado, on May 4th of that year. The school was the result of a collaboration of police administrators from four of the state's larger agencies. It was established to train new officers in police procedures, laws and tactics. The school was a precursor of the Colorado Law Enforcement Training Academy in Golden (CLETA) that is still in existence. Law enforcement basic training is now offered by a score of departments and colleges throughout the state.

Chief Grady's administration also saw the introduction of many contemporary innovations, such as the acquisition of a "tear gas" delivery system for use against barricaded suspects and riot situations in 1926; the placing into service of a police ambulance which could speed emergency medical service to any point in the city on a moment's notice in 1931; and the installation of a modern police radio system in 1933.

The radio system was the result of an agreement between Chief Grady and the members of a local service club called the "30 Club," which agreed to raise funds through a public subscription to supply the expensive equipment. Acceptance by the city of the plan was announced by Edward Redmond, the city's commissioner of police and finance, and details of the fund-raising program were announced by 30 Club President E.C. Fox. The *Pueblo Chieftain* opined in a January 1933 article that "efficiency of police departments in many cities has been greatly increased by radio. Installation of a system here will add much to the protection of this city."

Early in and throughout Chief Grady's tenure, the United States faced a surge in crime and public corruption brought about by changes in public attitudes concerning social, political and economic conditions of the time. Mass immigration with the ingrained distrust of law enforcement by those fleeing oppressive and brutal conditions in their homelands were factors. Others included Prohibition and the repeal thereof, the Great Depression and the associated failure of financial institutions. Adverse weather conditions, along with onerous agricultural policies, plunged a major portion of the country into drought (historically referred to as "the Dust Bowl"). All were factors that led to difficulties for police administrators everywhere, Pueblo being no exception.

An early manifestation of those difficulties was the emergence of what was called the "motor bandit." Motor bandits were gangs of outlaws who utilized motor vehicles to travel from jurisdiction to jurisdiction, committing their robberies with seeming impunity. Local law enforcement officers were often unable, or frequently reluctant to pursue them across jurisdictional lines where the officers' authority was in question. Many of those bandits, such as John Dillinger, Machinegun Kelly, Baby Face Nelson and Bonnie and Clyde, made national names for themselves, and due to public attitudes, frequently were viewed as "Robin Hood" figures who were merely stealing from the unpopular banks.

To combat those bandits, Chief Grady outfitted the Pueblo department with a complete armory of the most modern weaponry available, including the acquisition of a Thompson submachine gun with which local officers could match the firepower enjoyed by the bandit gangs of the 1920s and 1930s. Though apparently never deployed against a criminal, that Thompson submachine gun remained in service with the department until the mid-1970s when it was sold to help fund contemporary programs, a move that was considered by many, me included, to be a major mistake considering the historic value of that weapon.

Pretty Boy Floyd

The best-known of the gangsters of that era to have a Pueblo tie was Charlie Arthur Floyd, who made it to the top of the Justice Department's most-wanted list as "Pretty Boy" Floyd—Public Enemy Number One. Floyd was a hardened criminal from Oklahoma's Cookson Hills known to have been involved in numerous bank robberies and murders throughout the Midwest during his relatively short criminal career.

In 1929 Floyd was holed up in an upstairs rooming house on North Union Avenue in Pueblo. He had been released from jail in Kansas City a few days earlier, then accompanied three women and another man to Pueblo in a reportedly stolen car. Kansas City officers had sent a telegram to Pueblo stating they believed a wanted robber named "Red" Sheehan was believed to be in that stolen car. The vehicle was spotted behind the rooming house by an alert police officer. Considering the nature of the wanted robber, Chief Grady took personal charge of the operation to apprehend those believed to be in the room. He sent four well-armed and burly detectives: W. L. McDonald, Joseph Zeller, John Hench and John Hamrick to make the arrests. They did so without incident.

Once in custody, Floyd and the others, were photographed by the Pueblo Police Identification Bureau, then lodged in Pueblo City Jail while Kansas City authorities were notified. It turned out the car was not stolen—the payments were just not up to date in accordance with the purchase contract—and "Red" Sheehan was not among the arrested parties. Floyd and the others, not being wanted themselves, were merely charged with vagrancy. They were fined the following day by Municipal

Judge Crossman, and being unable to pay their fines, they were placed in city jail. To avoid the expense of having to feed and house the ne'er-do-well detainees, they were released and told to "get out of town." The car was held for the Kansas City finance company. Four years later, an incident involving the murder of four law-enforcement officers, two of them federal agents, and their prisoner who was being transported to Leavenworth Penitentiary, occurred in Kansas City, Missouri. Charlie "Pretty Boy" Floyd was identified as one of the gunmen involved in what became known as the "Kansas City Massacre" and the U. S. Justice Department was in a hurry to publish a wanted poster for display in every police station and post office in the country. As the photograph of Floyd taken in Pueblo in 1929 was the most recent one available, it was used on that poster.

On October 21, 1934, Pretty Boy Floyd and a fellow gangster, Adam Richetti, were seen by a citizen resting in the woods near Wellsville, Ohio. The two had wrecked their car and sent their female companions on foot into town to find assistance. The suspicious citizen notified police and four officers were sent to investigate. When they approached Floyd and Richetti, one of the officers who had seen the wanted poster recognized Floyd. The officers pulled their guns, but Floyd was quicker on the trigger. In the ensuing firefight two of the officers were injured. Floyd fled into the woods and Richetti was captured.

Word of the encounter was quickly relayed to Melvin Purvis, the G-man credited with bringing down John Dillinger and his gang. He quickly took a team of federal agents and flew to Ohio to take charge of the manhunt for Pretty Boy Floyd.

The next morning, October 22nd, Purvis and a group of heavily armed agents and local police from East Liverpool, Ohio, tracked Floyd down to a farmyard in woods north of East Liverpool. Tired and disheveled from a night in the dense woods, Floyd had happened upon the farmhouse where he was given food and promised a ride out of the area. As he got into the farmer's car, the passing agents spotted him and moved in to make the arrest.

Floyd fled across a corn field adjacent to the farmhouse and foolishly pulled a .45 caliber pistol in a vain attempt to evade capture. He was shot down by the team of agents and officers. As he lay dying, he looked up at Purvis, gasped for breath, and in a weak and labored voice denied that he had been involved in the Kansas City Massacre. He was carried to a nearby meadow and laid beneath a tree where he passed away before medical help arrived.

Other Depression era gangsters also had ties—though minor ones—to Pueblo. Eddie Green was a member of the John Dillinger gang. He served as the gang's getaway driver and "jug marker." A jug marker was a criminal term for a man assigned to case a bank, formulate a plan for the commission of a robbery and then plot escape routes to facilitate a getaway. Green was born in Pueblo in 1898. His father was an employee of the local steel mill, and he grew up on the rough streets in the Bessemer neighborhood. Attracted by newspaper accounts of the exploits of Midwest criminal gangs, he left Pueblo to seek his fortune as a bank robber.

Green became an associate of several roving gangs of outlaws in the late '20s and early '30s, including the vicious Barker–Karpis gang and Frank "Jelly" Nash's bank robbing crew. Jelly Nash would be killed in the aforementioned Kansas City Massacre. When he joined Dillinger, Green would work with such infamous bandits and killers as Baby Face Nelson, Homer Van Meter, Harry Pierpont and Charles Mackley. Like others of his kind, he met an untimely death in 1934 when he stepped into an ambush laid by federal agents in St. Paul, Minnesota.

Bonnie and Clyde

Bonnie Parker and Clyde Barrow were also well-known gangsters of the era who visited Pueblo during their flight from relentless law enforcement pursuit. In her book about her days with the deadly duo, *My Life with Bonnie and Clyde*, Blanche Barrow, Clyde's sister-in-law, and fellow gang member, revealed that the gang made it to Pueblo on July 4, 1933. She wrote that they spent the night in the mountains near Pueblo but divulged no further information about their escapades in Colorado. Bonnie had been severely burned in a traffic accident in Texas in June, and the gang was laying as low as possible in out-of-the-way places to tend to her injuries. They still had to eat, though, and the men of the gang frequently visited urban areas to purchase or steal food and medical supplies. Whether they committed any robberies in or near Pueblo, as they did almost everywhere they visited, will never be known. Interestingly, though, two armed holdup men in their 20s forcibly boarded an automobile at a stop sign at Lake and Northern avenues on Saturday, July 1, 1933. They forced the driver, Frank Allen and his lady friend, Audrey Hopkins, to take them southwest of Pueblo to Burnt Mill Road where the couple was forced out of the car and left on foot to make their way back to town. The two bandits told the pair they needed the car to "pull another job." They took the vehicle and headed back toward the city.

The case was never solved and no other robbery was reported in Pueblo that week. Further, there was no information in the media about the purloined vehicle being recovered. Could the two criminals have been Clyde and his brother Buck? The men of the gang frequently stole vehicles to use in robberies or when foraging for supplies, later to abandon them and be picked up by other gang members in another vehicle.

Bonnie and Clyde, who were credited with the murders of 13 law enforcement officers during their short career on the road, perished in a May 1934, ambush near Gibsland, Louisiana. The deadly ambush was orchestrated by a team of retired Texas Rangers appointed by the Texas governor specifically to track them down.

Marauding bank robbers were not the only challenge facing Chief Grady as his administration entered the first years of his tenure. The continuation of mafia activity, still contemporaneously referred to by the public as "Black Hand" activity, and the police response to the issue; the continuing public discussions about the horrific lynching that occurred just a few years prior to Grady's appointment; public concern over alleged police corruption following revelations, factual or not, about the McCafferty and Sullivan administrations; and questions about Grady's perceived involvement in those situations were leftovers he had to address.

In addition, some of the country's most gruesome and disturbing murder cases, widely reported by the national news media, occurred in Pueblo during his time in office. A series of terrifying axe murders in Pueblo's Bessemer neighborhood occurred between 1934 and 1936. Another was the horrific 1942 abduction and torture murder of 16-year-old Alice Porter, the daughter of retired Pueblo Police Detective Marvin Porter.

Arrests in two of the cases were rapidly made by officers acting under the direction of Chief Grady, and in both cases, he personally oversaw interrogations that elicited confessions that landed the perpetrators on Colorado's death row.

AXE MURDERS

It all began in a small adobe farmhouse about twelve miles north of the town of Walsenburg in Huerfano County on August 3, 1934. The home belonged to William and Flora Evans. William was an active 71-year-old farmer who sold milk, butter, eggs and other products produced by his small herd of cattle and his dozen chickens. He also did handyman work when requested by neighbors. Flora Evans, 65, sold butter and other farm products from their home. The couple was known throughout the Walsenburg area as a friendly and sociable family that would occasionally take in and feed hitchhikers and travelers down on their luck. Often, those they took in would be allowed to stay a day or two doing odd jobs around the Evans farm to pay for their keep. Though dangerous, that practice was common during the Depression years.

Shortly after 10 a.m. on Friday, August 3, Mr. and Mrs. Fred Speed, who lived by the Huerfano River about two miles from the Evans property were driving north on the Walsenburg–Pueblo road. Fred Speed was driving, and his wife and two small children were riding with him. As they passed the Evans home, Mrs. Speed was surprised that the house looked very quiet. Usually, by late morning the car was in the driveway, their chickens were active in their coop next to the house and William Evans was working in the yard.

Mrs. Speed then saw a bundle of ... something, something that looked like a woman lying on the ground by the north side of the house. She looked closer, then told her husband to stop. "I think Mrs. Evans is sick," she said, then almost immediately gasped, "She might be dead—she must have had a stroke or something!"

Fred Speed pulled to the side of the two-lane dirt road that ran about 150 feet from the front porch of the house. He backed up until he was able to see what had drawn his wife's attention. "Stay here," he cautioned as he alighted from the vehicle. He went directly to where Flora Evans was lying. As he got closer, he saw that her head was face down in a large pool of blood, and there were blood stains all around her head and upper torso. He knew immediately she was dead.

Shocked by the ghastly scene in front of him, he looked toward the front porch of the house. He later said he half expected to see William Evans come out the front door, but instead he saw the bloody bare feet of a man lying partially out of the front doorway. He figured the man was William Evans, and that he too was dead. A freezing fear overcame Fred Speed as he realized the Evanses had been murdered, and that the killer might still be on the premises. He turned and ran back to his parked vehicle, certain that a mad killer was closing in on him.

As he explained to his wife what he had discovered, a

second car, an older coupe with Texas license plates approached from the south. Fred excitedly ran out in front of the coupe and flagged it down. He relayed to the young couple inside the coupe that a murder had occurred, and law enforcement had to be notified right away. He was about to ask them to go for help when a state highway truck and a road grader coming from the north pulled up. They were headed about a quarter mile south of the Evans home where a new bridge over a small ravine was being constructed. Mr. Speed knew the men from the highway department, Ollie Scott and Eugene Brinker, and he ran to them. Upon hearing Speed's story, Brinker asked if the Evanses had a telephone. Upon hearing that they did, Brinker suggested going as a group to the house and calling the sheriff.

After some brief discussion, the small group consisting of Fred Speed, the two road workers and the Texas couple, all quietly and fearfully approached the house. Not wishing to step over the bloody body of Mr. Evans in the doorway, the group went to the rear of the house where they all saw "splotches of blood" on the door and on the ground. They also noted a large smear of blood on the frame of the windmill located about six feet outside the rear door. Both rear doors were closed. Eugene Brinker pulled the screen door open and slowly turned the knob of the main door. The door was unlocked, and he was able to easily push it open.

Brinker was very uneasy as he stepped into the kitchen at the east side rear of the house. He looked around and saw nothing remarkable in the kitchen, but since there was a straight shot between the front and back doors, he was able to see the body of William Evans protruding about two feet into the house at the front door. He noted that Evans's head appeared to be crushed, and the body was lying face down in a large puddle of blood.

Brinker carefully walked into the sitting room, then into the front bedroom which he believed to be the bedroom used by the Evanses. He saw what he later described as evidence that a terrific struggle had occurred there. The bed was soaked in blood. There was blood splattered on the walls and there were two wide trails of blood leading from the bedroom—one to the front door where the body of Mr. Evans lay and one to the back door. He also located the telephone in the bedroom, and he picked up the receiver to reach the Schlink Store in Walsenburg. He knew Anna Schlink was the telephone exchange operator who would put his call through to the proper authorities. It took a couple of minutes for Mrs. Schlink to answer, but when she did, Brinker told her Mr. and Mrs. Evans had been killed and asked her to notify the sheriff.

Zelma Sefton was in the Schlink store when Brinker's call came in. Upon finishing the conversation with Brinker, Anna Schlink told Miss Sefton that the Evanses had been murdered. She then called Sheriff Harry Capps, who said he would round up some deputies and head to the Evans house.

It took the sheriff several minutes to gather up a small posse of men, including Shorty Martinez, Bob Lee and Max Townley, and another twenty minutes or so to get to the scene of the murder. Upon arrival they found a large crowd of neighbors gathered at the Evans property. It seems word of the killings had spread very quickly after the call to the phone exchange, and about twenty people had beaten the sheriff to the crime scene.

Interestingly, Eugene Brinker, Ollie Scott, Mr. and Mrs. Speed and the couple from the Texas car, whoever they were, were not among those present. All later testified that they had to go to work and couldn't stay, apparently leaving the crime scene unattended until neighbors started arriving. Fred Speed also testified that the "Texas couple" had said they didn't want to get involved in something that would take up a bunch of their time, so they sped off in their coupe heading toward Pueblo as quickly as their 1920s model car could take them. No one had bothered to get their names or license plate number.

When Sheriff Capps arrived on scene, he went into the house to check it out. He looked closely at the visible wounds on the bodies, and he surveyed the condition of the interior of the house. He noted that a rocking chair had been knocked over in the sitting room and was lying on its side. That knocked over rocking chair became a major clue to the sheriff, but at the coroner's inquest three days later, Eugene Brinker testified that the chair was upright when he went into the house to phone the authorities. It was never determined whether others had entered the house before the sheriff arrived, or whether any other evidence had been disturbed or removed from the property. No appreciable amount of money was discovered during the initial search.

The sheriff, being unfamiliar with what personal items belonging to Mr. or Mrs. Evans should be present, or whether anything was missing, went outside and asked the assembled crowd if anyone was familiar enough with Flora Evans to know what jewelry she had. A couple of neighbor ladies said they were, so the sheriff invited them into the house to go through drawers in the bedroom to determine if anything of value appeared to be gone. They went through everything, and pronounced that everything of value was there, including a diamond ring they said William had just recently bought for his wife. No large sums of money were found, but 30 cents lay on a table next to the bed. The sheriff thus concluded robbery was not the motive for the killings.

Checking the exterior of the house and the property, including the corral and the nearby barn, outhouse, garage and chicken house, the sheriff noted that William's horse was saddled up and was roaming the property outside the barn. Neighbors told the sheriff that Mr. Evans would never leave his horse that way overnight since he was very diligent in his care of the animal.

The sheriff also noted that dogs belonging on the property were barking at the crowd and the activity taking place around the house. When the sheriff asked if the dogs normally barked, a number said they would loudly bark at anyone who approached the house, except for people they knew. The sheriff then reached out to the watchman who stood guard overnight at the bridge construction site just over a quarter mile south of the house. The watchman said he had heard the dogs barking in the past but did not hear them bark on the night of the murder. He said all he heard that night was "pounding noises" coming from the general direction of the house about midnight.

The instrument used to inflict fatal injuries on the victims was at first deemed to be an axe, or possibly a hatchet. When autopsies were conducted by Dr. S.J. Lamme the following day, it was determined that both victims suffered both sharp-force and blunt-force injuries, which could indicate two different weapons were used, possibly by two assailants, or that a single weapon with both a sharp edge and a blunt edge like a hatchet was wielded. It was further found that large puncture wounds, deep enough to penetrate to the brain, were located on both victims.

That finding caused speculation that a corn knife or a beet knife could have been used to kill both victims. The countryside around Walsenburg contained many sugar beet farms, so beet knives with their sharp protruding front spur were plentiful in the area.

A typical beet knife used in the 1930s. Note the protruding spike on the front of the chopping blade. The "spur" is used to bring the cut crop up to the harvester, so the worker doesn't have to bend over to pick it up.

The closest neighbor to the Evans house was Curtis Needham. He lived alone in a small house on the Miller ranch across the road one quarter mile from the deceased couple's home. He stated he had gone to see Mrs. Evans to buy some butter at about seven o'clock the evening before the grisly discovery. He said he paid 30 cents for the butter, chatted briefly with Mrs. Evans, then went home. When asked if he saw Mr. Evans, he said he did not see him, but he heard him working in the basement.

The home had no basement, but there was a small cellar where produce and dairy products were kept immediately to the northeast of the house. Mr. Evans churned butter and separated milk in that cellar, which stayed cool. Needham further stated he saw a light on in the Evans home at 8:10 p.m. just before he went to bed. He then dropped a bombshell by saying he saw a car in the Evans driveway early in the morning of the 3rd. He thought it was William's car, as Mr. Evans frequently pulled his coupe out of the garage and parked it in the sun in the driveway to warm up so it would start more easily.

This information was very important to the investigation since the car was found still in the garage. Under questioning, Needham said he just assumed it was William's car that he saw, but that it was too far away, and his eyes were too bad to tell exactly what type of car he saw in the driveway.

Sheriff Capps then began questioning others about a strange car in the driveway early that morning. Charles Biddle, a farmer who lived on the Dick ranch on the Huerfano River about two miles to the southeast, stated he was driving past the Evans house between 8:00 and 8:15 that very morning. He said he was going slowly, looking for some calves that had strayed from his property. He said individual cows and calves occasionally strayed on to the Evans property, and he thought he might find them there mingling with the neighbor's small herd. As he passed the Evans home, he saw a touring car in the driveway along the south side of the house, and a man dressed in dark clothing wearing a low-brimmed, dark hat leaning against the car's door as though he was waiting for someone. He thought nothing of it, as he frequently saw people there to buy milk, eggs and butter.

He drove past the house as he did not see his missing calves and proceeded farther north on the Pueblo Road.

About 10 minutes later as he was returning to his home, he drove past the Evans property again. He said the man and the touring car were still there. Oddly, he did not see Flora Evans lying on the ground just north of the house. The dark clad man and the touring car immediately became an important element of the investigation. But a few days later, a newspaper article reported that Sheriff Capps had solved the mystery of the touring car, and it had nothing to do with the murders. No further information about the man or the car was ever released.

The biggest concern of Capps's investigation was information from Pueblo about the escape of a dangerous inmate from the Colorado Insane Asylum. George Scholl, who hospital authorities said was violently dangerous, slipped away from a guarded ward at the Pueblo asylum. He was manacled when he made his escape on July 27, and he had induced a 16-year-old fellow inmate to accompany him in his escape. The youth was found a couple of days later south of Pueblo on the Walsenburg Road, and he stated Scholl told him, "Everyone at the state asylum was to be killed."

Concern about Scholl increased when a home in the Rye area was reported broken into and ransacked just two days prior to, and less than 20 miles from the Evans murder house. News reports of the hunt for the "escaped maniac" caused panic in the Walsenburg area until it was reported that Scholl had been apprehended in California, and information developed from him indicated he had gone west instead of south from Pueblo indicating he would never have been anywhere near Rye or Walsenburg.

A disappointed Sheriff Capps also organized a posse to search the prairies surrounding the Evans home to look for anything that could have been used as a weapon. The search covered an area of over a mile in diameter but proved fruitless. The press at the time settled on the murder weapon being an axe, but the officers closest to the investigation seemed to believe it to more likely be a beet knife, or possibly a corn knife, or two or more different instruments.

The murders of William and Flora Evans were never solved. A different sheriff thought he had identified a likely suspect but was unable to convince a court of the man's guilt. To this day, Huerfano County youngsters talk about the Evans house as being haunted and even though they know next to nothing of the crime that occurred there so many years ago, they regale their peers with spook stories of mad axe men prowling the property late at night looking for victims, especially on Halloween.

So, what does the Evans case have to do with Pueblo and the Pueblo Police Department? The answer to that question was revealed on the front page of the *Pueblo Chieftain* three months to the day after the Evans killings when the November 4, 1934, headlines screamed AXEMAN SLAYS PUEBLO WOMAN.

Julia Halasz Hatchet Murder

Pueblo's Bessemer neighborhood in 1934 was located near the south end of the city. What everyone called the Walsenburg Road, officially known as Highway 85, was the same road known in Walsenburg as the Pueblo Road. It ran through the western end of Bessemer on Lake Avenue, then turned to the northeast through the former South Pueblo, over the Arkansas River bridge on Main Street. It then turned north on Grand Avenue, eventually shifting two blocks west to Elizabeth Street, and continuing through the northern end of Pueblo to become the Colorado Springs Road.

At the south end of the city, the Minnequa Hospital, built in the beautiful Spanish-Mission style, marked the transition between Bessemer and the Minnequa Heights residential neighborhood which ran approximately a half mile to the southern city limit of Pueblo. The massive Minnequa

Steel Plant of the Colorado Fuel and Iron Corporation was the eastern boundary of Bessemer.

It was in this bustling neighborhood that Julia Halasz, a 66-year-old retired grocery store operator and cook for wealthy Pueblo families, met her fate during the chilly night of Friday, November 2, or the early morning of Saturday, November 3, 1934. Halasz (pronounced Halash) lived alone in a modest cottage-style home at 1628 Pine Street, about six short blocks, or 1,500 feet, from the main entrance to the steel mill. She lived directly across the street from the Bessemer Ditch, the waterway that once brought copious amounts of water into the mill to cool the steel making machinery and the hot byproducts of the steelmaking process. Now, the ditch runs through the mill to irrigate farms east of Pueblo.

Elizabeth Horvath, a close friend and neighbor of Julia's, went to her house a little before 9:30 on the morning of November 3, 1934. It was the custom of the two women to have coffee together on Saturday mornings, and Elizabeth was surprised to find Julia's house quiet. When Julia did not answer her repeated knocking at the front door, Elizabeth thought that she might be sick. Being a bit frightened of what she might find, since Julia was rather elderly, Elizabeth went to Antonia Smelich's home at 1620 Pine, and asked her to help get into Julia's house.

The two women went to Julia's back door and found it had been forced open. Quietly they entered to find the house ransacked. Though they called her name repeatedly, Julia seemed not to be there. Elizabeth left to summon the police. While she was gone, Antonia carefully made her way to the bedroom at the front of the house. Julia was not in her bed, but the bed was mussed as though someone had torn the bedding apart, as if they were searching for something. There was also a large blood stain on the pillows and sheets and a noticeable trail of blood leading to a small closet in the corner of the room.

She held her breath as she slowly opened the closet door. What she saw inside caused her to reel and flee the house screaming. The body of Julia Halasz, battered and bloody, was stuffed into the closet. It appeared she had been attacked in her bed, and then fled to the closet in an attempt to shield herself from her attacker. She obviously had been hacked to death with a heavy sharp weapon in that closet.

Police arrived within moments and quickly surveyed the interior of the small house. It appeared that an intruder had been intently looking for something, presumably money. Elizabeth and Antonia told the officers Julia had a rather large bank account, and although rumors abounded that she had a sizable stash of money and negotiable bonds in her home, she never really kept much cash in the house.

Chief Grady responded to the scene along with every detective in the city. A thorough search of the home and adjacent property uncovered very little in the way of clues. Elizabeth, Antonia and other neighbors were unable to give detectives any information which could lead to a suspect. The wounds on Julia's head indicated she had been repeatedly struck with an axe or hatchet of some sort, most likely the latter. No weapon was found inside the house or in the area around the property.

The Pueblo detectives were aware of the Evans atrocity in Huerfano County just three months prior to the Halasz murder and placed a series of calls to the Huerfano authorities, seeking information that could produce a suspect but got little to no information of value. It seems Sheriff Capps was fighting hard to retain his position as sheriff in the election that was just days away, and he likely had little time to bother himself with such mundane things as murder investigations. He would be decisively defeated by Claude Swift, who reportedly won the election by criticizing Capp's inability to solve the Evans case and promising that, if elected, he would rapidly bring a successful conclusion to that investigation.

Meanwhile, Pueblo Police detectives placed hope in obtaining fingerprints from inside the Halasz house, particularly from a small bowl found on the woman's bed. It apparently had been placed or thrown there after the woman had been killed.

Detective Richard Anderson, the head of Pueblo's Identification Bureau, the forerunner of today's scientific investigation unit, carefully dusted the bowl for prints. He found several. He then took the post-mortem fingerprints of the body of Julia Halasz and determined some of the prints on the bowl were not hers. Those fingerprints were sent to the Bureau of Identification of the Justice Department in Washington D. C., the forerunner of the FBI laboratory. It was hoped the Justice Department could find a match with the prints of a known criminal whose prints were on file. Unfortunately, no match could be found.

A careful canvas of the neighborhood, during which detectives interviewed people in every house within a two-to-three block radius of the Halasz home, revealed nothing of substance though a vigorous investigation continued for the next two months. Known local burglars, peeping Toms and other "people of interest" were aggressively questioned, however no solution to the mystery was found. The Halasz case went cold, but a lingering fear prevailed in the neighborhood, particularly among elderly women who lived alone and those who felt vulnerable in their own homes. Those fears came to a dubious fruition just two years later when a brutal and vicious killer struck again just over two blocks from the Halasz home. This time, two women were the targets of the fiendish attack.

Sally Crumpley Case

R.O. McMurtree spent a relaxing Saturday afternoon, August 1, 1936, in the Beulah area, likely hiking, picnicking and exploring in the beautiful mountain community southwest of Pueblo. He had gone on the outing with friends to allow his wife, Lillie, to spend some quality time with her 72-year-old aunt, Sally Crumpley, who was visiting from Osawatomie, Kansas. The McMurtree house was small and crowded since the McMurtree daughters, LaVerne, 20, and Rose Beach, 23, and her four-year-old son, Burton, also lived there. LaVerne and Rose had also gone to spend the night with friends, so their mother could enjoy the overnight visit with her aunt. Little Burton Beach remained in the house with Lillie and Sally.

Mr. McMurtree, though, was not going to spend the entire night elsewhere. He had likely decided to sleep on the living room couch when he got home, leaving the bed in the bedroom for his wife, her aunt Sally and his grandson. He arrived home from his long day outing at 2:15 a.m. He expected the women, and hopefully his grandson, to be asleep. He quietly entered the front door to find the house dark. When he turned on the living room light, little Burton Beach came running into the room. The child was crying and told Mr. McMurtree his grandmother was sick. He led his grandfather to the bedroom, where the man was aghast to find both women lying in a blood-soaked bed. Lillie was semi-conscious and was whispering over and over, "Oh, I am so sick." McMurtree could tell immediately that Sally was likely dead, and Lillie was critically injured and near death. Having no telephone, he ran to a friend's home at the corner of Division and Orman, about 1,600 feet from his house and called for the doctor at the CF&I Steelworks dispensary. He then ran back to his home to care for his wife. A few minutes after he got there, his son, 22-year-old Floyd McMurtree, arrived at the house. He had been to a dance and stated he stopped at his father's house with the hope of getting some money, since he had spent what little he had at a local beer parlor afterward with some friends. It was he who called the police.

Police and an ambulance arrived in less than ten minutes to find both women still lying in the bed. Both were bleeding from massive wounds to their heads and from their mouths. Sally Crumpley's arms were covered with a series of ugly bruises and the marks of blows from a blunt instrument were apparent on her head and face. A large gash had caved in her skull near her right eye. There were also several small, sharp-force injuries on her face. She was pronounced dead shortly after the arrival of the ambulance.

Lillie McMurtree had apparently only been struck a couple of times, but the blows fractured her skull. She was immediately rushed to Corwin Hospital just six blocks away by Dutcher Ambulance, a private ambulance company serving Pueblo at the time. Doctors at Corwin's emergency room pronounced her condition as extremely critical and gave her little chance of surviving.

Pueblo Police Officers John Hopkins and Thomas Easton began the initial investigation under the direction of Captain Ruba E. Pratt. The county coroner, Dr. C.N. Caldwell, took charge of Sally Crumpley's body. He ordered an inquest into the death. Detectives W.L. McDonald, Everett Horne and Richard Anderson were called out, and they arrived on scene within 30 minutes, along with Chief Grady, District Attorney French Taylor and his deputy John Marsalis.

The investigators spoke at length with the injured woman's husband and son. They were told the son, Floyd, had gone to the house earlier in the evening, about 11 or 11:30 p.m., to ask for money, but found both women sleeping soundly in bed. Little Burton Beach was also sleeping in the same bed. Floyd left the house without waking anyone. He saw no one else in the vicinity and could give no further information about the case to detectives. He immediately became what we would today call a "person of interest" as he was apparently the last person to see the victims before they were so hideously attacked. His presence at the house on two occasions near the time the crime was committed also seemed odd to the officers. Within the following two days he would be taken into custody for "suspicion of murder" and subjected to vigorous questioning for the next several days.

Mrs. Fred Johnson of Osawatomie, Kansas, daughter of the murdered woman, told officers her mother was in the habit of carrying a large amount of cash pinned inside her dress. Captain Pratt reported the woman had only a small amount of money in her dress, and it appeared to have not been disturbed. As nothing else in the home appeared to be missing, detectives discounted robbery as being a motive for the attack.

Little progress was made in the investigation during the next two weeks, even though detectives questioned people in every household in the area. The fact that Julia Halasz had been murdered in a similar manner in the same working class neighborhood two years previously was not lost on the officers, and their inquiries intently focused on those living in the roughly three blocks between the two crime scenes.

Chief Grady, known for his uncanny ability to elicit confessions from guilty suspects, questioned Floyd McMurtree for hours about both crimes. The answers he got from Floyd seemed to indicate a lack of knowledge about either attack, and the chief began to think Floyd was not involved in either offense. District Attorney Taylor, however, fervently believed Floyd was guilty of the Crumpley killing and he ordered the young man held for further investigation.

Nevertheless, the murder inquiry seemed to be stalled despite concerted efforts by a score of police officers and district attorney's investigators. But then, just two weeks after the Crumpley murder, residents of the city were shocked by the commission of another brutal murder just six blocks from the scene of Crumpley's slaying. This time two young girls fell victim to what the *Pueblo Chieftain* called an "axe-wielding maniac" in one of the most notorious and revolting crimes in Pueblo's history.

The Drain Case

Riley Drain, 38, a Works Projects Administration foreman and his wife, Peggy, had gone out on the town on the evening of Saturday, August 15, 1936. They went dancing, had a few drinks, and then stopped for a late-night meal at the Grand Café in downtown Pueblo. After finishing, they headed for home at 1536 Stone Avenue in the Bessemer neighborhood, not far from the CF&I steel mill.

They had left the home just after 10:00 p.m. with their 9-year-old son, Billy. They took him to a nearby friend's home where he was to spend the night. Riley's two daughters, 12-year-old Barbara, and 15-year-old Dorothy, being old enough and very mature for their ages, were left at their home. When the Drains left for the evening, Barbara was busy making a cake, and Dorothy was engaged in some needlework. The back door of the small Drain home was locked, but the front door was left open, and the screen unlatched, as was their practice during summer months.

Upon arriving back home at about three o'clock the next morning, both Riley and Peggy were surprised and rather unsettled to see the house in darkness. Peggy later testified in court that they always left a light on in the living room, and she said the girls would never turn that light off. Cautiously they entered the house and made their way toward the small back bedroom where the two girls shared a bed.

As they neared the bedroom, they both heard what they later described as a moaning sound. Riley immediately rushed into the room and turned on the light. There he saw his two daughters lying in a horribly blood-soaked bed. Barbara was writhing in agony and breathing in short gasps. It was her moaning the parents had heard. Dorothy was lying across the bed and not moving. Both girls had ugly head wounds and facial bruises that betrayed the utter brutality of the assault they both had endured.

Riley called out to his wife and told her to go for help. She ran to their neighbor's house and banged on the door. The neighbor, Perry Dunlap, was Riley's first wife's father and the grandfather of the two girls. Perry called the police, then hurriedly dressed, and ran to assist his former son-in-law.

Police officers Claude Clark and John Hopkins were first to arrive. They observed Riley Drain outside the front door of his house with Dorothy in his arms. They directed him to return her to the house where they briefly checked the condition of both girls. As other officers entered the scene a few minutes later, he begged them to get Barbara to the hospital fast. Officers immediately placed her in a police car and rushed her three blocks to Corwin Hospital. When Riley Drain asked why they didn't take Dorothy too, officers paused in silence but didn't answer. The look on Officer Clark's face told Riley what he already feared. Dorothy was dead.

When the initial report from the patrolmen on scene reached headquarters, calls went out to Chief Grady, District Attorney French Taylor and several on-call detectives. All responded within 30 minutes, as they realized they were faced with another immensely high-profile murder investigation, the second in the same neighborhood in just two weeks. As Grady sped to the scene, he had to think this attack and the Crumpley slaying on August 2nd were related. Also aware of the Halasz case two years earlier, and the still unsolved Evans case north of Walsenburg, he just shook his head as if to say, "We have to solve this one, and fast."

Upon arrival at the Drain home, Chief Grady took immediate charge and assigned primary responsibilities of the investigation to Detective Sergeant Everett Horne, a resourceful investigator who was next in line for promotion to police captain. The interior of the home, as well as both front and rear doorways, were carefully gone over by detectives. It was discovered that the back door was unlatched, though Peggy Drain said she remembered locking it before she and her husband left the residence the prior evening. Barbara's two dolls were found beneath the side of the bed and, as it appeared they may have been thrown there by the assailant during the attack, both were fingerprinted by Detective Richard Anderson of the Identification Bureau. Only unusable smudges of what appeared to be adult prints were found on the dolls. Detective Anderson discovered what he described as a "perfect man's palm print" on the floor near the bed. Anderson also discovered and photographed the clear print of the heel of a man's shoe on the bed sheet, and a smudged fingerprint on the bedroom door.

Thinking that tracking dogs might find the killer's trail in leaving the house, Chief Grady called for bloodhounds to be summoned from the state penitentiary in Cañon City, some 35 miles to the west of Pueblo. The chief also placed a call to Fire

Chief Luther Willis and asked for assistance of fire personnel in securing the crime scene, and a wide area around the scene. Police officers and firefighters quickly set up a two-block perimeter to keep back the crowd of several hundred people that began gathering shortly after dawn. The dogs arrived by late morning, and handlers began the tracking process in an attempt to follow the route taken by what was then thought to be a single killer. Though the dogs alerted on several homes in the general area, and several neighborhood men were briefly detained and intensely questioned, no viable suspect was identified.

City Highway Department Director H.E. McFarlane assigned several workmen to assist police officers in a detailed search of alleyways and vacant lots in the area, looking for anything of value to the investigation. Nothing was found. The Bessemer Ditch in front of the Drain residence was blocked off and drained, and mud at the bottom was raked through without finding anything connected to the crime.

As detectives began going door to door, interviewing neighbors in the block of the Drain home, Chief Grady began checking police records of known sex-offenders and peeping Toms. Seven men, identified by the records search, were taken into custody by midnight of the day of the crime. They were all questioned regarding their whereabouts at the time of the murder, but all seven were able to provide solid evidence that exonerated them. They were all released within hours.

Three days after the murder, Riley Drain was approached by a man named Frank Aguilar who had previously worked for him at the Works Progress Administration. Aguilar, who Drain had fired for poor job performance, offered Drain five nickels, and asked for permission to attend Dorothy's funeral. The encounter bothered Drain and he mentioned it to Perry Dunlap who reported it to Chief Grady. Aguilar thus became what we would today call a "person of interest" in the murder investigation, and detectives began gathering information about Aguilar's whereabouts and movements during the past few days.

Aware that murder suspects frequently attend the funeral services of their victims, and sometimes clandestinely visit their victims' graves after internment, Chief Grady assigned several teams of officers to attend Dorothy Drain's funeral. The service was held on Thursday, August 20—five days after the killing at the George F. McCarthy Funeral Home. The officers were instructed to watch for anyone who appeared "out of place" or suspicious in any way. Deputy District Attorneys Joe Botleman and Dick Cooper were also asked to attend the funeral to be available should officers need legal advice regarding the detention of persons who aroused suspicion. Motorcycle officers Nick Mikatich and Earl Butler were present in the midst of a crowd of well over a hundred people outside the front of the funeral home. Other officers were inside the chapel.

As members of the public began filing into the chapel, Officer Mikatich called Butler's attention to a fidgety man who appeared to be out of place in the crowd moving toward the doors to the building. On a hunch based on the man's dress, appearance and demeanor, Mikatich told Butler, "There's the killer," as the man walked directly toward the two officers. The man asked Mikatich for permission to enter the chapel to see Mr. Drain. Butler asked the man his name. Frank Aguilar was the reply. The officers held Aguilar and motioned for Deputy District Attorney (DDA) Dick Cooper to approach them. Neither Mikatich nor Butler had any knowledge of Aguilar being a suspect in the crime, but Cooper did. He immediately ordered Aguilar to be detained and taken to police headquarters for questioning.

Confronted with their suspicions, Aguilar denied any involvement in the homicide. As he was questioned by Chief Grady and Sergeant Horne, DDA Cooper prepared a search warrant for his home at 211½ Division Avenue, just blocks from the Drain home. Mikatich and Butler, along with other officers, were detailed to conduct the search. Officer Butler was the one who found an axe head, or more accurately, a hatchet head, with no handle under some rags in a bucket at the side of the Aguilar house. It appeared to have been washed.

It was taken to police headquarters for examination. Police Identification Bureau Detective Richard Anderson noted that the hatchet head was from a type of tool known as a roofing hatchet with a nail-pulling claw at the end of the blunt, or "butt" end. He also noted that both claws, or "peens," had been broken off at differing lengths. One was almost completely missing.

Detective Anderson went to Corwin Hospital and took photographs of the wound on Dorothy Drain's head. He then blew the photographs up to actual size and compared the mark left by the weapon with the hatchet head recovered at Aguilar's house. The missing claw peens were very evident on the wound, and the impression left by the weapon on Dorothy's head was the exact size as the one recovered.

 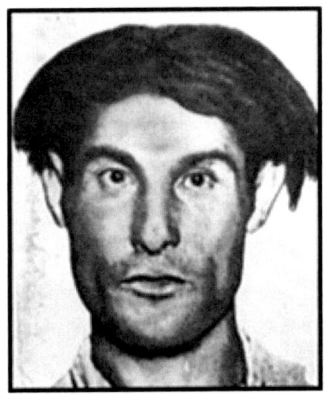

The murder weapon. Note the broken claw peens (arrow) that left very distinctive marks on Dorothy Drain's head. Pueblo Police photo. Right: Frank Aguilar

Aguilar continued to deny involvement in the attack on the Drain girls, even though he was confronted with the hatchet head found at his home. Chief Grady and Detective Sergeant Horne subjected Aguilar to intensive interrogation but were unable to elicit a confession. The officers continued to assemble physical evidence to support a solid, though circumstantial case against Aguilar. They were all certain Aguilar was the killer they had been seeking.

Joe Arridy

On Wednesday evening, August 26, ten days after the murder of Dorothy Drain, 21-year-old Joe Arridy of Pueblo was arrested for trespassing in the railroad yards in Cheyenne, Wyoming. He had hopped on a freight train in the Pueblo rail yards some days earlier and alighted in the Cheyenne yards when the train passed through that city.

The Larimer County (Cheyenne) sheriff, George Carroll, was aware of the Drain murder in Pueblo as he had read newspaper accounts of the tragedy. Along with law enforcement officers throughout the Rocky Mountain region, he had also received telegraph messages advising officers to be on the lookout for suspicious people from Pueblo in their respective areas. He did not know the specifics of the Pueblo crime, other than those in the newspaper.

When Sheriff Carroll heard his deputies had a man from Pueblo in custody, he had that man brought to his office for questioning. A long-time western lawman, Sheriff Carroll had a reputation as a tough but fair officer who had solved many crimes and wrung confessions from numerous recalcitrant criminals.

The moment he began talking with Joe Arridy, it was apparent to him that the young man's mental capacity was considerably diminished. Arridy told the sheriff he had walked away from the State Home for Mental Defectives in Grand Junction (that's what they called it in the 1930s) and spent the past two weeks or so in Pueblo where his parents lived. Sheriff Carroll asked Arridy if he had been involved in the attack on the Drain girls. He readily admitted that he had. "I killed the two little girls," he said. "I'm sorry now and if they let me alone, I'll be good after this."

Sheriff Carroll immediately placed a call to Chief Grady in Pueblo. "Chief Grady," he said, "We are holding a fellow here who says he killed the little Drain girl in your city. He's a nut—he can't even read or write—and he's told us two or three different stories, but he seems to know all about the Drain murder, and I wouldn't be surprised if he is the man you want."

Chief Grady was shocked. He was certain the Pueblo Police already had the killer in custody. Grady later said he was torn between two thoughts. "If this man seemed to know all the details of the crime and he couldn't read to get them from the newspapers, then he must be guilty. On the other hand, feeble-minded men frequently get a confession complex and admit every crime they are asked about." He knew he had to check out the man's story. As District Attorney French Taylor and Detectives Everett Horne and W.L. McDonald were at that time in Denver witnessing the scientific examination of evidence in the case, Grady telephoned them and sent them "post haste" to Cheyenne, Wyoming. Within a few hours, DA Taylor called Chief Grady back and said, "Looks like this is our man, Chief."

Taylor identified Joseph Arridy as a 21-year-old youth from Pueblo who had been confined for all but one week of the last 11 years in the State Home for Mental Defectives in Grand Junction. He had escaped from that institution on August 8th. He told the detectives he had seen the Drain girls' parents leave their house, so he entered the home through the unlocked front door and attacked both girls in their bed. He claimed he attacked the big girl (Dorothy), then killed both girls with an axe.

Arridy said he then went to his parents' home at 1604 Cedar, about four blocks from the Drain home. He said his mother took his bloody clothing, then beat him and locked him in the attic. He said his family left him there for about a week, then released him, gave him a dollar, and told him to leave town.

Chief Grady sent detectives to find Arridy's parents who were attending the 1936 Colorado State Fair. They answered a page over the fair's public address system and were immediately arrested and taken to the police station. Under questioning, they denied having seen their son for six years, and denied that he had been confined in their attic following the Drain murder. They said they did not even know their son had escaped from the state home. A check by detectives revealed that the attic of their small house on Cedar Street did not look like it had been recently entered. Arridy's parents were released from custody but remained under suspicion.

After speaking with Arridy, District Attorney Taylor was convinced that he was the actual killer of the Drain girl, and that Aguilar, the fellow they had in custody in Pueblo, must be innocent. But then Arridy changed his story. He told District Attorney Taylor that he had met a man named "Frank" in the Bessemer business district, and that Frank was his accomplice in the murderous attack. He said Frank had carried the death weapon, an axe head, in the hip pocket of his trousers. After they left the Drain house, he said he helped Frank wash the weapon at a hydrant at the rear of Frank's home before they separated.

Chief Grady would later say, "The name of Frank and the story of the axe head seemed to clinch our case against Aguilar. But we could not lose sight of the fact that Arridy was an imbecile" (a term freely used at the time to describe a "mentally deficient" or "retarded" person, or a person who does or says stupid things). Grady further stated he felt a lot of work would have to be done to either confirm, or refute claims made by Arridy. He was concerned that if the Arridy story leaked out to the public it could arouse a lynch mob that he said, "would undoubtedly storm our jail to get at Aguilar."

The investigation conducted by Cheyenne authorities revealed that Arridy had arrived in Cheyenne on August 20, four days after the Drain attack. It was learned from Mrs. Glen Gibson, who operated a kitchen car at the Cheyenne rail yard, that Arridy was dirty and very hungry when he got there. She and her husband befriended him, gave him some food and cleaned him up. For six days he washed dishes and performed menial tasks for the Gibsons. On August 26, the Gibsons had to leave Cheyenne. They left Arridy on his own in the rail yard. Railroad detectives arrested him that evening and turned him over to the sheriff.

It was determined that he walked away from the state home in Grand Junction with three other inmates who claimed they all hopped a train to Pueblo on August 10. The three claimed Arridy remained by himself in Pueblo on August 11 when the others hopped a westbound train back to Grand Junction. Where Arridy was between August 11, and August 20, remained in doubt. His parents continued to deny that he had been at their home.

On August 27, Sheriff Carroll and Cheyenne Police Chief Joe Cahill drove Arridy the 200 miles to Pueblo. He was turned over to Chief Grady. The next day Detectives Horne and McDonald, along with District Attorney Taylor and Chief Grady, took Arridy to the Drain house. They asked him to walk them around the home and explain what had happened on the evening of the attacks. Arridy readily maneuvered through the house to the back bedroom where the girls slept.

He described in some detail what had transpired in that bedroom, even asking where the "two dolls" were. The officers looked at each other. Two small dolls that belonged to Barbara Drain had been found on the floor beside the girl's bed when the crime was discovered. Unfortunately for the investigation, a photograph of the dolls had appeared in the *Pueblo Chieftain* the day after the murder. The officers wondered if Arridy could have seen that photo, and if he did, could he comprehend the significance of it? Arridy showed the officers where he first saw the dolls, and where he left them on the floor when he and Frank fled the home.

Arridy was then taken to Frank Aguilar's home. He went directly to a water pump beside the house where he said he helped Frank wash the hatchet head. Chief Grady stated he even showed them a pile of gravel in the backyard where he claimed Frank rubbed the blade of the hatchet in dirt after washing it.

He was taken back to the police station and placed in a chair in the chief's office. Frank Aguilar was then brought into the office. "Who's that man?" Chief Grady asked. Arridy brightened up and said, "That's Frank." Aguilar quickly denied knowing Arridy saying, "I've never seen him before."

Frank Aguilar was taken to the Colorado State Penitentiary for safekeeping. On September 2, after hours of questioning, he verbally confessed to the crimes committed in the Drain home. He described how he and Joe Arridy had entered the home after seeing the girl's parents leave for the evening. He told the interrogators how he had struck the "little girl" (Barbara) with the hatchet head he carried with him, then beat and sexually assaulted the "big girl" (Dorothy). He said he then offered Dorothy, who had been beaten into unconsciousness, to Joe Arridy. He said Joe removed his clothing and he too sexually assaulted her. He said he then struck Dorothy with the sharp edge of the hatchet head.

Aguilar later gave a four-page written confession that was printed almost verbatim in the *Pueblo Chieftain* on September 3. Both Aguilar and Arridy signed the written confession.

Prior to, and at his trial, Aguilar would repudiate his confession saying it had been forced from him by threats and physical abuse. Despite the overwhelming physical evidence, which tallied with details he divulged in his confessions, Aguilar repeated his earlier claims that he did not attack the Drain girls and was innocent of any wrongdoing. "I did not kill her," he said. He insisted he was home in bed at the time the murder occurred. His elderly mother, who lived in the same home, and his wife, would both back up his claim.

The details he had revealed in his confessions, however, seemed to render his denials, and the statements of his family, totally unbelievable. Because justice is compassionate, Aguilar's loved ones were not charged with giving false information to protect him.

His family's love and devotion could not help Frank Aguilar evade prosecution. Left to right: Mother Lupe, children Victor, 4, Ignacio, 7, Baby Victoria, 2, and wife Mary. His wife and mother would attempt to deflect suspicion from him by lying to provide him an alibi for the night of the murder.

First degree murder charges were officially filed against both Aguilar and Arridy. Aguilar's trial was set to begin the week of December 14, 1936.

CHAPTER 8

TRIALS & SPECULATION

The trial of Frank Aguilar for the wanton murder of Dorothy Drain began on the morning of Tuesday, December 15, 1936, in Pueblo District Court with the Honorable Judge William B. Stewart presiding. District Attorney French Taylor, who had participated in the investigation of the crime since the beginning, led for the prosecution. The defense attorney was the legendary Vasco Seavy, one of Pueblo's best known and respected trial lawyers.

Seavy launched objection after objection to the introduction of Aguilar's two confessions, arguing they were coerced and involuntary. He also objected to the testimony of Riley Drain, father of the murdered girl, who had gone to the state prison on August 27 to talk with Aguilar. Drain wanted to ask Aguilar why he had violated and killed his daughter and how the evening's events transpired. His conversation with Aguilar was compelling. Seavy objected on the grounds that the conversation was improper, involuntary and forced.

The judge also heard Aguilar's claim that he had been assaulted by Detective Everett Horne, and that Warden Best had threatened to "come into his cell and kill him." After two days of testimony and considerable deliberation, Judge Stewart ruled the Drain-Aguilar conversation was voluntary and Drain's testimony was admissible. He also ruled there was no evidence to indicate Aguilar was abused in any way.

The most damning testimony against Aguilar came on December 21 from Barbara Drain, the younger of the girls attacked on August 16. In perhaps the most dramatic moment of the trial, she walked across the courtroom to stand directly in front of Aguilar. She pointed at him and told the court he was the man she had seen enter her bedroom to attack her.

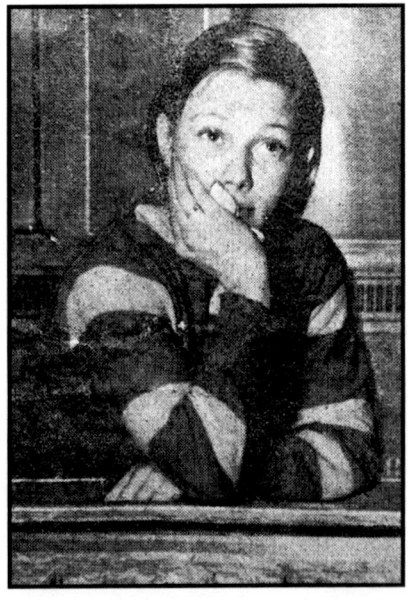

Left: District Attorney French Taylor – the prosecutor

Right: Barbara Drain in the courtroom after pointing out Frank Aguilar

That evening Aguilar confessed to Seavy that he was guilty of the attack on the Drain girls, and he asked if he could change his plea from not guilty to not guilty by reason of insanity. Seavy made the motion to amend his plea the next morning in open court. Judge Stewart immediately denied it.

The jury found Aguilar guilty of first degree murder and Judge Stewart sentenced him to death in the Colorado gas chamber. There was no appeal. Aguilar was transported immediately back to the state penitentiary.

The next day Frank Aguilar was visited in his cell by Lillie McMurtree, the surviving victim of the August 2nd attack that killed her aunt, Sally Crumpley. Lillie wanted to see if she could recognize Aguilar as the man responsible. Her memory was still clouded from the severe injuries she had sustained, and she was unable to recognize him or identify him as the fiend who had attacked her. She claimed her mind was completely blank after being struck in the head.

Shortly after, Aguilar confessed to Pueblo Police detectives and to Sheriff Lewis Worker that he was the intruder who entered the McMurtree home. He said he had seen the two younger women who lived there—McMurtree's daughters LaVerne McMurtree and Rose Beach. Aguilar said he was attracted to them and forced his way into the home hoping for a chance to sexually assault one or both of the girls. He had watched the house that day and was convinced the girls' father was not home. As the girls had also left the house to allow their mother to spend time with her aunt, Sally Crumpley, they were spared the ravishing he had intended for them.

Aguilar said the weapon he used to batter Lillie McMurtree and Sally Crumpley was a ball peen hammer head. He claimed he washed the hammer head and placed it in the same basket in which Officer Butler had found the hatchet head used in the Drain case. That hammer head had been found in the basket and had been in police custody since the search of Aguilar's home. Police had not realized that they had the Crumpley murder weapon in their evidence room since the search of Aguilar's house.

With Aguilar's confession to the Crumpley murder, Lillie McMurtree's son, Floyd, was released from custody. He had been held for investigation for over two months at the direction of District Attorney Taylor, who was convinced he was guilty of the crime. Taylor stated he was not convinced that Aguilar had committed the Crumpley attack, even though he had confessed. Taylor did not file charges against Aguilar for the Crumpley–McMurtree crimes, saying he needed time to think about it. Though faced with direct evidence as well as a coherent confession, the district attorney continued to believe Aguilar was not guilty of that outrage.

Left: The hammer head found at Aguilar's house.
Center: Lillie McMurtree—she survived the hammer attack
but was dismayed her son Floyd was accused of the crime.
Right: Floyd McMurtree—He spent over two months in jail,
but was exonerated when Aguilar confessed to the attacks.

The day before his execution, Aguilar was visited on death row by his aged mother Lupe Aguilar. When the realization that he would soon die hit her, she collapsed to the concrete floor. Aguilar looked on in seeming unconcern as she was removed to Fremont County Hospital. Frank Aguilar was executed in Colorado's lethal gas chamber with little fanfare on August 13, 1937. Riley Drain and his brother Vernon, a Colorado State Patrol officer, witnessed the execution.

Prior to going to his death, Aguilar was also questioned about the 1934 Halasz case. He denied involvement in that crime and the Halasz murder remained unsolved. Rumors that Aguilar had once chopped wood and done chores for the Halasz woman were never confirmed. There is no indication he was ever questioned about the Evans murders though some thought he may have been involved. That speculation was strictly due to the similarities in his confessed method of operation.

The sanity trial of Joe Arridy began on February 8, 1937, in the courtroom of the Honorable Judge Harry Leddy. Newly-elected District Attorney Ralph Neary prosecuted. By pleading insanity, the defendant, through his attorney C. Fred Barnard, admitted committing the crimes charged, but denied criminal culpability. At issue was the question of whether Arridy had the mental capacity to tell right from wrong and good from evil.

After two days of testimony by a panel of three renowned psychiatrists, and the officers who investigated the case and interviewed Arridy, the jury ruled that Arridy did understand the difference between right and wrong and was legally sane at the time of the commission of the crimes. Another jury was then chosen to determine whether he was guilty or not guilty of murder.

The trial on that issue began on April 12th and lasted through April 17, 1937. Remarkably, the issue of sanity was rehashed before the new jury, and, for the second time, the insanity defense was rejected. Under our system of justice, the jury is the final arbiter of fact, and the question of a defendant's sanity is an issue of fact to be determined by the jury, not by the judge. Arridy was again determined by the jury to be sane at the time of the crime. He was further found guilty of murder and sentenced to death.

A group of prominent Colorado citizens, including Denver attorney Gail Ireland, incensed by the notion that an "obviously retarded" man would be executed, fought hard to save Arridy. Their efforts were unsuccessful. Though Ireland managed to gain nine stays of execution, the Colorado Supreme

Court affirmed the trial court rulings on July 11, 1938, setting the stage for Arridy's execution.

After a "last meal" of vanilla ice cream, Joe Arridy took the long walk to the lethal gas chamber on January 6, 1939. Pueblo Deputy Sheriff John Krutka was one of only 50 people to witness his execution. That was the fewest number of people to view an official execution in Colorado's history. As the cyanide fumes rose from beneath the execution chair, Arridy took three deep breaths and went limp. He was pronounced dead a few minutes later by prison physician Dr. R. E. Holmes.

In 2011 a group of citizens calling themselves "Friends of Joe Arridy" convinced then Governor Bill Ritter that Arridy had been falsely convicted based on official misconduct. The group alleged that a corrupt Wyoming sheriff had fed information to Arridy, which he innocently repeated to Pueblo authorities. That information allegedly convinced the local court of his guilt. Apparently, the signed confession of Frank Aguilar, as well as that of Joe Arridy, along with the reenactment at the Drain home, Arridy's knowledge of where the axe head had been washed, as well as other direct evidence, did not matter. Governor Ritter granted Arridy a posthumous pardon exonerating him of the murder of Dorothy Drain.

In addition to allegations of improper conduct by the Wyoming sheriff—in essence "framing" Arridy for the crime—the group also questioned the reasonableness of executing a person of diminished mental capacity. The law at the time, however, allowed such an execution to go forward. It was not until 2002 that the U.S. Supreme Court ruled that "executions of mentally retarded criminals are cruel and unusual punishment prohibited by the Eighth Amendment." So, today the execution of Arridy, even if proven guilty beyond a reasonable doubt, would be prohibited. However, in 1937 it was legal and the sentence was upheld by two appellate courts.

In issuing the posthumous pardon of Arridy, the governor wrote in part: "granting this pardon demonstrates that Colorado has, in fact, matured in its understanding of mental disability." He, in other words, applied 2011 emotion and law to 1936 standards of justice and law.

The fact is Joe Arridy, aided by the best criminal defense available at the time, was legally tried, convicted, sentenced and executed in accordance with the law of the time. Larimer County, Wyoming Sheriff George Carroll, who had no reason to concoct false evidence or lie about Arridy's initial confession, was vilified and defamed years after his death with no way of defending his reputation.

In 1995 Deputy Police Chief Ron Gravatt, then the official historian of the Pueblo Police Department, and I sought out and interviewed Barbara Drain. She was then a woman of 75, married with children about my age, but still living in Pueblo. She stated she remembered that horrific day like it was yesterday. She told us her father had built an addition onto the rear of their small house on Stone Avenue, and it was in that addition she and her sister slept. The kitchen window that once looked out upon the back yard, then looked into the small bedroom she and her sister shared.

On the night of the attack, Barbara said she was awakened by noise she thought was the sound of people talking and by a light turned on in the kitchen. She said she at first thought it was her father she saw through the window, but quickly realized it was a stranger. That stranger rushed through the door to her room and immediately took the three or four steps to the bed. She said she had time to yell "get out" and to recoil from the advancing attacker, but then everything went dark. She had been struck on top of her head with the hatchet. The blow put her in a coma for over two weeks, and she said, gave her nightmares from that day forward.

What she next told us made the hair on the back of our necks stand up. She said, "I'll never forget the face of that man—it will be with me forever. He will always be the hatchet man to me." She was referring to the image of Frank Aguilar. Though she did not see anyone else at that time, she was sure she heard voices just before the kitchen light came on, and it was her impression there were at least two assailants in that kitchen just before Aguilar rushed into her room.

Was Arridy guilty of participating in the murder of Dorothy Drain? A court of law, after hearing the evidence, thought so. So did the detectives who interviewed him about his specific knowledge of things only a conspirator or active participant in the crime could have known.

Did Sheriff Carroll frame an innocent but developmentally disabled young man for a capital crime just to enhance his reputation as a "tough" lawman? There seems to be only speculation that he may have and there is no evidence that he did. If he did, Chief Grady and the other Pueblo detectives would likely have discovered it and quickly set the record straight. Chief Grady at first doubted Arridy's confession, but slowly began to accept it as direct evidence mounted and Arridy's knowledge of the intricacies of the crime pointed without a doubt to his guilt.

Should Arridy have been executed? Probably not. He wouldn't be today but the mores at the time, as well as existing law, made it legal and proper to do so.

Was justice served in this case when Governor Ritter commuted Arridy's sentence? You, the reader, must decide for yourself.

Fred McBride Trial

Meanwhile, in Walsenburg, newly elected Sheriff Claude Swift made it his mission to solve the Evans murder case. He interviewed hundreds of people in and around Walsenburg in the years following his election. One of those interviewed was a rancher who had property on the Cucharas River near Walsenburg. The rancher, Fred Romero, told the sheriff that at about the time of the Evans murders a transient "willow chair maker" had occupied an abandoned shed at the rear of his property. He said the transient had asked him for an axe or large knife to cut willows along the river bottoms.

Romero said he gave the man an old "beet knife" with the end "hook" sawn off. A beet knife was reported by the county coroner, Dr. Lamme, as possibly being used to kill the Evanses. Romero said the day following the murders, he became suspicious of the transient, and ordered him off his property. The beet knife was not found when the transient left. He said the transient had given the name of Fred McBride.

Further inquiries by the sheriff indicated that a Fred McBride had been sentenced to the state industrial school in Golden for the theft of a saddle in the 1920s. A check with personnel who had worked at the Golden facility revealed that McBride may have learned how to make willow chairs while detained at the school.

In 1940, six years after the murders, Undersheriff Carl Swift, brother of the sheriff, located a half-sister of Fred McBride in Pueblo. She told the undersheriff that Fred was employed in a mine in White Pine County, Nevada. A check with that facility revealed that he had moved on to Durango, Colorado. He was located in Durango on June 23, 1941. He was arrested by Durango authorities on a warrant issued by the Huerfano County Court based on a sworn affidavit from Sheriff Swift. No information concerning McBride's connection with the Evans case was released to the press at that time, and no official law enforcement reports about the case have survived.

Fred McBride—
Sheriff Swift's suspect
in the Evans murders.

Fred McBride was returned to Walsenburg by Claude and Carl Swift. He was lodged in the Huerfano jail. His trial was set to begin by the end of the summer, 1941. However, a case involving corruption in local government was being heard by the court and the judge declared the jury pool had been tainted. All jurors empaneled that year were dismissed, and McBride's trial was postponed until after the first of the year when a new jury could be empaneled.

His trial began in January 1942. The prosecution's case hinged on the testimony of two witnesses who stated they had seen blood stains on McBride's clothing about the time of the Evanses murders, and on testimony that he had borrowed a beet knife just before the murders occurred. The coroner testified that a beet knife could have caused the deep puncture wounds evident on both bodies. However, the beet knife "loaned" to the man who claimed his name was Fred McBride had the spur sawn off, leaving it incapable of inflicting the puncture wounds. In addition, the defense produced several witnesses who said McBride was in Durango at the time of the murders. Additionally, one of the witnesses who initially said she saw blood on McBride's clothing, took one look at him in court and stated he was not the Fred McBride she had seen with the bloody clothing. The trial ended with a hung jury.

A second trial was set for March 1942. The prosecution's evidence presented at that trial was basically the same as that presented at the previous trial. Judge Ralston ruled out the death penalty as the evidence was strictly circumstantial. After a very short deliberation, the jury returned a verdict of "not guilty," and McBride was released.

The acquittal of McBride angered Sheriff Swift. He and his department had spent weeks putting together information and evidence, though circumstantial, that he felt proved McBride guilty. Though he was unable to secure McBride's conviction, he thoroughly believed Fred McBride was the elusive killer—or did he really believe that?

Marie Manners Murder

Sheriff Swift rushed to Pueblo six years later on Thursday, October 2, 1947, when he read a *Pueblo Chieftain* report of the brutal murder of 81-year-old Marie Manners. Manners was murdered in her home at 1707 Palmer on Pueblo's south side by being struck in the head by some type of heavy object. The circumstances were similar to those in the Evans case, and the sheriff felt the same killer might be involved.

The killing of Marie Manners was initially investigated by Pueblo police as a suspicious death. Preliminary inspection of her home indicated she had fallen, struck her head on a buffet drawer that had been left open, then crawled to her bed. However, it appeared that her body had then been drug across the floor back to the dining room where a neighbor, Helen Lindvay of 1701 Palmer, found her.

It was possible, the police reported, that she may have tried to crawl from her bed back to the dining room where a telephone was located, thus leaving the drag marks in blood on the floor. No weapon that could have been used to club her was found in or near the home.

Pueblo County Coroner C.N. Caldwell and his assistant, Henry McCarthy, announced the results of the autopsy the next day. They concurred that Mrs. Manners had died of a heart attack either just before or just after falling against the buffet. They felt the death was caused by an accidental fall resulting in cardiac arrest and they discounted the murder theory.

However, the investigating detectives felt there were too many holes in the story of an accidental fall. One was that the front door to her home was found open by Mrs. Lindvay, and the other was that numerous drawers in the kitchen and bedroom had been left open. Those who knew Manners said she would not leave drawers open that way.

Further, her purse was found open and in a pan of water in the kitchen sink, which the officers considered strange. It was also reported that two other houses within a block of the

Manners home suffered attempted break-ins that same night.

Sheriff Swift of Walsenburg, along with Pueblo Detective Virgil Clifton and Captain Ruba Pratt, felt the death was due to foul play. Sheriff Swift was eager to assist the Pueblo authorities as he thought a solution to the Manners case could also solve the Evans case. He obviously was not as convinced of Fred McBride's guilt as he had once been.

After conferring in depth with the coroner's investigators, police and sheriff's detectives seemed to buy into their assertion that the Manners death was the result of a tragic accident. Sheriff Swift went back to Walsenburg disappointed that he still had not solved the Evans case.

But then, on October 30, 1947, just 28 days after the Manners mystery, Police in Tacoma, Washington, responded to a report of a woman screaming. When they arrived on scene they were horrified to find a brutal axe murder in progress. Two women were being hacked to death by a lone man who ran when he saw the arrival of police. The officers took the killer into custody after a short foot chase. The man identified himself as Jake Bird.

During the investigation that followed, Bird confessed to 22 murders in numerous states during the past few years. The latest one, prior to the double murder of the Tacoma women, was the murder of Marie Manners in Pueblo. Bird said he was a transient who went from city to city supporting himself by burglary. When he found someone at home after breaking into the house, he would kill them with whatever weapon was readily available. Today, we would call him a serial killer.

He said he entered the Manners house, found her in bed, and struck her with either a wrench or a club, he was unsure which. He said he later discarded the weapon in a nearby alley. According to Bird, Manners managed to get out of the bed, and at that point he strangled her to death and drug her body into the dining area. He claimed he went down the street to a corner house which he broke into, but found nothing of value. He said he then went back to the Manners home and searched through drawers, again finding nothing but a few dollars. His take from the woman's home totaled only 47 dollars.

Admitted serial killer Jake Bird. He confessed to the brutal 1947 murder of Marie Manners in Pueblo.

Washington State detectives, conferring with Pueblo authorities, were convinced Bird knew too many details of the crime to not have been the perpetrator. Marie Manners became one of 11 confirmed murder victims slain by Bird. His involvement in the other 10 crimes could not be confirmed, but detectives believed he likely had committed them all. Prior to his execution, Bird was injected with sodium pentothal, allegedly a truth serum, and questioned again about his claims. Warden Tom Smith of the Washington State Prison then stated Bird's "testimony," drowsily chanted under influence of the drug, supported his earlier claims of committing multiple murders throughout the country. Jake Bird, 48, was executed by hanging at the Washington State Penitentiary on July 15, 1949.

The admissions by Bird naturally brought law enforcement inquiries concerning unsolved homicides from throughout the country. Two of those were the November 1934 murder of Julia Halasz in Pueblo and the August 1934 murder of the Evans family near Walsenburg. It was learned though, that Jake Bird was incarcerated in the Iowa State Prison when those crimes were committed. Again, Sheriff Swift was disappointed that the Evans case would remain unsolved. He would later say he still believed Fred McBride had committed that crime.

Research into the Evans Murders

In 2019, my friend Michael A. Ragulsky and I began researching the Evans murders for a presentation I had agreed to do for the Pueblo County Historical Society. We were intrigued by the story of a "haunted house" in the prairies near Walsenburg in which a gruesome axe-murder had reportedly been committed years before. We decided to check it out.

We found old newspaper accounts of the Evans murders and determined they were the basis of the spook stories we had heard. We did quite a bit of research to familiarize ourselves with the case. We further found that the Evans house, though abandoned and boarded up, still exists. We located the current owner of the property, and we were allowed entry to the house. We discovered it had gone through several renovations over the years and looks nothing like the 1934 building. We decided to pursue other aspects of the case to hopefully find the truth about those murders.

Unfortunately, police and district attorney reports about the case no longer exist. However, we were very courteously provided a copy of the coroner's inquest by the current coroner of Huerfano County, Vonnie Valdez.

In reading and rereading the inquest document, we were surprised to find varied opinions about the weapon used to slay the couple. Area lore is that the weapon was an axe or hatchet with both a blunt end and a sharp end. After all, the crime is known as the "Huerfano County axe murders," and most people living in the area today have been brought up believing an axe was involved.

The coroner at the time, Dr. Lamme, felt a beet knife or a corn knife, both bearing hooks or spikes on the end of the blade may have been used. That belief was apparently based upon the presence of puncture wounds on both victims. In reading the coroner's description of the wounds we found the punctures were large and penetrated, in some cases, through the skull and into the brain.

Mike and I bought some Styrofoam heads (the kind used to display hats in clothing stores), and following the descriptions of the injuries indicated in the coroner's report, marked the heads to give us a graphic image of the actual wounds. What we saw inspired a theory about the murder weapon.

We checked our theory with former coroner and county commissioner Mark Ritz from Las Animas County. He was familiar with the Evans case having grown up not far from the scene of the crime, and he concurred with our supposition. As coroner, he had once been involved in a murder case in which the weapon used was a common fireplace poker. He said the injuries we had placed on the Styrofoam heads looked very similar to those on the victims of the case he had attended.

Mike and I purchased a typical 1930s style fireplace (or metal stove) poker. When we placed the poker against the Styrofoam heads, we were astonished about how closely the spiked end matched many of the marks on those heads.

Is it possible the killer picked up the poker at the fireplace in the front room of the Evans home and used it in his attacks? Could he then have either washed it off and placed it back in the fireplace or in the fireplace tools stand? Is it possible the murder weapon was hiding in plain sight the entire time the officers were searching for it? I doubt we will ever know.

Additionally, after some exhaustive research, Mike located Fred McBride's son living in Kansas. We contacted him by phone. He was 87 years old when we interviewed him and his memory was failing. He did remember his father's trial though, which occurred when he was nine years old. He recalled that his father told him he did not commit the Evans murders. He also said his father was an iron worker and had never made willow chairs or anything else fashioned from wood or willow branches. He further said that the trial was very traumatic for his dad, and he became sullen and perpetually distrustful and withdrawn from that time on. He did not think his father had committed the crimes.

We also developed a theory about William Evans's horse being saddled and led out of the corral, but not ridden away by the suspect. We feel the murderer may have saddled the horse and ridden it to another location, possibly the nearby railroad tracks (just three-and-a-half miles away) or to the then active Lascar Rail Station (four miles away) then released it. The horse, being on its own, would likely have wandered back to its home.

Several ranchers and "horse people" with whom we checked, confirmed that a horse would likely return to its stable if left unattended nearby. Could the murderer have been a transient or hobo who illegally rode a train to the area of the Evans home north of Walsenburg—probably to get some food and a comfortable place to lay low and sleep? After the murders, could the killer have hopped the train north to Pueblo and alighted in the south side rail yards at South Pueblo Junction—not far from the Halasz home? Nothing in news accounts of the time indicate any investigation was launched to pursue those theories.

This is all speculation, but it makes sense to both Mike and me, and to those with whom we have shared our theories. If any of this was considered by the original investigators, we will never know since none of the official sheriff's reports have survived. None of this makes any difference, as the Evans case is cold—as is the Halasz case.

Halasz Case: Still a Mystery

Though the Halasz case remains unsolved after over 80 years, many theories have been advanced concerning who may have killed her. However, no solution to the murder has ever been discovered. Arridy obviously was not involved, since he was incarcerated when Halasz was attacked. But did Aguilar enter her house and slay her with his notorious hatchet? Possibly, even likely, but he denied it and there is no evidence that he did.

What about Fred McBride? It appears he was never considered as a suspect in the Halacz case even though the Swift brothers knew about that crime while they were pursuing him for the Evans killings. While it is unlikely McBride was involved in either murder, it is interesting to note that Fred McBride's parents and siblings lived, at the time of the Halasz slaying, in the 2000 block of Routt Street in Pueblo—just over four blocks from the Halasz home. A coincidence that was never probed.

It remains doubtful that two of the most heinous crimes occurring in two Southern Colorado counties in the early 1930s will ever be solved. However, the 1940s would present the Pueblo Police Department with some additional mysteries and some much greater and less contentious successes.

CHAPTER 9

THE CISTERN

Marvin Porter was worried. His daughter Alice was supposed to be home around nine o'clock, but it was now approaching 11 p.m. and she hadn't made it there yet, nor had she called. Marvin was a retired Pueblo police detective, and even though the middle-class east side of Pueblo was, in 1942, considered a safe neighborhood, he knew it could be dangerous for a lone teenage girl on the streets late at night.

Sixteen-year-old Alice Porter and her two friends, Margaret Driscoll and Eileen Muhic, had been attending home nursing classes at Pueblo Catholic High School on Pueblo's south side. After the classes, she and her friends would take the Eastside streetcar to 8th and Norwood, then walk the few blocks to their homes. Alice lived at 1608 East 11th—a four-block walk from the streetcar stop.

Margaret Driscoll lived at 1515 East 9th Street, a little over a block from the stop, and Eileen Muhic lived at 1920 East 7th, six blocks east of the streetcar stop. Normally Eileen would take the car to the next stop at Reading Street and walk the two blocks home from that location.

However, that night of Wednesday, April 22, Margaret Driscoll had told the other girls her mother had made some snacks and she invited them to stop at her house for the refreshments. Eileen accepted the invitation, but Alice said she had promised her mother she would be home early. She declined the invitation and set off alone for her house. She never made it.

By 11 p.m., the Porters had called the families of the other girls and discovered that Alice should have been home a little after 9 p.m. Marvin Porter called the police.

Several officers responded to the call. They began checking the route Alice would have taken to get to her house. Though it was late and many of the homes along that route were dark, the officers began knocking on doors. At 1540 East 11th, the corner house at 11th and Ogden, just doors from the Porter home, a Mrs. McKinney reported she had heard what sounded like a girl scream at about 9:30. When she looked out her window, she saw a light-colored coupe speed down 11th Street and turn to the north on Norwood. She thought the car was a light tan color.

It was apparent to the investigating officers that Alice had been forcibly abducted. They sent a call out for additional officers and a massive search began. By mid-morning on Thursday, hundreds of people, including many of Alice Porter's classmates, a troop of Boy Scouts, members of the Pueblo Fire Department, County Sheriff Murphy and his staff and members of the District Attorney's office were engaged in the search. The front page of the evening newspaper, the *Pueblo Star-Journal*, reported the story of the missing and presumedly abducted girl. Before nightfall nearly everyone in Pueblo was aware of the situation.

Offers of help poured in to police headquarters. A pilot flew over the prairie areas adjacent to Pueblo searching for anything pertinent to the investigation. But heavy rain, which started a little after midnight Wednesday night and continued sporadically through Thursday, forced him to return to the airport. By Friday morning April 25, the FBI entered what everyone feared was a kidnapping case with dire possibilities.

The first break in the case came on Saturday afternoon when a rancher reported to the sheriff's office that a disheveled man walked up to his home about 10 miles southeast of Pueblo at about 7:30 a.m., Thursday, the morning after the presumed abduction. The man said he had been rabbit hunting and his car got bogged down in mud. He requested some food and a ride to Pueblo. The rancher complied and the man paid him five dollars for a sandwich and a ride to Pueblo's east side.

When the rancher heard about the missing girl later that day, he became concerned. The encounter with the disheveled man bothered him. He would later say, "no one hunts rabbits at night—especially in a rainstorm." He also thought the dress of the man was strange. After thinking about it for another day, he decided to report his suspicions. He told the sheriff, "No one goes rabbit hunting in 'city slicker' clothes." The man who came to his house was covered in mud, but he was wearing corduroy trousers. "No one traipses about the prairie in corduroy," he said.

Sheriff Tom Murphy sent several deputies to the rancher's home in an area called "the Broadacre" to get more information about the unusual encounter. The deputies began a systematic search looking for indications of a car stuck in mud. They continuously widened their search through the day along Doyle Road and several intersecting lanes in a small community called Undercliffe without finding anything.

Then, on Sunday morning, April 26, Boyd Whaley, owner of a garage and tow service in the 1900 block of East

4th Street in Pueblo, called the sheriff. He said a man he knew came to his shop in the afternoon of Thursday, April 23, and asked if Whaley would tow his car out of some mud. Whaley took the man in his wrecker to a location about 25 miles southeast of Pueblo where the car was stuck deeply in a mud hole. He pulled the car out of the mud and the man got it running again. Whaley said the man was acting strangely and seemed nervous. He had told Whaley he had been rabbit hunting when his car got bogged down. He also said he had to burn the clothing he had worn because it was covered in mud. Whaley thought that was odd.

This was the information the sheriff needed to find the place where the man got stuck. He called the police and the district attorney, and within a short time a multi-jurisdictional posse, along with Boyd Whaley, was headed south on the Doyle Road. That road became the road to Rattlesnake Buttes on State Highway 10 running east from Walsenburg.

Near the abandoned pioneer settlement known as the Finn Place (the Finn cemetery is still there), Boyd Whaley showed them where he pulled the car free from the now dry quagmire. Within sight of that spot was a dilapidated shack that had once been used by a religious sect known as "the Penitentes." Members of the posse entered the shack, and in a far corner of the building they found a small fireplace in which it appeared something had recently been burned.

Sifting through the ashes in that fireplace, deputies found several "bobby pins" and partially burned pieces of cloth that matched the description of clothing reportedly worn by Alice Porter when she disappeared. They also noted what appeared to be blood stains on the dirt floor in front of the fireplace. The officers now felt certain Alice Porter had been murdered, and the shack in which they were standing was the location of that crime. But where was the body? Right next to the shack was a deep gully, but a thorough search of that ravine failed to find the girl or any further evidence.

The shack where Alice Porter was raped, tortured, and slain

The posse split up and began widening a search around the shack. It was just 10 minutes later that searchers focused on an abandoned house about 1,200 feet east of the shack. Behind that house was a cistern—an underground collection point for rainwater, frequently used in rural areas to store water for agricultural and even domestic purposes. The area of the Finn Settlement had, at one time, been dotted with cisterns. All had been dry for years and many had been knocked down and filled in with dirt to prevent cattle from stumbling over or into them.

Officers looked down into the cistern and saw that it was filled with branches, tumbleweeds and pieces of wood from a nearby fence. There were also some ashes on top of some of the debris in the cistern. Posse members looked at each other ominously, their expressions betraying their collective fear that Alice Porter was under that debris.

Undersheriff Riley Drain was the first to speak. He said he would go down into the 10-foot-deep cistern to search for the girl. Drain was the father of Dorothy Drain who had been viciously murdered six years earlier. He had joined the sheriff's office afterward in the hope he could help find future perpetrators of the type of crime that took his daughter's life.

The Cistern
*Standing behind the cistern where Alice Porter's ravished body
was found are, left to right: Sheriff's officers Walter Christman,
Leo Broux, Bill Young, Undersheriff Riley Drain, Deputies Maurice
Forrester and John Greenwell, City Detective Richard Anderson,
and Deputy Phil Muhic. The photo was taken by D.A. Investigator
E.A. Morse. As of July 2022, the cistern is still there.*

District Attorney Chief Investigator E.A. Morse did not
want Drain to have to relive the slaying of his own daughter by
finding another teenage murder victim. A length of chain was
looped around Morse's waist and hooked to the rear bumper
of a sheriff's car. The car was backed slowly toward the cistern
as Morse was lowered into the pit. He began pulling tumble
weeds and debris aside as he descended. As he cleared his way
downward the odor emanating from below told him Alice was
there. It took him only a few additional minutes to find the
battered, nude body of the once-pretty teenaged girl.

A radio call requesting the response of the county coroner
and a police identification bureau detective immediately went
back to Chief Grady at Pueblo police headquarters. Soon
thereafter, four detectives: Everett Horne, W.L. McDonald,

Alice Porter—brutally murdered and dumped in an abandoned cistern.

D. A.'s Investigator E. A. Morse—he found Alice's body in the cistern.

Oscar Olson, and Thomas Matthews were knocking on Donald Fearn's door.

Twenty-six-year-old Donald H. Fearn was the man Boyd Whaley said had hired him to pull his car out of a mud hole near the cistern. Fearn was arrested without incident. His car, a 1940 light blue Ford sedan, was recovered in the garage behind his home at 1629 East 13th Street—about two blocks from the Porter home. The car had been meticulously washed since Fearn had brought it home, but it still contained evidence of the grisly crime. The car was impounded by police.

Fearn was taken to Chief Grady's office where he was questioned about his involvement in the abduction and murder. At first, he denied everything but when he was confronted with the evidence obtained from a search of his car and his home, he broke down and admitted he had killed Alice Porter. He said he had "always wanted to torture a young girl" and his wife's absence gave him the chance to do just that.

Donald Fearn's wife was in Parkview Hospital where she had given birth to their second child just two days earlier. Her mother was watching the couple's first child as Donald had to work. He was employed as a railroad brakeman during the day, but his evenings were free to fulfill his fantasies in his wife's absence. He claimed he had urges to hurt people ever since he was a child of about six years old. "Why do I have these urges?" he rhetorically asked.

He knew his wife would be home with their new baby shortly, so he took the opportunity of her absence that Wednesday to seek out a girl to "attack" and torture. (Attack was a term used colloquially and by the press at the time to mean rape). Fearn said he put together a "kit" of materials he would need to facilitate his planned crime. The kit consisted of, among other things, nine 12-to-16-inch sections of bailing wire, some two-inch-wide adhesive tape, a claw hammer and a .32 caliber revolver. He had borrowed the revolver from his mother during the afternoon of the day of Alice Porter's abduction.

Fearn said he began driving around the east side of Pueblo Wednesday evening looking for a potential victim. He spotted Alice Porter walking alone at Norwood and 11th Street and decided she would be his target. He pulled his car alongside her, got out and pointed the gun at her. She let out one scream when she saw the gun, but he said he told her to be quiet and get into the car. She reluctantly complied and he drove off with his quarry. He headed toward the abandoned Finn settlement. He said he was aware of the Finn property as he had once lived near Rattlesnake Buttes and had frequently taken the Buttes Road to and from Pueblo. The road passed by the abandoned Finn colony and cemetery.

He claimed he had a flat tire on the drive down Doyle Road southeast of town. He threatened to kill Alice if she tried to get away while he changed the tire. She remained in the car. After changing the tire, he went directly to the abandoned shack. He said he forced the girl into the shack where he built a fire in the small fireplace in the back corner of the room. He then made her disrobe. He used the adhesive tape to bind her hands and feet and cover her mouth. Fearn said he then "went wild" and began pummeling her with his fists and anything else he could get his hands on.

He claimed he placed several pieces of the bailing wire in the flames of the fireplace and heated them until they were red hot. While the wires were heating up, he went to his car, removed the rear seat cushion, and took it into the shack. It was on that cushion that he raped Alice. He then continued the beating, and also began whipping the girl across the body and legs with the hot wires. The torture, he said, went on until way after midnight.

He was asked by Chief Grady if Alice cried out and he said she remained quiet through the whole ordeal. Of course, her mouth was taped shut so she could not scream or cry out. He admitted to the chief that he had beaten her with his fists in between periods of lashing her with the scorching wires.

*Fiendish murderer Donald Fearn.
He readily admitted to the sexual
assault, torture, and brutal killing
of 16-year-old Alice Porter.*

While Fearn was inside the shack subjecting poor Alice Porter to the most atrocious abuses, it began to rain. The rain quickly became a downpour, melting the clay soil of the surrounding prairie into a stew of thick mud. Fearn was unaware of the rain until he had finished his gruesome assault on the unfortunate girl. He said he had not initially intended to kill her, but after raping and injuring her, he decided he had to do away with her.

He went to his car and obtained the hammer. When he reentered the shack, he said Alice was sitting in front of the fireplace with her back to him. That is when he walked up behind her. When she turned to look up at him, he struck her in the forehead with the claw hammer. He said he struck her three or four times. Just to be certain she was dead, he then shot her twice in the back of the head with the .32 caliber revolver. He said he then picked up his tools and what "evidence" he felt he had left at the scene and drove away, heading back to Pueblo. He only got about a fifth of a mile when his car sank in the deep muddy clay.

Fearn said he worked for two or three hours trying to free his vehicle from the mud but realized he would need help to get it out. Not wanting Alice's body to be found near the spot where his car was stalled, he went back to the shack and picked up the battered corpse. He carried the body across the muddy prairie until he found the cistern. He dumped Alice's body into the cistern. He then began the long walk toward Pueblo.

He hiked approximately 10 miles until he found a small ranch house near the road. Hungry and exhausted, he knocked on the door and asked the rancher for some food and a ride into the city. The next day he went to Whaley's Garage and asked Boyd Whaley to tow his car from the mud. The car was brought back to his house late that Thursday afternoon.

Fearing the body could be seen by looking into the cistern, he returned to the scene of the crime that Saturday morning on April 25. There he gathered up some tumbleweeds which were prevalent in the area, as well as some sticks, branches, and other debris, and threw them into the cistern to cover and hide the body. He also returned to the shack where the killing had occurred, scooped up much of Alice's burned clothing and a scoop of ashes, and took them back to the cistern where he deposited them on top of the other debris. He said he thought he had scrubbed the crime scene to totally conceal his presence there.

He then returned to his home where he washed away what he thought was every trace of prairie mud, and every trace of Alice Porter's presence in his car. He scrubbed the back seat cushion to remove all traces of the sexual assault and barbaric torture to which he had subjected poor Alice. Of course, he could not erase all the evidence of his wicked crimes. His car proved to be a treasure trove for police Identification Bureau Detective Richard Anderson and other officers who spent hours going over every inch of the vehicle.

The car used by Fearn to abduct Alice Porter was a 1940 light blue Ford sedan. A meticulous search of the vehicle yielded considerable evidence of the horrendous crime, as did a search of Fearn's house and garage. Police Captain Ruba Pratt and D.A. Investigator E. A. Morse are shown above discussing the evidence obtained from the car.

The gun and the hammer used to slay Alice Porter were recovered. The hammer was found in a toolbox in Fearn's house, and the gun, a .32 caliber nickel-plated revolver with a short barrel, was turned in to police by Fearn's mother. She had loaned the weapon to her son on the day of the abduction and he returned it to her the next day.

News of the arrest was released by Chief Grady shortly after seven o'clock Sunday evening. The chief said the confession dictated by Donald Fearn was "the most amazing, most gruesome confession he had heard in his 38 years on the force." By eight o'clock that evening, a small but threatening mob had begun milling about outside police headquarters. Another angry mob had gathered outside the county jail as well.

As a safety precaution, Fearn was secretly transferred to the Colorado State Penitentiary following his confession. Though it had been almost 25 years since a mob had acted to forcibly remove from custody and lynch a prisoner, Chief Grady wanted to take no chances. Fearn was held in solitary confinement at the state prison in Cañon City until May 11th when he was returned to Pueblo for a secret arraignment before Judge J. Arthur Phelps.

Donald Fearn (center) awaiting arraignment in court. He was brought back to Pueblo from the Cañon City prison by Sheriff Thomas Murphy (left) and Undersheriff Riley Drain (right). Undersheriff Drain was the father of 15-year-old Dorothy Drain, the victim of a similar horrifying murder six years earlier.

Fearn's court-appointed attorney, O. G. Pope, entered two pleas in his behalf—not guilty and not guilty by reason of insanity at the time of the commission of the crime. The judge accepted both pleas and also appointed a second attorney,

E. E. Pierson, to assist Pope in defending his client. Because of the insanity plea, an 18-day period of observation at the Colorado Psychopathic Hospital in Denver was ordered by the judge. The trial was set to begin during the week of June 8, 1942.

On the opening day of the trial, Fearn, through his attorneys, withdrew the insanity plea and entered a plea of guilty of first degree murder. He said he wanted to pay for his crime. As he had just spent 18 days in psychiatric observation, it was assumed the psychiatrists had found him sane, though their finding was not initially made public. The change of plea meant the jury would only have to decide between first degree and second-degree murder. If found guilty of first degree murder, the jury would have to fix the penalty at either death or life in prison. No plea deal had been made.

Donald Fearn took the stand at his trial and nonchalantly told the jury how he had kidnapped, assaulted, tortured and killed Alice Porter. Testimony from Boyd Whaley and H.O. Johnson, the rancher Fearn had asked for food and a ride, as well as the physical evidence and photos of Alice's horribly abused body, sealed his doom. Fearn was convicted of first degree murder and sentenced to die in Colorado's gas chamber.

On the day of his scheduled execution, Fearn was asked what he wanted for his last meal. He replied, "Strawberries." When told strawberries were out of season and not available until June, Fearn jokingly said, "I'm willing to wait." He chuckled at his own joke then became more somber and said, "Why would I want to wait—if I must die, why not get it over with quick—that's what I want—I'm better off out of the way because I'm a nuisance when that urge comes over me."

His last meal was a hearty steak dinner and a bottle of beer. He silently consumed it all before joining Assistant Warden Vincent Donahue and prison chaplain Father Schaller on the long walk up the hill to the small yellow building containing the death chamber. As he entered the building, he paused briefly and commented about how interesting Colorado's gas chamber looked.

At a few minutes after eight o'clock that Friday evening, October 23, 1942—just six months to the day after the murder of Alice Porter—Donald Fearn went quietly to his death in that chamber. Marvin Porter, Alice's father, and two of her uncles, Thomas Connors, and Thomas Nogle, were among the fifty witnesses who observed the execution.

Fearn's mother and wife claimed his body after the execution. He was taken to Rouch Funeral Home in Pueblo for a brief private service followed by interment in Mountain View Cemetery. Alice Porter had been interred across town in Roselawn Cemetery. Hundreds of people attended her service.

The *Pueblo Chieftain* reported that "an act of God" in the form of the heavy rainstorm was what brought about Donald Fearn's downfall. Investigating officers agreed that had it not rained, causing his car to become stuck in the mud, he would likely have never been identified as the perpetrator of one of Pueblo's most vicious atrocities.

Though the shacks and barns and a small church that had once comprised the Finn pioneer settlement are long gone, the cistern remains. Though inaccessible since it is on fenced-in private property, it is a gruesome reminder of the heinous attack on a 16-year-old girl by what the newspapers called a "merciless monster" on a rainy, early morning in April 1942.

The CISTERN

CHAPTER 10

GRADY'S FINAL YEARS

When J. Arthur Grady was named police chief in 1922, he swore to himself that he would do everything in his power to keep his officers safe. He had experienced too many police deaths during his tenure as a detective. The murders of his friends Jeff Evans and John Dunleavy particularly bothered him. He was also concerned about the conduct of officers that often led to their ouster from the department. When new recruits were hired, he would meet with them and give them some specific warnings.

The late Ronald P. Jackson was hired by Chief Grady in 1950 and served for over 39 years. He rose to the rank of captain. He was a good friend of mine. We frequently had lunch together, and as I was curious about the history and lore of our agency, he freely answered my many questions. Ron once told me about his first meeting with Chief Grady. He said he and two other recruits were ushered into the chief's office and seated before his huge oak desk.

So great was Grady's reputation that Ron said he expected to see a giant of a man behind that desk. He was surprised to see a gaunt, older man of average size sitting there. At first there was silence. Then Grady sat up straight and stared into the eyes of each recruit. They all sank in their chairs.

"Booze and broads, gentlemen," he boomed. "Booze and broads—those are the things that cost officers their jobs more than anything else." Though he had some other admonishments, those words were the ones Ron Jackson remembered about the chief forever.

It was well known by department members that some officers occasionally took a drink while on duty. Some even engaged in on-duty extramarital infidelity which caused problems when infuriated wives found out. Grady disapproved of such behavior. He acted swiftly to discipline errant officers when their indiscretions came to light. He had fired several officers for such offenses.

Though Grady was intimidating to most younger officers and recruits, Ron Jackson liked him. He felt Grady was doing his best to provide the guidance officers needed to stay out of trouble and succeed at their jobs. Over the years though, he knew many officers who took an occasional drink on duty. He also knew of rumors in the community that police officers were corrupt and "in the pockets" of organized crime. He told me the latter was untrue.

"When witnesses won't cooperate or when they change their stories under oath in court," he continued, "it becomes very frustrating." He also felt corruption had existed in upper levels of government and in the court system in earlier days. When police made an arrest for criminal activity that everyone in town knew existed, and the "defendants" got the proverbial slap on the wrist, or "walked" altogether, it looked bad for the officers in the eyes of the community. "Most officers were scrupulously honest and thoroughly dedicated to their jobs," he said.

When Esco Billings joined the force in 1926, there were several bars and pool halls in the downtown area and in Bessemer where illegal activity was widely known to take place. Those places were outlets for bootleggers to sell their products and engage in other crimes. Billings once told his grandson, Jim Billings, who would become a Pueblo police chief in 1998, that Grady advised his officers to "leave the black handers alone."

Some officers interpreted that as a form of corruption and thought Grady had been compromised by organized crime. Others, Esco included, thought Grady was just protecting his officers. "Why put yourself at risk or put a lot of work into something that will lead to nothing in court?" he questioned. With the lack of local resources, and federal agencies conducting their own investigations, Grady felt his officers' time would be better spent on other community problems— which were many.

More importantly, Grady didn't want his uniformed officers stumbling into federal undercover operations. That could mess up months of work for the federal agency, and could place the officer or the undercover operative in physical danger. "Grady was shrewd and deliberate," said Esco, and he was never officially alleged to be collaborating with the criminal element or corrupt in any other way. Esco knew of his reputation as a good cop and thought of him as a good police chief.

Billings Wounded in Gun Battle

I have always felt the most important attributes of a good cop are honesty and the personal trait of caring about the job they do and about the people they serve. From the time of his appointment, Esco Billings was a very hard working, honest and caring police officer. For that reason, he was assigned to some of the busiest and most active beats in the city. He handled himself well, and he was admired by most of the people who lived and worked on his beat. Like other beat cops of the 1920s through the 1960s, the ones who didn't admire him, feared him.

Esco carried a big .45 caliber revolver, and a nightstick, or billy club. The troublemakers on his beat did their best to avoid him. They knew he wasn't afraid to tangle with them, and they knew he would always come out on top.

When officers were assigned to a foot beat, they quickly got to know all the bartenders, shop owners, waitresses and street people on that beat. Usually, those people would assist the officer if he needed it, even if that assistance merely amounted to placing a call to police headquarters. The people also knew they could count on "their" officer if they needed help.

Esco Billings was the Bessemer beat officer in 1947. He knew virtually everyone on the streets and in the many taverns and cafés along Northern Avenue. The Bessemer beat was known as Beat 93 and was one of the busiest beats in town. The cop on that beat had to be tough and Esco Billings filled the bill. But he also had a compassionate heart, and he frequently paid for a meal or a bus or streetcar token for the less fortunate habitués of the area.

Forty-two-year-old Roberto Perez was one of those street people. He was usually drunk and, though he had a job, he frequently found himself without funds for a meal. Esco felt sorry for him in a way and tried his best to steer him away from the bars. He occasionally chipped in to get him a snack or a cup of coffee and then herded him toward his home. He never had any trouble with Perez.

On Sunday afternoon, November 9, 1947, Perez had money. By early afternoon he had also had a few drinks and was "buzzed." He met up with an acquaintance, Victor Ybarra at the corner of Northern and Evans in front of a business called Pachak Hardware. Ybarra saw a revolver tucked into Perez's belt at that time, but he didn't question Perez about it. Perez asked Ybarra to accompany him to the Brown Derby Bar across the street to have a few drinks. Ybarra went with him. It was then a little before two o'clock in the afternoon.

The two men sat at the bar and drank one beer and one shot of whiskey each. Ybarra said Perez then noticed a couple of his friends seated in a booth toward the back of the room, and he suggested they go and join them. The men in the booth were Julian Gallegos and Ezequiel Jimenez. Perez sat down directly across from Gallegos.

Gallegos also noticed the gun in Perez's waistband but said nothing about it. Gallegos later said Perez started talking about politics and arguing with the others. He became louder and more boisterous as he did so. He was buying the beer and whiskey, though, so the other men remained there with him even though he was causing a disturbance. They were there for about an hour when the Bessemer beat cop, Officer Billings, entered the barroom.

The officer looked at the bartender, William Amicantonio, who nodded toward the boisterous back booth. Billings then slowly walked back to the booth and motioned with his finger for Perez to come with him, saying, "I want to talk to you." Perez stood up and Gallegos noticed that he had the revolver in his hand. Before Billings could react, Perez started firing. Billings ducked and turned away to draw his own weapon. At that time two of Perez's rounds struck him in the back, and he fell to his knees. Perez bounded from the booth as Billings drew and fired four rounds at him. Perez ran toward the front door of the tavern but fell to the floor in the doorway.

The bar patrons were all sure he had been shot, but Perez got up and ran out of the building. Billings fell back and was bleeding profusely. The bartender and other patrons quickly went to his aid with towels to stop the bleeding. Several police officers arrived on scene within minutes, as did the Fire Department's First Aid Squad, the forerunner of today's Rescue Squad. Rather than wait for an ambulance, Billings was loaded into the First Aid vehicle and rushed to St. Mary's Hospital. He was admitted in critical condition.

Police Officer Esco Billings
—Photo courtesy of the Billings Family

Several witnesses followed Perez as he fled and they told officers he had gone to Valencia Café, across the street and two blocks to the east. Numerous officers descended on that restaurant to be told Perez had left the gun, a .38 caliber Smith and Wesson revolver, with a waitress there. He then ran toward the alley between Elm and Box Elder Streets. The gun was recovered at Valencia by Sergeant Roy Harper. Upon inspecting the six-shooter, he found that five chambers were empty, indicating that five rounds had likely been fired. The remaining chamber was loaded with a flat-nosed target round.

A few minutes later, Officers Cleo Sell and Ernie Walker spotted Perez in an alley behind Elm Street where the Interstate 25 freeway is currently located. He offered no resistance when the officers approached him. He was arrested and taken to police headquarters where it was noticed that he too had been shot. The Fire Department was called, and Perez was taken to Corwin Hospital on Pueblo's south side. He was placed under guard while emergency room personnel worked to save his life.

Perez suffered two bullet wounds, one to the abdomen and one to his leg near the knee. Emergency surgery was performed and the bullets were removed. He was admitted to the hospital in very critical condition. He died two days later without making any statement about the shooting.

St. Mary's Hospital officials reported Officer Billings had been shot in each lung and had lost a considerable amount of blood. He was given several transfusions. The bullets used by Perez were soft, flat-nosed bullets commonly called "wad-cutters" and generally used for target practice. They did considerable damage as they tore through Officer Billings's lungs. Hospital personnel added that they had received several calls from people volunteering blood for the highly respected officer.

Officer Billings remained in the hospital for several weeks. It was later determined by the police retirement board that he had been totally disabled by the shooting and he was granted retirement effective August 1, 1948.

It was never determined why Perez fired at Officer Billings. The witnesses seated at the table with him, as well as the bartender and the waitress, all said Billings had said or done nothing to provoke the attack. It is also unknown why Perez was carrying the revolver on that fateful day, and from where the money he was so freely spending came.

Though never able to return to the work he loved, Esco Billings had a profound effect on the future of public safety in Pueblo. His sons, Esco Junior and Jim, would become Pueblo firefighters, both rising to the rank of assistant chief. His grandsons, Esco III and Jim would also become public servants for the city. Esco III was a deputy fire chief, and Jim was police chief in the late 1990s and the first decade of the 2000s. The influence and leadership of the Billings family is still evident in the agencies they served for over 80 years.

Footprints in the Snow

Dan Badovinac was a big, tough but affable beat cop, and he rapidly became known and admired by almost everyone in the Bessemer area. The children loved him. He took over the foot beat in that tough neighborhood after his friend Esco Billings was tragically shot and had to retire. Knowing that Esco loved the Bessemer beat, Dan promised him he would take good care of it for him.

Dan's father, Nick Badovinac, served with the Pueblo department in the early 1900s. He joined the department during the administration of Chief Griffin and soon became a detective during the regime of Chief Shoup. Dan followed in his father's footsteps becoming a Pueblo police officer in 1926.

One cold winter evening in 1949, a passing motorist called to Dan to tell him a burglar had just broken the front door glass of a pastry shop just off Northern Avenue. Dan ran through the three inches of snow on the ground to the location. He found someone had indeed broken into the business—wet and snowy prints were on the floor throughout the interior of the small store—but the perpetrator was gone.

As Dan approached the store, though, he noticed some distinct footprints in the snow. The footprints came from north of the business, went in, then out of the broken door, then headed back toward the north. "They probably went to a car," he thought, as most burglars used a vehicle to make their getaway. But, as he followed the prints, he soon realized they were heading toward the next block. There was no indication anyone had tried to obscure or erase the prints.

Dan had called for additional officers from the donut shop, and soon the Bessemer car crew joined him as he followed the footprint trail to a small garage at the rear of a house in the 1100 block of Pine Street. A flickering light emanated from a window in that garage. He also heard chatter and laughter coming from inside.

As Dan pushed open the door, he saw three boys in their mid-teens seated around a fire in a large trash can. They were smoking, drinking bottles of beer and eating day-old donuts from a display tray, obviously taken from the pastry shop. There was no indication where the beer came from, but the wet trail on the floor revealed the youth who had earlier raided the donut shop.

"How did you find us?" one of the young burglars asked as they were led to a police car in the alley. "I followed you," said Dan. "Followed me? You must be really good because I didn't even see you," replied the youth. Dan and the other officers just laughed.

Incredibly, many criminals have forgotten that officers can follow footprints in snow, or mud, or even in simple dirt. It seems every year or so stupid crooks are caught because they leave a trail from their crime scene right to the location of their arrest.

Dan was very shrewd in other ways too. In a situation reminiscent of the Caspar Zweifel incident, he arrested a man who had passed a counterfeit coin in a local business. He told the story this way:

"We had been getting reports of a man passing bogus dimes, quarters and dollar bills. One day a girl clerk became suspicious of a dime she received from a customer and called me in. The coin was phony, though it looked pretty good." Dan arrested the man and began walking him to the corner call box to summon a car. The man suddenly called out in Italian to another man on the street.

"Though I'm of Croatian origin," Dan later said, "I did understand the Italian language, and I knew the man told his friend to go home and get the valise. Valise in Italian is valigia, pronounced valisa. We beat his friend to his rooming house and got the valise—in it were the molds and the whole counterfeiting layout. He got three years in Leavenworth for that one," Dan said. "Apparently it didn't cure him though. We heard later that he tried the same thing in Pennsylvania and was sent to the federal pen in Atlanta where he died."

The arrest of the counterfeiter earned Dan the nickname "Valisa" among his fellow officers. Good-natured Officer Dan just smiled when friends teased him and called him by that moniker.

Dan Badovinac had a long and varied career in law enforcement. Wanting to serve with his dad, he joined the Pueblo department initially in 1920. He became interested in federal law enforcement shortly thereafter. He resigned from the Pueblo department to take a job with the Federal Prohibition Agency, a division of the Treasury Department, in Denver in August 1921.

He excelled in that job and was soon acclaimed one of the leading agents on the staff of the agency's director for the district of Colorado. His work in the Denver office, which frequently resulted in assignments to Southern Colorado, earned him several special commendations from agency bigwigs in Washington, D.C. It seems he had a special sense for finding illicit stills and running down bootleggers and other criminals, and his bosses took notice. Many of his seizures of illegal liquor production operations occurred in Pueblo.

The fact that he had lived in Pueblo and knew many of Pueblo's police officers gave him an edge in ferreting out such activity. At the height of the moonshine wars between the Carlinos and the Dannas, Dan made several arrests of people associated with them. In 1923 U.S. marshals arrested Ben and Joe Bacino, F. Bacino, Paul Yerkovich and Krist Raketich and several others on warrants sworn out by Prohibition Agent Dan Badovinac. All were arraigned in Denver before U.S. Commissioner Vates. The arrests cleaned up much of Pueblo's moonshine activity at the time.

When Dan tired of his federal job, he reapplied to the Pueblo Police Department. Carl Jackson, Division Chief for Prohibition Agents for the Western United States tried hard to dissuade Dan from leaving. When he became convinced of Dan's desire, he reluctantly accepted his resignation. Dan Badovinac was reinstated as a Pueblo patrolman in 1926.

Dan Badovinac's Federal Prohibition Agent's credentials in 1921. He served throughout a five-state region for seven years. Photo courtesy of the Badovinac family—obtained by them from the Ancestry.com collection of prohibition agents ID cards.

On Sunday, June 7, 1940, several Pueblo officers, including Dan Badovinac, got to meet George Herman "Babe"

Ruth. The former New York Yankees outfielder was in Pueblo performing a special batting exhibition at Pueblo County Park, now Runyon Field. His appearance was to kick off the opening of Colorado's fourth annual semi-pro baseball tournament. Two Pueblo teams, the Walter's Brewery *Brewers* and the Pepper Furniture *Furniture Men,* emerged victorious in the event. A crowd of several hundred people packed into County Park to view Ruth's demonstration of batting prowess. It was the largest crowd of Pueblo's 1940 baseball season.

Though Babe Ruth's major league baseball career was over by 1935, he remained very popular with fans until his death in 1948. He engaged in many demonstrations and fund-raisers throughout the country well into the 1940s. While in Pueblo, he posed for photos alongside the patrolmen assigned to crowd and traffic control at County Park. Dan had his picture taken with "the Babe," as did his friend Officer J. A. Starasinich, seen below at the ball field.

Officer J. A. Starasinich with Babe Ruth in 1940. Note the typical police uniform of the time with the "suicide strap" across the shoulder. It was called a suicide strap because it was easy for an assailant to grab and use to pull the officer off balance during a scuffle. Pueblo Police photo

By the early 1950s Dan wore police badge number 1, meaning he had the most seniority of any patrolman on the department. He spent 28 years on the Pueblo Police force, seven of those as the Bessemer beat cop. When he retired in December 1954, he was lauded by Chief Roy Harper who succeeded Chief Grady in 1952.

The chief commented that "everyone knew Officer Dan—most of them loved him—the others were afraid of him." It was a common saying about strong and determined street cops, but there couldn't be a better tribute to a kind but tough and dedicated police officer.

Police Officer Dan Badovinac, known by his many friends as "Valisa" and simply "Officer Dan." He was known on the streets as an honest, fair, shrewd, and gentle (but tough when he had to be) cop who was respected by many but feared by the criminal element.
Photo courtesy of the Badovinac Family

The Late 1940s

As he neared retirement, Chief Grady made several moves to improve and modernize the department. He instituted a motorcycle traffic squad to pursue speeding motorists and patrol the city's numerous parks, many of which were inaccessible to cars.

He was successful in convincing city council to fund a new police station, which he said would be ultra-modern and efficient.

It would be built at 130 Central Main beginning in 1949 and opening in 1950. To save money, the structure was designed with input from Chief Grady, and built entirely by the Pueblo Public Works Department. The building, with many modifications, still exists and currently houses Brues Alehouse Brewpub, The Clink Lounge and the Station on the Riverwalk hotel.

Construction of the "new" police station began in 1949. The large building in the background is the old Riverside School.

On February 18, 1949, Chief Grady had members of his department assembled on what was then Grand Avenue across the street from the police station. He had a photograph taken of the group with Pueblo Memorial Hall in the background. It was deposited, along with several other items, behind the cornerstone of the new police station.

Front Row, left to right: *Police Chief J. Arthur Grady, Commissioner of Safety E. D. Rickords, Capt. R. E. Pratt, Capt. Robert L. Mayber, Sgt. Roy Blackwell, Sgt. G. D. Roberts, Matron Minnie Goodwin, Court Clerk Frank Kolbezen, Sgt. John Hamrick, Sgt. Harvey Neilson, Sgt. Marshall Stephenson, Sgt. David Davenport, Sgt. Oscar Olson, Sgt. H. G. Hutcherson, Sgt. Thomas Matthews, Capt. E. C. Horne*
Second row: *Patrolmen Harold Sell, Arthur Gray, Max Graff, Robert Urban, Earl Butler, Clyde Harrell, Guy McCrery, Sgt. James Rafferty, Patrolmen R. E. Pieratt, James Hayes, Fred Hegler, Thomas Easton*
Third row: *Sgt. Jack Stiffler, Patrolmen J. A. Starasinich, Dan Badovinac, Roy Mayber, Mike Chorak, Steve Secora, W. H. Hawkins, Capt. Roy Harper, Patrolmen Herman Huskins, Ray Marshall, R. A. McIntosh, Dan Black*
Fourth row: *Patrolmen Nick Mikatich, Cleo Sell, W. F. Brown, A. R. Avery, John Busia, John Meachum, A. A. Germ, Duncan McDonald, E. W. Walker, Sgt. Harold Jones*
Not present when the photo was taken were Sgt. Virgil Clifton, Patrolmen M. F. Berry, Jerry William, Pete Buchi, Roy Disbrow, Maurice Maytott, W. R. Hunter, and Claude Clark

Chief Grady's motor patrol squad in 1948. The officers are, left to right: R. L. "Bob" Mayber, Earl Butler, Nick Mikatich, John Busia, and Harold Bowlds

Trouble on the Horizon

Though Grady had served with distinction for close to 47 years, rising through the ranks to become chief of police, there were some groups of citizens and a few officers who were not impressed. As he neared the end of his career, he began to face criticism for what many said were irregularities within the department.

On February 19, 1952, Chief Grady and Captain E. C. Horne were both suspended from duty by City Manager John Hall for 48 hours each. City Council then added to the suspensions, giving Grady a 60-day suspension for negligence in performance of his duties and Horne a 30-day suspension for improper performance of his responsibilities as inspector of police uniforms.

In his position as uniforms inspector, Horne had received an additional day's pay each month since 1943. That additional pay amounted to approximately $1,000. It was alleged by the local police union in a letter to Hall that Horne had accepted that additional pay but had never performed a uniform inspection. The union further alleged that Grady had certified, on a monthly basis, that Horne had performed those duties, but did not maintain any documentation of any inspection or any action taken as the result of a uniform inspection.

The mayor, Marion Hunter, who was actually the president of city council since the transition two years earlier to a city manager-council form of government, recommended only a suspension for Horne, but the City Manager and a vote of the entire council included the chief in the disciplinary process. It was 73-year-old Grady's first disciplinary action since he had joined the department.

Captain R. E. Pratt was named acting chief for the first three weeks of Grady's suspension. The job was then rotated between Captain Roy Harper and Captain Robert L. Mayber for the remainder of the term of the suspension. The Police Benevolent Association voted not to pay for legal representation for Grady and Horne. On April 23, Grady and Horne filed a lawsuit against Hall. Seven days later, Hall resigned and the hunt for a new city manager began.

Things did not get better for Grady after he returned to work following the suspension and several weeks of medical leave for a required surgery. On August 27, 1952, Grady suspended police officers Herman Huskins and Raymond Marshall for insubordination, conduct unbecoming an officer and conduct detrimental to the peace and safety of the community following an alleged noisy and public argument between the two officers and members of the police vice squad.

According to Huskins and Marshall, they were off duty and driving down Santa Fe Avenue when they spotted the vice squad's unmarked vehicle parked in front of the Grove bar and pool hall. They said they pulled up next to the car and waited for Detective Sergeants Marshall Stephenson and Roy Blackwell to leave the hall and approached their car. They then confronted the detectives, saying there was a rumor that gambling was going on in the Grove and the vice officers were being "paid off" to do nothing about it.

Raymond Marshall allegedly told Stephenson that "we will raid any place we want to and arrest anyone committing crimes—regardless of what the chief says." He claimed Stephenson then told him, "When he was a young man, he obeyed the chief and did what Grady told him to do." Marshall said he then told Stephenson, "Times have changed." The implication was that Grady had instructed the officers to "leave the gamblers alone," and the younger officers resented that.

Chief Grady held a hearing in his office concerning the confrontation and directed every captain to attend. He later stated that Marshall and Huskins became boisterous, profane, and disrespectful at that meeting, and that's what led to their 48-hour suspensions.

Marshall and Huskins disagreed and said there was nothing wrong with their conduct at the meeting, which they thought was just convened to "bring them into line." They even stated that Captain Horne had "pulled a gun" on them during the meeting. Grady countered that Horne never pulled a gun on anyone but did remove his revolver from its holster and placed it on the table in front of him when it looked like Huskins and Marshall, who were also armed, might become violent.

Blackwell and Stephenson vehemently denied taking payoffs to not enforce the law. They pointed out that the owner of the Grove Tavern had been arrested three months earlier for possession of a slot machine but was released by the court when no one could testify they had seen anyone actually putting money into the machine. They said they checked the Grove and other trouble spots regularly and took appropriate action when it was warranted.

The meeting in the chief's office and the suspensions of the two officers became the subject of a public city council meeting held on September 13. Vice Squad Detective Sergeants Blackwell and Stephenson, as well as Chief Grady and all five police captains, were subpoenaed by the city to attend the meeting. Five officers: Harlan Allen, James Yenko, Ronald Jackson, A. R. Avery, Alfonso Sandoval, and Duncan McDonald also attended the meeting to support Huskins and Marshall.

It was announced in the local press that city council member Georgia Farabaugh requested a county-wide grand jury to look into gambling, illegal liquor sales and other vice activity allegedly occurring throughout Pueblo County. She said a complete investigation of the police department was in order as there was "noticeable suspicion of the chief, the five captains and the vice squad." Newly appointed City Manager W. T. Loman pointed out that, though there had been several allegations, only unsubstantiated charges, denials and countercharges came out of the council meeting. He also stated "tangible evidence" would have to accompany any request for a grand jury probe, and there was none.

After due consideration, council voted on September 16 to reverse the suspensions of Marshall and Huskins. The chief was ordered to return them to work. Grady did so reluctantly. Simultaneously, City Manager Loman announced that the city would begin its own comprehensive investigation of the police department.

Just days later, on September 23, the city manager gave Sergeant Roy Blackwell an "indefinite suspension" after receiving complaints from two officers, whose names were not released. The officers alleged Blackwell had destroyed evidence in a drunk-driving case and released the errant driver from custody. The name of the driver was also withheld from the public. City Manager Loman asked council to uphold the indefinite suspension, which amounted to a dismissal of Blackwell for the offense of "tampering with evidence and misconduct." Council complied and Blackwell was required to turn in his badge and all departmental equipment in his possession.

Blackwell was livid, and announced on October 1, that he was filing a suit against the city, the city council, and the city manager. Chief Grady was left out of that controversy, and never consulted about the situation.

Shortly thereafter, the city manager publicly announced that the much-discussed, full-scale probe of the police department would begin on October 18. He said it would likely take at least three months to complete. A few days later a tired and disillusioned Chief J. Arthur Grady announced that he would retire effective November 1, 1952.

Civil service examinations had been given several months earlier to establish promotional lists for each position within the city. At that time, candidates for department head positions, including police chief, had to score high on the civil service exam to secure the appointment. Traffic Captain Roy F. Harper had scored highest on the police chief examination, and City Manager Loman announced that Harper would be promoted to chief upon Grady's retirement. Sergeants James Rafferty and Jack Stiffler would simultaneously be promoted to police captain. The "indefinite suspension" of Sergeant Blackwell was also rescinded.

In March 1955, the Colorado Supreme Court sided with the City of Pueblo and denied Chief Grady's claim that he had been improperly suspended three years earlier. It was a sad denouement to the story of many successful criminal investigations, and a long and often successful, but provocative career as Pueblo's longest-serving police chief.

Traffic Captain Roy F. Harper was appointed Chief of Police to replace the retiring J. Arthur Grady on November 1, 1952.

CHAPTER 11

THE HARPER YEARS

Roy F. Harper began his term as Pueblo police chief at a time when the department was under scrutiny from city council members who believed many officers were "in the pockets" of organized crime. Chief among the department's detractors was council member Georgia Farabaugh, a thoughtful but strong-willed and fiery councilor who had fought hard for an investigation into what she perceived as rampant police corruption during the Grady administration.

Though Chief Harper had escaped suspicion of involvement in criminal activity, he felt his actions in his newly appointed post would be under a microscope with city administrators watching him closely. Accordingly, he dropped a lawsuit he had filed against the city for rotating the position of acting chief between three captains during the period of Grady's suspension nine months earlier. He felt he should have been the one to exclusively serve in that position, since he was the one who had scored the highest on the civil service examination for chief, but he did not want to rock the boat. He maintained a low profile and made few public announcements during the first few months of his tenure, but he did stay busy.

Actions he took as chief in those first months included an internal department directive that receipts would be issued to those people posting bond to secure release from jail or to forestall being booked on charges. Astonishingly, that order was the first of its kind in department history.

Harper also directed that Pueblo residents would not be required to post bond on traffic complaints, except those involving drunk or reckless driving. Offenders would be ticketed and released after signing a promise to appear in the appropriate court or pay a prescribed fine for the violation charged.

Harper's confidence in knowledge gained by his experience as captain of the department's traffic division guided his approach to several new policy developments. He had a new microfilm camera installed in the city jailer's office at police headquarters. His accompanying directive mandated that all prisoners booked into city jail would be photographed by the new system. He announced in an interview with a reporter for the *Pueblo Chieftain* that the black and white photos would be rapidly developed and mounted in standard slide frames. They would then be filed in a new cross-reference system for identification purposes. It was the latest law enforcement identification system available at the time.

The camera, he announced, would be permanently mounted with focus and shutter speed set in place. The prisoner would sit on a hydraulic stool which could be raised or lowered to bring the subject's face to the proper level to be captured on film. The system went into operation in early February 1953, just three months after Harper was sworn in. It was successfully used for many years until a more efficient mug-shot system utilizing a Polaroid camera was adopted. The mounting apparatus and hydraulic stool, though no longer functional, was still in place in the jailer's office well into the 1970s.

Responding to reporters' questions about an apparent surge in local crimes committed by juvenile delinquents, Harper opined that curfew laws must be strictly enforced. He followed his public comments by ordering all department personnel to pay particular attention to youths roaming the streets after hours set by the long-standing but frequently ignored curfew ordinance. That ordinance made it illegal for children under 16 years of age to be on the streets after 10 p.m. unless accompanied by a parent or a responsible adult. He further ordered that violators of the ordinance were to be taken into custody until parents could be located. The parents would be required to appear in court with their children when they were taken before the judge.

Many officers who worked under Harper would later say he was a strict disciplinarian who expected compliance with his directives. Some officers were afraid of him, but none failed to obey his orders. Arrests for curfew violations skyrocketed during early 1953, and late-night juvenile crime concurrently declined.

In another situation involving a juvenile, Chief Harper was required to discipline a police officer who sold a firearm to a 15-year-old boy. The boy's mother found the .38 caliber revolver in the youth's coat pocket. Under her questioning, the boy said a police officer had sold him the gun. She complained to Chief Harper.

A quick investigation revealed that Officer Alfonso Sandoval had sold the firearm to the boy. Sandoval said the youngster had admired the gun and asked if he could purchase it. At the time there was no law prohibiting such a sale and

Sandoval said he knew the boy and felt he was "a good kid." He claimed the boy was very mature and he had no thought that the boy would ever use the gun for an illegal act.

The chief suspended Officer Sandoval for 48 hours, stating the sale of the gun to a 15-year-old constituted conduct unbecoming an officer. It was the first suspension imposed by Harper, who angrily declared, "we can't curb juvenile delinquency if a police officer is going to put a pistol in the hands of a juvenile."

Harper did acknowledge though that the boy who bought the gun had never been involved in any criminal activity and had a stellar reputation at his school. Sandoval wisely did not appeal the suspension. He went on to a successful career with no further disciplinary issues, rising through the ranks and retiring as police captain in 1979.

The FBI National Academy

Early in 1953 Chief Harper moved to take advantage of a training opportunity that had been offered by the federal government since 1935. In July of that year, FBI Director J. Edgar Hoover established the "National Police Training School" in response to a 1930 study by the Wickersham Commission which cited the need for standardized training for all law enforcement agencies in the country.

The Wickersham Commission was a committee launched by President Herbert Hoover in 1929 to study law observance and enforcement in the United States. It focused primarily on enforcement of Prohibition laws. Though it made many recommendations to the president, most were ignored. FBI Director Hoover, however, focused on the commission's findings regarding inconsistencies in law enforcement procedures. He felt the FBI would be the best agency to provide the training needed to bring local departments into compliance with "best practices" of the time.

Director Hoover designed the police training school to accommodate high-level police professionals from throughout the country who could return to their respective departments and pass the training on to other agency members. Two training sessions were offered in the first years of the school's operation. That number increased to three, then four sessions per year by the early 1940s.

The FBI, under Hoover, established a training program in Washington, D.C. for bureau personnel as early as 1929. The courses of study taught there were the genesis of the courses developed for the Police Training School which would be renamed the FBI National Academy in 1940. Courses were initially taught in facilities in the nation's capital but were moved to the U.S. Marine Base in Quantico, Virginia, in late 1940. That move would allow the students to use the Marine Corps weapons ranges for firearms training.

The result of an agreement with the Marine Corps in 1940 was the construction of a classroom building for exclusive use by FBI personnel and National Academy students on the main Marine base. It wasn't until 1965 that funds were allocated for the building of a larger academy compound with a large firearms training facility just west of the main Marine complex. Construction was begun in 1969, and the academy we know today was opened in 1972. It has continued to grow since that time.

Today the FBI Academy occupies almost 550 acres of the Marine base at Quantico. The National Academy program accommodates approved law enforcement executives and professionals from throughout the free world. Students earn university credits that can be transferred to a plethora of accredited colleges and universities. The National Academy is today considered the premier law enforcement training and research facility on earth and is the most esteemed leadership-based opportunity for ranking law enforcement officials worldwide.

When the initial national training school opened in 1935, every law enforcement agency in the country was notified and encouraged to submit applications for a high-ranking officer to attend. Chief J. Arthur Grady apparently was not interested in participating as there is no record of him applying for or requesting information about the process. He had already assisted in establishing a police training school in Colorado and likely felt outside schools like the National Academy were redundant.

Several other Colorado agencies did send candidates to the National Academy in the early years of the program. The first Colorado officer to attend was Bill Barlow, a deputy sheriff from Jefferson County. He attended the tenth session from January through April 1939. Two other Colorado officers, one from Prowers County and one from Denver, attended the twelfth session in late 1939. Chief Pueblo County Deputy Sheriff Ralph Thompson was sent to the 14th Academy session which graduated in June 1940.

Chief Harper was the first applicant from the Pueblo Police Department for the FBI Academy. After passing a thorough background investigation by the FBI, his application was approved, and he was invited to attend the 52nd academy session in August 1953. He graduated on November 20th after 10 weeks of intensive training covering such topics as investigative and scientific techniques, traffic enforcement, management principles, police administration and firearms and self-defense tactics. Captain Robert L. Mayber served as acting chief during the three months Harper was away.

When Chief Harper returned following his graduation from the National Academy, he announced his plans for improving department performance. He approached newly appointed City Manager Russell Rink for approval to purchase newly developed radar equipment for detecting speeding motorists. He based his proposal on statistics he had learned at the National Academy that convinced him the use of radar was practically foolproof in drastically reducing serious traffic accidents and injuries. He further cited figures he received from the North Carolina Highway Patrol. Those figures, he said, showed that officers using radar there greatly reduced the number of traffic accidents, the number of injuries and the number of fatalities in one year. His proposal was approved by the city manager and the city purchased a radar speed control system in mid-1954.

Harper said he also learned that pre-drawn schematics of troublesome city intersections could be used by officers to diagram serious accident scenes more accurately and in less time. Rink approved his plan to collaborate with City Traffic Engineer Paul Johnson to produce mimeographed scale drawings of intersections where the most traffic accidents occurred. The drawings were completed within the year and successfully used by officers for several years. Inevitable changes in street construction and traffic patterns by the end of the decade would render many of the drawings obsolete.

Harper reported he was impressed by the quality of the training offered by the FBI, and he established a list of applicants he would propose for attendance at future training sessions. Two additional Pueblo officers would go to the FBI National Academy during Harper's tenure as chief.

A New Look for Pueblo Officers

Since before the turn of the last century, Pueblo police officers, like officers in cities throughout the country, wore very dark blue uniforms made primarily from wool serge. Serge is a heavy worsted woolen fabric used for centuries to make military uniforms, trench coats and certain heavy suits. Serge uniforms were very hot for those who wore them, particularly in summer months and in warmer climates.

By the late 1940s the heavy serge had given way to a lighter weight woolen uniform, but officers still complained they were too hot. Some said the wool fabric also caused an itchy rash, especially when they got wet.

As a nasty prank, some officers were known to occasionally rub gasoline on the car seat of one of their fellow officers. When the target of their prank sat in the seat and set out for a drive, the gasoline would slowly soak into their trousers causing their back side to begin itching and burning. It was a funny joke—except to those who suffered the burning and itchy rash.

Prior to 1950, former Chief J. Arthur Grady authorized officers to wear a light gray, long-sleeved uniform shirt during the summer months. The heavier dark uniform trousers remained, as did the dark blue shirt in winter months and the requirement to wear a necktie year-round.

Grady also allowed officers to ditch the Sam Browne shoulder strap, known as a "suicide strap." The Sam Browne was a leather belt with the attached supporting strap that passed over the left shoulder of the wearer. The belt held the holster, handcuff cases, ammunition pouches and other equipment carried by officers. It was named after Sir Samuel Browne, a British army officer in the 1800s.

After losing his left arm in battle, Browne devised a shoulder strap to support the right side of his belt where he continued to carry his sword. Sam Browne belts were adopted by police agencies worldwide because of their official appearance. As the strap was frequently used by opponents to grab and pull arresting officers off balance, most agencies abandoned them by the 1950s as being unsafe.

While at the National Academy, Chief Harper's exposure to personnel from many different law enforcement agencies afforded him the opportunity to see different police uniforms. He liked some of the light-colored uniforms worn by officers from other departments. Within a few months of his return, he began exploring the transition to a completely different police uniform—one he thought would be more comfortable and one he believed would look more contemporary.

Feeling he had to create a new image to accompany changes in the uniform, Harper chose a new style badge that had been highlighted in a catalogue from a badge company called Entenmann-Rovin. The new badge would replace the badge worn since 1914. The new badges, or shields made their debut in late 1954.

Within another year, Harper moved to change to a lighter-colored, French-blue trouser that sported a one-inch-wide black stripe down each side. A French-blue shoulder patch bearing the Colorado state seal and yellow lettering proclaiming "Pueblo Police" completed the new uniform. It was topped off by a French-blue, eight-point police cap. Officers appeared on the streets with their new look in 1956.

Officers wearing the 1956 French blue and gray uniforms standing for roll call and inspection. Back row, left to right: Officers Tim Sutton, Tim Pepin, Bill Washburn, Les Tooker, Front Row: Dave Macias, Jerry Salazar, Greg McCaulley, and Lynn Murray. I am the good-looking sergeant conducting the inspection in 1975.

Aside from the brutal attack on Officer Max Graff that resulted in his early retirement (see chapter 3), the streets of Pueblo were fairly quiet through the late 1950s. However, one sickeningly violent crime dominated regional news broadcasts toward the end of the decade. It was a torture murder unlike Pueblo authorities had encountered since the Alice Porter case in 1942.

Mecca Motel Murder

The Mecca Motel was a ten-unit motor court located at 2415 Lake Avenue on what was then known as Highway 85/87, or the Lake Avenue strip. The motel was owned by the Dominic Pighetti family that lived in quarters behind the small motel office. It was one of the nicest of the small lodging houses along South Lake Avenue. During the cool evening of Wednesday, March 26, 1958, a little after 7 p.m., a lone young man rang the bell at the office door. Mrs. Pighetti quickly responded to the office. She admitted the man who asked if a room was available. She nodded and presented a registration card to him. The man asked if he could have a corner room and requested permission to turn the unit's television volume up very loudly. He said he was hard of hearing. Permission was granted and Mrs. Pighetti signed the man into room number 7 located at the far rear corner of the complex. The room had no common walls with any other room. He signed the register book as "Bob Martin" and listed his address as a home on Lowell Street in Denver.

Mrs. Pighetti noticed that the man nervously hesitated before writing down his automobile license plate number on the card. Because of that hesitation she doubted that he had written down the correct number. After the man went to room number 7, Mrs. Pighetti mentioned her doubts to her 14-year-old son John. He decided to walk by the carport next to the room to get the correct license plate number. He did so, then returned to the office, erased the number the man had written on the registration card, and replaced it with the actual 1958 Colorado license plate number: L over 10–145.

When Dominic Pighetti returned home from work at 11 p.m., he noted that the man's car was not in the carport and the room was dark. About a half hour later, he and his wife retired for the night. Neither heard anything from room number 7 during the night. Nor did they know when "Bob Martin" returned to the room, but said it had to be late.

The next morning, Thursday, March 27, the motel maid began the task of cleaning the rooms from which people had checked out. When she got to room number 7 at 11 a.m., she noticed that Martin's car was not in the carport. She could hear the television playing very loudly in the room and wondered if someone was inside. She knocked and got no response but did not make any attempt to enter.

After tending to other rooms, she returned to room 7 at 12:40 p.m. She knocked again and still received no answer. She could still hear the television blaring. Feeling uneasy, she notified Dominic Pighetti. He responded and also knocked but received no response. Pighetti then used his passkey to enter the room. What he saw when he walked in sent him scurrying back to the office to telephone the police.

Detective Sergeants David E. Davenport and Roy Blackwell responded immediately. After listening to Pighetti's account of what he had seen, they cautiously entered room number 7.

The case-hardened detectives were shocked to find the bloodied nude body of a young woman with her hands and feet tied to the corner bedposts. The body was partially covered by the bedding. A washcloth had been stuffed into the woman's mouth and wired into place. There was a section of wire wound tightly around her neck, and what appeared to be an ugly stab wound in her chest. The detectives requested assistance and secured the room as a major crime scene.

As Pueblo's Identification Bureau officers began processing the scene for evidence, Sergeants Davenport and Blackwell interviewed the Pighettis at length. They found that the man calling himself Bob Martin had written the wrong license number down on the registration card, but that young John Pighetti had obtained the correct number.

The detectives checked with the Colorado State Patrol which obtained the license listing from the Colorado Department of Revenue (DOR). In those days before computers, it took 30 minutes or more for DOR to obtain a registration listing. Within the hour, the State Patrol reported the plate listed to a Randolph Montgomery of 4535 South Grant Street in Englewood, Colorado.

The most recent driver license photograph of Montgomery would later be obtained from DOR, placed in a photo array, and shown to Mrs. Pighetti. She pointed to the photo of Montgomery as being the man who used the name Bob Martin and checked into the motel the previous day. The hunt was on for Randolph Montgomery.

Back at room number 7, Deputy County Coroner Fay Rouch examined the body and determined the woman had been horribly tortured before being strangled by the wire ligature and stabbed with a sharp instrument, most likely a knife. Death resulted from the strangulation. Two unopened soft drink bottles were found in the bed with her—one a Coke bottle, the other a 7-Up. In 1958 soft drink bottles did not have twist off caps—the bottle caps were pressed on and had to be removed by a bottle-opener. The edges of the bottle caps were serrated to allow the bottle-opener to catch a raised edge to pry the cap off.

It appeared to the coroner, later to be confirmed at autopsy, that the bottles with the serrated caps had been repeatedly shoved in and out of the woman's vaginal orifice. This action caused profuse bleeding which soaked the sheets and bedding beneath her. It would have been an extremely painful torture. Her screams would likely have been muffled by the washcloth wired into her mouth and by the television volume being turned up so high.

The victim was identified as Beverly Jean Bair, a waitress at the Chief Bar and Grill at 326 North Union Avenue in downtown Pueblo. Bair had worked there Wednesday night. She was seen leaving the tavern by other bar employees shortly after the 2 a.m. closing hour. They had noticed she was in the company of a man. When later shown photographs of Randolph Montgomery by police, those witnesses would identify him as the man seen with Bair.

Responding to the all-points bulletin issued by Pueblo officers, police in Lamar, Colorado, spotted Montgomery's vehicle in that city on the evening of the day Bair's body was discovered. He was taken into custody and the Pueblo Police Department was notified. Chief Harper was among a team of officers that quickly responded to Lamar, some 100 miles to the east. Montgomery and his vehicle were returned to Pueblo before midnight that night.

Montgomery vehemently denied any involvement in the sadistic slaying. The closest he came to admitting anything was when he was taken to Rouch's mortuary the following day by Detective Sergeant Thomas Matthews. Montgomery was shown the body of the murdered woman, and he said he had seen her Tuesday or Wednesday evening at the Chief Bar, where he had stopped for a drink. He remained calm and stoic during his questioning. Though faced with mounting evidence against him, he continued to deny that he had killed the woman.

Randolph C. Montgomery

Montgomery went on trial for first degree murder before the honorable Judge S. Philip Cabibi on June 16, less than three months after the brutal killing. The prosecutor was District Attorney Matt Kikel. Montgomery was represented by attorney Vasco Seavy, assisted by his son, attorney Jack Seavy. Montgomery's mother, brother and wife were present in the courtroom during the trial. The victim's mother and sister also attended.

Though Kikel presented an air-tight case against Montgomery, the Seavys reminded the jury that under Colorado law the death penalty could not be imposed if the only evidence placed before the jury was circumstantial in nature. The lawyers told the jury that no direct evidence, such as an eyewitness to the commission of the crime or a confession by the accused existed.

The Seavys' impassioned arguments to save their client's life worked. On Friday, June 20, the jury found Montgomery guilty of first degree murder but rejected the death penalty. He was sentenced to life in prison by Judge Cabibi on June 25. Ten minutes after the sentence was imposed, Montgomery was taken from the courtroom, placed in a sheriff's car, and taken to the state penitentiary in Cañon City. Members of his family were not present in court for his sentencing.

Chief Harper praised his detectives for their hard work and quick solution to the crime. He also credited 14-year-old John Pighetti and his mother for providing the crucial piece of evidence that led to the capture of the killer. Without the true license plate number, he said, it would have been extremely difficult to have identified and apprehended the perpetrator.

The early 1960s presented the Harper administration with several noteworthy cases to tackle. Two of those involved high-profile crimes that occurred in the sheriff's jurisdiction outside the city limits but involved the participation of Pueblo city officers.

The first was a crime the *Pueblo Chieftain* called in an editorial, "the most inexcusable crime in Pueblo's history." It was the unnecessary and senseless murder of a Pueblo taxicab driver during an armed robbery that netted the killer only $22.

The Cabby Killing

The Pueblo office of the Colorado State Patrol received a call a little after 9 p.m. on Friday, March 25, 1960. The caller reported a possible auto-pedestrian traffic accident at Highway 96 and County Lane 27 just east of the city. State Patrol Officer Lee Grater made an emergency run to that location. Upon arrival he found the body of a young man lying next to Lane 27, about a quarter block from the much busier Highway 96. Highway 96 led to Pueblo Memorial Airport. Inspecting the body of the presumed hit-and-run accident victim, Grater noted what appeared to be a gunshot wound in the back of the man's head. He realized he was dealing with a homicide rather than a traffic accident.

Grater notified the sheriff's office, reporting the obvious murder in the county's jurisdiction. Sheriff's officers were on their way to the scene by 9:16 p.m. As Grater further examined the body, he found a City Cab Company trip sheet between the dead man's legs and a "hack" license lying nearby. He notified Pueblo police at 9:25 p.m.

Police Captain Jack Stiffler, along with a contingent of detectives, responded. A check with the two local cab companies revealed that City Cab driver Roy Don Bussey, assigned to cab number 46, was not answering his radio. Bussey had been dispatched to the Western Union office to pick up a message. He was to deliver the message to the *Pueblo Chieftain* at 211 West 5th Street.

Bussey had called in a little after 8 p.m., saying he had delivered the message, and had then picked up a man who had flagged him down in front of the *Chieftain*. The fare wanted to go to the Pueblo Airport east of the city. Bussey was then told by the cab company dispatcher to first go to the Central Bus Depot at 5th and Court streets a half-block away from the *Chieftain*. He was told to pick up a fare there who wanted to go to 811 East 2nd Street.

He had picked up his second fare at the bus depot at 8:11 p.m. He had then told his dispatcher he would be en route, first to 811 East 2nd Street, then on to the airport. He had not reported in since that 8:11 p.m. transmission, nor had he answered repeated calls from his dispatcher.

A BOLO (Be on the Lookout) was broadcast for City Cab number 46. It took officers about 45 minutes to find the cab abandoned in the 1700 block of East 7th Street. It was towed to the basement of the police station for processing by the Police Identification Bureau. The interior, particularly the driver's seat, was covered with blood. The driver's cap was on the floor of the back seat, and there were two .380 caliber shell casings on the back seat. It appeared the assailant was in the back of the cab, behind the driver, when the shooting took place.

Twenty-seven-year-old David Tafoya was contacted by police at 811 East 2nd Street. He stated he was the one who called for a cab to pick him up at the bus depot. When the cab arrived at the depot, Tafoya said there was already another fare in the cab. When Tafoya climbed in, the man was sitting to his right in the back seat. Tafoya was able to provide a good description of the man.

He said the man was about 25 years old, had dark wavy hair, was about 5-feet, 8-inches tall, and was of medium build, about 150 pounds. He said the man did not speak while Tafoya was in the cab. Tafoya was dropped off at 811 East 2nd Street, and he paid the driver just over a dollar for the ride.

Tafoya was later taken to the Davis Mortuary to view the body of Roy Don Bussey. He identified Bussey as the driver who took him home, then headed eastward with the lone suspect in the back seat.

Roy Don Bussey was an employee of the Southern Colorado Power Company. He was supplementing his income by working part-time for the City Cab Company. He had worked for the company for less than a month. When his body was found, his wallet was missing, presumably taken by his killer. It would later be determined that only 22 dollars had been stolen by his assailant.

Assuming the murderer would have left the abandoned cab on foot, all rooming houses and hotels on the east side of Pueblo and in the downtown area 15 blocks away, were checked by teams of officers. They were looking for a lone man who had rented a room on the late evening of the crime, or who matched the description provided by David Tafoya, or who had aroused suspicion for any reason. It was a daunting task.

Hopes were high when a man officers recognized as having just been released from the State Penitentiary was found to have rented a room that evening in a seedy downtown flophouse. He was taken into custody for questioning but released when his claimed whereabouts at the time of the murder were confirmed.

Meanwhile, four teenage boys who were playing in the prairies near the eastern city limits, found a suitcase hidden under a bridge that crossed Dry Creek, one of the many arroyos in the area. They turned the suitcase into the Sheriff's

Office. Inside the suitcase were several rounds of .380 caliber pistol ammunition, some clothing and a wallet containing a photograph of a young man.

Of particular interest were the Remington pistol cartridges that were identical to those found in the cab. The photo was shown to David Atencio, and he identified it as the man with whom he had shared the cab ride. Officers now began looking for the man in the photograph. Simultaneously, surveillance was established at the bridge where the suitcase had been found.

On Monday, three days after the slaying, Deputy Sheriff Ted Nicolet, driving an unmarked sheriff's car, spotted a man hitchhiking on Highway 50 near the Salt Creek bridge, just east of Pueblo. Nicolet, who had seen the picture found in the suitcase, recognized the hitchhiker as the man in the photo. He pulled over. The hitchhiker hopped into the car. Only then did the man apparently realize it was a sheriff's car. He jumped out and ran over a small hill near the highway. Nicolet radioed for help. Several officers responded, and within ten minutes the man was tracked down and arrested by Police Officer Ray Marshall. He was taken to Pueblo police headquarters.

The man identified himself as John Bizup Jr. Under questioning by Chief Harper, Captain Stiffler, Sheriff Krutka and Deputy Nicolet, Bizup denied any involvement in the Bussey murder. When confronted with the suitcase, he admitted it was his, but said the ammunition was for a gun he no longer owned. When he refused to answer any further questions, he was taken from the interview room and led to an elevator. As he entered the elevator, Chief Harper put his hand on Bizup's shoulder, pulled him closer to him, and said, "Boy, I wish you hadn't done it." Bizup's eyes teared up. He lowered his head and quietly said, "Take me back—give me a cigarette and I'll tell you about it."

He then calmly told the interrogators how he had driven to Englewood, Colorado, from California in a car he had stolen from a girlfriend. The car had run out of fuel in the Denver suburb of Englewood, so he abandoned it and hitchhiked to Pueblo. He said he got rides from four different motorists on the way.

As he had no money for a room, Bizup said he hid his suitcase under a bridge just outside the city. He felt it would be safe there while he explored the city and sought a way to get some money. He claimed he couldn't find the suitcase when he later went back to retrieve it. It had most likely already been found by the teenagers.

Bizup stated he had hailed the cab to take him east of town near the airport that Friday so he could hitchhike from there. Being short of cash, he said he decided to rob the cab driver when he got a chance. That chance came when the cab passed the city limits and entered a stretch of highway where no other cars were in sight.

He pulled his pistol and told Bussey to pull off at the next intersection. Bussey did as he was told when he reached Lane 27, a narrow unpaved lane that ran to the south off the highway. Bizup said he ordered Bussey to give him all his money and he fired one round into the rear floorboard of the cab to show Bussey he meant business.

Bizup said he took Bussey's wallet and what little cash there was in a pouch in the front seat of the cab. He said his take totaled 22 dollars. He then paused, choked back some tears, and told Harper he then started to get out of the cab intending to leave Bussey stranded on that lonely road. He instead shot Bussey in the back of the head. He claimed the shooting was an afterthought—that he had not initially intended to shoot the cab driver and didn't know why he did so.

He said after the shooting he pulled the body out of the vehicle and drove the cab to a residential area in the city where he abandoned it. He then walked to the downtown area and rented a room. He paid for two nights rent with some of the money he took from Bussey, and also visited several bars and cafes, paying for drinks and meals with his ill-gotten gains.

After two days, he became nervous, believing he would be caught if he stayed in town, so he decided to hitch a ride with a motorist headed east.

He said he made his way on foot to Highway 50 and there began "thumbing it." He didn't realize it was a law enforcement officer who stopped to pick him up until he saw the two-way radio in the car and Nicolet's badge on his belt. He jumped out and ran over a hill. He said he still had the gun on him at that time.

Bizup told the officers he scratched out a small hole in some loose gravel and buried the gun when he was out of Nicolet's sight. He said he would show officers where it was. He was taken by Chief Harper, Deputy Nicolet, Officer Marshall and District Attorney's Investigator Joe Foreman to the area where Santa Fe Drive and Northern Avenue intersect near the Salt Creek bridge. There he led them over a small hill where he pointed out the spot where he buried the gun. It was recovered by Officer Marshall where Bizup said it would be.

Bizup went on trial for first degree murder in December 1960. He was quickly convicted and sentenced to die in Colorado's gas chamber during the week of March 19, 1961. When the verdict was read Bizup grinned widely, shook his head, and said, "Well how about that?" He was transported to the State Penitentiary in Cañon City after his sentencing.

Bizup was less jovial when he got to the old territorial prison. He spent the next three years on death row. During that time, he received six stays of execution. He was said by the warden to have been a model prisoner, and he did not want to die. His final attempt to avoid the death penalty was a personal plea for mercy to Governor John Love. He asked the governor to commute his death sentence to life in prison. Incredibly, though he vigorously fought for his life and clearly wanted to live, he opined that a life behind bars was a worse punishment than a quick death.

Noting that Colorado law prevented the execution of an insane person, Governor Love ordered a psychiatric examination of Bizup. After meeting with Bizup's mother and sister, along with his Pueblo lawyer James Phelps, Governor Love said he would only commute a death sentence if he found ameliorating factors, or if it was clear that there had been a miscarriage of justice.

The psychiatric examination returned an opinion that Bizup, though of low intelligence, was sane at the time of the commission of the crime. The governor denied clemency, saying there was no compelling reason to second guess the trial court. Bizup was then scheduled to die during the week of August 10, 1964.

Colorado executions were traditionally held on the Friday evening of the week set by the court, or, in this case, by the governor's refusal of a reprieve. Bizup rejected the offer of a last meal but did will his eyes to a Denver eye bank. He spent his last day alone in his cell.

At 7:50 p.m., Friday, August 14, 1964, the 30-year-old John Bizup was escorted to the building housing the gas chamber. He entered the chamber at 7:58 p.m. with a rosary wrapped around his hand, and a religious medallion on a chain around his neck. He was blindfolded by guards and strapped into the metal chair in the center of the chamber.

Prison Warden Harry Tinsley, Associate Warden Fred Wyse and Catholic Chaplain Justin McKernan each spoke briefly with Bizup before the heavy metal door to the chamber was closed. At 8:02 p.m. sulfuric acid was dropped into a basin below the chair. Fifteen sodium cyanide pellets were introduced to the acid at 8:04 p.m. Bizup was pronounced dead, the rosary still in his hand, at 8:06 p.m.

The Roy Don Bussey case was lauded by the press and the public as an example of what officers from multiple jurisdictions could accomplish by working together. Expressions of satisfaction for the performance of Pueblo's criminal justice system poured in from a grateful public.

Unfortunately, with the unfolding of the next high-profile murder case, that satisfaction would yield to ridicule.

Local people still laugh, shake their heads in disbelief and joke about a court ruling that freed a notorious local murder suspect. The suspect was widely known as one of the state's top Mafia bosses.

No One Saw the Bullet Leave the Gun

The Five Queens was a nightclub and dance hall at 2301 Lake Avenue on the southwest corner of Lake Avenue and Highland Avenue in south Pueblo. As the city limits ended at Highland Avenue, the Five Queens was in the county. Though outside the city limits, it was frequently surveilled by Pueblo police vice squad officers as it was known to be a hangout for local organized crime figures and visiting thugs, many from the Denver area.

Officer Richard "Dick" Shorter and his partner, Officer Oscar D. "Ozzy" Schmidt were checking businesses on their beat, then called District 2, near Lake and Highland. It was nearing 2 a.m. on Thursday, September 15, 1960, and the many bars and nightclubs on the Lake Avenue strip were beginning to close. Being early Thursday morning, there was not as much traffic on the streets as there would have been at 2 a.m. on a Saturday or Sunday morning.

The experienced officers knew, however, that there would be a few intoxicated individuals on foot trying to make their way home. They also knew some of those stragglers would occasionally commit a minor theft, property damage or even a burglary on the way, so they were quite diligent in checking the area for that type of problem.

Shorter had turned the headlights of the patrol car off as the officers slowly passed through the alley in the 2200 block of Lake Avenue. Though cool outside, the car windows were down allowing them to hear the sounds in the night. As they rounded the corner onto Highland, they heard some shouting coming from the area of the Five Queens, a half block away. They pulled into a position from which they could see the front of the nightclub.

They observed a man lying on his back on the ground directly in front of the club. Two men, later identified as Harry Ricci, an entertainment booking agent, and Milford Watson, the leader of the band at the Five Queens, were standing nearby. The officers went to investigate. As they pulled alongside them, both men approached the police car. Watson asked them to call an ambulance. Officer Schmidt asked what had happened, and Ricci said, "He's been shot and he's dying." Shorter immediately radioed headquarters to request an ambulance and a Sheriff's Office response.

As the officers went to the unconscious man, Shorter asked who had shot him. Ricci said he didn't know. He claimed he had been inside the club when he heard what he thought was a car backfire. He then heard some shouting, so he went outside. He saw the man lying on the ground and stooped to see if the man was drunk or injured. That's when he saw what he thought was a bullet hole in the man's face.

The officers attempted to assist the injured man who was bleeding profusely from an injury near his nose and a wound through the palm of his right hand. Shorter checked the man's pulse and breathing and found he was alive.

Schmidt questioned Ricci further and Ricci told him he had seen the victim inside the club several minutes earlier and the man was arguing with two other "Negro" men and one White woman. He had seen all four leave the building, then heard the backfire a few minutes later.

Schmidt broadcast a "pick-up" for a car containing two Black males and one White female. Within 30 minutes the El Paso County Sheriff's Office reported they had stopped the car just south of Colorado Springs and were holding the people who had been with the victim at the Five Queens.

Back at the crime scene, officers Shorter and Schmidt briefed arriving sheriff's deputies with what little information they had, then returned to service and resumed patrolling their district. Sheriff's officers and district attorney's staff launched a comprehensive investigation into the shooting.

The victim of the shooting was quickly identified as one James Scott who lived in Colorado Springs. He had been the piano player with the band hired by the club, but the night of the shooting was his night off. He was visiting the club with friends. According to witnesses, friends of Scott began arguing with a bartender over a quarter they had put into a juke box that apparently was out of order. Scott became involved in the argument on the side of his friends.

Scott and his friends were then pushed out the front door of the club by the bar manager, a man named Parlato, and other bar staff. The argument continued outside and Parlato and Ricci began a physical fight with Scott. Watson jumped in and separated the combatants. That's when Joseph Scotty Spinuzzi, who had earlier been sitting with Ricci in the club, arrived on scene. He began waving a handgun around and hollering at Scott and his friends. He angrily ordered Scott's friends to leave. Using extremely foul language he said he would "blow their brains out" if they did not leave. They drove away, leaving Scott in front of the club. They slowly drove around the block and therefore did not see what happened next.

As Scott's friends drove away, Spinuzzi reportedly advanced toward Scott, pointed the gun at his head and began hitting and kicking him. Scott tumbled backward with his hand in front of his face. He fell to the ground with Spinuzzi, still holding the gun, on top of him. Spinuzzi then disengaged from the fight and began to stand up. At that time several witnesses heard a shot fired. Spinuzzi stood up, put his revolver in his waistband, got in his car and drove away.

Scott's friends drove back by at that time and saw Scott lying on the ground, obviously injured. They stopped briefly, intending to load Scott into the car and take him to St. Mary-Corwin Hospital about three blocks away, but fearing further trouble with the bar staff, decided to leave. They drove away and headed back toward Colorado Springs. Pueblo police officers arrived on scene at that time.

Sheriff's deputies immediately began looking for Scotty Spinuzzi. A contingent of deputies went to Spinuzzi's house just three blocks away to the east, but his wife told them he was not at home. Though they checked numerous known haunts of the wanted man, deputies were unable to find him during the weekend.

On Monday morning, four days after the shooting, Spinuzzi and his attorney, Vasco Seavy, walked into Pueblo County Jail. He turned himself in saying, "I heard you were looking for me." He was booked on a charge of first degree murder, but quickly released after posting a $50,000 bond.

Judge S. Philip Cabibi recused himself from hearing the case, claiming he personally knew Spinuzzi. Cabibi appointed a visiting judge, George H. Blickhahn from Alamosa, Colorado, to preside. District Attorney Matt Kikel announced he would seek the death penalty. The trial of Joseph D. "Scotty" Spinuzzi commenced on March 15, 1961.

Joseph D. "Scotty" Spinuzzi

Prior to the trial beginning, Attorney Vasco Seavy made a motion to vacate the trial because prosecution witnesses had refused to talk with the defense. Judge Blickhahn admonished the witnesses to talk with Seavy about the case or they would not be allowed to testify. Kikel objected, but his objection was overruled.

The first witness to testify was the band leader, Milford Watson. He said he saw a gun in Spinuzzi's hand immediately before and just after he heard the gunshot, but he did not actually see the shot fired.

Scott's friend from Colorado Springs, Carol Algien, identified Spinuzzi as the man she had seen holding the gun. However, when Seavy cross-examined her, she admitted that Spinuzzi had been pointed out to her when she went to county jail to look at possible suspects. Blickhahn ruled her identification "tainted" and threw it out.

The next to testify was Scott's other friend, Vincent Pinkston—also from Colorado Springs. He was one of those told to leave the area or get his brains blown out. When asked if he could identify the man who made the threats with the gun, Pinkston said, "I'm not sure, but I think I'd recognize him." Seavy immediately jumped to his feet and said, "If he's not sure, then he has disqualified himself." The judge agreed and excused Pinkston from testifying. A frustrated Kikel protested the ruling, stating the matter of identification was an issue for the jury, not the judge, to determine. The judge overruled him.

When the prosecution then attempted to introduce a crime scene photograph of the deceased Scott to establish his identity and to show the path the bullet would have taken through the head, the judge stopped it. He ruled against the use of the photograph for anything other than identification purposes.

As Kikel rested his case against Spinuzzi, Seavy moved for a directed verdict of acquittal. Judge Blickhahn granted the motion regarding the charges of first and second-degree murder. That left only the charges of voluntary and involuntary manslaughter to be considered by the jury.

Seavy then rested his defense case and again moved for a directed verdict of acquittal to those charges. Blickhahn threw out both of the lesser charges and ordered the jury to return a directed verdict of "not guilty on all counts."

The jury so ruled, and Spinuzzi left the court a free man. Judge Blickhahn was beseeched for an explanation by reporters following the ruling. He replied that "Nothing can be left to conjecture. No one actually saw who fired the shot that killed James Scott." The implication was that the shot could have come from anywhere in the vicinity—the fact that Spinuzzi had a gun in his hand at the time was not proof that he fired the weapon. He pointed out that no one had seen the path the bullet had taken before it struck Scott.

A headline in the *Pueblo Chieftain* the following morning stated, "No one saw the bullet leave the gun." It was clearly a reporter's tongue in cheek comment on the verdict, but it reflected the sentiment of nearly everyone who had followed the case through the court. District Attorney Kikel, in particular, was livid. He immediately filed an appeal with the Colorado Supreme Court citing numerous errors he believed the judge had made during the trial.

A year later the supreme court handed down a unanimous decision that severely criticized most of Judge Blickhahn's rulings. The court listed numerous errors the judge had made. Prominent among them was the direction to the jury to find Spinuzzi not guilty. The court said the issue of guilt or innocence should have been submitted to the jury, not decided by the judge.

Blickhahn also erred when he told prospective witnesses they would be prohibited from testifying if they did not talk with defense attorneys. The court said, "Neither statutes nor common law gave authority to exclude a prosecution witness's testimony because they refused to discuss that testimony with defense lawyers."

Regarding Pinkston's testimony, the supreme court ruled that it was an error to reject his identification of the defendant because he said he was "not sure." The court said, "It is not essential that a witness be free from doubt as to the correctness of his opinion nor that he be able to positively identify the accused—the certainty or uncertainty of identification goes to its weight rather than to its admissibility."

Blickhahn also erred when he restricted the use of a photograph of the deceased for the purpose of identification only. The court said photographs are competent evidence of anything a witness may describe.

It should be noted here that had the photograph been allowed as evidence, it could have shown "the path taken by the bullet when it entered Scott's body" and been used to trace the bullet to its origin—the location where Spinuzzi was seen holding the weapon.

The court did not find fault with Blickhahn's statement that "no one saw the defendant pull the trigger and no one saw the path of the bullet as it left the gun," but it did rule that it was a mistake to acquit on those grounds. It said, "such precision of testimony is not necessary to convict a defendant of a crime. Convictions could be made based on other evidence before the trial court."

*District Attorney
Matt J. Kikel*

He served as DA from January 1957 through December 1962. He was appointed District Judge in 1962 and served in that capacity through 1983.

Kikel asked the supreme court whether a retrial would be appropriate, or if that would constitute "double jeopardy." The court did not address the issue, so Kikel had Spinuzzi arrested again and lodged in county jail. Vasco Seavy then filed a writ of habeas corpus (a petition to the court on behalf of a person being held in custody regarding the circumstances of detainment, usually based on allegations that the rights of the defendant have been violated or there were factual errors surrounding the arrest or confinement).

Another out-of-town judge, Max Wilson of Cañon City made the writ permanent and ruled that any attempt to retry Spinuzzi would constitute double jeopardy. Kikel appealed that decision to the state supreme court, but in September 1963, the court upheld Wilson's ruling. Spinuzzi could not be tried a second time for the murder of James Scott.

Joseph "Scotty" Spinuzzi would rise through the "ranks" of the Mafia to become the head of the Colorado faction of La Cosa Nostra in 1969. He would die of natural causes in September 1975.

The story of "no one saw the bullet leave the gun" has become a local legend. It's been told and retold by incredulous citizens who firmly believe criminal intervention, in the form of bribes or threats by the local Mafia was responsible for the failure of justice in one of the most notorious murder cases in Pueblo's history.

MORE CRIMES OF THE '60S AND A NEW CHIEF

It seemed that Detective Sergeant Edson Lutes knew everybody in town—at least every criminal. He also had a photographic memory. From the late 1950s through the early 1970s other detectives would go to him if they had a question about a particular offender from years past, or if they wanted to know about a case Lutes had previously worked. He always had an answer.

A few minutes after 6 p.m. on Sunday, September 16, 1962, Sergeant Lutes was in the Bessemer neighborhood working one of the several cases he had been assigned during the week. He was only a couple of blocks south of 800 East Abriendo Avenue when he heard a radio call dispatched to the district 2 beat car. The desk sergeant told the patrol officers to go to 800 East Abriendo on a disturbance. The responding car crew was also told the fire department's first aid squad was en route to 802 East Abriendo on a serious injury call. It was believed the two calls were related.

Detective Sergeant
Edson Lutes

Ed Lutes recognized the 800 East Abriendo address as being Joe Segura's home. He knew Joe Segura since he had arrested him eight years earlier for a narcotics violation. Segura had been convicted of that charge and sentenced to federal prison. He had done time at Leavenworth and been released on parole within the past few weeks.

Lutes arrived at the scene before the other responders. He pulled his car to the curb on Bicknell Street north of the Segura home. As he stepped out of his vehicle, he saw Joe Segura walking down the three steps from his backyard toward Bicknell. Lutes saw that Segura was bleeding profusely from an injury on the side of his neck. Lutes approached him and asked, "What's the matter, Joe?"

Segura held his hand to his neck and Lutes noticed his forearm was also bleeding. "Just a little family trouble," Segura replied. "Better come to the garage." Lutes radioed the police station for an ambulance for Segura, then followed him to the small garage at the rear of the property. He told Segura to wait outside as he entered the partially open door. Once inside he saw a young man he believed to be Chris Segura, Joe's son, lying face down on the dirt floor at the rear of the garage. It appeared that the 27-year-old Chris was dead, or close to it. The back of his head appeared to have been crushed by repeated blows from a heavy blunt instrument.

Patrol officers Warren Dodson and Frank Grubb arrived at that moment, and Lutes told them to hold Joe Segura while he checked on what was happening next door where the fire department's first aid squad had just arrived. He went to the front porch of 802 East Abriendo where he saw a woman he recognized as 47-year-old Lorraine Segura, Joe's wife. She was being tended to by fire department medics who told Sergeant Lutes she was in critical condition, having suffered a probable skull fracture from a severe beating. She also had a broken arm. The medics had called an ambulance for her, and they continued their efforts to stop her bleeding. She was unable to speak with Lutes at that time.

Lutes radioed police headquarters to report the situation was a probable murder case and he requested an Identification Bureau response. He was accompanied by one of the fire medics as he returned to the back yard. He again asked Segura what had happened. Segura repeated, "Just some family trouble Ed—a lot can happen when you're gone for eight years."

"And what happened to you?" Lutes asked. "I cut myself with that razor," replied Segura, pointing to a straight razor on a shelf just inside the garage. He then began coughing as the firefighter started working to stem the bleeding from a nasty gash on the side of his neck. He refused to say anything else. After being bandaged by the fire department medic, he was placed into custody and taken by police car to St. Mary-Corwin hospital.

Chris Segura was also examined by fire department medics. They detected a very slight heartbeat, so he was treated at the scene then transported by Hurley Ambulance Company to St. Mary-Corwin Hospital. He was pronounced dead on arrival by Dr. Pierce.

Deputy County Coroner Allen Chamberlain took charge of the body at the hospital. He had it removed to T. G. McCarthy Funeral Home for an autopsy. That autopsy would disclose multiple skull fractures and severe internal injuries to the brain. The cause of the injuries was several hard blows to the back of the head with a heavy object. The manner of death was homicide.

Back at the murder scene, Detective Sergeant Lutes and Identification Officer Jim Ruggieri processed the garage and surrounding area for evidence. The interior of the garage was awash in blood. There were blood droplets leading from the garage to the house where blood was found in several rooms. A trail of blood also led from the house to the neighbor's house next door.

One broken baseball bat was found on the floor of the garage. A second ball bat, also broken, was found near the garage door. Splinters from that bat were strewn across the floor. Pieces of both bats were covered with blood. Tufts of hair were clinging to the splintered end of one of the bats.

The neighbor, Loretta Lewis of 802 East Abriendo, was interviewed by Sgt. Lutes and Sgt. Bill Hurley. She told the officers she had just arrived home from work when she heard what she initially thought was the whimpering of a child coming from the Segura's backyard or garage. The whimpering continued for several minutes and caused her to become concerned that Segura might be beating his preteen grandson, whom she had seen earlier in the backyard.

She said she then heard a very weak scream coming from the garage, and she decided to go to the Segura home to tell Lorraine that her husband Joe was beating the child in the garage. As she started toward the Segura home, she saw Joe

Segura emerge from the garage. He was holding some sort of stick with what appeared to be blood on it. She knocked on the front door of the Segura residence.

She said she was met at the door by Chris Segura, and she told him his father had beaten the child in the garage. She claimed Chris then angrily went out the back door of the Segura home and into the garage. Mrs. Lewis said she then went home and didn't hear any further noise. A few minutes later she said she saw Lorraine leave the garage and run to her house. Lorraine then came over to the Lewis house. She was bleeding terribly and appeared to be severely injured. That's when Lewis called the fire department for a first aid response. She said Lorraine was almost incoherent and would only say, "Going to the garage to look at the tomatoes." The officers had seen a box of tomatoes in the garage.

Lorraine Segura was taken by ambulance to St. Mary-Corwin Hospital. There she was seen by Dr. Pierce and Dr. Williams. They would opine that, though critically injured, she would probably survive. She did survive and had recovered enough by the next afternoon to answer questions.

Lorraine was interviewed by Captain Ernest Walker and District Attorney Investigator Joe Foreman. They reported she spoke very rationally when they questioned her. She told them her husband had been beating her with a bat for "a long time" when her son Chris entered the garage. She said Joe saw Chris approaching the garage and hid behind the open door. When Chris entered, Joe struck him from behind with the bat. Chris fell forward to the floor. At that time, she ran from the garage and went to her home. She said she realized she needed help, so she went to the Lewis home next door. She said she did not see what happened after she left the garage.

Two days later, on September 18th, Sergeant Hurley interviewed Joe Segura in his room at St. Mary-Corwin Hospital. Segura told Hurley he remembered confronting his wife about a box of tomatoes in the garage. He said she had allowed the tomatoes to spoil. He claimed, "something just happened to me, and I grabbed the bat and started hitting her." He claimed the tomato incident was just the last straw as there had been family troubles ever since he returned home after getting out of prison. He couldn't recall how many times he struck her, but said it was more than once.

Segura said he remembered seeing Chris enter the garage, and he saw him fall, but he did not remember hitting him. He said, "I must have hit him though." He then launched into a lengthy story about the family troubles he had since he was released from prison. He claimed his wife had been entertaining men in the house while he was away, and the whole family has been on one long party ever since he was incarcerated. He even claimed his son Chris had been providing men for his wife, acting as a pimp while his wife served as a prostitute. He alleged that Chris had beaten him up twice since he came back from the penitentiary and the other members of his family would not help him.

Segura was formally charged with murder by District Attorney Matt J. Kikel. However, Kikel was appointed District Court Judge in November 1962, and Carl Parlapiano, an assistant in the DA's office, was selected to fill the vacancy created by that appointment. It fell to Parlapiano to lead the prosecution of Segura.

On March 7, 1963, Joe Segura was found guilty of first degree murder in Pueblo District Court. The jury fixed his penalty at death. He was transported to the state penitentiary and placed on death row. During the next few months, he requested and was granted two stays of execution to allow his attorney time to prepare arguments for an appeal.

It took almost two years for an appeal to be filed with the Colorado Supreme Court. The appeal alleged several significant errors in the conduct of the original trial. After hearing arguments, the judgment of the trial court was affirmed and

Segura was ordered executed during the week commencing Saturday, June 25, 1966.

He then filed a motion for post-conviction relief under the Colorado Rules of Criminal Procedure. That motion was denied on June 29, 1967. Review was again sought in the Colorado Supreme Court which again affirmed the original trial court. A petition for a rehearing was also denied.

He then received a stay of execution by executive order pending a vote of the people regarding the abolition of the death penalty in Colorado. The people voted to retain the death penalty and Segura was returned to death row.

Then in 1971, the United States Supreme Court reversed the death sentences of 35 men, Joe Segura included. The decision was based on an earlier ruling that "jurors may not be disqualified solely because of their attitudes against capital punishment." Several potential jurors had been rejected from serving on Segura's original trial jury. They had all claimed they had a "conscientious objection" to the death penalty or were just opposed to the state-sanctioned killing of a person in the name of justice.

Though Segura's death sentence was reversed, the Supreme Court allowed his conviction to stand. A rehearing on the question of punishment was ordered by the court. At age 60, following a short rehearing on the issue of "penalty," Segura was sentenced to life in prison.

Margaret Rose Murder

Many people think of a murder case as involving only one victim, or as many victims as are actually killed or injured during a given incident. Every police officer, though, knows that a single murder produces many victims. Friends, relatives, children, coworkers, classmates, friends of relatives, friends of friends, neighbors, employers, employees—virtually everyone involved with both the person slain and the perpetrator of the lethal crime are themselves victims in one way or another. Murder is more than a manner of death—it is a life changing event for a great number of people. The Margaret Rose murder is only one of the tragedies that perfectly illustrate how a single crime can impact an entire community.

It began in the early morning hours of Thursday, October 6, 1966. Police Sergeant Alfonso Sandoval was working the desk at police headquarters. Up until 1973, when non-sworn police dispatchers were hired, the desk sergeant was responsible for answering phone calls and dispatching patrol units. At 6:50 a.m., Sgt. Sandoval received a call from the Fort Collins Police Department. They were holding a 16-year-old boy who identified himself as Leo Kopasz from Pueblo. He had been stopped in that city by officers who became suspicious of someone so young driving a luxury Chrysler sedan (plate number GR-108) through their city at such an early hour. He told the officers the car belonged to his aunt, but he couldn't tell them any specific details about the woman. As the Fort Collins officers were questioning him, Kopasz admitted he had stolen the car from a "Mrs. Rose." He then added that he had stabbed the woman to death.

Sandoval sent officers to the county courthouse to get a listing on the plate. At that time police had a key to the vehicle registration department to allow them to obtain registration information in emergencies after business hours. The listing was quickly obtained. It showed the Chrysler was owned by a Margaret Rose of 133 Cornell Circle in the upper-class Sunset Park subdivision on Pueblo's southwest side.

Sandoval relayed the information to Sergeant Walter Prior who responded to the Cornell address. Sgt. Prior went to the front door of the residence, knocked, and rang the bell repeatedly. He got no answer. He then entered the open door of the attached garage and found the door leading from the garage into the home standing wide open. He called to Mrs. Rose several times but got no answer. The home was eerily quiet.

Prior went back to the police car and radioed for assistance. A short time later Officer Gus Gourdin arrived. The officers entered and began looking through the house. Sgt.

Prior found the body of Margaret Rose in a bedroom off the main hallway. He checked her vital signs and determined she was dead. He and Gourdin then secured the scene and notified Desk Sergeant Sandoval to contact the proper people. Proper people in Pueblo police jargon means the shift commander, the chief of police, the district attorney's office, the captain of detectives and the coroner. All were notified.

During the ensuing forensic investigation, it was found that the telephone wire in the kitchen had been cut, but the phone in Rose's bedroom was in working order. There was a broken floor lamp lying across Rose's body. She was lying diagonally across the bed on her back. The body was covered with dried blood. Mrs. Rose was clad in her night clothing and was not covered by any of the bedding. The top of a nightgown or blouse stained with blood was found on the floor next to the bed. Rose's right arm was extended over the edge of the bed and her left arm was partially under her body.

A padded backrest, used for support while reading in bed, was on the floor between the bed and the dresser. On the nightstand next to the bed were a pair of glasses and a wristwatch. On the floor in front of the dresser were sections of a rope that had apparently been cut from the covering of a boat parked in the garage. Blood stains were noted in the bathroom and on a couch in the study adjacent to the bedroom. A towel on a rack in the bathroom was also heavily stained with blood.

Sergeant David E. Davenport photographed the crime scene which was then checked for fingerprints. Detective Sergeants Lutes and Shorter arrived to handle the investigation, as did Captain Mayber, Joe Foreman from the DA's office and Assistant County Coroner Dr. F. W. Barrows. Mayber was serving as acting chief at the time. The body was eventually taken to St. Mary-Corwin morgue and an autopsy was ordered.

Since Chief Harper was out of town when the crime was committed, Acting Chief Robert L. Mayber was tasked with the difficult job of notifying the parents of the youth being detained in Fort Collins. Mayber found the parents had already been contacted by the Fort Collins Police Department and had even been allowed to briefly converse with their son by telephone. Though devastated by the story of the incident to which their son had confessed, Steve and Louise Kopasz agreed to fully cooperate with the police investigation. They immediately gave their permission for Pueblo officers to return their son to Pueblo from Fort Collins.

The suspect, 16-year-old Leo Kopasz, who lived with his parents near the Rose residence, was brought back to Pueblo by Sergeant Edson Lutes and Sergeant Dick Shorter. Because of his age, his parents would have to be present when he was questioned by the detectives.

Leo Kopasz told detectives he had received a traffic ticket a few days earlier and was afraid to tell his parents. His father was a highly respected Pueblo schoolteacher, and he knew he would be in trouble at home if he confessed to errant driving and then asked his parents for the money to pay a fine. He said he was desperate to not incur his father's wrath.

On the night of the killing, he decided to sneak out of his home and try to find some way of getting cash to pay the anticipated penalty assessment. He said he crawled out a basement window in his home about 10 o'clock that evening and began prowling through the neighborhood. He noticed some lights were on in the Rose home and the garage door was open. He knew an "old lady" lived alone in the house, as his brother had delivered newspapers in the neighborhood and he himself had occasionally filled in on the paper route.

He said he entered the home through the garage door with the intention of rifling drawers to find money. He claimed he must have made a noise or something to attract the attention of the woman. When she saw him, he knew she would later be able to identify him. Frightened of what his father would do if he were caught, he decided to kill the woman. After doing so, he became even more concerned that he would be caught, so he took the woman's car. He intended to get as far away as possible in the hope that he could delay his inevitable capture. His account of his actions at the crime scene tallied with what the physical evidence revealed to the detectives.

A charge of first degree murder was filed against Leo Kopasz by Assistant District Attorney Joe Losavio. Kopasz would be tried as an adult, which is a common practice in Colorado when first- or second-degree felony crimes, or crimes of extreme violence, are charged against a youth at least 12 years of age.

Attorney Vasco Seavy entered pleas of not guilty and not guilty by reason of insanity on behalf of Kopasz, and the young man was ordered to undergo a psychiatric evaluation prior to trial. He was determined to be sane at the time of the commission of the crime. The trial was scheduled to begin in January 1967 in Pueblo District Court before the Honorable Judge S. Philip Cabibi.

Seeing the futility of a not guilty plea, as Kopasz had confessed to committing the crime, attorney Seavy changed Kopasz's plea from not guilty to guilty of first degree murder. Leo Kopasz took the witness stand shortly thereafter to tell the court he had discussed the change of plea with his parents, and it was his desire to plead guilty. The *Pueblo Chieftain* reported that Kopasz showed a great deal of courage as he stood erect before the court and answered pointed questions by Seavy.

Seavy explained to Kopasz that such a plea required the judge to impose a mandatory sentence of life in prison. Kopasz nodded that he knew that and understood the implications of pleading guilty. Seavy then asked him if he still wanted to change his plea. Kopasz replied, "It is my desire to enter such a plea." The youth's father, sitting near the front of the courtroom, lowered his head and wept silently.

In the ensuing very brief trial, several prosecution witnesses, including two Fort Collins police officers, were questioned about their interactions with Kopasz in connection with the case. One of the Fort Collins officers, Officer Daniel Joseph, who first questioned Kopasz after he was stopped by officers in Fort Collins, told the court, "The boy was very repentant—it seemed he wanted to get it all off his chest."

Doctor Bennett Sewell was the St. Mary-Corwin Hospital pathologist who performed the autopsy on Rose's body. He testified that she had been stabbed seven times. Three of those stab wounds were in her chest, three were in her back, and one was in her neck. Death resulted from loss of blood and shock.

Norman Butorac, a son-in-law of Margaret Rose, testified about the last time he had seen her. "My wife Jean and I had just brought her back from Denver on October 5th where she had been in the hospital for treatment in connection with open-heart surgery she underwent in June." He further reported that she had taken them out to dinner that evening and remembered that she commented about only having $3 and some change left after paying for the meal. He said she was always doing nice things, like buying their meal for them. "We took her home at 8:15 p.m. and that was the last time we ever saw her."

As Butorac completed his testimony, he paused for several seconds and stared at Kopasz. He then shook his head slightly and walked away from the witness stand.

Seavy offered no defense testimony and asked that the judge dispense with the usual pre-sentence report. Since the verdict was predetermined by law, his request was approved. Then, with Kopasz standing silently at his side, Seavy addressed the court.

"I think this is the most tragic occurrence I have seen in all my years of practicing law. I personally knew Mrs. Rose for many years—she was a wonderful woman—one of the finest persons I've ever known. Leo Kopasz is one of the nicest boys I have ever met—he has been a perfect gentleman at all times."

Margaret Rose's family, seated in the courtroom gallery, looked away and shielded their eyes. They likely wondered if she thought he was such a nice boy when she met him in her bedroom that October morning.

The *Pueblo Chieftain* reported that there was obvious pain in Judge Cabibi's voice when he pronounced the life sentence. The courtroom was eerily quiet when the words, "for the rest of your natural life" were spoken. Judge Cabibi rose, swallowed hard, called for a recess, then hurriedly left the courtroom.

Kopasz was immediately taken to county jail. Within the hour he was in a sheriff's car on his way to the Colorado State Penitentiary in Cañon City.

Mayber Appointed Chief

Roy F. Harper successfully completed almost 15 years of service as Pueblo's police chief and announced his retirement in early November 1967. His administration had seen little controversy or public expressions of dissatisfaction, even though several of the issues that had raised the hackles of citizens as well as city council members during the previous administration, remained. Chief among those issues was the widespread belief that the influence on public institutions by the Mafia still existed.

Allegations of corruption in local and county governments were also perceived as having been ignored, nor had concerns about police ineffectiveness and brutality been addressed. Mayber, who had frequently served as acting chief during Harper's absence, swore to address those issues.

Police Chief Robert L. Mayber at his desk. He served as chief from 1967 through 1973.

He was appointed chief on November 16th.

While Harper had been less transparent in his dealings with the local press, Mayber invited representatives of the news media into his office every morning to view reports generated during the previous 24 to 72 hours. First, he would read the reports, sign them indicating his approval, then hand them to the reporters gathered in front of his desk. They could read the reports and take notes but were discouraged from asking questions. Mayber would just tell them, "You read the same report I did." Occasionally, he would sign a report, then quickly stash it in his upper desk drawer. If a reporter had the temerity to ask why it was being withheld, Mayber would curtly reply, "It's not done yet." And that was that.

During his seven years in office, Chief Mayber oversaw an expansion of the department to over 160 officers and the creation of the position of deputy police chief to assist in the daily management of operational activities. A seasoned and tough senior captain, Jack Stiffler, was promoted to that position in 1968.

The position of police inspector was also created by Chief Mayber. Inspector was not a rank, but a designation awarded to selected senior police captains. The inspectors would be charged with, in addition to their regular duties, the obligation of handling citizens' complaints and allegations of serious or criminal misconduct by department personnel. The assignment would serve as forerunner of the later full-time Internal Affairs Section.

The inspectors would also oversee special assignments, which at the time meant protracted investigations relating to narcotics violations and organized crime. Two revered police captains, William T. Hurley and Robert E. Simon were chosen to serve as the inspectors. Both men had served long and distinguished careers with the department and both had successfully handled many of the most important cases of the 1960s and early 1970s.

*Inspector / Captain
Robert E. Simon*

*Inspector / Captain
William T. Hurley*

Patrolman Enloe Murder

Captain William T. Hurley stretched back and relaxed in his easy chair. He and his wife Shirley usually watched the 10 o'clock local news on television before turning in for the night. He hoped this night, Monday, January 8, 1968, would be no exception to their routine, but he knew an urgent call summoning him back to work could come at any time—that was the nature of his job.

Hurley sat straight up in his chair when the news began. The lead story was about a Colorado State Patrol officer (now called a trooper) who had just been shot and killed near Trinidad. The news reporter announced that the killing happened on Interstate 25 north of the city of Trinidad, about 80 miles south of Pueblo. As he listened intently to the breaking news his mind was racing ahead. He knew that if the killer headed north on the Interstate the first larger city he would reach, and his most logical stopping off point, would be Pueblo.

Hurley called the police station and asked on-duty Detective Sergeant Richard Bravo if there was anything he could do. "I think we could use all the help we can get," Bravo told him. Hurley grabbed his gear and quickly headed to the station. It took him just ten minutes to get there.

At approximately nine o'clock that evening, Colorado State Patrol Officer Larry B. Enloe, just six days shy of his 29th birthday, had stopped a 1967 Mercury station wagon for erratic driving just north of downtown Trinidad. The driver and sole occupant of the car was later determined to be a 16-year-old escapee from a mental hospital in Kansas named Edward C. "Eddie" Cosgrove. The station wagon had been stolen by Cosgrove the previous day.

As Enloe radioed the information of the stop to his dispatcher, Cosgrove jumped out of the station wagon and ran back to the patrol car. Before Enloe could react, Cosgrove shot him with a .38 caliber revolver he had purchased that day. He then took the officer's sidearm, rifled through his pockets, and took a small amount of change.

Colorado State Patrol Officer Larry B. Enloe. He was shot and killed when he stopped a stolen vehicle near Trinidad. He was the 13th CSP officer to die in the line of duty— the 4th in history (as of September 1, 2022) to be slain by hostile action.

Cosgrove crouched behind the parked patrol car. A few minutes later he saw a Volkswagen approaching. He stepped out in front of the car and waved the driver down. The driver, seeing the State Patrol car at the side of the road and feeling it was safe to stop, pulled over.

Cosgrove shoved his revolver in the man's face and hopped into the car. The driver was a sergeant with the U.S. Army, and he had his infant son in the car with him. Cosgrove snarled that he had just killed a state patrolman, and he threatened to kill the sergeant's child unless he did as he was told. He instructed the young sergeant to head north on the highway. The man complied.

As Cosgrove and his hostages neared Pueblo, they encountered a police roadblock. Cosgrove concealed his gun and told the man to cooperate fully and get them through the roadblock. The sergeant told the officers manning the roadblock he and his two sons were returning to Fort Carson after visiting out-of-state family. Seeing an army sergeant, a young man and a small baby, the officers discounted them being involved in the shooting of their comrade. They allowed the car to proceed.

The terrified army sergeant drove to a point on the highway adjacent to Pueblo's downtown area. Cosgrove told him to stop. He then jumped out of the car and fled toward the Pueblo business district. The sergeant turned his car around at the next exit and sped back to the roadblock where he told the officers there what had happened. Fortunately, he was able to provide a good description of Cosgrove. The information provided by the shaken man was radioed to Pueblo police.

Upon arriving at the police station, Captain Hurley was briefed with the available information, including the description of the armed criminal. He then teamed up with Officer Richard Paglione. The two then began checking bars and hotels in the downtown area. In the 600 block of North Main Street Hurley and Paglione encountered Officer David A. Davenport who was walking the North Main beat (Beat 45). Davenport accompanied them as they went to the Avalon Hotel, a cheap second-floor rooming house at 620½ North Main.

As they entered the first-floor landing, Hurley noticed wet footprints of what appeared to be a man ascending the narrow staircase. The officers cautiously went up the stairs to the hotel manager's office. Seeing the wet footprints in the hallway, they quietly aroused the manager who told them a young man had only moments ago checked in. The officers were told the man had signed his name as "Paul Johnson" and he was in room number 6. They also determined the man matched the description of the wanted murder suspect.

The three went to room 6 and knocked. A male voice answered from inside. Hurley ordered the man to open the door. The man replied that he first had to dress. Davenport said he would return to the manager's office to get a passkey. As Davenport neared the stairwell adjacent to the manager's room, he heard a loud crash. Cosgrove had broken out the window in his room and dropped to the sidewalk below. He then ran as fast as he could toward 7th Street.

Davenport ran down the single flight of stairs and onto the sidewalk in time to see a running figure rounding the corner onto 7th Street. He gave chase. When he got to the corner, he saw the wanted party about a half a block ahead of him. He was headed toward Santa Fe Avenue. Davenport ran to the corner. When he saw Cosgrove cross 7th Street, he yelled for the man to stop. When he didn't, Davenport took careful aim and fired one shot at the fleeing felon. His bullet struck Cosgrove in the right leg just below the knee. Cosgrove fell hard to the pavement. Hurley and Paglione ran up at that time to help Davenport handcuff him.

Cosgrove was treated at the scene by the Pueblo Fire Department First Aid Squad. His leg injury, determined by medical personnel to be minor, was bandaged. He was then taken by officers to police headquarters. The State Patrol was notified that their murder suspect was in custody.

Captain Ernest Walker and Detective Sergeant Richard Bravo briefly spoke with Cosgrove while they waited for the arrival of sheriff's investigators from Las Animas County, the jurisdiction in which the fatal shooting had occurred. Cosgrove spoke freely with the Pueblo police investigators. He readily admitted to killing the patrol officer and kidnapping the army sergeant and his baby. He said he was afraid because he was in a stolen car when the officer stopped him. He said he just wanted to get away.

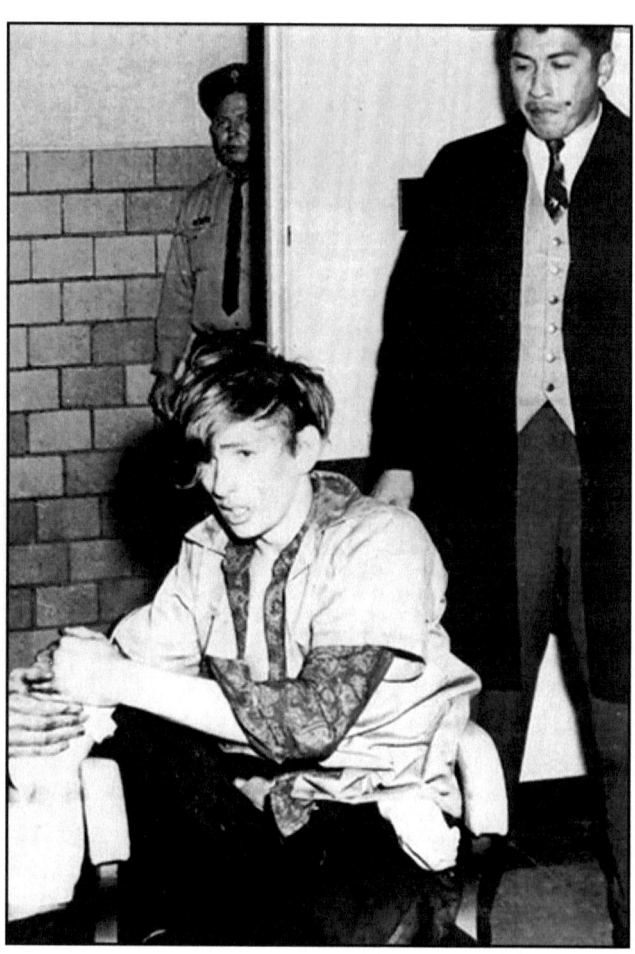

Detective Sergeant Richard Bravo watches over murder suspect Eddie Cosgrove in the Pueblo Police captain's office. Officer John Meachum stands guard in the hallway. Sergeant Bravo would rise through the ranks to retire as deputy chief.

Cosgrove was determined to be sane enough to stand trial for second-degree murder. He was tried as an adult, found guilty, and sentenced to a term of 34 to 50 years in the Colorado State Penitentiary. He arrived at the Cañon City facility on January 30, 1969. He began serving his time at the old territorial prison in the medium security unit at that complex.

Cosgrove escaped from the Colorado State Penitentiary in 1974. He remained at large for nearly seven years. On June 12, 1981, local authorities were notified that a man killed in a motorcycle accident in Florida had been positively identified as Eddie C. Cosgrove.

Mayber Makes Changes

Noting an emerging trend in smaller town law enforcement, Mayber approached City Manager Fred Weisbrod in 1972 with the prospect of instituting a new position in the police department—that of policewoman. Weisbrod was intrigued by the idea and gave Mayber permission and a budget to proceed. Three non-sworn parking enforcers, then called meter maids, were officially sworn in as policewomen that year.

Judy Leach, Nancy King and Charlene Marino, later to marry and become Charlene Graham, turned in their gray meter maid uniforms for new French blue skirts and jackets topped by white caps resembling sailor hats. Each was issued a snub-nosed revolver to carry in their shoulder bag purse.

The three were initially assigned to duties it was felt females were capable of handling. Accordingly, one was assigned to the Juvenile Section, as it was believed a female could relate well to children; one was assigned to the Identification Section, because women could certainly take photographs and do general lab work; and one was assigned to the Investigations Division where she could assist with the investigation of sex crimes as it was felt female victims would only divulge sensitive information about their victimization to another female.

The three new policewomen following their graduation from the police recruit training academy. Left to right: Judy Leach, Nancy King, Charlene Marino (Graham). The male recruits in the background are Carl Higbee and Charles Hicks. Larry Billesbach is just visible at far right.

As the law enforcement community and society at large became more enlightened, the policewomen were allowed to assume an equal role with their male counterparts in the department. The policewoman position was dropped on January 1, 1975, and the three were reclassified as police officers.

Judy Leach would leave the department to assume directorship of the city's data processing department, now called the Information Services Department, and Nancy King would leave to accept employment elsewhere. Only Charlene Graham would remain with the department for the long run. She would retire as Deputy Police Chief in 2003.

Deputy Chief Charlene B. Graham would have an amazing career in local law enforcement. She was one of Pueblo's first three "policewomen" and the city's first female deputy police chief. She served as chief of the Investigations Bureau and retired in 2003 to go into private business. She later served as division chief for the Pueblo County Sheriff's Office.

CHAPTER 13

THE BURGLARY SCANDAL

I always wanted to be a cop. My fascination with law enforcement began when I was a very young child growing up on South Lake Avenue in Pueblo, which in those pre-Interstate 25 freeway days was the main north-south highway running through the city. My home had a large fenced-in front yard in which I would play. I remember running to the fence whenever I heard a siren approaching. I loved to watch the emergency equipment race by. I could only imagine the thrill of driving those vehicles with their red lights flashing and their screaming sirens directing other traffic to pull over and give them the right-of-way.

That fascination with police cars and fire trucks was only enhanced when my family got our first television in the early 1950s and I was introduced to the many popular police procedural shows like *Dragnet, Code 3,* and a bit later, *Highway Patrol.* They became my favorite TV programs. I was particularly taken by the integrity, the bravery and the professionalism displayed by the TV cops, who were always the good guys. I was determined at that youthful age to someday become one of the good guys.

As soon as I turned 21 years old, I applied to become a member of the Pueblo Police Department. It took a few months for the Civil Service entrance exam to be given, and I took that exam with enthusiasm, obtaining a score that placed me number eight in consideration for being hired. As there were only six vacancies to be filled in the department, I feared that I had failed to make the grade. Fortunately for me, two candidates who had placed above me either dropped out of the process or were eliminated from consideration. I was thrilled beyond belief when I was notified that I was in line to be hired contingent upon passing a background investigation and a polygraph exam.

The year was 1970 and polygraphs, also known as lie-detectors, were just starting to be used in the hiring process for police officers. I was anxious to go through that process, knowing I had nothing to fear. At the time, I was working as a news reporter for KDZA radio. One day while at work, I received a phone call from the fellow who had placed number one on the police civil service exam. He introduced himself and asked if I had yet taken the polygraph exam. I told him I had not but was scheduled to do so the following day. He told me that I should "refuse" to take the exam and said there was "something wrong" with the test because everyone who had taken it had failed. He told me there was a meeting that very evening at the Branch Inn, a local tavern on Union Avenue, to discuss what to do about the situation. He asked me to attend. I felt very uncomfortable and very suspicious of the caller's motivations. Though I had no intention of attending such a meeting or refusing to take the polygraph exam, I told him I would try to be there. I did not attend that meeting, nor did I fail to show up for the scheduled lie detector test the next morning.

I sailed through the polygraph exam and was told to go ahead and give my current employer two-week's notice, as I would soon become a Pueblo police officer. I was so proud and so excited about the new career upon which I was about to embark that I literally forgot about the phone call I had received the previous day. I was therefore surprised a few days later when an announcement was made by the Civil Service Commission that the polygraph exams given to prospective police candidates were all being discounted as being "unreliable." I was a bit troubled by that decision, but since it didn't appear to affect my position on the hiring list and since I had a whole lot more to occupy my mind, I dismissed it as unimportant.

The *Pueblo Star-Journal* and *Pueblo Chieftain* both reported a few days later that six new police officers were to be sworn in on January 4, 1970: John Rusick, Michael Marino, Carmen Port, William Dreibelbis, Norman Morris, and John Ercul. It was official; I was a Pueblo cop.

After taking the oath of office from City Clerk Mary Weaver, we were issued a .38-44 revolver (a .38 caliber weapon built on a larger .44 caliber frame), our badge (mine bore the number 109) and a police whistle. The subsequent week-long training consisted primarily of learning how to fill out a police report form, how to properly wear the police uniform, how to use the two-way radio in the police cars and listening intently to Captain Harold Sell read aloud the entire city traffic code in monotone. We were then paired with senior officers whose job it was to break in a rookie, and then turn us loose on the public.

The most exciting call to which I initially responded was a burglary in progress at some railroad boxcars near the *Pueblo Chieftain* and Midtown Shopping Center. It was my first night on the street, and I was working with a senior officer named Jack Lowe. He and I quickly rounded up three juveniles who had forced open the door of one of the boxcars and were presumably looking for something inside to steal. The boxcars were all empty and we simply took the three into custody for minor property damage. To my parents' delight my name was in the newspaper the next day as being one of the arresting officers. I too was delighted.

My second or third night on the job found me working with Officer Bill Schonlau. The first stop we made after leaving the station was the south side Dunkin Donuts on Prairie Avenue. Schonlau told me to go in and get us some coffee and a couple of "sinkers" (that's what the cops called donuts in those days). I got out of the patrol car and made my way toward the front door of the donut shop. Suddenly I was struck hard in the back from behind. Schonlau had gotten out of the car and thrown my nightstick at me as hard as he could. "Don't you ever get out of the car without your stick!" he bellowed at me. I learned the lesson well—I never again went anywhere without my 18-inch-long hickory nightstick.

The closest I came to being involved in a major criminal investigation in my first few months on the job began when I stopped a taxicab for going through a red light in the Mesa Junction business district. My senior partner at the time was Warren Dodson, known by the nickname "Stony." He was grading me on writing a traffic citation, apparently unaware that I had successfully written several before being assigned to work with him.

I duly pulled the cab over, approached the driver, obtained his driver license and the vehicle registration and wrote the ticket. The cab driver, John Henry Schwader, politely accepted the citation and went on his way. Three weeks later John Henry Schwader would figure in a brutal murder that occurred about two blocks from where I stopped his cab. I would be questioned by detectives about the traffic stop, observations I made during the stop and Schwader's demeanor when he was contacted.

Nellie Belle Prince Murder

Rose Swearingen was worried. She had been trying to reach her daughter, Nellie Belle Prince, by phone since early morning but Nellie was not answering. Rose thought that was strange because she and Nellie had planned to have coffee together at 9 a.m., and Nellie never missed their morning coffee.

It was now a little after 3 p.m. on Thursday, April 9, 1970. Rose telephoned Nellie's landlady, Delores Schwader. After hearing Rose's concerns, Dolores went up the stairs of her narrow two-story home to the small living quarters rented by Nellie. She could hear a radio playing in Nellie's apartment, but she got no answer when she knocked on the slightly ajar door.

Slowly, Delores Schwader pushed the door open. She called out but again got no response. She quietly stepped into the apartment. She initially saw nothing out of the ordinary but noticed the door to the bedroom was standing open. She slowly made her way toward the bedroom, calling Nellie's name as she did so. She had only taken a couple of steps into the bedroom when she saw Nellie Belle Prince lying nude on the floor in a pool of blood. She turned and ran downstairs to the phone. Rose Swearingen was still on the line. "I think your daughter's been murdered," Delores said. She told Rose she would send her husband John Henry Schwader over to pick her up. Delores then called the police.

First on the scene were officers Robert Curtis and Tony Trujillo. They found Delores Schwader, accompanied by Nellie's son, 17-year-old Dallas Wayne Prince, waiting on the front porch. Dallas had just returned home from school. He had been restrained from entering the house by Delores. He was noticeably upset by the news of his mother's death.

Delores told the officers of the phone call from Nellie's mother, and of finding Nellie dead. When she mentioned that Nellie's body was devoid of clothing, Dallas interjected that his mother had been fully dressed when he had left for school at 7:45 that morning.

Officer Trujillo called for the patrol supervisor, Sergeant J. C. Grace, then he and Curtis went up to Prince's apartment. After assuring themselves they were dealing with a murder case rather than an accidental death, they secured the scene and requested the proper people be notified. Detective Sergeants Ben Williams, Robert O. Silva, Earl Pieratt and Richard Paglione, along with Investigator Joe Forman of the District Attorney's office, arrived on scene within ten minutes.

Photographs and videotape of the crime scene were taken by Identification Sergeants David E. Davenport and Ray Magan. Video of the exterior of the house, garage and yard were also taken. The scene was dusted for fingerprints. It was then measured, and a detailed schematic was prepared.

Sergeant Williams interviewed both Delores and John Schwader. John Schwader said he had gotten off work at the City Cab Company a little after 6 a.m. He claimed he went directly home and to bed. He said he was awakened by the telephone ringing about 11 a.m. but found no one on the line when he answered it.

He said he then went back to bed but got up a short time later and began cleaning up and shaving. He said he was distracted when the couple's two pet cats began fighting and that distraction caused him to cut his face with the shaving razor. He then left the house about 11:45 a.m. and walked to the Mesa Junction about five blocks away to get a haircut. He then went to the city civil service office downtown to pick up a job application.

He told Sergeant Williams he then went back home, arriving about 2:45 p.m. He said he went directly to the garage behind the home to work on some lawn furniture which had previously been damaged. He became aware that his wife had returned home from Colorado Springs a little before 3 p.m. so he went into the home to see her. At that time, he saw her running down the stairs from Nellie Prince's upstairs apartment. She went to the phone, talked with someone, then asked him to go to an address on the east side to get Rose Swearingen. He said he did not know who Rose was.

After hearing about John Schwader's account of his movements during the morning of the murder, Deputy Chief Jack Stiffler spoke further with Delores Schwader. A major inconsistency was noted when Delores told the deputy chief that upon arriving home a little before 3 p.m., she had seen her husband John coming down the back stairs of the house. She said at that time the phone rang, and she answered it. It was the call from Rose Swearingen inquiring about her daughter.

Assistant Coroner Dr. Harper Kerr examined the victim at the scene. He found numerous bruises on Nellie's throat, face and shoulders. He also pointed out to the investigating officers a large laceration on the top of Nellie's head. He opined that she had been bludgeoned with some sort of heavy blunt instrument sometime during the early morning hours of April 9th.

A later autopsy performed by Dr. Baitlon at the St. Mary-Corwin Hospital morgue would reveal the cause of death as being ligature strangulation. He believed the ligature used was a small cord with a rough edge. Dr. Baitlon further reported that some scratches on the victim's head, shoulders and chest appeared to have been caused by an unknown type of instrument with a sharp edge.

While at the scene, Dr. Kerr observed the scratch marks on John Henry Schwader's face and reported that they appeared to have been inflicted by human fingernails—not from the cuts of a razor blade. Fingernail scrapings from each of Nellie's fingers were collected at that time.

Interviews with Nellie Prince's son and daughter, as well as the interviews with Delores Schwader and the evidence at the scene, indicated that John Henry Schwader and the victim were likely the only ones in the home after 7:45 a.m. No signs of forced entry to the home or to Nellie's apartment were discovered.

John Henry Schwader was taken to police headquarters where he was advised of his Miranda rights. After acknowledging he understood his rights, he agreed to talk with Captain Ernest Walker and Sergeant J.C. Grace without the presence of an attorney. Simultaneously, Deputy District Attorney Cecil Turner, working with the cadre of detectives at the Madison residence, prepared a search warrant for the entire premises. The warrant was signed by Judge Bollinger.

Delores Schwader was cooperative with the detectives during the execution of the warrant. It was obvious to those present that she suspected her husband had committed the crime. She told the detectives that she had been married to John for approximately two years, but during that time she had become concerned for the safety of her daughter from a previous marriage who lived with the couple. She said her daughter had complained that Schwader would parade around the house in his underwear when she was present and that he had, on at least one occasion, tried to put his arm around her when her mother was not there. Delores said she had recently filed for a divorce from John Henry.

During the search of the Schwader's main floor living quarters, police found a pair of light blue men's jeans with several blood spots on them. They were wrapped around a white t-shirt that was also stained with blood. Both Delores and her daughter identified that clothing as belonging to John Schwader.

Near where the bloody clothing was found, officers discovered a heavy 18-inch-long hardwood nightstick, similar to the type police officers carried at the time. A short length of rope was found in the same area along with some men's leather gloves. The gloves had stains that appeared to be blood on them. A pair of women's silk stockings was found stuffed inside one of the gloves. Several pair of women's panties that did not belong to the Schwader women were also found in the basement of the home. A satchel containing several soft-core pornographic magazines was located near the panties.

Under careful interrogation by Captain Walker, John Henry Schwader became visibly confused. He at one point said he did not remember committing the murder "but may have done it." He acknowledged that he had "a problem" stemming from when he served in the army in Vietnam. He continued to deny that he even knew Nellie Belle Prince. He said he thought the tenant in the upstairs apartment was named "Price— or something like that." He did, however, consent to take a polygraph test.

The polygraph exam was conducted by certified examiner Sergeant Richard Paglione at 8:15 on the evening of the murder. Sergeant Paglione reported that Schwader's responses to certain questions indicated deception. Specifically, Schwader appeared deceptive in his negative answers to the following: "Did you fight with the woman upstairs today?" "Did the woman upstairs scratch your face today?" "Did you kill the woman upstairs?" It was the opinion of Sergeant Paglione that Schwader had indeed committed the crime and that he remembered doing so.

As the investigation progressed, it was discovered that Schwader had been listed as a suspect in four house burglaries in the area of the Schwader home dating back to 1966. Schwader had been interviewed by police in each case but had denied committing the crimes. In all four cases, items reported stolen included ladies' undergarments. Victims had known of Schwader, and all described him as "simpleminded." They all stated he had been seen prowling in the area at night which is why they listed him as a suspect in their burglary cases.

Schwader was also listed as a suspect in the thefts of women's undergarments from clotheslines in the neighborhood during the past year or so. The thefts had been considered so minor by the victims that they hadn't reported them until contacted by police during a neighborhood canvas following the Prince murder.

The Nellie Belle Prince attack also brought John Henry Schwader into focus as a suspect in two recent late-night attacks on women in the Mesa Junction area. Both victims had been attacked from behind and had not seen their assailant. Accordingly, neither could identify Schwader as her attacker. One of the women had suffered multiple superficial stab wounds and cuts from a sharp-edged weapon. Schwader was questioned about both attacks. He initially denied committing the crimes, then exercised his right to remain silent. Authorities were unable to connect him with either crime, though detectives believed he had committed both.

Schwader was also listed as a suspect in an indecent liberties incident that had occurred on April 2, 1970, just one week prior to the Prince homicide. The reporting party was a 13-year-old girl who had taken a cab from Pueblo's east side to her home in the 1500 block South Prairie Avenue—a block of low-rent project housing locally known as "the bricks." She reported that the cab driver drove her past her home to an unknown location at the edge of town. It was 4:30 a.m. and she was not familiar with the area to which she had been taken.

She said the cab driver grabbed her by the blouse and told her to take off all her clothes. She said she was frightened so she completely disrobed and sat quietly in the cab as the driver fondled her for a few moments. He then allowed her to get dressed, and he took her home. She said she told the driver she would have to go into her apartment to get the money for the cab fare. He waited outside while she went in. As soon as she entered her home, she called the police.

Officer Art Durning arrived on scene within minutes and contacted the cab driver, John Henry Schwader, waiting at the curb. Schwader told Officer Durning he had been dispatched to the east side to pick up a fare, and he had taken that fare to the apartment on South Prairie. He said she told him she would get the money for the ride in her house, but that she had not come out and he figured he had been "stiffed." He said he was about to call the police to report the fraud when Durning drove up.

Both the reporting party and John Henry Schwader were taken to the police station and questioned. Neither deviated from their original account of the incident. Schwader came across as forthright and confident while the alleged victim appeared confused about details of the reported molestation and the location where it occurred. As it was difficult to determine whether the girl was telling the truth, attempting to evade having to pay the cab fare or just embarrassed about having to relay details of a sexual assault, no immediate action was taken. The south side district patrol car was called to the police station to take the reporting party home. Corporal Bob Hudgens and I were the officers assigned the district 2 car—we were given the transport task.

It was the second time in two weeks I had encountered John Henry Schwader—this time as he left the captain's office at the police station. He had been released pending further investigation and the possible filing of charges by the district attorney's office. That case was still pending when Schwader was arrested for the Nellie Belle Prince killing.

I was not involved in the trial of John Henry Schwader, but my brief encounters with him taught me that one cannot determine a person's true character by their meek appearance and pleasant demeanor. Schwader was a proverbial wolf in sheep's clothing.

After months of legal wrangling over the issue of his sanity, John Henry Schwader was tried and convicted of second-degree murder in Pueblo District Court. The state was unable to prove the killing was premeditated, or if it occurred as the result of the unexpected resistance of the victim of an intended sexual molestation. Schwader was sentenced to 10 to 25 years in state prison. Probation was denied.

CLETA Training

After working the streets about four months, my turn came to attend CLETA—the Colorado Law Enforcement Training Academy at Camp George West in Golden, Colorado.

In 1970 there was no Pueblo Police Academy—all recruit officers had to await an opening for the three weeks (yes—just three weeks) of basic training at CLETA. Officer Mike Marino and I were detailed to attend the May 1970 class along with recruit officers from throughout the state. There we learned a bit more than we had during our week-long training in Pueblo, though it was a Colorado State Patrol lieutenant who read the state traffic code to us verbatim—in monotone.

The May 1970 CLETA graduating class. I'm the baby-faced cop seated at the far right in the middle row.

A few days after graduating from CLETA, I showed up at work for the 9 at night to 5 in the morning shift. Three older officers had called off sick that night and there were not enough senior officers to pair up with rookies. A young officer named Ray Flieger, only on the job about six months longer than I, was thus assigned to work with me. We were told to work in District 6, the predominately middle-class Belmont residential neighborhood that was considered the least busy part of town. As the sergeant was nervous about two newer officers working together, we were told to just drive around, do nothing, don't stop any cars, and don't get into any trouble.

We tried hard to comply, but about halfway through the shift we jumped a burglar trying to break into one of the shops in the Belmont Shopping Center. He ran, we chased and caught him, and the fight was on. Before other officers arrived, we had the miscreant trussed up and in custody. The sergeant just shook his head.

American Serial Killer

Pueblo Police Officer David Martinez, working the single officer District 6 patrol car, was checking businesses in the Belmont Shopping Center on the city's northeast side on a very quiet early Tuesday morning in April 1973. He had just made a pass through the parking lot when he heard a radio call directed to the District 5 car crew.

Officers Tano Roybal and Pat McCoy, assigned to the two-officer District 5 car, were directed to go to the phone booth located at 21st Street and Norwood. They were told by dispatch that there was a man in that phone booth on the line with the Santa Cruz Police Department confessing to a series of murders in the California jurisdiction.

Dave Martinez was much closer to the phone booth than the other Pueblo officers, so he sped to that location, intending to set up surveillance before the other officers arrived. As he turned onto Norwood, he saw the phone booth. He first had the impression that there were two people crowded inside—the booth looked so full.

He then realized there was only one man in the booth—a big man—a really big man he thought. The man turned toward him, and David decided he needed to take him. Martinez drove up to the phone booth, got out of the police car, pointed his service revolver at the man and told the man to get out of the phone booth and put his hands up. The man complied.

Left: California serial killer Edmund Kemper

Above: Pueblo Police Corporal David M. Martinez. He arrested Kemper in a phone booth at 21st Street and Norwood.

The man in the phone booth was 24-year-old Edmund Emil Kemper III, who stood 6 feet 9 inches tall and weighed almost 300 pounds Kemper found himself in Pueblo about midnight on Tuesday, April 23, 1973. He had left Santa Cruz two days earlier; he would later say that he didn't know where he was going—he was just driving. A day earlier he had been stopped by a Colorado state patrolman on the state's western slope. He had been issued a speeding ticket and released.

He drove around Pueblo for a short time trying to decide what to do. He was seething inside, and he wasn't thinking clearly, but he knew he needed help. He also knew that if he didn't get help soon, someone—perhaps many—would die. He knew that because just three days earlier he had killed his own mother and another woman in Santa Cruz County, California. And they weren't the only victims—there had been many others—so many others.

For the previous year, the Santa Cruz area had been plagued by a series of brutal, sexually-oriented murders. Many of the victims had been beheaded and otherwise mutilated. The press had labeled the series of crimes "the Coed Killings" as most of the victims were young female students hitchhiking in the Santa Cruz area.

The coed killings began on May 7, 1972, when Kemper picked up two hitchhikers, Mary Ann Pesce and Anita Luchessa, both 18 years old, near Berkeley, California. He drove them to a secluded area near Alameda where he stabbed and strangled them to death. He then took their corpses home to his room in Santa Cruz. There he took photographs of the bodies before dismembering and decapitating them. He then performed irrumation (oral sex) on their severed heads and sexual intercourse with their mutilated bodies. The bulk of the remains were bundled into plastic bags and hastily buried in a wooded area on Loma Prieta Mountain, north of Santa Cruz. The heads and some internal organs were kept for a while to satisfy Kemper's perverted sexual desires, then thrown into a ravine near his home.

Next to die was Aiko Koo, 15, who had been picked up by Kemper as she hitchhiked near the Santa Cruz campus. Aiko was a small girl—no match for the massively built Kemper. The large man simply overpowered her and smothered her with his massive hands. He raped her corpse then took it home for mutilation and dissection.

A similar fate befell Cindy Schall, 18, on January 8, 1973. She was forced into the trunk of Kemper's car where he shot her. Her severed head wound up in a shallow grave behind Kemper's home.

Next in line for slaughter were 23-year-old Rosalind Thorpe and Alice Liu, 20. They were shot by Kemper, then decapitated and sexually assaulted in his usual manner.

Finally, as Easter Sunday 1973 neared, Kemper's mind gave way altogether. He began fantasizing about murdering everyone on his block. He quickly decided that would be impractical and he settled on murdering his mother.

Like so many of his kind, Kemper was the product of a broken and abusive home. He harbored an intense hatred for his mother that stemmed from his childhood. Physically abused and locked in a damp cellar for hours on end as a child, Kemper entered a world of fantasy. Most of those fantasies involved violent death. He butchered and ripped apart at least two pet house cats as a child. He also decapitated and sexually mutilated several of his sister's dolls in much the same way as he did the coed victims.

In 1963, at the age of 15, Kemper shot and killed his paternal grandparents. He was quickly packed off to Atascadero State Hospital, California's maximum security mental health facility. He lived there until 1969 when he was paroled to the custody of his mother—the mother he hated. He lived with her for almost four years, during which time he began his murder spree.

On the day before Easter 1973, he apparently felt it was time for her to pay for her "crimes" against him. He crept into her room while she was napping. He stared at her a moment, then crushed her skull with repeated blows from a hammer. He then cut off her head, raped her headless corpse, and dismembered it. After toying with her severed head and various body parts for another hour, he telephoned his mother's close friend, Sally Hallett, and invited her over for a "surprise dinner party" in his mother's honor. Though she was at first hesitant, Hallett finally accepted the invitation.

When the unsuspecting Ms. Hallett arrived, Kemper clubbed her to the floor. He then strangled her to death, cut off her head, mutilated her corpse, and threw it in a closet along with the remains of his mother. His mother, Clarnell Kemper Strandberg and her friend Sally Hallett were the last of his 10 murders.

The next morning, Easter Sunday, Kemper left home and started driving. When he got to Pueblo, he pulled over into a parking lot. He later admitted that he originally intended to use the 30.06 caliber rifle he had with him to shoot law enforcement officers "sniper style." He claimed he realized that he would likely be shot and killed if he attempted that but said he didn't care.

He decided, however, that enough was enough, and he placed a call to the Santa Cruz Police Department from a phone booth located near the intersection of Highway 50 West and North Elizabeth Street. The operator who answered the phone told him to call back after 9 a.m. when the detectives handling the coed murder case would be on duty.

Frustrated, he drove around town for another hour, then pulled over and napped in his car for a short time. When he awoke it was nearly 5 a.m. and time to try another phone call. This time the phone was answered by Santa Cruz Detective Joe Brown who immediately realized the gravity of the call. Within minutes, the California authorities were on the line with the Pueblo Police Department, and the radio broadcast that brought Corporal David Martinez face to face with Edmund Kemper was aired.

"He's pointing a gun at me!" Kemper told Detective Brown on the other end of the line in California. Kemper then hung up the phone, opened the phone booth door and meekly surrendered to Martinez and the other officers who had arrived to assist.

Kemper was taken to police headquarters where he was fingerprinted and mugged (photographed) by Officers J. Emilio Trujillo and Tom Cullen of the Identification Section. The rental car in Kemper's possession was located and towed to the police station for processing. In the trunk of the vehicle officers found a Remington bolt-action 30.06 rifle, a Winchester 12-gauge shotgun, a .30 caliber carbine rifle and one 100-round belt of 30.06 ammunition. Also found in the trunk was a dark blue jumpsuit which Kemper voluntarily stated he had worn when he murdered his mother and her friend.

Kemper submitted to an interview with Detectives Frank Grubb and Oscar Schmidt later that afternoon. He was cooperative with the detectives and forthcoming with his answers to their questions. Their interview with Kemper was transcribed word-for-word and forwarded to the Santa Cruz District Attorney's office. It became an integral element of the prosecution. Kemper was declared sane and convicted of eight murders by a jury of six men and six women on November 8, 1973. He was sentenced to seven years to life in prison for each count. He remains incarcerated in the California Medical Facility in Vacaville.

I was not involved in the capture of Edmund Emil Kemper in 1973, but I spoke with those who were. Corporal Dave Martinez told me Kemper was the scariest man he had ever encountered during his career as a police officer.

I thoroughly enjoyed my first few years in the police department. I made many good friends and worked with some remarkably proficient officers. I was very proud to be a Pueblo police officer—one of the "good guys." At that time the thought that some officers might be "crooked" never crossed my mind. I didn't realize how naive I was.

The Scandal

It was a warm afternoon in May 1972, when Joseph A. Concialdi, co-owner of the Branch Inn, a well-known tavern located at 301 South Union Avenue, sauntered unannounced into the office of Police Chief Robert L. Mayber. He placed a large stack of official police reports on the chief's desk. Concialdi told Mayber the reports had been purloined from the police records division by two corrupt police sergeants, Richard Harpel and William Schonlau, and taken to his tavern. Included with the written reports was a tape recording of a confidential telephone conversation between police narcotics detective John Koncilja Jr. and a federal narcotics agent relating to a planned bust of drug traffickers in the Pueblo area. In explaining his reason for bringing the documents to the chief's office, an angry Concialdi reportedly said he "just didn't want them lying around his bar, and he wanted the chief to be aware of what his officers were doing."

Shocked by the situation and suspicious of the real reason Concialdi had brought the matter to his attention, Chief Mayber immediately assembled a team of senior investigators including Deputy Chief Jack Stiffler, Captain Robert E. Simon and Sergeant Edson Lutes. He instructed them to begin a comprehensive internal investigation into departmental corruption.

Both Harpel and Schonlau initially denied taking the reports to the Branch Inn but faced with numerous inconsistencies in their answers to the intense questioning, the truth began coming out. The two sergeants eventually revealed that Concialdi was operating a "brokerage" operation, taking money to "fix" minor violations of the law, and to provide confidential information that would compromise the prosecution of more serious crimes. The crimes in question included attempted murder, theft and burglary. One Pueblo teenager was identified as having paid Concialdi $300 to make a traffic ticket "disappear." Schonlau admitted that he had removed the ticket from both the records file and the municipal court file but denied receiving any money for doing so. He said tickets were frequently "adjusted," meaning turned from a citation to a warning at the request of other officers. He saw nothing wrong with the practice and continued to deny any wrongdoing involving the matter.

It was alleged by the two sergeants that Concialdi was also "brokering" certain civil service promotional examinations and tests to establish an initial employment list for the city. It was alleged that for a fee, applicants would be instructed to answer only the questions on the exam they knew to be correct and to leave the others blank. When the test was graded by the personnel office clerk, Mary Ann Wurster, a cousin of

Concialdi's, she would fill in the correct answers to guarantee the applicant's high position on the test. Personnel Director Doug Ulmer trusted Wurster's grading and did not check on it. Both Harpel and Schonlau had recently been promoted to sergeant after having "come out high" on their respective promotional exams. Both Harpel and Schonlau were fired by Mayber.

In the following month, the Pueblo County grand jury entered the investigation, and it was announced that Chief Mayber and other members of the department would be subpoenaed to testify about alleged police corruption. It was revealed that the grand jury was working on information that several local attorneys had been illegally receiving confidential crime reports smuggled out of the police station and sold to them by Concialdi. District Attorney Carl Parlapiano confirmed to the local press that he and members of his staff had been suspicious for some time concerning the amount of information prematurely in the hands of certain defense attorneys in criminal cases handled by the police. Further, the illegal wiretapping aspect of the investigation brought the FBI into the case because wiretapping is a federal offense.

In his testimony before the grand jury, Concialdi leveled allegations of numerous other crimes committed by Schonlau, Harpel and three or four other Pueblo officers acting in conjunction with them. Allegations included burglaries, procurement of at least one illegal abortion, receiving stolen property, ticket-fixing, arson and insurance fraud. Schonlau and Harpel continued to deny their involvement in illegal activity and they both appealed their firings to the Pueblo City Civil Service Commission.

At a subsequent hearing before the commission, Concialdi testified that Schonlau and Harpel had brought numerous stolen police reports to his tavern, but he downplayed his own involvement by saying he knew nothing about the contents of the reports. He said the reports, along with a confidential document identifying suspected organized crime figures from throughout the state, were kept out of sight under his bar for several months. He said he eventually became concerned about the material being in his establishment and instructed both Harpel and Schonlau to get them out of his bar or he would "take them to Chief Mayber." Schonlau testified that he saw police reports at the Branch Inn, and he admitted making some hand-written notes regarding one of them, but he denied stealing the documents or delivering them to Concialdi's bar.

At the same hearing, another police officer, Corporal Dan Studen, alleged that Schonlau had attempted to entice him into illegal gambling activities in the Pueblo area. He testified that he was approached by Schonlau about six months previously and asked if he was still interested in running for the office of Pueblo County Sheriff. He said Schonlau then asked him what he thought about gambling, and whether he would be willing to cooperate with "his people" involved in illegal gambling activities.

When asked by City Attorney Thomas Jagger if Schonlau ever mentioned any names, Studen replied that Schonlau said a man named "Grandpa" was the leader. He later said that "Grandpa" was Scotty Spinuzzi, the well-known and frequently alleged organized crime leader in Pueblo. Schonlau reportedly told Studen that he could get him elected sheriff, but that Studen would have to agree to cooperate with the gambling operation. He allegedly told Studen that there would be a great deal of money involved in gambling payoffs.

When asked by Jagger if any threats were made against him, Studen said he was told that he would have to be cool and quiet about "all this," and that if he ever said anything about it, Schonlau would call him a "God-damned liar." He said Schonlau further told him that Spinuzzi was the "number one man," and that Concialdi was "nothing but a bartender, and would never be nothing but a bartender," and that "I would be wise to go with him (Schonlau), and to stay away from Concialdi. Studen said the conversation did not frighten him but did cause him some concern for his safety.

Studen further testified that he was a frequent customer of the Branch Inn, and that Concialdi had recently shown him the box of purloined reports he kept under the counter. Studen said he told Concialdi to "take them to Chief Mayber and report what's going on." When braced about Studen's allegations, Schonlau reportedly said they were all "bald-faced lies" and Studen was "a God-damned liar." The firings of Schonlau and Harpel were upheld by the Civil Service Commission.

In September, the grand jury indicted both Schonlau and Concialdi on bribery and conspiracy charges and both voluntarily surrendered to the Sheriff's office to be booked into county jail. The grand jury probe continued into subsequent years with numerous witnesses called to testify, including several local organized crime figures and at least one known criminal tied to the Smaldone organization, an alleged organized crime outfit operating in Denver. It emerged that a small group of Pueblo officers were involved, directly or indirectly, in numerous felonies over a three-to-five-year period. Those crimes included numerous burglaries during which two or more officers would commit the actual break-in while another officer, or a corrupt sergeant would distract honest cops working in the vicinity of the planned offense to prevent them from happening upon the crime in progress.

Other crimes included conspiring with an illegal abortion operation in the Walsenburg area, committing a phony burglary at a local electronics store to defraud an insurance company, the arson fire of another electronics firm to drive it out of business and reduce the competition for the firm that had hired corrupt cops to commit the insurance scam and "fixing" civil service examinations to get "cooperative people" hired or promoted to supervisory ranks within the department.

Officers who were convicted and sentenced to the Colorado State Reformatory or state or federal prison for their parts in the police scandal of the 1970s were Captain J.C. Grace (who admitted to secretly recording the conversation between narcotics officers and prematurely releasing the information to allow drug traffickers to evade capture), Sergeants William Schonlau and Richard Harpel, Corporal D.A. Davenport and Officer Russell Longgrear who admitted to committing more than one burglary. Several others, including Officer Al Stasco, were subjected to departmental discipline, but avoided criminal prosecution. Stasco admitted to buying some tires from officers involved in thefts, but he denied knowing the tires had been stolen.

Former Officers John Rusick and Ray D. Pearce, who both resigned from the department at the height of the corruption probe turned witnesses for the prosecution and were granted immunity in return for their testimony. Rusick admitted to paying Concialdi $500 to rig the police entrance exam he took in late 1969 to make him the top candidate. He claimed he was told to answer only the questions to which he knew the answers and to leave the ones he did not know blank. He answered only 115, or 76 percent of the 150 test questions. Rusick said he paid Concialdi $50 a month until the $500 was paid off. John Rusick was the one who called me at KDZA when he reportedly failed his polygraph exam in 1969. I guess there was really nothing wrong with the lie-detector tests given that year after all.

Also indicted or listed as unindicted co-conspirators in crimes related to the corruption probe were Pueblo organized crime chieftain Joseph "Scotty" Spinuzzi and local citizens, business owners or city employees Mary Ann Wurster, Joseph Concialdi, Michael Anselmo, James Cozzolino, Eugene Cozzolino, Jerome Vellar, Sam Vernon, Jay Baird, John Foderaro and Gloria Savage. Some were sentenced to jail or prison terms.

Several officers were disciplined for rule and regulation violations, mainly failure to report suspicions about the activities of fellow officers. In some cases, officers were disciplined for being "less than truthful" with investigators working the case.

In its review of the investigation, the Pueblo County grand jury publicly expressed a "lack of confidence" in the top-level management of the police department. It noted that most of the testimony it heard revealed a severe lack of administrative guidance evidenced by several questionable practices and policies on behalf of the agency. It pointed out, however, that the vast majority of Pueblo officers were honest and dedicated professionals who played no part in the type of illicit activity receiving daily reportage in the area press. The grand jury praised the untiring efforts of the officers who worked hard to ferret out the bad apples among them and restore public confidence in local law enforcement.

Chief Mayber received the brunt of public criticism, and he retired in 1973. After a contentious nationwide search, during which Pueblo police investigators and state investigators from Colorado's organized crime task force scrupulously vetted several out-of-town applicants for the position, a new police chief was chosen. Elbert L. "Bud" Willoughby, then a major with the Kansas City, Missouri, Police Department, was hired as the new Pueblo police chief.

Within weeks of his appointment Chief Willoughby orchestrated a complete reorganization of the department and put into place many regulations and procedures which would make it much more difficult for the type of corrupt activity that ran rampant during the early 1970s to continue.

CHAPTER 14

THE WILLOUGHBY YEARS

Police Corporal Tom Hanson and his partner Jim Askey had become good friends since being assigned to work the graveyard shift downtown patrol car together. Tom, the older and more experienced of the two, made Jim laugh. He made everyone laugh—that's the way Tom was—bright, cheerful, fun to work with. But Tom was also a very diligent and shrewd seven-year officer who knew when it was time to joke around, and when it was time to be serious.

Tom was driving their assigned car, unit number 8, on the morning of Saturday, December 29, 1973. It had been a busy night for the officers, and Tom's stomach was starting to bother him. "Some milk would fix that up," he thought, as he steered the cruiser toward the 7-Eleven store-at 8th Street and Grand Avenue. As they drove their cruiser southbound on Grand past 10th Street, Jim noticed a white Volkswagen turn off Grand and proceed west on 8th Street. It was the only vehicle other than the police car at 1:45 a.m. and Jim mentioned it to Tom. The two made a mental note of that car as they pulled their vehicle into the parking lot in front of the store.

Corporal Tom Hanson   *Officer James Askey*

As Tom pulled to a stop directly in front of the double doors, he noticed that the clerk was not visible inside the store. Under most circumstances that would have raised a red flag for both officers but neither thought much about it on this night because, being familiar with their beat, they knew the clerks working at this store were usually in the rear storage room stocking the coolers just before 2:00 a.m.

Jim remained in the patrol car to work on a crime report he had taken earlier in the shift while Tom went into the store for a small carton of milk. Upon entering the store, Tom stopped cold—something was just not right. Jim sensed it too and he looked up from his paperwork to see what was going on in the store. He observed a masked figure stand from a crouched position behind a display counter. As he watched, the party sprang from where he had been hiding and ran toward the front doors. That path took the masked man directly toward where Tom Hanson had paused. Jim also saw that the shadowy figure was clutching a pistol in his right hand. He reacted immediately. He drew his service revolver and stepped from the police car.

Tom saw the figure too. He drew his weapon but was unable to bring it into play in time. He also reacted by extending his left arm toward the party in what was probably an attempt to parry away the pistol that was now pointed directly at him. The running figure fired. The .22 caliber round went through Tom's shoulder, then entered his chest cavity, went through a lung, clipped a major artery and lodged in Tom's esophagus.

Police car number 8 parked in front of the 7-11 convenience store at 8th Street and Grand Avenue. Officer Jim Askey fired through the plate glass window striking and bringing down the robber who had just shot Cpl. Tom Hanson on December 29, 1973.

Tom staggered, then fell backwards to the floor. Jim had a perfect view through the store's plate glass window and he fired—two rounds at first, then a third when the suspect did not immediately react. His rounds all found their mark. The third round struck the assailant in the head, bringing him down hard. Jim ran into the store and went to Tom. Tom partially raised himself on one arm and said, "I'm all right." Jim knew better—he held his breath as he watched his friend and partner lapse into unconsciousness.

Chief Bud Willoughby had only been in bed a short while when he was awakened by the telephone call from the dispatch center. There had been an officer involved shooting, and an officer had been shot. It was the worst possible news a new police chief could possibly get. However, Willoughby was an experienced law enforcement administrator from the Kansas City Police Department who had only been named Pueblo police chief a few months earlier. He had experienced officer shootings before. He knew exactly what to do.

The chief directed that every off-duty Pueblo officer be notified and asked to report for duty. He then went directly to Parkview Hospital where Tom Hanson had been taken. There he learned that Tom had passed away from loss of blood due to massive internal bleeding. He also learned that the one known suspect, 19-year-old Bernard Meehan, was also dead but that the absence of a getaway vehicle parked in the vicinity of the crime indicated there was at least one additional suspect on the loose.

Within the hour, over a hundred officers had gathered in the lobby of the police building. All were clamoring for information about what had happened. Chief Willoughby called for everyone to gather in the assembly room for a briefing. His intention was to bring all officers up to date regarding the situation, dispel rumors and orchestrate an immediate, comprehensive investigation to identify and capture the illusive getaway driver.

Chief Willoughby had been hired in the wake of an unfolding scandal involving corruption and dereliction of duty that was still casting the shadow of suspicion over much of the department. Most of the officers did not know him well and many were unsure of him. "Why," they asked, "did we need an outsider to clean up the department? Didn't we have honest and competent ranking officers here that could do the job?"

Pueblo Police Chief Elbert L. "Bud" Willoughby, 1973

The assembly room was uncannily quiet as the chief entered. Without hesitation, he began laying out the details of what had happened at that 7-Eleven store and who some quick-acting officers had determined was a probable second suspect—one who had been with the dead robber earlier in the night and may have acted as a getaway driver who fled when the shooting started. The chief then passed out keys to every police vehicle in the fleet—marked and unmarked—and ordered everyone to team up, grab a vehicle and "hit the streets" looking for the wanted party. As a finale, he asked for a moment of silence for

Tom Hanson. He then led the gathering of officers in a prayer for their fallen comrade. When he finished the prayer there wasn't a dry eye in the room—even experience-hardened officers were sobbing, and when he ended with the directive, "Now go get him," the officers enthusiastically emptied to the parking lot, each of them sure of their mission. As the officers rushed to the cars, one was heard saying, "I think our new chief is great." Another replied, "Right now I think he could be elected president."

The getaway driver, a 17-year-old youth, was tracked down in his white Volkswagen and taken into custody by 8:00 a.m. and the case was quickly and successfully wrapped up. Tom Hanson was given a hero's funeral—small compensation for the sacrifice he had made. Jim Askey was also proclaimed a hero for the quick and appropriate actions he had taken. He remained with the department for several more years before taking a medical retirement for a back injury.

The Tom Hanson case and the way Chief Willoughby handled it—particularly the way he interacted so quickly, so professionally and so sincerely with the other members of the department—solidified his reputation internally. His actions helped establish a level of trust that enabled him to easily make major and needed changes in the organization and the operation of the department.

Chief Willoughby was born in Pueblo in 1930. He spent his early years in Pueblo until his parents moved to Missouri. In 1954, he was hired by the Kansas City, Missouri, Police Department. He swiftly rose through the ranks of that organization to achieve the position of major—second in command to Kansas City Police Chief Clarence M. Kelley. On June 27, 1974, Kelley was appointed by President Nixon to be the 2nd national director of the FBI. (Clyde Tolson, L. Patrick Gray and William Ruckelshaus had served short terms as "acting director" following the death of J. Edgar Hoover in 1972, but Kelley became the 2nd permanent director).

Prior to Kelley's appointment, Willoughby, with Kelley's backing, had applied for the chief's job in Pueblo. His impeccable reputation as an honest, forward thinking, hardworking and extremely competent police administrator elevated him to the top of the list of applicants and all but assured his appointment. When he was notified that he would be offered the job within the month, he requested a list of names of all personnel of the Pueblo Police Department, along with a photograph of each. The requested material was delivered to him.

On August 9, 1973, Willoughby accepted his appointment. When he arrived in Pueblo to assume his new duties, department employees were shocked when he was able to recognize and greet each one of them by name. He had memorized the photographs and names of each employee.

Reorganization

Almost immediately after assuming command, Chief Willoughby announced a complete reorganization of the department. He created two bureaus, Administration and Operations, each to be overseen by a deputy chief whose rank title would be changed to major. The two positions of major were filled on an interim basis until the city's Civil Service Commission could arrange for a qualifying examination. Captain Harold Jones, who was about to retire, and Captain Robert O. Silva, who did not have the required time-in-grade to compete for the full-time position, were selected as the interim majors. Jones assumed command of the Administration Bureau, and Silva took the Operation Bureau post. After the civil service testing process was completed and certified, Captains William T. Hurley and Robert E. Simon were promoted to the full-time position of major.

Chief Willoughby also appointed the department's first full-time public information officer, then called a press and projects officer. I got that appointment. In addition to being responsible for media relations, my duties as press officer were identified as arranging for publicity and advertisement of police programs, issuance of identification cards, organizing press conferences, writing articles and news releases and ensuring media exposure of projects such as the newly created Law-Explorer program and the "Cops on Campus" program, a forerunner of the later School Resource Officer Section. I held the position of press officer until November 1974 when I was promoted to sergeant and moved to a supervisory position in the Patrol Division.

Chief Willoughby also appointed a task force consisting of newly promoted Captains Ben Williams, Robert O. Silva and several other experienced officers to assist him in researching, writing and distributing a new department manual. It took approximately three months to complete that process.

The manual was made up of three four-inch-thick loose-leaf binders. One of the binders would contain *general orders*—those directives that would govern the general conduct of personnel on a day-to-day basis. The second binder would contain *special orders*—those directives that would address special activities and events and one-time operations not covered by the general orders. The third binder was for *procedural instructions*—"how to" directives spelling out methods of accomplishing specific tasks. The manual replaced the former *rules and regulations* booklet, a short list of prohibited conduct that had been in use since anyone could remember. Every member of the department was issued a copy of the manual, and all were required to read and sign a sheet to indicate they had read the entire manual and understood what was expected of them.

As the manual writing process was winding up, the chief created a planning, research and development section to be responsible for staff work essential for the development of policies, programs, procedures and activities. That section was responsible for the maintenance of the department manual, for the drafting and publication of new or changing directives and for providing the acquisition and coordination of grant money available to law enforcement organizations. A special crime analyst was hired to examine crime trends and to plan for the focus of police resources and strategies according to current and changing needs. The crime analyst would also conduct research to identify successful programs employed by other agencies that could lead to development of programs for Pueblo.

Chosen to be the department's crime analyst was a brilliant 29-year-old former military police major who had experience as a nuclear weapons depot commander and as commanding officer of the Criminal Investigations Division, the primary federal law enforcement agency of the U.S. Army. Fred Newton III had also served as a crime analyst for police departments in Dallas, Texas, and Kansas City, Missouri, where he had worked with Willoughby to identify crime patterns there. With Willoughby's support, Newton suggested several changes in policy that would bring the Pueblo department in line with contemporary best-practices for American law enforcement agencies.

Newton would serve in Pueblo for four years before moving on to jobs with several other local and federal law enforcement agencies. He would go on to serve as senior advisor to the director of FEMA, the Federal Emergency Management Agency, the Department of Defense, and the President's National Security Council. At the time of his death in 2011, he was special advisor to the chief of staff for the Undersecretary of Defense for policy.

Fred Newton III was chosen by Chief Willoughby as the department's first crime analyst in 1973. He was a brilliant police strategist whose progressive ideas helped shape the future of American law enforcement.

Newton family photograph used in his obituary in 2011.

To quickly act upon urgent recommendations presented by Newton, a new street crime unit, called the Special Operations Section, or SOS, was formed. Captain Richard Bravo, who was well known as a smart, tough and aggressive commander, and two sergeants—Tom Crowell and Bill Stewart—were appointed to the unit, which was patterned after very successful street crime units in operation in larger American cities. The focus of the ten-officer unit was perpetrator and location-oriented patrol, which meant that the unit would use informants, investigative techniques and research from the planning unit to identify those individuals and gangs that were actively committing violent crimes. Locations, particularly businesses that appeared most likely to be victimized, were also identified. The unit would then establish surveillance on people and locations to allow the officers to quickly intervene in violent crimes in progress. The mission was to save innocent victims placed in danger and to make rapid and appropriate arrests. The unit was equipped with special weaponry (Uzi submachine guns and scoped Remington .223 caliber sniper rifles), riot control equipment and safety and rescue apparatus that made SOS the forerunner of today's SWAT Team.

Capt. Richard Bravo   *Sgt. Tom Crowell*   *Sgt. Bill Stewart*

One of several items of electronic equipment acquired for use by SOS was the Bell & Howell TAC-II portable alarm system. That system allowed officers to place manually, or in some cases, automatically operated alarms in businesses or private residences identified by the planning unit as extraordinarily vulnerable, or in imminent danger of victimization.

The system would transmit an activation code to a portable receiver in an unmarked SOS vehicle in the area. Activation of an alarm would trigger the immediate response of tactically trained and equipped SOS officers. The system was quite successful in bringing about the swift arrest of numerous armed-robbery or burglary suspects. The TAC-II system was the genesis of much more sophisticated and effective systems used very successfully by law enforcement agencies to this day.

The centerpiece of Chief Willoughby's reorganization, however, was the complete revamping of the police patrol system. For many years, the city had been divided into five districts, each served by a one-officer patrol car during the daylight hours then expanded to eight districts each served by a two-officer patrol unit from 9:00 p.m. to 5:00 a.m. Those units were supplemented by two to four cars dedicated to traffic enforcement and accident investigation from 8:00 a.m. to midnight, and up to six "foot-beat" officers who patrolled relatively small areas of the business districts during certain hours—two during daylight and five during nighttime hours.

The Willoughby plan called for the city to be divided into two sectors, each with a sector sergeant supervising four one-officer basic patrol cars, at least one two-officer support unit and one van-style paddy wagon. There was also a captain serving as a watch commander on each of the three shifts. The foot beats were eliminated, but the basic car officers were required to leave their vehicles to check out defined areas of their beats on foot as time permitted.

Further, the reorganized Traffic Division was responsible for fielding at least one accident investigation unit (called an AIU) on each shift, and at least one traffic safety unit in each sector. The safety units were staffed with traffic specialists schooled in selective enforcement of traffic laws. Their specific assignments were primarily governed by recommendations from Newton's crime analysis section and were based on an examination of the number of serious accidents at specific locations, and the underlying causes of those accidents. The Traffic Division also deployed a trained and specially equipped DUI (driving under the influence) officer during specified hours to focus upon the frequently complained-about problem of drunk or impaired driving in the community. The radio number of the DUI car was 555. It was frequently referred to by officers as the "triple nickel" unit. Triple nickel was responsible for a major increase in DUI prosecutions, and fewer DUI related traffic accidents.

Under Chief Willoughby's reorganization, a regional police training academy, largely funded by the Federal Law Enforcement Assistance Administration (LEAA) was opened. The emphasis of the new Pueblo Police Academy was the provision of top-notch recruit and in-service training designed to bring local and area law enforcement officers up to standards then being set by the state. The academy staff included trained and highly skilled Pueblo officers and guest instructors from other agencies and related disciplines. Among the first classes to graduate from the academy were three in-service detective training classes that were to provide candidates for the department's reorganized Investigations Division. The classes were also open to students from other area law enforcement departments. As the largest law enforcement agency in southern Colorado, Chief Willoughby saw it as Pueblo's responsibility to assist neighboring organizations with their training and operational needs.

Up until early 1974, Pueblo's detective squad was not organized into specific areas of expertise and the working detectives were all sergeants. Willoughby felt the sergeants should exclusively serve as supervisors and specifically trained detectives should be recruited from the ranks of patrol officers and corporals. The newly created Investigations Division under the command of Captain Raul Prado was thus organized into three specialized sections: crimes against persons, crimes against property and the juvenile section. An ad hoc major case squad, consisting of detectives pulled from the persons and property sections, was also established to focus an immediate attack on a specific major crime.

Lewis M. Rhoades Murder

The major case squad, consisting of detective sergeants and newly appointed detectives still in training, was first activated in December 1973 when local entrepreneur and civic leader Lewis Marvin Rhoades was found bludgeoned to death in the backyard of his East 8th Street home. An expensive diamond ring had been wrenched from his finger by at least one attacker who assaulted Rhoades as he returned home from a local tavern. Though it appeared that a length of pipe, crowbar or similar instrument had been used to repeatedly strike the 69-year-old victim, the murder weapon was never found.

Robbery was initially considered as a motive for the crime, but other factors, including numerous financial and business entanglements involving Rhoades, muddied the waters of the investigation. Though thousands of hours of investigative activity were devoted to the case, the murder of Lewis Marvin Rhoades remains unsolved. As with other unresolved crimes, the case file continues to be open and is periodically re-examined as additional information or ideas are developed. It is hoped someone with knowledge of, or critical information about, one of Pueblo's most baffling crimes will come forward.

Certain crimes can be easily predicted by a careful analysis of previous crimes of the same nature in the same neighborhood. Robberies, burglaries and other street crimes are known in law enforcement circles as "suppressible crimes." A concentrated effort to allocate resources to address those crimes is generally successful in reducing the number of them and increasing the chances of apprehending perpetrators. Some murders can be prevented by such tactics too. By focusing upon reducing armed robberies, for example, police can reduce the number of homicides that may occur incidental to them.

The body of Lewis Rhoades lies covered near the rear corner of his small garage. He had been dragged to that location from the steps at the rear door of his home where he had been attacked. As a streetlight directly in front of his garage cast a light into the backyard, it was speculated that the killer(s) pulled him into the shadow of the garage in the dark before rifling his pockets. The above Pueblo Star-Journal *photo shows Sergeant Ray Magan videotaping the crime scene while I, as press officer, observe the activity.*

However, murders that are not associated with suppressible street crimes (those not associated with a series of crimes in a particular area) cannot be accurately predicted. They are therefore much more difficult, if not impossible, to anticipate. Police, therefore, cannot develop a plan to intercede to prevent or stop the crime in progress, or to apprehend the criminal in the process of committing the crime or in the immediate flight.

Beginning in 1973 and continuing into the early 1980s, Pueblo police were confronted with a string of unrelated murders of elderly people who lived alone in modest homes, many on Pueblo's Eastside. The Lewis Rhoades murder was one of those crimes; the only one that remains unsolved. The next audacious homicide occurred within three blocks of the Rhoades home and less than eight months later. That crime fueled the public's fear that a homicidal maniac might be loose on Pueblo's Eastside.

Robinson Hammer Murder

Joseph Vernon Robinson had a loving family and many friends. The 77-year-old widower was also very popular with his neighbors. In the wake of the still unsolved Lew Rhoades murder, those neighbors would periodically visit him at his small, cottage-style home at 1345 East 8th Street. They just wanted to make sure he was okay. He always had coffee ready, and he frequently left the front door unlocked or standing open to welcome his callers. Violet Covington lived just two doors from Robinson. She was one of the neighbors who checked on the man on a regular basis.

Saturday morning, August 17, 1974, was warm in Pueblo. Violet Covington decided to walk down to the corner drug store to see what new magazines were on the shelves. Her friend, Mr. Robinson, lived right next door to the pharmacy. She decided to first drop in to see him. She knocked at his door; it swung open. Cautiously, she entered the house.

She was only a few steps inside when she saw the older man lying on the floor between the home's kitchen and dining room. She also saw a large pool of blood around his head. She approached him and noticed he was still breathing, but laboriously. She picked up the phone and called 9-1-1. The emergency services operator asked her what had happened. In her haste to get medical help for her friend, she blurted out, "He must have shot himself!" The call then went out as an "attempted suicide—gunshot."

Several officers, a fire rescue crew, and an ambulance were on scene within minutes. The first officers in the room saw the gaping wound on the side of Robinson's head. "Yep," they surely thought, "It looks like a large bullet wound—but where's the gun?" As medical personnel started performing life saving measures, the officers began looking around for a weapon. There was none—not near where Robinson lay; not in the dining room or kitchen; not anywhere in the house. The officers realized this was not a suicide attempt. They called for a homicide investigation.

As Joseph Vernon Robinson was rushed to St. Mary-Corwin Hospital by Alert Ambulance, Chief Willoughby activated the major case squad. Major William T. Hurley was called back from vacation to head up the inquiry.

Robinson made it to the hospital, went through emergency surgery, but expired from his injuries. Deputy County Coroner Dr. Robert Stewart said death resulted from a blow to the side of the head that shattered the man's skull. The experienced eyes of the major case detectives told them the murder weapon was probably a hammer.

A check of the victim's backyard revealed tennis shoe prints. Robinson did not wear tennis shoes. As the detectives were examining and photographing the prints, a 10-year-old boy called to them from the alley. He informed them he had been playing in his tree house just over a block from the murder scene. From his elevated perch he had seen a young man quickly walking from the direction of the Robinson home. He said the man was carrying a hammer. He further said he could show the detectives where the hammer had been discarded.

The officers carefully followed the boy westbound in the alley, observing additional tennis shoe prints that appeared to match those seen in the Robinson backyard. They finally reached the youth's home and saw the tree house in a large elm tree, standing like a sentinel above the neighborhood. "It's up there," the youngster said—pointing to the roof of a small shed in the yard next door to his home directly below his tree house.

The detectives secured the property and soon recovered the blood-stained, steel-shanked, claw hammer with a rubber handle on the roof of the shed—right where their young witness said it would be. Bingo—they had the murder weapon and a witness who had seen the murder suspect; now they needed to find that suspect.

The 10-year-old boy was questioned extensively. He was able to provide an excellent description of the young man he had seen discard the hammer. He further said he saw the suspect cross through a yard at 8th and Joplin—right across the street from the Lew Rhoades murder scene. The suspect appeared to be headed north to Joplin.

Footprints found in that area and elsewhere between 9th and 12th Streets led detectives to believe the suspect had headed back to the east in the alley off 12th. Observations made by citizens along that route took the search party to the 1600 block of East 12th Street.

Major Case Detective Eloy Roybal had been a lifelong resident of the eastside. He knew many of the denizens of that part of town. He was aware of a 16-year-old boy named Rudy Saiz, who lived with his mother at 1633 East 12th. Saiz closely matched the description given by the 10-year-old witness. Saiz was contacted by the officers.

At 9:30 p.m. on the Tuesday following the Saturday morning murder of Joseph Vernon Robinson, Rudy Saiz was arrested. He and his mother were taken to the police station where Rudy was advised of his rights. With his mother's consent, he agreed to answer questions about the crime, and said he would submit to a polygraph examination.

On Wednesday afternoon, August 21, 1976, Rudy Saiz confessed to the crime. He said he had entered Robinson's home through an unlocked front door with the intent of find-ing something to steal. He apparently surprised the napping Robinson who jumped up and confronted him. He said he panicked and repeatedly struck the septuagenarian with the claw hammer. A polygraph examination administered by Captain Richard Bravo substantiated his statements.

The district attorney determined that the 16-year-old would be tried as an adult—common practice in murder cases. He would be convicted of murder, robbery and burglary and sentenced to life in prison. Chief Bud Willoughby praised the work of the major case squad. He also publicly commended those citizens, including the young boy who provided information that led to the arrest of the perpetrator. He further reported that no evidence was developed to link Saiz with the earlier murder of Lewis Marvin Rhoades. That case would remain unsolved.

I served as Chief Willoughby's press officer for just over one year. During that time, I studied for the civil service promotional exams for the ranks of both corporal and sergeant. I came out number one on both tests. (Prior to the late 1980s, a competitive exam was required to attain the corporal rank. As the duties of corporal were virtually the same as those of patrol officer, the system was changed to allow the rank of corporal to be filled by seniority and the testing requirement was eliminated. The sergeant's exam remained as a supervisory position with much different responsibilities).

A police corporal position came open on October 1, 1974, and I was promoted to that rank. A month later, a sergeant's position was opened, and I received that promotion. I served as corporal only 39 days before receiving my sergeant's stripes from Chief Willoughby at a promotional ceremony in the department's assembly room. Officers Steve Port and Don Williams were promoted to corporal at that same ceremony.

My first assignment as sergeant was North Sector (Sector 1) patrol supervisor under Captain Al Sandoval. Al was a fair but demanding captain, and I learned a lot from him. I also learned from my incredibly talented team of eleven officers. During one month in the spring of 1975, we arrested 14 criminals in the process of burglarizing businesses in the downtown area. I received a written commendation from the chief for the results attained by my team that month. Gosh, the graveyard patrol shift was fun.

Chief Willoughby presented me my sergeant's badge at a ceremony in the assembly room at the police station on November 9, 1974. Promoted to corporal at the same time were officers Steve Port and Don Williams.

Pueblo Police Photo

Maude Ruddick Ceramics Shop Murder

For more than a decade, 77-year-old Maude E. Ruddick operated a small neighborhood ceramics shop at 1615 East 8th Street in Pueblo. In addition to the stock of ceramic figurines she displayed on the shelves in her store, she kept a treasured personal collection in her attached apartment behind the business.

On Sunday afternoon, October 26, 1975, Maude's close friend, Madge Eyestone, stopped in to see if she was alright. Madge's husband, Ernest, accompanied her to the Ruddick residence, but Ernest walked around the side of the building to check the backyard and the detached garage which faced the alley, while Madge went in the side door leading to Maude's living quarters. Ernest did not hear the commotion inside the home when Madge walked in.

As Madge Eyestone entered the small apartment, she was immediately met by a violent attack. A young man grabbed her and furiously knocked her against a table in the front room. Her head struck the corner of the table causing a serious injury to one of her eyes. The attacker then struck her a couple of more times, then leaned over and said, "You know where the money is—get it or I'll kill you!"

He then pulled Madge up from the floor and pushed her into her friend's bedroom. Though blood flowed freely from several head lacerations and barely able to see due to her severe eye injury, she was able to pull a folder from a drawer. She gave it to the man.

Inside the folder was an undetermined amount of money belonging to Maude Ruddick. The man took the money, then knocked Madge Eyestone to the floor and told her to get under the bed until he was gone. He then fled from the home.

Madge, bleeding profusely, crawled from under the bed and called 9-1-1 from Maude Ruddick's phone. At that time, Ernest Eyestone entered the apartment, unaware that anything had happened. He ran to his prostrate wife, pulled off his shirt, and attempted to stop the bleeding from her ugly head wounds. That's when he noticed the body of poor Maude Ruddick lying nearby. He looked around in horror, half expecting to be assaulted by a lurking fiend, but he did not see the perpetrator who had committed the outrageous attacks. As the sound of approaching sirens filled the air, he did what he could to comfort his wife.

When police and emergency medical personnel arrived a few minutes later, they found that Maude had been strangled by a length of electrical cord cut from a nearby lamp. The cord was wound around her neck and through her mouth into which a sweater had been stuffed to gag her. It was also apparent that she had been viciously sexually assaulted.

Madge Eyestone was transported to Parkview Hospital by ambulance. She was admitted in critical condition with a fractured nose, several deep lacerations to her head and face and a very serious eye injury. Despite the efforts of hospital personnel, she would permanently lose her sight in that eye. She was, however, able to give investigating officers a good description of the attacker.

Police patrol officers and detectives, led by Major William T. Hurley, fanned out in all directions searching for any sign of the killer. They theorized that the suspect had to be covered with Madge Eyestone's blood. They began questioning people they encountered on the street.

A group of small children playing in the front yard of a nearby residence told officers they had seen a man run by earlier. They said he "had blood all over him." The children pointed to a home in the 1800 block of East 8th and said, "He went in that house."

Officers quickly surrounded the house pointed out by the children and contacted a woman who answered their knock. After some hesitation, she told the officers a man known to her as Norman Pacheco had come to her home and asked for a ride to Salt Creek, a small residential area just southeast of the city. She said her husband had taken Pacheco to a location there, but she did not know the address.

At that time, the woman's husband drove up. Confronted by officers, he told them his friend, Norman Pacheco, who lived in the apartment complex at 2002 East 12th Street, had come to his house and asked for a ride to a relative's home in Salt Creek. He did not know the address but said he would show officers where he had taken Pacheco. He said Pacheco appeared agitated and had what appeared to be blood stains on the front of his shirt. He went with a team of officers to Salt Creek and showed them the house.

Occupants of that home told the detectives Pacheco had stopped there briefly. He had changed clothes, borrowing a shirt from his uncle there, then asked for a ride to his home. He and his uncle had left just moments before the police arrived.

Pacheco stopped at a store en route to his apartment, then went on to his home. He was confronted in the parking lot of his apartment complex by Major Hurley, Sergeant Ed Arriaga, Sergeant Ruben Archuleta, Officer Rich Lipich and District Attorney's Investigator Don Shafer. He was placed under arrest. Faced with Madge Eyestone's identification and other evidence located at the scene of the crime, Pacheco confessed.

He was tried in Pueblo District Court, found guilty and sentenced to life in prison for the murder of Maude Ruddick, and 35 to 38 years for the brutal assault of Madge Eyestone. The sentences were ordered to run concurrently.

A little over a year later Pacheco appealed his conviction to the Colorado Court of Appeals. His quest for a new trial failed, and his convictions and sentences were upheld.

Both the Joseph Robinson killing, and the murder of Maude Ruddick were quickly solved when children, who had witnessed the flight of the perpetrators, gave police the information they needed to track down suspects. Officers were fortunate those children were trusting of the police and anxious to assist them.

The changes made by Chief Willoughby during his term as department head were well received by most officers. They felt the department had been brought current with the mainstream of contemporary law enforcement philosophy. They also felt a renewed sense of pride in the department following the embarrassing revelations of corruption that stained the reputations of every department member—even the honest and dedicated officers. Officers were happy the stigma of the scandal of the early 1970s had been all but overcome by 1977 when Elbert L. "Bud" Willoughby was offered a position he could not refuse. He was appointed police chief of Salt Lake City, Utah, and he left the Pueblo department with what he said was "a heavy heart" but a "sense of pride" in what the department had accomplished during his tenure. He was particularly happy that public confidence in the department had been restored.

CHAPTER 15

THE TRANSITION

A group of local sportsmen had set out on the morning of August 18, 1976, to catch some fish in the sprawling Pueblo Reservoir just west of the city. By 11 a.m. they spotted an ideal place to settle and cast their lines. One of the fishermen noticed a large, overstuffed dark green plastic trash bag beside a lonely access road near the western shore of the lake. Curious about the contents of the bag, the fisherman approached it and pulled it open. The objects that spilled out sent him staggering backward in horror.

Stifling an urge to regurgitate his earlier breakfast, he turned to his friends and excitedly told them to go immediately to the nearest telephone and call the sheriff. He had just discovered the dismembered remains of a human body.

Pueblo County Sheriff's deputies, the district attorney's investigators and county coroner's representatives arrived on scene within 30 minutes. The contents of the bag were found to consist of the legs, handless arms and neatly sliced off breasts of a human female. The head, torso and hands of the poor woman were missing. Nothing was found in the bag that could identify the victim.

A sheriff's check on recently reported missing persons revealed a report taken two days earlier by Pueblo Police. The report concerned a missing divorcée named Sharon Marie Copp. Ms. Copp had left her three small children with a babysitter two evenings earlier. She told the babysitter she would be home in a few hours. When she hadn't returned by morning, the babysitter contacted Copp's mother, Mrs. Don Bowman. Bowman immediately made several calls in an attempt to locate her daughter. When she was unable to do so, she notified the Pueblo police, and a missing person report was taken.

At a little after 4 p.m. on August 18, just hours after the discovery of the body parts in Pueblo County, a woman in the 1300 block of East 18th Street called police to report that someone had discarded a trash bag containing what she believed to be a dead dog in the alley behind her home. At that time, the police department operated the city animal control unit, and the police dispatcher sent an animal control officer (ACO) to pick up the dead dog's carcass.

Upon arriving in the alley, the rather petite ACO attempted to lift the bag into her truck. The bag was too heavy for her to handle alone, so she called for a police officer to assist her. Officer Gilbert Abeyta, the Eastside patrol officer, was dispatched.

The bag lay against a fence and had partially split open exposing a tuft of yellowish hair. It also emitted the unmistakable odor of death, thus prompting the belief that a large dead animal, most likely a dog, was inside.

With the ACO's assistance, Officer Abeyta lifted the bag to the side compartment of the animal control truck. As he began to stuff the bag into the compartment, the split in the bag widened and a human head dropped out. It landed at the feet of the horrified officer and ACO. Officer Abeyta called for assistance. The remainder of the dismembered body discovered earlier that day near the reservoir had now been located.

Teams of city detectives quickly arrived at the scene. The bag and the severed head were photographed in situ and removed by Assistant County Coroner Robert Stewart to the morgue. There, the bag was opened to reveal the horribly mutilated torso of a woman, along with two severed hands. The head, which showed signs of having been savagely beaten prior to being cut from the torso, had been separately transported to the morgue. It too was examined by Dr. Stewart.

Also in the bag was a golf club, the head of which had been broken from the shaft which was bent and damaged. It would later be determined that it was probably the golf club that had been used to administer the terrific beating that ended the victim's life.

Detectives, working with the coroner, discovered a blood-soaked tank-top shirt, known at the time as a "wife beater," in the bag. It bore the image of a crude cartoon soccer player kicking a ball while holding a much smaller African American player by the throat. The shirt was sold by Kmart stores, but Kmart did not collect identifying information about their customers. The local Kmart's inventory indicated they had sold only one of the shirts, but no one there could remember anyone buying it.

The purchaser was never identified. A photograph of a shirt bearing the same image was released to the press, and it appeared in newspapers and television news programs throughout the area. Citizens were asked to contact the Pueblo Police Department if they had seen anyone wearing such a shirt, or if they knew anyone who owned a shirt sporting such an image. No one came forward.

A bloody, size small shirt, yellow in color, bearing the ugly caricature seen at right, was found in a trash bag along with Sharon Copp's body parts in 1976. As the case is still open in 2024, Pueblo Police would like to hear from anyone who knows anything about a shirt bearing this image.

Despite the passage of time, cold case detectives still would like to talk with anyone who remembers anything about a shirt like the one pictured. Pueblo officers felt the image on the shirt could reveal a bigoted suspect. They hoped that could help identify the individual who committed the horrible crime. So far, it hasn't.

The brand of the trash bags used by the killer(s) was checked, and it was found to be a mass-produced product sold by virtually every supermarket and convenience store in the state. Again, no local store employee could remember anyone specifically buying a box of the bags within a few days of the finding.

Dr. Stewart reported that the numerous cuttings on the body indicated the victim had been tortured prior to being battered to death. He determined the cuts were made with a very sharp knife or similar cutting instrument, and the body was dismembered by a large, serrated knife or possibly a saw.

It didn't take long to identify the victim of the unspeakable crime as the missing Sharon Marie Copp. The investigation of what the press called "the most gruesome homicide case in Pueblo's history," was just getting started. It would continue for decades.

That investigation quickly disclosed that Sharon Copp had been married three times; her first two marriages ending in divorce. Further, she had recently filed for a divorce from her estranged third husband, Donald Copp. He reportedly was serving time in Pueblo County Jail at the time of her disappearance. Having been wanted for failure to appear in court for a drunk-driving charge, he had turned himself in to county jail personnel just days earlier. It would later be disclosed that he had been allowed work-release status and may not have actually been present in jail at all times relevant to the investigation. He became one of many persons of interest in the case.

Detectives did learn that Sharon had visited several taverns in south Pueblo during the evening of August 16. She was seen by several patrons of Jeanie's Bar at the corner of East Evans and Jones Avenues near the Colorado Fuel and Iron Corporation steel mill. She had been seated at the end of the bar near the front door and was alone when seen. She reportedly spoke to no one in the bar other than to order a drink. No one, not even the bartender, remembered seeing her leave the establishment. He said she must have left about 7:30 p.m. because he doesn't remember seeing her after that. No one noticed any creepy or otherwise suspicious people hanging around the bar that night.

Her car, however, was discovered parked in a streetside lot in front of Jeanie's Bar on the evening of August 18—the day her body was discovered. Bar personnel had noticed it there at closing time on the 16th. At that time, they did not know who the car belonged to and just assumed an intoxicated patron had left it there and gotten a ride home—something that was not unusual. No one could say whether the car was running when it was first observed at that location.

Detectives inspected the car and found that the key was in the ignition and the battery was dead. It appeared that Sharon had gotten into and started the car when someone must have approached and abducted her, leaving the car to run until it ran out of gas. Was it possible someone familiar with her car spotted it parked there and waited for her to emerge from the bar? The answer to that question was never determined.

The location where Sharon was dismembered was never found. The coroner said much of the blood had been drained from the body before it was stuffed in the trash bags. He indicated the crime scene would have been awash with blood and bodily fluids. He said it would be next to impossible to clean up such a scene without leaving considerable evidence of the slaughter that occurred there. The absence of a crime scene frustrated the efforts of detectives.

Donald Copp's brother was found to own a boat moored at Pueblo Reservoir not far from where the body was found. A search of that boat did not reveal any evidence that Sharon had been there or that the crime had been committed on or near the boat. An in-depth search of the reservoir shoreline was conducted by both police and sheriff's personnel, but no evidence of a crime scene was discovered.

Pueblo officers also reviewed reports of torture, dismemberment, mutilation and sexually driven murders that occurred in other parts of the country within a few years of the Copp killing. They were attempting to identify similarities that could link the Copp case to one or more crimes committed elsewhere, or to identify persons of interest whose names turned up in other investigations.

One particularly gruesome slaying, the one that most closely resembled the Copp case, was the Ruth Masters homicide in rural Massachusetts. That crime occurred in May 1977—nine months after the Copp killing. Other than dismemberment, which was not present in the Masters case, the injuries suffered by the Masters woman were very similar to those inflicted on the body of Sharon Copp.

Though vigorously investigated by Massachusetts authorities, the Masters case was not quickly solved. Pueblo officers began checking to determine if any evidence linking the two crimes existed. None was found.

It was not until 1998 that a suspect was arrested, tried and convicted of killing Ruth Masters as she bicycled through a wild area of Miles Standish State Park near Plymouth, Massachusetts. The Stoughton, Massachusetts, man convicted of the crime, Eric Anderson, died in prison in 2016. No information was found to indicate he had ever been in or near Colorado.

Suspects in the Copp case included serial killer Henry Lee Lucas. Lucas had been jailed in Texas in 1983 after confessing to upward of 600 murders throughout the country. Since it was determined that Lucas may have traveled through Pueblo about the time of the Copp murder, Pueblo Detective Rich Lipich was sent to Texas to interview him. Though Lucas initially confessed to the Copp murder, Lipich, a skilled interrogator, quickly determined he did not know, or was totally inaccurate concerning details of the killing. Lucas was eliminated as a suspect.

Lucas was later found to have lied about the majority of the crimes to which he had initially confessed. It was found he most likely had committed the murders of only three people—none of them in Colorado. His false confessions appear to have been driven by a desire for publicity, and by extra jailhouse privileges afforded him as over-zealous investigators from a multitude of agencies anxious to close difficult unsolved homicide cases, were allowed to interview him. Almost all of his admissions were discounted in later years by DNA evidence and other revelations about the crimes in question. Henry Lee Lucas died from heart failure in a Texas prison in 2001.

The Sharon Copp murder investigation has been reviewed on at least three occasions by profilers from the FBI Behavioral Sciences Unit in Quantico, Virginia. They were unable to provide any suggestions concerning the conduct of the investigation or means of identifying a perpetrator, other than those already done by Pueblo detectives. Pueblo detectives had received training from the FBI regarding criminal profiling several times prior to the Copp case. They were already conversant with the FBI's approach to identifying possible suspects through analysis of various aspects of the crime, a profile of the victim and a thorough evaluation of the crime scene. The FBI did report that the extent of torture suffered by Sharon, and the disfiguring injuries to her face and other parts of her body, would tend to indicate the killer was someone who knew and intensely disliked—even hated her.

In 2003, Pueblo Police Identification Detective Clint Thomason and I took the Copp case file to Philadelphia, Pennsylvania, where we presented it to the Vidocq Society for their review and examination. That society is named after Eugène Francois Vidocq, a famous French criminalist credited with founding the renowned French Sûreté Nationale (the former French national security police) in 1912. He is widely considered the world's first private detective. The Vidocq Society was established in 1990 to further the resolution of unsolved homicides nationwide.

Vidocq (pronounced Vee-dock) Society membership is made up of volunteer forensic experts, specialists in criminal profiling and murder investigation techniques, active and retired law enforcement professionals, medical examiners, prosecutors and practitioners of other disciplines relative to cold case homicide resolution. Their mission is to provide confidential assistance to detectives working long-unsolved murder cases and to suggest tactics to employ to solve those cases.

Vidocq Society members carefully considered aspects of the Copp case and the investigation. Over a period of several weeks, members provided Pueblo detectives with numerous theories and suggestions regarding how to proceed with the investigation. Their input, though valid, added nothing new to the list of investigative strategies Pueblo officers had already employed during the years following Pueblo's most revolting and disturbing homicide case.

Though unsolved as of early 2024, the Sharon Copp murder, as with other unsolved Pueblo murder cases, remains an open and active investigation. Nearly every newly-appointed detective and supervisory officers from throughout the department, are granted access to the investigative file. They are encouraged to look at it with a "new set of eyes" and to bring forth any thoughts or ideas regarding a solution.

Chief Willoughby repeatedly reviewed the Copp case file and the files of the other unsolved crimes that occurred during his tenure. He was a perfectionist, and he wanted to assure himself that everything possible had been done to successfully conclude those investigations.

As he neared the end of his fourth year as Pueblo's police chief, he told me that his greatest source of pride since accepting the chief's job, was the rapidity with which department personnel had risen to the levels of professionalism he had set forth. He further stated he was grateful that Pueblo officers were supportive of his efforts to make the department more transparent in its dealings with the public.

He said his biggest regret was the department's inability to solve some of the city's most egregious crimes— particularly the Lew Rhoades and Sharon Copp homicides. "I looked at those cases myself," he told me as his final day approached, "And I can't see anything we didn't do that we could have done—I just hope time and persistence will give us the answers we need."

Following Chief Willoughby's widely publicized departure from Pueblo, his second in command, Major William T. Hurley was named acting chief. Major Hurley served for two months. An aggressive and talented officer admired by Willoughby was then appointed to succeed the popular chief. Having served as one of Willoughby's trusted and best-known commanders, Captain Robert O. Silva's appointment was praised internally by department members and externally by a supportive public.

During the transition from the Willoughby to the Silva administrations, the police department would be drawn into another high-profile investigation that originated in a neighboring county. As the complex inquiry involving investigators from six area law enforcement agencies progressed, it became obvious that the execution style murder of a popular Southern Colorado businessman and celebrity had begun in Pueblo.

Tom Turcotte Case

Rudy Force and his wife Winona, better known by her stage name Trixie, sat at a small table in the barroom of the Three Thieves Restaurant across from the ornate stone and iron entrance to Pueblo City Park. Three Thieves was considered one of Pueblo's best restaurants, specializing in perfectly prepared steaks. Though it was a typically busy weekend evening on Friday, May 27, 1977, the Forces weren't interested in having steak dinners. They told members of the bar staff they just wanted to have a few drinks.

The head bartender thought that was strange as the Three Thieves bar was just not that sort of place—it was a quiet lounge where people could relax before being shown to their dinner tables—not a beer joint that catered to people with the rough appearance of Rudy and Trixie Force. Trixie was a stripper who worked at a Lake Avenue adult nightspot called the 85 Club—and she looked the part.

Other patrons of the classy restaurant noticed the grubby couple too. Tony Langoni, who later became assistant city manager, was one of them. His attention was drawn to the couple by their shabby appearance that made them stand out from the other clean and well-dressed restaurant patrons.

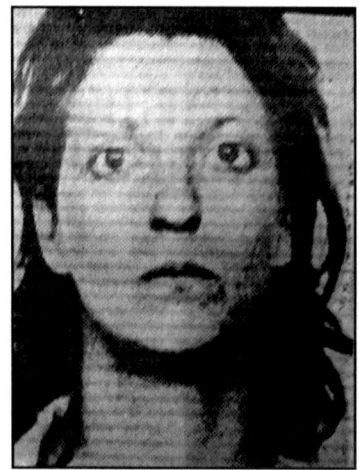

Ralph (Rudy) and Winona (Trixie) Force

Thomas Turcotte was a popular radio disc jockey and television personality in Colorado Springs—about 45 miles north of Pueblo. For several years, Tom had owned and operated a successful advertising agency, Turk Productions, in that city. He was well known throughout Southern Colorado due to his appearance in television commercials. His voice was highly recognizable to anyone who listened to Colorado Springs area rock and roll radio or heard radio ads on other stations throughout the state. Tom had a very distinctive radio voice. He was very charismatic—people who didn't even know him liked him based on his TV ads.

Pueblo businessman Rich Goodwin's educational background was in mass communications and public relations. He owned a Pueblo ad agency called R.F. Goodwin and Associates. Eleven months earlier, Goodwin had purchased Turk Productions from Tom. Turcotte agreed to stay with the agency for one year to assist with the ownership transition and service his existing accounts. The two had bought a $50,000 "key-man" term insurance policy to protect their individual interests should one of them die or become incapacitated and unable to complete their contractual obligations to each other. The policy offered double indemnity if either should die from an accident or misadventure.

Tom Turcotte and Richard Goodwin were also patrons at Three Thieves that evening.

The two had earlier attended a meeting in Colorado Springs, but Goodwin's car broke down and was taken to a repair shop. As it would require the acquisition of parts before it could be repaired, Goodwin asked Turcotte for a ride back to Pueblo. The two left Colorado Springs a little after 3 p.m. for the approximately 50-mile drive to Goodwin's office in downtown Pueblo. As thanks for the late afternoon ride to Pueblo, Goodwin offered to treat Turcotte to a fine steak dinner at Three Thieves. Turcotte accepted.

Goodwin picked up his second car at his Pueblo office. He suggested to Tom that they stop for a few drinks along the way to an evening steak dinner. Turcotte followed in his black, 1977 Porsche as Goodwin drove to the lounge of the Ramada Inn. According to Goodwin, they had two or three drinks there, then drove separately to a large but dark and cozy lounge called The Colonial House on South Pueblo Boulevard, not far from their dinner destination. After a few drinks there, they headed for their dinner engagement. Goodwin later estimated they had seven or eight drinks each prior to going to Three Thieves.

It was just shy of 8:30 p.m. when the two arrived in the busy parking lot in front of the restaurant. Tom parked his Porsche in the lot, while Goodwin parked along the street at the side of Three Thieves. Neither seemed to notice the out-of-place couple in the barroom adjacent to the front lobby as they walked into the restaurant. According to other patrons, the Forces stared at them as they entered the front door. They were immediately shown to their table toward the rear of the establishment. They each ordered a medium rare T-bone with baked potato and a salad with the Three Thieves famous Italian style dressing. They talked, joked, laughed and drank as they consumed their meals.

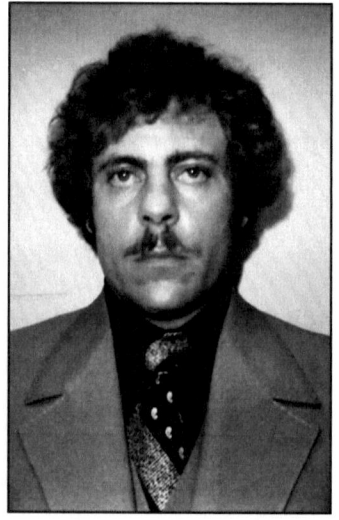 

Richard Goodwin   *Thomas Turcotte*

As they walked out of the restaurant a little before 10:30 p.m., they ran into a gentleman Goodwin knew. Goodwin introduced Turcotte to Dr. Harry Bowes, president of the University of Southern Colorado (now Colorado State University Pueblo). They spoke for a few minutes, then Goodwin excused himself saying he had left his sunglasses at the dinner table. He went to retrieve the sunglasses as Turcotte left the restaurant, saying he had to get home.

When Goodwin returned to the lobby, Turcotte was already gone. As Goodwin left, he reportedly saw Tom's car pulling out of the lot and heading through the gated entrance to City Park. That road would traverse the park, pass the large fountain with color-changing lights and the placid lake and emerge at the west park exit onto Pueblo Boulevard. From there, one could go north or south to reach Interstate 25.

When later asked if he actually saw Tom in the car or if there was anyone with Tom when the car pulled out of the parking lot, Goodwin said, "No, the windows of Tom's car are tinted so darkly you can't see anything inside."

Richard went to his home on Brentwood Drive about three blocks west of the park, got some additional cash, then went to the Stadium Lounge on South Prairie Avenue to meet his ex-wife, Martha. He and Martha, accompanied by two of her friends, spent the rest of the night barhopping and dancing. He returned to his home at 3 a.m. on May 28th.

About 8 a.m. that morning, he was awakened by a telephone call from Tom's wife, Joanie. She was concerned that Tom had not yet made it home. She asked Richard if he knew where Tom was. He said he did not, but he would start checking around. He told Joanie the last time he saw Tom was at Three Thieves, and he told her Tom was heading home, but that he might stop at the dog track, referring to the greyhound racing track at Lake Avenue and Pueblo Boulevard on Pueblo's extreme south side.

Having never known Tom to visit a dog racing facility, she was skeptical of Goodwin's remark, but said nothing. She made several more calls to Tom's business associates in Pueblo but found that no one could tell her where Tom was, or what might have happened to him.

A little before 7:30 a.m. Saturday, May 28, 1977, a self-employed cement and masonry contractor on his way to work in Pueblo, spotted what looked to him like a human body. It was in a borrow pit beside R Street, just a half mile north of Highway 50 near the small community of Penrose, 20 miles west of Pueblo in neighboring Fremont County. He stopped to check it out.

As he approached, he saw that it was indeed the body of a man. It was bound by wide, white adhesive tape, had white medical tape covering the face like a mask, and had what appeared to be a bullet hole in the side of the head. The body was lying in a pool of blood about four feet from the west side of the road.

The contractor called the Fremont County Sheriff in Cañon City, about 15 miles away. Sheriff's deputies and the Fremont County Coroner were on scene within 20 minutes.

They first checked the body and discovered it was quite cold, indicating it had been dumped in the roadside pit several hours earlier.

There was no identification on the body, but when the contents of the victim's pockets were checked, two Texaco credit card receipts were found. Both indicated that the card in question had been issued to a Thomas Turcotte of Monument, Colorado. A State Patrol officer on scene opined that the name Turcotte was familiar, "maybe from TV ads." By a little after 1 p.m., the Fremont County Sheriff had determined who Tom Turcotte was. Within the hour, sheriff's investigators from El Paso County, the county that encompasses Colorado Springs and the town of Monument, were talking with a near hysterical and sobbing Joanie Turcotte.

A teletype was sent out to all area law enforcement agencies regarding Tom's new missing black Porsche. A previously filed Pueblo police report was immediately discovered. It indicated that Tom's Porsche had been reported as illegally parked and obscuring a residential driveway on Highland Avenue just 100 feet off Lake Avenue on what was then called the "Pueblo Strip," a seedy, several block area of bars, nightclubs, cheap motels and strip clubs near the south city limits. The car was found parked in a driveway bordering a night club called The Broken Dollar a little after 2:30 a.m.

Pueblo Officer Robert Montoya noted the car was unlocked and the keys were in the ignition. He checked The Broken Dollar, which had recently closed, and the small restaurant, The Little White House, across the street. The car owner could not be located nor could anyone who saw the person who parked the car at that location. Montoya moved the vehicle to allow access to the residential driveway, secured the vehicle and placed the keys in a proper receptacle at the Pueblo Police Property Section. He also wrote a short report detailing his actions.

By early afternoon, Pueblo detectives had reviewed the report and recovered the car. They had it towed to the police garage and were beginning a forensic examination of the vehicle checking for fingerprints, blood stains and other indications of murder. Based upon where the victim's car was found, and upon statements from the victim's wife, it began to appear that the crime may have originated in Pueblo.

By late afternoon on Saturday, the news of Tom Turcotte's murder hit the airways. Television and radio stations in Pueblo and Colorado Springs premiered the story on their evening newscasts and the *Star-Journal,* Pueblo's afternoon newspaper, headlined the story on their front page. By five o'clock that afternoon, it seemed everyone along Colorado's Front Range was talking about the crime—many were publicly speculating about who might have killed the popular young media personality.

Privately, law enforcement officers were also speculating. Their speculation, however, was based upon interviews with employees of Goodwin's and Turcotte's ad agencies. Those interviews disclosed financial difficulties and disagreements between the two ad executives. It emerged that the two fought constantly and did not like each other. Their public persona appeared to be a facade put on to dissuade distrust of their business ventures by potential clients.

But no information directly incriminating Richard Goodwin was developed.

The big break in the case came on Tuesday morning, May 31, 1977. Neva Audine Hennessee, a waitress at the Little White House Café, contacted a Pueblo police officer who frequented the café and whom she knew and liked. She told Officer Dave Roberts that she knew who had killed the man whose body had been found near Penrose. Roberts immediately took her to police headquarters.

There Neva Hennessee told detectives that her son, 22-year-old Terry Hennessee, had been doing odd jobs for a man named Rudy Force. She said Force owned a cabinet-making shop located in a rented garage directly behind the Little White House. She further stated that her son had abruptly left town on May 17. She said he went to Chicago and told her not to tell anyone—especially Rudy Force—where he was.

She further said Rudy contacted her the following day, May 18, and demanded to know where Terry was. She claimed she told Force she did not know. Force then demanded that Terry return $1,750 he had accepted as a down payment for doing a job for Rudy. She told Rudy her son never had $1,750 in his life.

The following day, Rudy's wife, Trixie, contacted her and told her Terry and her husband had been hired to kill someone, but Terry chickened out and left town with his half of the down payment. Trixie said she would have to perform the task Terry had been hired to do if Terry could not be found. Neva said she told Trixie she did not know where Terry was. That conversation bothered Neva, but she dismissed it as some sort of bad joke.

She was again contacted by Trixie Force on May 28th. Trixie again asked where Terry was but said there was no problem because the job "had been taken care of." She appeared to be heavily disguised at that time, wearing heavy makeup and a dark wig. Trixie told Neva that she and Rudy were going out of town in a couple of days.

Neva continued, saying she became worried for her safety and for the safety of her son after she heard about the Tom Turcotte murder later that day. That's when she contacted Officer Roberts. She voluntarily gave investigating officers Terry's address and phone number in Chicago.

Contact was quickly made with Terry Hennessee in the Windy City. He agreed to meet with officers in Chicago but said he was afraid to come back to Pueblo until the case was resolved. He did agree to discuss the case over the phone with Captain Bravo and detectives assigned to the murder case. The information he gave to Pueblo investigators strongly implicated Rudy and Trixie Force in the murder of Tom Turcotte. He agreed to discuss the matter face to face with a

Colorado detective, but only if the interview could take place in Chicago.

Shortly after that initial telephone interview with Terry Hennessee, a strategy meeting was held in District Attorney Joseph E. Losavio's office to determine if enough probable cause existed to arrest the Forces. Detectives Mike Downs and Jimmie Smalley, Captain Bravo and I met with Losavio and members of his staff to review the evidence and information so far developed. I assigned Detective John Sheehan to watch the movements of the Forces. He sat up surveillance on their home at 1305 Illinois Avenue. That residence is one block off Lake Avenue, and about two blocks from the 85 Club where Trixie had earlier been employed.

District Attorney Losavio requested that Neva Hennessee be brought to his office so he could personally talk with her. After a short interview with Hennessee, Losavio and Deputy District Attorney Charles Malouff determined that sufficient probable cause existed to justify Rudy and Trixie's arrest, but he wanted to prepare affidavits and arrest warrants setting forth that evidence for a judge's review. As the process of preparing the necessary paperwork began, Detective Sheehan radioed to me that the Forces appeared to be preparing for a departure from town.

I left the meeting and responded to the south end of Pueblo to assist Detective Sheehan in tailing the Forces until word was given by the DA's office that warrants had been signed by a judge. I met Detective Sheehan at Pueblo Boulevard and Lake Avenue. He said Rudy and Trixie, along with their two dogs, had just left town, heading south on Interstate 25 in a black over brown 1967 Buick Electra.

I parked my car and jumped in with Sheehan. We sped up to overtake the Forces. I radioed the police dispatch center and asked that they call the Colorado State Patrol and request an officer meet us near the Colorado City freeway exit 22 miles south of Pueblo.

Traveling at what seemed like warp speed, Sheehan and I caught up with the Force vehicle about ten miles south of

Pueblo. We pulled a few hundred feet behind the vehicle and slowed to match the speed Rudy was driving.

As we approached the Colorado City exit, we noticed the marked white state patrol car parked at the top of the southbound exit ramp. Sheehan pulled off there and let me out. I jumped in the patrol car as Sheehan moved to close in on our prey. I filled in State Patrol Officer Terry Godsey, and he sped to assume a position behind Sheehan's unmarked police car.

About five minutes later, Detective Smalley called me and said the warrants had been signed and we could make the arrests. We pulled the Force vehicle over near the Apache City exit, about 27 miles south of Pueblo. Neither Rudy nor Trixie offered any resistance as we took them into custody.

Pueblo animal control responded to take charge of the two dogs and a wrecker was called to take in the car. Trixie Force was transported to Pueblo Police Department headquarters by State Patrol Officer Godsey. Detective Sheehan and I transported Rudy Force. He was quiet and obviously absorbed in thought during the half-hour drive to the police station.

Winona Sue "Trixie" Force was taken to an interview room in the Investigation Division office where I formally advised her of her Miranda rights. Detective Sheehan witnessed the advisal and Trixie Force indicated her understanding of those rights by affixing her signature to the advisement form. She then stated she wanted to exercise her rights, and she refused to talk with us without the presence of an attorney. She was taken upstairs to the city detention facility where she was allowed to call Attorney Darol Biddle before being booked for first degree murder.

Next to be advised of his rights was Ralph "Rudy" Force. He also signed the advisement form indicating he understood his rights but when asked if he wished to answer questions about the case, he stated he wanted to first talk with Joe Losavio. When he was reminded that Joe Losavio was the prosecutor rather than a defense lawyer, he said he knew that. He further stated he wanted a deal from the DA before he would consent to talk with investigators. DA Losavio was called, and he responded to the station.

However, before the district attorney arrived, Rudy indicated to the detectives that he first wanted to talk with his own attorney, Darol Biddle. Mr. Biddle was already at the station discussing the situation with Rudy's wife, and when told Rudy wanted to talk with him, he immediately sent word to Rudy to refuse to talk with the district attorney. Accordingly, Rudy Force was booked into the detention facility for first degree murder.

On Monday, June 6, 1977, Special Agent James Hardtke of the Colorado Bureau of Investigation was dispatched to Chicago, Illinois, to interview Terry Hennessee. The extensive interview took place that afternoon. A taped recording of the interview and a 29-page transcribed copy were delivered to Pueblo Police later that day.

The information given to Agent Hardtke, though more detailed, did not vary from that given to Pueblo officers by telephone a week earlier.

Terry Hennessee told Agent Hardtke that he had worked for Rudy Force at Rudy's cabinet shop for several weeks and had developed a rapport with Rudy. He claimed that around the middle of May, Rudy asked him if he would help him kill a guy. He said Rudy told him he had been hired by a businessman to kill his business partner, and for that he would pay Rudy $10,000. Terry said Rudy offered him half the money, $5,000, if he would drive the car they would use to kidnap and murder the man's business partner.

Hennessee said he told Rudy he would think about it, but he claimed he had no intention of getting involved in a criminal homicide. Rudy, however, pestered him about it for several days, and he finally agreed. He said Rudy gave him $1,750 as a down payment and promised him additional money after the job was completed.

Hennessee at first said Force did not mention any names, but finally told him the man who hired him to commit the murder was Richard Goodwin. Hennessee knew that Force had previously been retained by Goodwin to remodel his office at his downtown ad agency.

Meanwhile, other people familiar with Rudy and Trixie Force were interviewed by Pueblo detectives. It emerged that many of the employees of Goodwin's ad agency were familiar with Rudy Force, who spent several days in the office installing new cabinetry and making Goodwin's office look more opulent. Those employees told detectives the remodeling of Goodwin's office was one of the issues that irritated Turcotte. "Why would he spend the money to remodel his office when the agency is losing money due to his mismanagement?" Turcotte would rage.

On June 8th, twelve days after the killing of Tom Turcotte and eight days after the arrest of the Forces, Rudy Force agreed through his lawyer to discuss the case with the district attorney. The next day, I was notified that the district attorney's office was drafting an arrest warrant charging Richard Goodwin with first degree murder. It was disclosed that Rudy and Trixie had been told to position themselves at the lounge in Three Thieves to watch Goodwin enter the restaurant. They had been told the man with Goodwin was their target. The two killers were told to follow Goodwin's companion when he left the restaurant and to abduct and kill him when the chance to do so presented itself. They followed their instructions precisely.

Turcotte had been forced into his car in the restaurant parking lot and forced to drive to Highland Avenue. He was made to park adjacent to the Broken Dollar night club, then taken across the street to Rudy's cabinet shop. There he was struck over the head to render him unconscious, then bound tightly with adhesive tape. His eyes and mouth were also covered with tape, and he was shot in the head. The body was then wrapped in a blanket and driven to the location near Penrose where it was deposited in the borrow pit on R Street.

At 5:30 p.m. on Thursday, June 9th, Captain Bravo was notified that the arrest warrant had been signed by Judge Gordon Cooper. Bravo relayed that information to the Colorado Springs Police Department. Then he, Detective Downs, Detective Smalley and I, with warrant in hand, left for Colorado Springs.

As Colorado Springs officers had already taken Goodwin into custody, we met with them at Colorado Springs Police headquarters. There we formally served the warrant and Goodwin was released to our custody. Detectives Downs and Smalley transported Goodwin back to Pueblo where he was booked into the Pueblo city detention facility. He was then formally advised of his constitutional rights by Detective Downs. He stated he did not wish to talk with us, so he was immediately transferred to the Pueblo County Jail to await further proceedings and trial.

In accordance with agreements made with District Attorney Joe Losavio, Rudy and Trixie Force pled guilty to first degree murder. For their personal safety, they were sentenced to lengthy prison terms to be served at an out-of-state correctional facility.

Richard Goodwin pled not guilty, but after a long and controversial trial he was found guilty of first degree murder, conspiracy to commit murder and kidnapping. He was sentenced to life in prison.

Detectives Downs and Smalley and I received letters of commendation from Investigations Captain Richard Bravo for our parts in the Turcotte investigation.

The inquiry demonstrated conclusively that seven law enforcement agencies—the Pueblo Police Department, the Colorado Springs Police Department, the El Paso County Sheriff's Office, the Fremont County Sheriff's Office, the Colorado State Patrol, the Colorado Bureau of Investigation and the Chicago Police Department could work together to quickly solve a complex and difficult murder case.

CHAPTER 16

THE SILVA YEARS

Robert O. Silva was one of the youngest and brightest captains in the police department when Chief Bud Willoughby announced he had accepted the job of chief of the Salt Lake City Police Department. Silva had a lot of administrative experience serving as one of Willoughby's right-hand men during the 1973 reorganization of the department. He had also played a major role in the investigation of departmental corruption that had sullied the agency's reputation and led to Chief Mayber's departure and Willoughby's appointment that year.

Silva had also been a very successful detective who had risen to the position of captain of detectives in 1974.

Willoughby had further taken note of Silva's oversight of investigative activity concerning serial killer Edmund Kemper who had been arrested in Pueblo in April 1973 and his work on the Sharon Copp murder investigation. He seemed the natural successor to Willoughby, and he was selected as Pueblo's 20th police chief by City Manager Fred Weisbrod within weeks of Willoughby's departure in 1977.

Chief Robert O. Silva

Though celebrated as "the right choice for chief" by both department members and the public, Bob Silva faced numerous challenges as he stepped into his new role. Foremost was the deteriorating Pueblo economy weakened by a steadily declining CF&I steel operation.

Since the mid-1960s American steel production was suffering a downturn due to several factors. Cheaper foreign-made steel began flooding the market and orders for the arguably better products produced locally began falling off. Simultaneously, advances in technology in the steel making process, and a trend to rely more on the recycling of scrap metal rather than making steel from the raw materials produced by the company's mining operations, hit the local job market hard.

From a high of more than 12,000 employees during the post war 1940s through the '50s and '60s, the early 1970s saw less than 7,800 people on the CF&I payroll. Census figures in 1970 indicated two-thirds of Pueblo workers held high-paying manufacturing jobs. By 1977, when Chief Silva was appointed, that statistic had dramatically declined to about 10 percent. That figure would continue to decline throughout Silva's tenure. The resulting city budget cuts from loss of tax revenues would negatively impact all city department budgets, including that of the police department, from almost day one of his term.

Despite the worsening economy, Silva kept the department above water with innovative manpower usage—and he kept the city's crime rate low. But despite those aggressive programs and strategies, the fear of violent crime began to soar in Pueblo. The unsolved Sharon Copp dismemberment murder and recent attacks on elderly Puebloans in their own homes seemed to constantly be on the minds of friends, neighbors and families of older citizens who lived alone. That feeling of vulnerability only increased when a brutal and terrifying crime occurred in the shadow of an iconic local high school.

Rosey Bowman's Perfume Caught Her Killer

Rita Schneider worked as a caretaker for elderly people who lived alone and needed occasional assistance with their daily activities. She was frequently hired to spend the night with a client to assure the client's special needs were met and their dignity, emotional health and sense of independence was maintained.

Rosey Bowman was Rita's client on the cold winter evening of Thursday, December 14, 1978. Rosey lived in a ground floor apartment at 126 East Grant Avenue, diagonally opposite the historic Pueblo Central High School building. Rita stayed with Rosey from 6:00 p.m. until 7:30 a.m. every night except Saturdays.

Rosey was only 75 years old, but she had some medical problems that made it difficult for her to get around at night, fixing her evening meal, taking her prescribed medication and getting bathed and ready for bed. She also just needed and very much appreciated the companionship offered by her friendly and supportive caretaker, Rita.

Rita Schneider always arrived at Rosey's apartment a few minutes before 6:00 p.m., and she would let herself in the front door, which was usually left unlocked in anticipation of her arrival. This evening, however, she found the door locked. She knocked and rang the doorbell but got no response. She then went to the back door and found it unlocked—but something, later determined to be an open closet door, was wedged against it preventing her from gaining access. Rita called out but again got no answer. She was, however, met with the strong scent of Rosey's perfume.

Worried and concerned for Rosie's well-being, Rita went to a neighboring apartment to get a spare key from Rosey's friend, 57-year-old Florence Linn. The two women then returned to Rosey's front door and Florence unlocked it. As Rita Schneider pushed the door open, she immediately saw that the apartment appeared to have been completely ransacked—drawers opened, contents dumped on the floor and knickknacks knocked off tables. Suddenly gripped by fear, she backed away and told Florence something was wrong. Florence took a deep breath and stepped into the apartment. There, lying on a red couch against the front wall, was Rosey Bowman—a small decorative blanket wrapped around her face. Florence cried out to Rita, who reluctantly entered the apartment. Florence then picked up the phone receiver in Rosey's front room and dialed 9-1-1.

Rescue Squad number 3 responding from firehouse number 3 just five blocks away, was on scene in three minutes. Police Officers Jerry Thomas, Craig Dotson and Corporal Ray Avery followed two minutes later. The rescue crew checked Rosey and determined she was dead. It was obvious to the fire medics and to the initial officers that they were dealing with a brutal and senseless murder. The fire department team left the scene, and the location was secured by the officers.

Sergeant Jim Barnes, Deputy County Coroner Len McDaniel and identification officers Dave Marshall, Oscar Schmidt and Sergeant J. E. Trujillo were next to arrive. As they began photographing the scene and processing it for fingerprints and other evidence, Officer Dotson commented about the strong odor of perfume he immediately noticed when he entered the apartment. A quick examination of the debris on the floor of the living room disclosed that a bottle of Rosey's very distinctive perfume had been knocked off an end table and spilled on the carpet and on some of Rosey's clothing that appeared to have been thrown on the floor next to the couch where she was tied.

Rita Schneider was taken to a nearby apartment where Officers Dotson and Thomas interviewed her. When asked if she had seen anyone suspicious around the area within the past few days, she replied that she encountered a young man she knew only by the name Tim when she visited Rosey two days previously. She said Tim stayed with other men in an apartment somewhere on Colorado Avenue, about four blocks from Rosey. She said she had frequently seen him wandering the streets in the neighborhood.

She told officers that when she opened the door to Rosey's apartment that day, she saw Tim inside. She said Tim looked surprised and said, "Hi, Rita, I didn't know you worked here." She asked Tim what he was doing there, and he told her he was looking for a party named George, who he thought lived there. Rita said she told Tim no one named George had ever lived there and she told him to leave.

As detectives began their on-scene investigation, Officers Dotson and Thomas began trying to find out who Tim was and locate the apartment on Colorado Avenue where he was staying. The officers checked records at the police station but found nothing.

They then contacted the Narcotics and Intelligence Section and spoke with Detective Dennis Yaklich. He told them he had heard of a Tim who was allegedly trying to score some Demerol in the Mesa Junction area. (Demerol is a trade name for Meperidine, a narcotic compound popular with drug addicts.) Yaklich said he would check with a confidential informant and get back with the officers.

An hour later, Yaklich contacted the officers and told them a man named Tim Calhoun was staying with a man named "Ike" at 224 Colorado, apartment number 4. He said the informant told him Tim had just that day told the informant he wanted to steal some small appliances to sell to make enough money to leave town.

The officers, accompanied by Sergeant Jim Barnes, went directly to the apartment reported by Detective Yaklich. They knocked at the door. A man named Ike Leatherman admitted them to the apartment. Two others were inside the apartment. One of them appeared to be asleep on the couch.

As the officers entered the apartment, they immediately noticed a strong odor of perfume that smelled exactly like that they had detected at the murder scene. They awoke the man on the couch. They later testified he and his clothing reeked of the perfume. The man identified himself as Timothy Calhoun. He was taken into custody, and along with the others there, was transported to the police station for further investigation. Detectives, some of whom were still working at Rosey Bowman's apartment, were summoned to the scene and the Colorado Avenue apartment was secured until a search warrant could be obtained and a forensic examination conducted.

At police headquarters, Tim Calhoun was advised of his rights and then interviewed by Major Bill Hurley. Hurley noticed that he signed the advisement form "Timothy Callis," and he asked Tim to explain.

Timothy Raymond Callis said he was on federal probation for a conviction of drug trafficking, and he used the fictitious name Timothy James Calhoun to avoid being contacted or tracked by federal authorities and by his probation officer. He further admitted to going to Rosey Bowman's apartment with a man named Pat to steal merchandise to sell for money to buy dope. He said he did not know Pat's last name.

"Pat had tied the victim up and put a blanket over her face to stifle her screaming," Callis told Major Hurley. He said Pat then allowed him to rape the victim. He said he did so for one or two minutes, then began looking through the apartment for money or jewelry—anything he could later sell. He said while he was conducting the search, Pat raped the victim for some time.

Under Hurley's deft questioning, Callis changed his story. He said he was alone when he entered Rosey's apartment. He admitted it was he who tied her hands to a table leg next to the couch, and he said he raped her for a considerable period of time until she stopped moving and making any sounds. He then got off her, ransacked the apartment and took money, jewelry, a bottle of Rosey's prescribed pills and other items. He went back to the apartment on Colorado Avenue and fell asleep. He denied that anyone else was involved in the crime and said he made up the character of Pat, who never really existed. The investigation also disclosed no evidence linking anyone else to the horrible crime. Timothy Raymond Callis was booked in Pueblo County Jail for first degree murder.

An autopsy revealed that Rosey Bowman died from suffocation, and that she had indeed been forcibly raped while being simultaneously smothered. Fingerprints lifted from the victim's apartment matched those of Callis and hairs found at the scene bore similar characteristics to samples taken from the defendant's head and pubic area. Testimony about the strong odor of perfume staining Callis's clothing being the same as that spilled in the victim's apartment, seemed to seal his fate.

Callis was convicted of first degree murder, felony murder, first degree burglary, robbery and first degree sexual assault. He was sentenced to life in prison. He would later challenge his conviction on appeal, saying authorities erred when they admitted his statement that he was on federal probation at the time of the killing, thus prejudicing the jury against him.

The appeals court ruled in the state's favor noting that the "rule of completeness" states a defendant's voluntary admission or confession, including all parts favorable and unfavorable to the defendant's interests, is admissible in its entirety. Callis's conviction and sentence were upheld.

Narcotics and Vice Staff Increased

Chief Silva understood that focusing the department's enforcement efforts on illegal drug sales, vice, illegal liquor operations and other suppressible crimes, could lead to dramatic decreases in more serious and violent offenses in the community. He therefore strengthened the department's already very successful narcotics and vice section with some additional manpower. The Rosey Bowman case demonstrated how the focus on the gathering and sharing of intelligence by narcotics officers could speed up the resolution of very serious crimes—like the murder of Rosey Bowman.

In late 1978, I was selected by Chief Silva to attend the FBI Law Specialist school at the FBI Academy in Quantico, Virginia. Graduation from the month-long course resulted in my certification as a constitutional law specialist by the University of Virginia.

In the spring of 1981, Chief Silva promoted me to captain and nominated me to attend the FBI National Academy. I attended the prestigious three-month course in the fall of that year and graduated with honors.

Upon my return from the academy, I was transferred from my supervisory role in the Support Services Division to command of the Administrative Division located in the chief's office complex. That division included management of the department's budget, oversight of the business office, staff inspections and internal affairs. My internal affairs investigator was Sergeant and future Police Chief Jim Billings. Little did I realize that our unit would soon become involved in a very high-profile murder investigation—the killing of a highly respected narcotics investigator, and the series of accusations that followed.

Dennis Yaklich Murder

Detective Dennis Yaklich had several things on his mind as he drove toward his home in eastern Pueblo County on the frigid morning of December 12, 1985. He was tired—it had been a grueling evening shift in the Narcotics and Intelligence Section of the police department where he worked—and he was anxious to get home to the arms of his loving wife. Though frequently asleep before he got home, she sometimes awaited his arrival and the two shared a drink or a snack and a little conversation before going to bed.

Their conversation, however, rarely revolved around his work in one of the most dangerous assignments in the police department. He didn't want to scare her with the details of his job, which frequently involved undercover meetings with drug dealers and other criminals, kicking in doors to serve search warrants, meeting clandestinely with potential informants and pursuing felons on the run who are willing to shoot it out with officers to evade capture.

He preferred to talk about much more mundane things, like the crop of delicious green chile peppers growing in the field behind the couple's rural home. Eastern Pueblo County is nationally renowned for its robust pepper crops.

Those chile peppers yielded additional cash for the Yaklich family during the growing season. Dennis's wife Donna helped in the harvesting of the crop. She frequently took a truckload of the popular and tasty peppers to the police station where she sold bushels to many of the officers coming and going during the afternoon shift change. Many of the officers knew her well and liked her, as they did Dennis. He had a reputation for being a very aggressive and successful narcotics detective but one who was willing to help younger officers wanting to increase their knowledge of undercover work and tactics in the narcotics field.

Narcotics Detective Dennis Yaklich was known and feared by members of Pueblo's criminal element. His size and muscular physique made him appear intimidating, but he was, in reality, a fair and dedicated professional.

Dennis was also a champion weightlifter and bodybuilder. He stood six-feet, four-inches tall and weighed over 230 pounds in his prime. He had won numerous bodybuilding championships, and he co-owned a gymnasium and exercise facility on Pueblo's south side. Though his sheer size intimidated some, those who knew him well thought of him as a "gentle giant" who used his strength and appearance to his advantage in his job to avoid roughness, and he seldom had to manhandle anyone.

The snow had subsided as Dennis neared his home and he noticed the house was dark—a sign that his wife had already gone to bed. He pulled into the driveway and alighted from his car, anxious to get inside the house and out of the cold. Suddenly he sensed something—movement in the brush adjacent to the driveway. He turned and instinctively reached for the pistol in his waistband. He probably didn't even hear the two shotgun blasts that tore numerous pellet holes through his head and torso. He was dead before his massive body hit the concrete driveway.

Chief Bob Silva was awakened by the phone call a little before 1:30 that morning. Though the shooting had happened in the jurisdiction of the county sheriff's department, Chief Silva assembled a team of city detectives, mostly from the Narcotics Section, and headed for the scene. As a seasoned detective who had come up through the ranks to become police chief eight years earlier, Silva knew better than to jump to conclusions prior to extensive investigative activity. He reasoned the execution style shooting may be connected to narcotics cases being worked or having been worked by Dennis Yaklich and the Narcotics Section. But he didn't discount other motives or suspects in the vicious crime.

The chief was soon sitting in a car near the blood-soaked driveway with Pueblo County Sheriff Dan Tihonovich. Tihonovich had several of his best detectives on scene but confided to Chief Silva that he needed the additional resources of the police department to conduct a thorough investigation. He asked the chief if he would take the lead in what both knew would be a protracted and time-consuming effort. Silva agreed and the two agencies thus began a mutual endeavor to find out who had killed Dennis Yaklich.

Though a major investigation began on many fronts, it was not until weeks later that an anonymous tip phoned into police headquarters provided the detectives with the break they needed. The caller advised that the officers should look at two brothers, 25-year-old Edward and 16-year-old Charles Greenwell. It was reported that both brothers began spending freely right after the Yaklich murder and that they had bragged in some circles of their involvement in the crime. Both were brought in. During intense grilling by Sergeant Steve Samek, Yaklich's partner in the Narcotics Section, both confessed that they were the hired triggermen in a plot by Donna Yaklich to murder her husband.

Donna was subsequently arrested, and the investigation revealed that she had paid the two brothers $4,000 to kill Dennis. The theory of District Attorney Gus Sandstrom was that she wanted the insurance money that would be forthcoming upon his death.

Donna Yaklich's trial for the murder of Dennis Yaklich commenced in January 1988 in Pueblo County, Colorado. During the trial, her defense pleaded that she was the victim in the case and that her husband was abusive towards her. She claimed that she hired the Greenwell brothers in self defense and to put an end to a long pattern of abuse. Meanwhile, the prosecutors argued that she orchestrated the gruesome deed to get the monetary gain of his insurance money.

After two trials, Donna was incredibly acquitted of first degree murder but convicted of conspiracy to commit murder. She was sentenced to 40 years in prison. The Greenwell brothers, in return for their sworn testimony against Donna, received slightly shorter sentences.

Donna Yaklich's attorneys presented a very aggressive defense at her trial. Many in the community believed the theories the lawyers proposed as to her motivation for orchestrating the murder of her husband. Those aspects of the case against her were compelling but seemed too unbelievable for most of the public to accept.

Many, however, did subscribe to the theory that she was a battered and frightened woman who saw no way out of an abusive relationship except murder. Some even believed that Dennis was a tyrant who had murdered his first wife and posed an imminent threat to Donna's safety.

Dennis's first wife had died from a heart ailment several years earlier. He had unsuccessfully performed CPR with chest compressions on her when she fell. The visible bruising from those chest compressions resulted in some people speculating that domestic abuse had led to her death. Those accusations, however, were discounted by the many officers who worked alongside Dennis and interacted with the couple on a personal basis, and by the doctor who had performed the medical examination of Yaklich's first wife's body at the time.

As Jim Billings and I were working Internal Affairs at the time of the murder, we both knew for certain that Donna had never made a formal complaint, or even a plea for help from the one departmental element that would have interceded in her behalf had she done so. We were obligated, however, to look into the allegations that arose during and after the trial of Donna Yaklich. After weeks of searching, we found no evidence to substantiate any of those accusations.

Donna Yaklich served almost 20 years in the Colorado State Penitentiary. She was released to a halfway house in Arapahoe County near Denver in 2005 and has since faded into obscurity. Charles Greenwell was released from prison in 2003 after serving 18 years of his 20-year sentence. His older brother Edward served out his 30-year sentence and was released from prison. He died of natural causes in 2017.

The truth is still a matter of conjecture in many circles, and it remains up to the individual reader to decide whether Dennis Yaklich deserved to be killed in such a ruthless and cold-blooded manner, and whether justice was served or denied in the Yaklich murder case.

Mass Layoffs

Chief Silva was at the helm of the department in June 1982, when drastic budget cuts within city government resulted in an across-the-board reduction of ten percent of department personnel. This was one of the darkest times in the history of the department and the first-time mass layoffs occurred. Personnel reductions occurred from top to bottom of the department hierarchy, starting with the abolishment of one captain's position. As the captain with the least departmental seniority, I was the one to go.

By city ordinance a person laid off in one position can use their seniority to "bump" a person with fewer years of service in a lower position. As four sergeants were simultaneously laid off, there were no sergeants left with less seniority than me, so I had to bump into a position as corporal—a demotion of two ranks in one fell swoop. The sergeants reduced in rank included future chiefs Ron Gravatt and Jim Billings, both of whom joined me as police corporals.

Several corporals were reduced in rank to patrol officer, and several patrol officers found themselves out of work completely. Some quit the department rather than wait until openings occurred and they could resume their service, albeit with less seniority than they previously enjoyed. Many found temporary employment elsewhere, and then returned to service with the force when the budget crisis abated.

Chief Silva fought to maintain the strength of the department, but his efforts were to no avail, as the city claimed to be almost broke. It was nearly a year before regular attrition began bringing people back to their former ranks and positions. It took me two years to regain my captain's rank. Chief Silva publicly expressed his pride and admiration of those who persevered and resumed their duties with a positive attitude and continued dedication to their jobs.

But the city budget, and consequently the police department budget, remained deficient for several years. A lack of monetary resources necessary to develop new and innovative programs continued to frustrate the chief in his efforts to maintain the high level of service the public had come to expect. Crime, however, did not decrease with the dwindling budget. In the spring of 1985, a one-man crime spree involving drug dealing, sexual assault, robberies and at least three murders brought the investigative resources of the Pueblo department and several other regional law enforcement agencies together to rapidly apprehend and convict a ruthless serial killer.

Ronald Lee White

Patricia Cruz was the night clerk at the Hampton Inn at 4703 North Freeway at 5:38 a.m. on Thursday, January 28, 1988. She was tending to paperwork in the small office adjacent to the front counter when she heard someone enter the front door. She stepped from the office into the reception area behind the counter and saw a young, bearded man in the lobby. Before the petite 19-year-old could say anything, the man asked if he could use the restroom located in the hallway adjacent to the office. She told the man he could.

As the man passed the door to the office, he drew a small, black revolver and stepped in. He pointed the weapon at Patricia and told her to get the cash register drawer from the front desk and take it to the office. Patricia complied with his demands.

The man took the contents of the cash drawer. He then told Patricia to open the safe. She told the man she did not have a key or any access to the safe. She said any money placed in the safe is pushed through a slot at the top of the safe. The man looked at the safe and noticed the last envelope deposited into the slot had apparently not dropped all the way into the safe. He told Patricia to pull it out and give it to him. She did as she was told.

The man told Patricia to get face down on the floor and not move until he had left the building. She said he threatened her by saying, "Do as I say, or I'll shoot you in the head." Again, she complied. After what she estimated as "a minute or two" she got up and ran into the lobby. There she came face to face with Catherine Collins, an employee of the Hampton Inn who had just arrived to begin preparing the hotel's complimentary breakfast for guests. Patricia told Catherine they had just been robbed. Catherine said she had seen the suspect leave the building when she was approaching. She also said she thought he may have left the parking lot in a light-colored Honda hatchback. The women called the police.

They described the suspect and vehicle to the police dispatcher who simultaneously conveyed the information to responding officers by radio. Dispatch procedure at the time was to initiate a "three beep" alert tone followed by an open mike during which the dispatcher questioned the caller then repeated the information given in real time, so all officers immediately heard the caller's responses concerning descriptions, directions of travel and weapons used.

The suspect from the Hampton Inn robbery was described as being a male Caucasian, about 25 years old, six feet tall, 190 to 200 pounds with a neatly trimmed full beard and mustache. The man was further described as walking with a pronounced limp.

Numerous police cars quickly swarmed into the area. Some fanned out on streets surrounding the hotel and four cars sped north on adjacent Interstate 25 all the way to Colorado Springs looking for a light-colored Honda. Despite the rapid police response, no contact was made with a suspect or vehicle.

Patricia Cruz was visibly shaken by the experience. The terrified woman was given some time off work by hotel management to recuperate. Some of her coworkers were recruited to substitute for her during her absence. One week later on Tuesday, February 2, Raymond Garcia agreed to fill in for his friend, Patricia, as night clerk. He likely thought of the ordeal Patricia had endured as he checked in for work at 11:00 p.m.

Right at 2:00 the next morning, Wednesday February 3, Garcia was behind the front counter when a man brandishing a handgun walked into the lobby. The man apparently announced that he was holding the place up and forced Garcia at gunpoint down the hall and into a storeroom next to the office.

At that time a security guard hired by the hotel walked in on the robbery in progress. Robert Martinez did not initially see Raymond Garcia, but as he approached the counter, he could see a man with a gun standing next to Garcia in the back storeroom. Simultaneously the armed man saw Martinez, turned the gun toward him and said, "I know you are armed—don't go for your gun!" He then took Martinez's weapon and led Martinez to a nearby conference room. Garcia was left in the storeroom but remained in sight of the gunman. He apparently felt he could not get out of the small office area without being seen by the robber and shot.

As the robber began to shove Martinez into the conference room he paused and, in a matter-of-fact tone said, "I think I'm going to kill you!" The comment caused Martinez to turn toward the man just as he fired the gun. The turning move caused the bullet fired at the back of his head to penetrate the left side of his face instead. The resulting wound caused Martinez to fall backward to the floor.

Apparently thinking he had killed Martinez, the man went immediately to the storeroom where the terrified Garcia still stood. The man fired again—this time into the side of Garcia's head near the temple. That round killed Garcia instantly. The killer then fled from the hotel.

Lying on the floor in the next-door conference room, Robert Martinez heard the shot that killed Garcia, and he heard the suspect leave the hotel. A few seconds later, he heard the sound of a car he assumed was the killer's vehicle drive out of the parking lot. He would shortly tell investigating officers the car sounded like a "muscle car" with the muffler removed or modified to make the engine sound very loud.

Martinez made his way to a telephone in the office, and he called the 911 emergency number. Within seconds police officers Rich Ashley and Gary Johnson were on scene. Robert Martinez was found to be seriously injured, but he was able to give the officers a full and coherent account of what had happened before being rushed to Parkview Hospital on North Grand Avenue by ambulance.

The description Martinez gave of the shooter was: Caucasian male, 6-feet to 6-feet-one-inch tall, with a full, well-trimmed beard and mustache. He also told the officers about the loud, unmuffled engine noise of the suspected getaway car. The information was broadcast to all city and county law enforcement units, and relayed to the Colorado Springs Police Department, the El Paso County Sheriff's Office and the Colorado State Patrol.

The similarity in the description of this night's killer and the man who robbed the hotel a week earlier was not lost on the officers. The information about the loud, unmuffled muscle car similarly attracted the attention of Colorado Springs Police officers who were working on an exceptionally cruel and vicious murder that occurred in that city just a week earlier.

The victim of that crime was a 31-year-old bicycle repairman named Victor Woods who lived in an apartment complex in southwest Colorado Springs. Two days before the first Hampton Inn robbery, a young female occupant of a neighboring apartment heard angry yelling coming from the Woods apartment. A short time later she saw a man leave the apartment. She told authorities the man drove away from the apartment complex in a blue Camaro. She characterized the vehicle as a "muscle car with a very loud, unmuffled engine." Moments later smoke began rolling out of the Woods apartment.

The Colorado Springs Fire Department arrived to find that several fires had been set inside that apartment. The fire crew quickly extinguished the flames, then discovered the partially burned body of Victor Woods under a pile of clothing on the floor. The clothing appeared to have been thrown over the victim then set afire. But Victor Woods had died from multiple stab wounds to the back and abdomen. Police began a murder investigation.

As both Pueblo and Colorado Springs woke up to the news of the Hampton Inn execution-style murder Wednesday morning, Pueblo Officer Gene Valliant of the Special Operations Section, the departmental unit that manages the Crime Stoppers program, answered a call. The anonymous caller told Valliant they "knew who was responsible for both Hampton Inn robberies." The caller said a man named Ron White, who lived in an apartment complex in Colorado Springs and walked with a limp, had bragged about doing the first robbery on December 28, and he said he planned on hitting the same hotel again shortly. The caller also said White drove a 1987 Camaro, blue with orange stripes, and very loud tailpipes.

Valliant ran a records check and found a 32-year-old Ronald Lee White whose criminal history and description matched that given by the caller and who was currently being sought for a sexual assault that occurred in May of 1987. The caller confirmed that Valliant had found the Ron White to whom the caller was referring. Valliant immediately wrote up the tip and forwarded it to detectives.

A photo array, or picture line-up, was assembled and quickly shown to Patricia Cruz and Catherine Collins. Both picked the photo of Ronald Lee White as being the man who held up the Hampton Inn one week earlier. Security guard Robert Martinez, in his hospital room, was shown the photo array and he also identified White's picture as being the man who held up the Hampton Inn on February 3rd and shot both him and Raymond Garcia during that robbery. An affidavit for an arrest warrant was prepared.

The Colorado Springs Police Department was given the information obtained from the Crime Stoppers caller, and they began searching for Ronald Lee White. Detectives in Colorado Springs were especially interested in the information about the car White was reported to have driven. It closely matched the description of the car seen leaving the scene of the Victor Woods murder.

Court records revealed that Ronald Lee White lived in an apartment at 1123 Verde Drive in Colorado Springs. Surveillance of that apartment was established by the Tactical Enforcement Unit of the Colorado Springs Police Department. They were quick to observe a blue Camaro Z28 with orange stripes parked in front of the apartment. They waited.

At 1:45 p.m., just shy of 12 hours following the robbery/ murder in Pueblo, Ronald Lee White walked out of his Colorado Springs apartment and right into the arms of 10 heavily armed CSPD tactical officers. He offered no resistance.

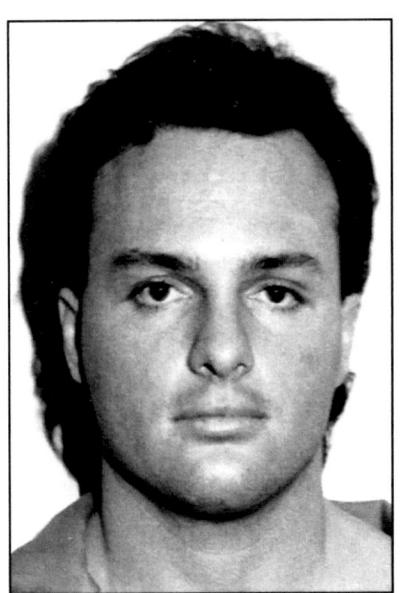

Ronald Lee White—he had shaved his beard and mustache shortly after the hotel robberies.

Faced with the mounting physical evidence against him in both robbery cases and the murder in Pueblo, the murder of the bicycle salesman in Colorado Springs and a pending consensual rape of an underage girl in Pueblo—White pled guilty to all counts to avoid the death penalty. On April 9,

1988, he was sentenced to life in prison. He would not have been eligible for parole until 2046, when he would be 91 years old. But this conviction and sentence would not be the last the justice system heard from Ronald Lee White.

In March 1988, a headless and handless decomposing male body was found by a rancher in a grove of trees alongside a country road about 15 miles south of Pueblo. The Pueblo County Sheriff's Office began an intensive investigation to first, identify the obvious homicide victim, and second, to determine what led to his death and disposal in the rough terrain a few miles east of the Interstate 25 exit to the mountain community of Colorado City.

Due to the removal of the victim's head and hands, it was speculated by sheriff's investigators that the body was mutilated in that manner to obscure the man's identity. It was quickly determined by the county coroner that the decomposed body also showed signs of animal predation. The coroner also determined the man had likely been killed by a close-range shotgun blast. Determining the identity of the unfortunate man would be difficult.

About six weeks later, a human skull was found in a ravine near the town of Rye, a picturesque mountain community a dozen miles west of where the decomposing body had been found. The skull was later determined to have been sawn from that body. A search of the ravine failed to find the victim's hands.

A check on all missing people in the Pueblo area disclosed one of extreme interest to sheriff's deputies. Paul Vosika had been reported missing by his father in September 1987. He had lived in an apartment complex on Bonnymede Road in the Belmont subdivision on the north side of Pueblo. Vosika was reported to have had a roommate named Ron. Sheriff's investigators began trying to determine who Ron was.

Working with Pueblo police detectives, it was discovered the elusive Ron was most likely Ronald Lee White. But definitive evidence that the severely dismembered corpse found south of Pueblo was Paul Vosika had not yet been conclusively determined. Similarly, direct evidence linking White to the disappearance of Paul Vosika was limited. Police continued their investigation until they were able to determine the roommate of Vosika's was indeed Ronald Lee White, and the two had been involved in narcotics sales in the Pueblo and Colorado Springs areas.

It took several months to shore up another murder case against White who was then incarcerated in the Colorado State Penitentiary. He was confronted with the evidence police had developed. At first, he feigned ignorance of the Vosika murder, but a few weeks later he wrote a letter to the judge of his previous trial offering to confess to the Vosika murder if he could be transferred to a prison in Wyoming. When asked why he wished to confess to a murder, he said he would do so only if he could be transferred to a correctional facility in Wyoming "where conjugal visits with females was allowed." Though authorities felt the prospect of a confession was compelling, no agreement was made.

Investigation continued, however, and by late 1990 police had enough information to charge White for the callous murder of Paul Vosika. He was tried and convicted, and on Friday, May 17, 1991, he was sentenced by Pueblo District Judge Eugene Halaas to death by lethal injection.

But again, this would not be the end of the saga of Ronald Lee White.

In May 1999, White's death sentence was overturned when information surfaced that some evidence held by the sheriff's office had been improperly handled and not turned over to White's defense counsel as required by law. District Attorney Gus Sandstrom publicly stated he was disappointed with the sheriff's office and emphasized that experienced deputies, rather than shoddily trained civilian clerks, should be responsible for the handling of evidence.

Ronald Lee White was resentenced to a third term of life in prison. He remains incarcerated in the state penitentiary. His additional sentence means White will not be eligible for parole until 2052. He will be 97 years old—if he lives that long.

As chief of police, Bob Silva presided over the introduction of two popular and innovative programs to the Pueblo department in the 1980s. First was the Crime Stoppers program, which had been receiving wide-spread attention since it was started in Albuquerque in late 1976. Crime Stoppers is a citizen based non-profit organization that offers anonymity to those who offer information concerning a crime or location of a wanted criminal and pays a reward to those whose information leads to the solution of the crime or arrest of the person or persons responsible.

Since its introduction, the Pueblo Crime Stoppers program has been extremely successful, especially in helping to solve the aforementioned crimes of Ronald Lee White and other high-profile murder cases. Many of those cases could have gone unsolved had it not been for the anonymous tips generated by Crime Stoppers. It continues as one of the most successful anti-crime programs ever.

The second program begun by Chief Silva was the DARE, or Drug Abuse Resistance Education program. DARE is an educational program based in the local school system that seeks to prevent illicit drug use, gang membership and violence among youth. The program uses specially selected and trained police officers to teach a carefully designed curriculum to young people in the community. It was very popular throughout Silva's tenure as chief, but it was curtailed in later years due to budget constraints. It did, however, serve as a precursor to the School Resource Officer program that is still in existence.

An operational element of the department initiated by Silva in the late 1980s was the SWAT, or Special Weapons and Tactics Team. Special purpose tactical teams were first formed in the late 1960s in major U.S. cities that were plagued by increased levels of violent crime and unconventional criminal activities such as hostage taking occurrences, barricaded gunmen, sniper incidents and riot situations. For some time in the 1980s, Chief Silva and his command staff had discussions about how the department could position itself to respond to the increased violence beginning to be seen, particularly in drug enforcement activities and in street crime in general. But due to a lack of funding for such a venture, no conclusive decisions were made.

Then in the summer of 1988, a young and energetic patrol sergeant named Eddie Rhodes approached me with a request to attend a basic SWAT school offered by the Denver Police Department. I looked the proposal over, liked it, and felt that this might be the opportunity for which we had been looking. I presented it to Chief Silva, and he concurred that getting a few of the right people trained in the SWAT concept could lead to more informed discussions concerning creation of a part-time special purpose team that could function within the then meager budget. Sergeant Rhodes's proposal was not only approved, but it was decided by the chief that I, along with two other officers who had expressed interest in serving in a tactical capacity, Sergeant Richard Goddard and Corporal Steve Samek, would also attend the Denver school.

The Denver Police Department had a reputation for having one of the best SWAT Teams in the country. It was a full-time unit, meaning SWAT was the only assignment for the 50 or so Denver officers so assigned. They worked exclusively on tactical training and unconventional operational assignments that exceeded the capabilities of traditional law enforcement responders and they were good at what they did. The two-week basic training course they provided was excellent and gave us the knowledge and skills necessary to develop a proposal for the creation of a team that could meet Pueblo's needs while not straying too far from the constraints of our budget.

Chief Silva liked the proposal but wanted additional information about capabilities our team members would need to confront most any threat we could possibly face. He wanted to be sure we would have the skills, abilities and equipment necessary to succeed safely in the changing environment he was sure we would be facing in the coming decades. Before approving the creation of a team for Pueblo, he sent the four of us to additional training, including the Denver Police advanced SWAT course and an FBI advanced SWAT tactics school. Only after completion of those courses and the preparation of a comprehensive outline of the selection process we would use for choosing team members, did he give us the go-ahead to launch a SWAT program for our department. As Captain, I would be the commander of the unit—Sergeants Rhodes, Goddard and Samek, who had just been promoted, would be the supervisors. Within the month, numerous officers interviewed and tested for the assignment, and fourteen were selected to begin training. By the fourth quarter of 1989, we had Pueblo's first fully functional SWAT Team up and running.

The first deployment of the team followed very quickly when a disgruntled, recently terminated employee of a local health care facility, threatened to kill everyone in his former work area. And he was seen skulking around the facility's parking lot. The facility was on lock-down status, and officers were alerted to be on the lookout for the man. He was found at his home later in the afternoon, but when officers attempted to contact him, he barricaded himself inside and began making threats that ranged from shooting anyone who came near his house, to killing himself.

The fledgling SWAT Team and trained departmental negotiators were called out and attempts to negotiate a peaceful resolution to the situation began. After several hours, it became apparent that a tactical intervention would be needed to resolve the incident. Chief Silva responded to the scene to get a first-hand view of how his SWAT officers were performing. As Sergeant Rhodes and I prepared the tactical plan and began briefing our team on the strategy we had formulated, I knew that if anything went wrong, our whole SWAT Team program would come to a screeching halt. I held my breath as I gave the order to execute the plan.

The door was breached, a distraction device was deployed, a rapid entry was made, and the suspect was taken into custody before he could bring a weapon into play or offer any physical resistance. It was a resounding success and displayed for Chief Silva that the team could utilize advanced tactics to resolve a very tense and dangerous incident safely, humanely and successfully without causing any injury to the subject or to any of the officers involved. The team was here to stay.

In the coming years the SWAT Team would be used an average of 50 times annually for everything from high-risk warrant executions to high-risk arrests, barricaded persons contemplating suicide, those seeking to avoid arrest through aggressive or armed resistance, hostage situations, VIP

The Pueblo Police SWAT Team upon receipt of the armored Peacekeeper. The vehicle was awarded to the police department in 1991 as part of a program that transferred surplus military equipment to American law enforcement agencies. That program was terminated in 2012 when concern was raised about "the militarization" of civilian law enforcement agencies. The vehicle served the SWAT Team for over 20 years.

protection and many other challenging operations. Chief Silva recently confided in me that creation of the SWAT Team was one of his career achievements for which he was most proud.

For several months in the early '90s, the SWAT Team practiced tear-gas-initiated entry tactics in an abandoned complex of buildings that had once been a state prison honor farm. The cluster of buildings stood on city-owned property just west of Pueblo along the Arkansas River. It had deteriorated to the point of being unusable for about anything else—no windows or doorways or frames for either, cracks in the walls and ceiling and very little roofing, etc. It was a perfect setting for firing tear-gas projectiles through non-existent windows and making dynamic entries.

Others appeared to have occasionally used the abandoned buildings for more nefarious purposes as well.

Devil Worship and Satanic Rites

Pueblo, like virtually every city in the country, has a very rich tradition of ghost stories and tales of the supernatural. And many of those stories center on the dark and thick, brush-entangled Arkansas River bottoms adjacent to City Park. Older Puebloans will remember the stories of the "pig-man of City Park," a rumored ghostly figure of a man with the head and face of a gigantic pig that generations of locals are sure is real. It is a story that has been told for years, but no one has ever admitted to having personally seen the elusive creature. Still the story persists, keeping many from violating the 10 o'clock park curfew or leaving the safety of their cars as they move through the park after dark.

Another local legend is that of the mysterious blue lights said to have been seen floating through the underbrush by numerous people, mostly teens visiting the "lovers' lanes" on the bluffs above the river. According to the stories, the lights would disappear whenever anyone scuttles down to discover what they are. Are they "ghost lights" of some sort? Maybe mystical orbs or clusters of fireflies?

Or are they something much more sinister like a throng of demons carrying blue lanterns to lure unsuspecting victims to their fate in the swirling waters. A local film producer named John Henry Johnson posited just such a theory in his low-budget film *Curse of the Blue Lights* shot mainly on location in the river bottoms below the park. The film has become a cult-classic in recent years and a heavily edited DVD version is available on Amazon.

The ghostly La Llorona—the "crying woman" who had drowned her own children in desperation after having been jilted by an unfaithful lover is also rumored to haunt the section of the river bottoms west of the park. One version of the legend dictates that "if you hear the wailing of La Llorona, you must run the opposite way as fast as you can." But which is the opposite way, and is La Llorona real, or just a mythical spirit conjured up to frighten naughty children?

Perhaps the most disturbing of the local spook stories to come forth during Ruben E. Archuleta's term as detective captain, centered on the old, abandoned prison honor farm located off 11th street near the north bank of the Arkansas. Tales of satanic worship, human sacrifice and terror surrounded the dilapidated buildings that once comprised a state prison farm. The property had been abandoned by the 1980s, and rumors of ghastly rituals abounded, occasionally bringing a police response to reports of bonfires and mysterious chanting. Mostly, those responses resulted in the discovery of teen drinking parties, known as "keggers," rather than more ominous activities.

But reality is often more terrifying and loathsome than any ghost story or horror movie could ever be. Such was the case on January 13, 1991, when a contingent of police officers rushed to the old honor farm in response to a reported kidnapping. The innocent victim of the reported crime was a four-month-old baby boy named Arturo Ortega. He had allegedly been taken from his home on Pueblo's south side by his 18-year-old uncle, Kenneth Galves Jr. Kenneth's mother had contacted the police after discovering that little Arturo, along with a blue Toyota pickup, was missing from the family home. She feared that her son had taken both the vehicle and the baby, and she feared that Kenneth might harm Arturo.

The frantic mother said Kenneth had recently been released from the state hospital, and that he was "not right." She further reported to Police Corporal Robert D. White that Kenneth had recently been talking about occult activities. Kenneth's father stated that his son had told him that he was "the chosen one" to inherit the kingdom of hell from Satan, but that to do so, he would have to sacrifice his own baby. The distraught parents said Kenneth did not have a baby of his own, but he had recently taken an increased and rather morbid interest in his sister's child. They opined that Kenneth would not harm the baby "if he was in his right mind," but they were concerned that he may not have been taking his prescribed medication. They also said Kenneth had been hanging around the old honor farm, and that he might have taken the baby there.

Silva's detective captain, Ruben E. Archuleta, was following the radio traffic concerning the initial kidnapping investigation. Archuleta was an experienced and savvy investigator who had worked some very dangerous undercover assignments that had taken him deep into many life-threatening international drug trafficking organizations and organized criminal enterprises.

Realizing that the Galves situation was potentially much more than a routine familial kidnapping, and sensing that time was not on the side of law enforcement, Archuleta dispatched several of his Crimes Against Persons Section and Juvenile Section detectives to the honor farm. He also responded to assume command of the search for both the victim and the suspect of what was shaping up as one of the most bizarre crimes in Pueblo history.

Several patrol officers also responded, and when Corporal Richard Harsch turned into the farm complex, he quickly discovered the missing vehicle but reported that neither Kenneth nor Arturo were readily seen in the area. Numerous officers arrived, and a massive search of the property was initiated. Shortly, Detective Sergeant Jim Barnes found Kenneth Galves hiding in some underbrush about 200 yards from the abandoned buildings. He was taken to Captain Archuleta's car where he was advised of his constitutional rights and Archuleta began asking him about the whereabouts of the child.

Galves was steadfast in his refusal to answer Archuleta's questions. Feeling he was getting nowhere with the defiant Galves, Captain Archuleta asked Sergeant Rich Lipich, the supervisor of the Juvenile Section, to try his hand at questioning the man. Lipich met with the same reticence from the suspect, and he suggested to Captain Archuleta that they take the extraordinary step of allowing Kenneth's father to interview his son. Kenneth Galves Sr. had by that time arrived at the scene and Archuleta agreed to allow him to speak with his son.

Generally, only trained and experienced officers are permitted to interview in-custody suspects. Family members and friends of suspects are usually not allowed to talk with them, as officers cannot control the conduct of the discussion and may open themselves to claims of coercion or illegal interrogation techniques that may negate the admission in court of the information obtained. But Captain Archuleta felt time was of the essence and there was still a chance the child could be found alive and unharmed if the information about his whereabouts could be quickly obtained.

After about 45 minutes, Galves Sr. emerged from the car and stated his son would show the officers where the child was. Galves Jr. was moved to Corporal White's car and a caravan of police vehicles left the honor farm to follow Galves's directions. He told White to head toward the reservoir and indicated he should take the Wetmore highway. Galves further said the baby might still be alive, but they would have to hurry.

White activated his red lights and siren, and the parade of police vehicles raced at break-neck speed west toward an unknown destination where young Arturo had reportedly been left. Though early in the afternoon, the January weather was chilly, and the officers were fearful for the child's welfare. And of course, there were grave concerns about wildlife, particularly bobcats and bears, both of which inhabited the woods in the area toward which the officers were headed.

When Lipich asked Galves if he thought the baby was still alive, Galves replied, "doubtful – doubtful." A sick feeling began eating at the officers as they hurriedly negotiated the tightly curved highway west of Wetmore toward Westcliffe. Suddenly, Galves said "here it is," and White skidded to a stop at the entrance to a short driveway that led to a small clearing that appeared to have been used as an informal camping ground. As White steered the police car into the drive Galves said, "I hope you brought a body bag."

Located at the center of the clearing was a crude circle of stones, similar in appearance to a firepit. Several officers, including Captain Archuleta, pulled into the clearing. The officers held their collective breaths as they quickly approached the ring of stones, afraid of what they might find.

Inside the placement of rocks lay Arturo's body, his small head crushed by a 30-pound rock that still obscured a portion of his scalp. It was apparent that Galves had placed his nephew in the stone circle, then lifted the large rock above his head and brought it down hard on little Arturo.

The gruesome scene brought tears to the eyes of many of the officers. Others stood silently in obvious shock at what they were seeing. Archuleta, who would rise through the ranks to become chief of police about four years later, recently confided in me that the image of "that beautiful little baby with that huge rock resting on his head" still gives him nightmares, and the case remains the one that disturbs his sleep to this day.

Galves was charged with first degree murder and kidnapping. He was adjudicated incompetent to stand trial, and was ordered confined in the state mental health facility. He has never faced a court of law for one of the sickeningly worst cases of wanton homicide in Pueblo's history, and the one case that haunts the dreams of every officer involved in the investigation. Captain Archuleta and Chief Silva led the call for demolition of the heavily graffitied honor farm buildings. Following some expected bureaucratic delays, the complex was unceremoniously razed to the ground in 1995.

The Cora Romero Tragedy

Just days after the Arturo Ortega outrage, another frighteningly tragic event occurred in Pueblo. This one was the direct result of the unbelievable carelessness of a law enforcement officer and the gross negligence of that officer's agency. That negligence led to the totally preventable and brutal murder of a Pueblo grandmother.

On February 8, 1991, Chaffee County Deputy Sheriff Chester Price was sent by his agency to pick up two of that county's prisoners at the Colorado State Hospital located on the northwest side of Pueblo. The prisoners, being held for separate crimes in Salida—a small town about 85 miles west of Pueblo on the Arkansas River—had each been sent to the state hospital for court ordered mental health evaluations prior to their trials. They were slated to be returned to Chaffee County.

Price, driving a sheriff's Chevrolet Blazer, was alone as he pulled into the state hospital complex. He first picked up 26-year-old Woody Ashfield, shackled him, and placed him in the Blazer. Ashfield, who had a long record of violent crimes, had been arrested for the armed robbery and brutal assault of a Salida motel clerk. He was considered extremely dangerous and an escape risk.

Price, with Ashfield in tow, then drove to a different building in the hospital complex to pick up the second prisoner. He left Ashfield in the sheriff's Blazer as he went into that building. Incredibly, he also left his .45 caliber revolver in the vehicle.

When he returned to the car a few minutes later, he found that Ashfield had the revolver in hand. He pointed the weapon at the surprised deputy and demanded the keys to the vehicle. Despite the shackles, Ashfield was able to drive away in the sheriff's car, leaving Price standing dumbfounded in the parking lot. The alarm was sounded and both Pueblo and hospital police were notified.

Within 15 minutes, the sheriff's Blazer was discovered wrecked near the railroad yards a few blocks southwest of the hospital grounds. Multiple officers swept through the huge rail yards and into Pueblo's midtown area. Ashfield was not found. It was assumed he may have caught an outward-bound train or found his way to the nearby Arkansas River bottoms and disappeared into the tangled underbrush.

Three days later, on the afternoon of Monday, February 11th, 61-year-old Cora Romero was preparing dinner in the kitchen of her modest home at 2314 Poplar Street in south Pueblo—about four miles from the state hospital. Her three-year-old grandson, for whom she had been babysitting, lay napping nearby.

Cora was an excellent cook who had once run the lunch counter at the Rexall drug store on Union Avenue. She was known for her excellent Mexican food, particularly her spicy green chile. On this day, she stood at her stove stirring a large pot of boiling hot refried beans. Her Chevy Lumina was in the detached garage next to the back door of her home. The garage door was open, exposing the car to the view of anyone who might pass by.

As she stirred the beans, a man suddenly forced his way through the back door. Evidence indicated the man probably demanded the keys to the vehicle, and Cora likely resisted.

The man then grabbed the bean pot and threw the steaming contents over Cora's face and shoulders, severely burning her. He then beat her with the pot, strangled her and finally stabbed her repeatedly with a butcher's knife he found on the kitchen counter.

The killer took the keys to the Lumina and fled in the vehicle. Neighbors and family members found the body of Cora Romero a short time later and called police.

The ensuing investigation did not uncover any evidence that could identify the mysterious killer. Cora's family and friends could offer no information about anyone who bore a grudge against her or with whom she had ever had a problem. It began to appear the case was shaping up as a very difficult stranger-on-stranger homicide. Detectives issued an all-points bulletin for Cora's vehicle.

Four days later, some alert officers in Los Angeles, California, spotted the vehicle and pulled it over. The driver was Woody Ashfield. He was taken into custody and quickly returned to Pueblo.

Ashfield admitted to killing Cora Romero for her vehicle. He was tried and convicted of first degree murder and received a life sentence. Cora Romero's family sued Chaffee County for gross negligence for allowing Woody Ashfield to escape. They were awarded $195,000 — $45,000 for the child for being placed in "the sphere of danger" and $150,000 for the family— the most allowable by law at the time for claims of wrongful death caused by a governmental agency.

Silva Retires

Police Chief Bob Silva served as chief for almost 15 years. During his tenure the department saw many ups and one real down, but his steady hand and steadfast leadership kept things running smoothly. He announced his retirement in 1992. He was succeeded by Robert E. Simon who served a brief term that year, followed by W.A. "Bill" Young who came to the department from the Houston, Texas, Police Department.

Young served from 1992 to 1995. Other than making some controversial personnel assignments, he made few changes in the operation of the department. He did oversee the change in officer uniforms from the dull gray and French blue, which many joked about making department members look like bus drivers, to the traditional dark blue uniforms still worn with a few contemporary modifications by Pueblo personnel.

Chief Young also created the position of "Night Commander" who would work the night shift and handle all major situations requiring top-level attention normally necessitating the after-hours call-out of the chief. He appointed me to that position which I held until Young's retirement.

But Bill Young was an unpopular chief. He was viewed by many department members as an outsider who did not understand the lore and traditions of the department. He was also viewed as racist by many of the Hispanic officers—particularly very aggressive supervisors and commanders of Latino heritage whom Young had assigned to lesser administrative positions housed in the neighboring police annex building. Some of those officers felt they had been "banished to Siberia" because of their race or national origin. They began referring to the annex as "Little Tijuana," and they complained bitterly to the city administration.

Though the disgruntled members were reminded that the city charter empowered the police chief with the authority to assign employees where he deemed necessary, they were not happy. Realizing department morale was declining rapidly and fearing political repercussions should the discontent continue, city management began exploring means of easing the chief out. Bill Young announced his retirement in early 1995. Administrative Deputy Chief Ronald A. Gravatt was immediately appointed chief. He served for a brief period until Ruben E. Archuleta was elevated to the position later that year.

Chief Ronald A. Gravatt. His name is frequently omitted from lists of Pueblo police chiefs because he served in that capacity for such a short time. Many do not realize he had been appointed chief, rather than acting chief, to maintain continuity of agency leadership while city management sought ways of restoring confidence in the department's top position.

THE ARCHULETA YEARS

The Galves and Romero cases depicted in Chapter 16 were just preludes to a series of senseless and tragic crimes, mainly involving gang activity, that plagued certain areas of Pueblo in the early 1990s. The murders of several young people beginning in the summer of 1993 and extending through 1994 became known as "the summer of violence," and severely taxed the resources of police investigators. Captain Ruben Archuleta realized early on that the majority of gang members in Pueblo were of Mexican American descent. He vowed to do whatever was necessary to change the propensity for young Hispanic people joining the many gangs that had taken hold in the city.

As captain of detectives, Archuleta had also been widely recognized as spearheading the investigation and ultimate resolution of a double murder case where the suspects had fled to Mexico. The bureaucracy involved in getting the suspects extradited to the United States to stand trial had been exasperating. Archuleta had spent days working with numerous governmental agencies on both sides of the border to orchestrate what would become the first ever prosecution of a Mexican citizen in Mexico for a crime committed in Colorado. That success was recognized by city officials as well.

As the population of Pueblo at the time was close to 45 percent Hispanic or Latino, roughly equal to the percentage of non-Hispanic Caucasian, Archuleta's popularity with the public soared. When he applied to be the next police chief, his application was greeted with excited approval by Pueblo's Hispanic leaders as well as by non-Hispanic citizens who were impressed by his positive connection with city, county, national and international officials and his successes in dealing with a significant demographic of the city. He was appointed by City Manager Lew Quigley as chief of the Pueblo Police Department on April 11, 1995.

Newly appointed Chief Archuleta went to work immediately to, as he put it, "bridge the gap" between the community and the department. He announced that departmental investigations, particularly those involving allegations of officer misconduct, would be thorough and wide open to public scrutiny so there could never be any allegations of a cover-up. He publicly opined that accountability was paramount if the department was to be successful. "If one of our employees crosses the line," he said, "they know there will be consequences. By the same token," he continued, "If someone falsely accuses an officer of wrongdoing, and we can substantiate it, they should also face legal and civil consequences."

As the department's first police chief of Hispanic heritage, Archuleta used his considerable knowledge of Latino culture and his long-standing personal relationship with Hispanic community leaders to vastly improve the department's image in Pueblo's multi-cultural environment. He was hailed as a role model for Hispanic youth. To this day, many young police officers of Hispanic descent point to Chief Archuleta as their inspiration.

Chief Ruben E. Archuleta

The chief had also been troubled for some time by the escalation of violence he observed firsthand on Pueblo's streets, so he moved to create a Youth Enforcement Section comprised of a new gang unit and the already highly successful School Resource Unit. Those functions would work closely with a newly created Crime Analysis Unit and the Juvenile Section, to form a concentrated multi-pronged attack on gang activity and youth violence. That approach proved to be remarkably successful. From a high of five gang-related murders in 1994, the number dwindled to only two over the next ten years.

Archuleta also improved officer training by bringing in some noted figures to conduct in-service training for every officer in the department. Those guest instructors were highly respected law enforcement professionals from throughout the country. He stated it was more economical to spend several hundred dollars to bring in a noted instructor who could reach almost every department member than it was to continually send two or three Pueblo officers to outside schools at a cost of three or four hundred dollars each time for each officer.

But some lingering problems remained from the previous administration. Prior to Archuleta's ascension to the chief's post, the city and county had experimented with a combined emergency services dispatch center. City dispatchers had been moved from the police annex building to a new dispatch center in the basement of the old county jail which had been remodeled by the sheriff's office. Dispatch consoles for both city and county operations had been installed so personnel could continue to handle calls from their respective jurisdictions. It was further felt that at busy times, both groups of dispatchers could answer 911 calls and relay the information to the appropriate radio dispatcher. The idea was to consolidate the duties of both entities to save money. It was a laudable goal, but not adequately thought out.

City dispatchers complained loudly that the sheriff's dispatchers would not answer emergency calls coming from within the city, and county dispatchers complained that city dispatchers were rude and condescending toward them. Negotiations revealed that the controversy was driven by the fact that the unionized city dispatchers were paid considerably more than their counterparts from the county. County dispatchers wanted parity, though city personnel pointed out that they were considerably busier as upward of 90 percent of the emergency calls came from the urban environment of the city rather than from the more rural county.

It seemed no one was happy with the situation—not city administration, not county commissioners and certainly not the individual dispatchers. Complaints consisted of calls being missed, lengthy response times due to a lack of communication, misunderstandings of how each group had been trained and calls being lost due to the differences in how equipment worked. These were major problems the politicians on both sides looked to Chief Archuleta to fix.

Though he thought consolidation could work in the future, he felt the time was just not right. He realized a thorough assessment would first be required before the problems could be fixed. That assessment, he felt, would be expensive and time-consuming. He also thought the way the two separate dispatch centers had operated prior to consolidation worked considerably better for a number of reasons. Each center was staffed with personnel uniquely familiar with the demographics, street layout and peculiarities of their respective jurisdictions; dispatchers from each center had been accustomed to the radio code system and operations manual of their own agencies; and personnel from each agency knew who their bosses were and to whom they were to report. Minor issues existed, like who had access to the locked center, who was authorized to obtain information from the various computer systems, why the disparity in pay and many more.

Archuleta pushed for a dissolution of the combined center and a return to two functional communications centers—one for the considerably busier city and one for the county. The two could conceivably work together when necessary, and dispatchers could temporarily move from one to another in the unlikely event of one center going completely down due to a disaster of some sort, or due to terrorist activity.

The challenging project was assigned by Archuleta to Deputy Chief Max Atencio. He was given a directive to involve the individual dispatchers with the design, selection of equipment, training and formulation of policies that would be necessary to make the move to a newly designed center at the police station for which they could all be proud. Sheriff's personnel did the same and within a couple of months the newly tooled "comm centers" were up and running with no major problems.

Archuleta would later state that he was "one of the luckiest chiefs around, because I was blessed with the best command staff anyone could ask for. Any of my command staff could have handled the chief's job well, so I knew we had a heck of a team put together," he said.

As the command staff of the department had slightly diminished in number due to attrition over the previous year or two, Chief Archuleta moved to reorganize the agency into six divisions, each to be overseen by a deputy chief. He reassigned the deputy chiefs to positions he felt could best make use of the talents they individually possessed. The result was a strong and cohesive staff that would work together to achieve the best results for the city.

Deputy Chief Jim Billings was appointed to command the Operations Bureau, the largest bureau of the department, consisting of the patrol and traffic divisions. Deputy Chief Charlene Graham was given the Investigations Bureau comprised of criminal investigation and identification services. Deputy Chief Max Atencio remained in the position of technical services commander, Deputy Chief Bill Stewart took over support services, Deputy Chief Ron Gravatt remained the boss of administrative services, and I was given command of Special Investigations and Tactical Services. Special Investigations was the Narcotics and Intelligence Division and the department's participation in interagency task forces, such as the Drug Enforcement Administration's southern Colorado drug task force and the United States Bureau of Alcohol, Tobacco and Firearms task force. Tactical Services was the SWAT Team, the crisis negotiators, and the explosives utilization and disposal unit.

Prior to his appointment, the chief had told the city manager he would not work with a shortage of officers. He said previous chiefs had used the money saved by vacancies in officer positions to make up for budget deficits and he felt that practice negatively impacted officer safety on the streets. He pointed out that the department was authorized 194 officers in 1976, and that in 1996 it was operating with fewer sworn positions. He was given permission to fill vacancies and to look for ways to acquire funding for additional officers and equipment.

Chief Archuleta's 1996 Command Staff, left to right: Deputy Chief John Ercul, Chief Archuleta, Deputy Chiefs James W. Billings, Charlene Graham, Bill Stewart, Max Atencio and Ronald A. Gravatt.

Deputy Chief Ron Gravatt was tasked with the responsibility for researching funding sources and writing grant applications. Within the year, the department was able to replace a major portion of the aging vehicle fleet by utilizing a lease purchase plan. Ron also applied for and received a grant to hire additional officers. The strength of the department was increased to 207 sworn officers.

But there were still crime problems in the community. On a Wednesday evening in August 1996, a particularly disturbing crime was discovered in Pueblo's predominately

Hispanic and Catholic Eastside neighborhood. It was a crime that immediately made news headlines throughout the world and thrust the city into the international spotlight. It was the killing of two respected Roman Catholic priests inside their home behind the iconic Saint Leander Church.

Killing of Two Catholic Priests

Saint Leander Church, with its blond brick, Spanish-style double bell towers, stands like a sentinel over the working-class neighborhood of east Pueblo. The church and the adjacent St. Leander school building cover the entire block between Monument and Norwood avenues and East 6th and 7th streets. The rectory is attached to the back of the church at 6th and Monument.

As was his custom, the Reverend Bill Powers, a retired priest who lived about a block from St. Leander, walked down to the rectory to visit his close friend, 65-year-old Thomas Scheets, pastor of St. Leander, on the warm evening of Wednesday, August 8, 1996. If he noticed the trail of blood leading away from the front of the parish home, he didn't pay much attention to it until he reached the door. There he stopped in his tracks—startled by what he now realized was blood on the doorstep. He knocked and called out to the two priests who were usually at the door to greet him. Getting no answer, he slowly opened the door. He didn't even have to step into the home—he saw Father Scheets on the floor just inside the door. He was covered with blood and Reverend Powers knew immediately his friend was dead. Powers went across the street and called the police.

As a precaution, the Pueblo Fire Department Rescue Squad was dispatched along with a contingent of police officers. One look told the fire crew that Scheets was beyond earthly help, a vicious slash had laid his throat open and the copious amount of blood that had run from the hideous wound and pooled on the floor next to the hallway wall was clear evidence that the beloved priest had expired.

Police began their investigation by checking the rest of the home. As officers entered the bedroom occupied by the retired priest Reverend Louis Stovik, they found him in a similarly shocking condition. It was obvious to the officers that both priests had put up a fight, and it was quickly determined from the appearance of blood stain patterns that the killer was most likely injured and bleeding as well. A call quickly went out to all local hospitals and urgent care centers asking them to report the appearance of anyone at their facility who had a serious cut or similar wound to their hands or arms.

By the time additional investigators arrived to begin a comprehensive forensic examination of the scene, a crowd of grieving citizens had assembled in the street in front of the home. The local news media had also gathered and were demanding information. Chief Archuleta, who had arrived on scene early on, could foresee that this case would attract national media attention. He established an area across the street for the news media to gather, and he began preparing for the periodic press conferences he knew would be coming. Little did he realize then that the story of the murder of two priests would, as we would say today, go viral. In less than an hour, media trucks with their satellite dishes would be flocking to that media staging area.

I was on vacation in London, England, when the crime occurred. London time is seven hours ahead of Pueblo time. When I woke up on the morning of August 9th and turned on the television in my hotel room, I was greeted by images of the crowd in front of St. Leander Church in Pueblo, and Chief Ruben Archuleta doing his best to assuage the curiosity of the world press.

Citizens from throughout the neighborhood also converged on the parish house in an eerily silent vigil, making crowd control difficult for police. As officers established an outer perimeter to keep the growing crowd at a reasonable distance from the crime scene and the dwindling trail of blood, a couple of people came forward to tell the officers of a young man who had occasionally done chores, like sweeping the floors and running errands for the priests. They felt uneasy about the youth, and they thought officers should check him out. His name was Douglas Comiskey and he lived just over a block from the church.

As Chief Archuleta conducted his first press conference, telling reporters the investigation was in its early stages and warning other local priests and ministers to lock their doors and take steps to increase their personal safety, detectives and crime scene investigators began gathering evidence in and around the home.

The blood trail observed at the front doorstep of the murder scene led officers south toward the home of the Comiskey youth. As the evidence began to point directly to 20-year-old Douglas James Comiskey as the killer, his home was placed under surveillance. Detectives began doing a background investigation on the troubled young man. It was discovered he led an unhappy life, punctuated with minor criminal activity, drug abuse and mental problems. Armed with an arrest warrant, police went to his home on Wednesday afternoon. He was arrested there just 28 hours after the discovery of the disturbing crime.

At first, Comiskey refused to talk with investigators. After several tries, Chief Archuleta was able to speak with the obviously disturbed young man personally but was unable to get him to talk about the attack on the two priests. Within an hour of interrogation, however, he began talking about hearing whispered voices that commanded him to do things.

Eventually he would tell officers that he had seen a large number 1 written on a file folder at his doctor's office that morning, and at that moment "werewolves" whispered to him that he would be killed if he did not kill someone else by 1 p.m. that afternoon. He said he began driving around the Eastside neighborhoods looking for someone to kill.

He further said he knew a girl who lived near his home, and he decided to kill her. He crept up to her house, peeked in a window, and saw that she had a male friend in the home with her. He decided he had to look elsewhere. He then went to the parish house of his church. He said he knew Father Scheets well, and as it was nearing the one o'clock hour, he said he "had to kill him in order to keep from being killed himself."

Comiskey admitted that he went to the door of the rectory and knocked. When Father Scheets admitted him with a smile, he immediately began stabbing the kindly priest. Comiskey said Father Stovik must have heard the noise, as he came out of his room and confronted him in the process of stabbing Father Scheets. He said he became enraged and chased the elderly priest down and stabbed him repeatedly. At some time during the attack, he received a minor cut on his hand. He knew he was covered with the blood of the priests, and he went to his home to clean up. He did not realize he had left a bloody trail directly to his front door.

Comiskey would later tell his appointed public defender that he was a werewolf in the process of being transformed into a vampire. Charged with two counts of first degree murder, Comiskey was found not guilty by reason of insanity on March 19, 1997. He was sentenced by Judge Eugene Halaas to one year to life in the state mental hospital.

He would remain confined for just over eight years before doctors were able to convince the court that he was no longer a threat to the public. He reportedly had been a model patient, had taken his medication faithfully, had participated in supervised visits to the community and had accepted therapy. He was granted unsupervised visits to his hometown and was eventually relocated to the Denver area. He has not reoffended as of 2023.

Chief Archuleta had always been an avid defender of Second Amendment (gun) rights and his stance was well known in the community. He was therefore appalled when New Jersey Senator Frank Lautenberg sponsored an amendment to the National Gun Control Act of 1968 which prohibited people who had been convicted of misdemeanor domestic violence from ever owning or carrying a firearm. The law went into effect on September 30, 1996.

The chief stated publicly that he had "a real problem with the law as it was written." Though politicians claimed otherwise, it appeared to Archuleta and others that it could be interpreted as being retroactive back to 1968, which meant that if someone had a minor tiff with a significant other, maybe some pushing and shoving or even a slap but not involving a firearm, they would not be allowed to have a gun forever after—even if that tiff happened 25 years ago. He felt the law was unconstitutional.

Part of his objection to the new law was that anyone who had been convicted of such a misdemeanor when they were very young but had passed psychological examinations and background investigations and been hired as a police officer years later, would automatically become unable to carry a gun. They would have to be dismissed from their employment with the department. Archuleta felt that was unfair. As such, he felt the law would be enforced mainly against law enforcement officers and military personnel—those who were required by their jobs to be armed. He opined that, with most gun control laws, the law-abiding citizens and responsible gun enthusiasts would obey them, while the law breakers would ignore them. "The people who respect the law are the ones being penalized," he stated.

Unfortunately, his stance on gun control laws—particularly the retroactive domestic violence law—put him at odds with many government officials and a certain segment of the public. He was publicly criticized by some groups that dealt with battered women and domestic violence. The executive director of the local anti-domestic violence group stated in a December 1996 article in the *Pueblo Chieftain* that she was "startled and disappointed because this was the wrong message to battered women and perpetrators—domestic violence didn't matter."

Archuleta responded that he was even more disappointed in her comments than she was in his because he had made the domestic violence issue a priority and had taken the lead locally to work with the various groups that were now criticizing him so loudly. He said the law could keep the very people it was meant to protect from having a weapon for their own protection should they ever be convicted of a misdemeanor domestic violence infraction.

He further stated that the law did a disservice to the victims of domestic violence by giving them a false sense of security. "Why not focus on consequences," he asked. "If a person uses a knife or a club, or a fork, or a beer bottle during a domestic fight, don't ban the instrument—pass a law that deals with stiff consequences and use it," he said. He reemphasized his contention that he favored preventing youth and domestic violence, not by passing more gun laws, but by enforcing the ones we already have. "We need to work on crime and violence prevention by emphasizing accountability, responsibility and consequences," he said.

Chief Archuleta held to his beliefs and refused to do background checks on Pueblo officers to ferret out those who may have had a misdemeanor conviction prior to their being hired. The criticism began coming in from all sides, especially from news organizations and from state and federal politicians. Some federal officials began issuing what Archuleta considered "veiled threats," reminding him that he was required to obey the federal law or face severe federal consequences, including huge fines and possible prison sentences if he did not comply.

Refusing to compromise his beliefs, and not wanting to cause problems for the city manager and council members who had supported him, Archuleta decided his best course of action was to resign his position rather than capitulate to his detractors. In December 1996, the chief rose to address the regular meeting of Pueblo City Council to announce his decision. He spoke slowly as he told council that he intended to retire and explained that he was unable to compromise on his position regarding the domestic violence law. He said he did not want to become a liability to the city. He further said he did not need the government, the feds and liberal politicians telling him how to run his department.

As he finished and turned to walk away, one of the councilmen, John Verna, rose to insist that council wouldn't allow him to retire. Verna was followed by every other council person who urged Archuleta to reconsider his decision.

Archuleta thanked them for their support, then walked out into the bitterly cold night.

He later wrote: "The large fluffy snowflakes were thick and beautiful, and I was noticing how peaceful and serene the evening was, when I heard a boy's voice behind me. I turned around and saw a young boy wearing a T-shirt standing in the falling snow. He pleaded with me not to retire . . . that I was a role model and a mentor for the kids in the community."

Archuleta said the encounter with the young boy touched him deeply and caused him to question whether he was doing the right thing by retiring. He slept uneasily that night.

Newspaper headlines the next day shouted the news of the chief's pending retirement and he began receiving phone calls from members of the community urging him not to go. The city manager even dropped in to tell Archuleta he owed it to him, and to the community to stay. A few days later, following what he said was "a lot of soul-searching," Chief Archuleta called a press conference to announce that he had changed his mind and would not retire. His announcement was well received by the community.

As the gun control controversy continued, and still does to this day, Chief Ruben Archuleta, Pueblo's first Hispanic police chief, would remain in that position for another year before deciding the time had finally come for him to step aside. His last day at work was August 31, 1998, but his official retirement day was January 15, 1999.

Deputy Chief Ronald A. Gravatt, who had held the position of chief following Chief Bill Young's hasty resignation four years earlier, was again installed as chief. He would serve for a little over a month until October 5, 1998, when City Manager Lew Quigley appointed Deputy Chief Jim Billings to become Pueblo's new police chief.

Billings would serve for 13 years and guide the department through the many complex and vexing challenges that faced law enforcement, both locally and internationally, in a rapidly changing world.

CHAPTER 18

THE BILLINGS ERA

The first plane struck its target at 8:46 a.m., Pueblo time. The news went out within seconds, but no one knew whether the incident was a terrible accident or a deliberate act of sabotage or terror. When the second building of the World Trade Center in New York City was struck by another plane at 9:01 a.m., local time, September 11, 2001, it was apparent that our country was dealing with an intentional terrorist act of monumental proportions.

Police Chief Jim Billings had been following the news since the initial attack on the first WTC tower, and as soon as he was sure the unfolding catastrophe was more than a tragic accident, he sent a message to every member of his command staff directing them to be in his office at 10 a.m. sharp for an emergency strategy meeting. He also contacted the Pueblo County Sheriff's Department and invited the attendance of the sheriff's command staff to insure a concentrated and unified local response to what he knew was shaping up as one of the deadliest criminal acts in the history of our country—one that would impact every law enforcement jurisdiction and every aspect of American society.

As additional information began filtering in and additional attacks occurred in Washington, D.C., and aboard a plane bound for Washington, D.C., but forced to crash in a field near Shanksville, Pennsylvania, the chief's intuition proved correct. Eventually, over 3,000 lives would be lost in the most unspeakably heinous act of coordinated terror in modern times, and one that would ultimately claim hundreds of additional lives due to the residual effects of the attacks and the rescue and life-saving efforts associated with it.

At the heart of the chief's strategy session was the establishment of emergency protocols to protect the City and County of Pueblo from any similar ideologically extremist inspired attacks. Chief Billings also was concerned about the possibility of misguided attacks on innocent people of Middle Eastern ethnicity by citizens angry about what was already being called "radical Islamic terrorism." Reports of brutal attacks on people of Middle Eastern and Asian heritage were already coming in from some cities, and since Pueblo had a vibrant Middle Eastern community made up mostly of foreign-born students attending the local university, Chief Billings directed the immediate establishment of a line of communication between local public safety entities, university officials and representatives of student organizations. He wanted to become aware of any developing tensions between student groups and others on and off campus. Fortunately, Pueblo did not experience any significant problems in that area.

Of special concern to the chief was the vulnerability of local utility companies, especially Pueblo's water supply and the security of our local airport and other transportation functions. The CEOs of local utility agencies were contacted and brought into discussions about how to protect their multitude of facilities across the county. Their individual interests became paramount to the department's planning process and within hours of the initial 9-11 attacks, the police department had in place a comprehensive set of directives dealing with all areas of concern. Those directives were issued to every member of law enforcement in the area. The communications center responsible for receiving 911 emergency calls and dispatching the appropriate fire, medical and law enforcement response, was also issued new directives covering all calls of suspicious activity in or near any local utility facility, the airport and other places of concern.

Over the coming days and weeks, additional concerns arose because of situations occurring in other parts of the country. When the national news reported certain people had received letters filled with a powdery substance that claimed in the letters to be anthrax—a pernicious and infectious disease of cattle and other mammals which is deadly to human beings—local people began reporting the reception of similar mailings. Fortunately, the department already had in place a protocol for handling biochemical hazards. The local calls all received an immediate and measured response, and none of the eight to ten local incidents involved actual anthrax or other toxic substances. All were thoroughly investigated to ensure the safety of the intended victims, and all were quickly determined to be cruel hoaxes.

Another concern was the potential use of "MANPADS," or man portable air defense systems, to take down aircraft entering or leaving Pueblo's airport. Several MANPADS had been reported stolen or missing from some military facilities around the country and the FBI had issued a warning to be on the lookout for such rocket-like weapons that could be used to shoot down an airplane at relatively close range. All approaches to Pueblo's airport runways were surveyed and measures taken to have them watched by airport security personnel during take-offs and landings. Further, all officers were made aware of what MANPADS looked like and given instructions on how to recognize signs of their presence when stopping suspicious vehicles.

Though resources were severely taxed by counterterrorism procedures, all local public safety agencies rallied to ensure, as much as possible, the safety of Pueblo citizens, and ease the public fear of becoming victims of terrorist assaults. The protocols developed by Chief Billings and his staff remained in effect for several years, and excerpts of them are still contained in departmental directives and the procedural instructions of local utility companies.

Chief Billings had only been at the helm of the department for about three years when the 9-11 attacks occurred, but he had already initiated several refinements to the organization and operation of the agency. Just months before the 9-11 attacks, the country was beset by another tragic event that shocked the consciousness of every American. The Columbine High School mass shooting incident, though not the first occurrence of its kind, ushered in an unprecedented public awareness of what law enforcement had been calling "crisis killing sprees," or "active shooters." The Pueblo Police SWAT Team had been doing some training in how to combat situations of this type, but that training intensified following Columbine.

Due to the department's close association with an organization known as the National Tactical Officers Association (NTOA), the chief became aware of that organization's research and initial policy recommendations regarding response to active shooter incidents. One of the members of NTOA's policy development team was a sheriff's deputy from El Paso County, just north of Pueblo. Due to Pueblo's close association with area agencies, including El Paso County, the department got a first-hand look at the developing policy regarding active shooter response. Pueblo therefore became one of the first agencies in the state to embrace and adopt NTOA guidelines with modifications to suit the local environment. For instance, NTOA recommended the formation of three-officer ad hoc teams to make an immediate entry into any structure where an active shooting incident was occurring and to move that team to contact with the perpetrators based on the sound of gunfire or other indications of their location.

Based upon Pueblo's documented response time matrixes, the command staff felt the department could field four officers as quickly as it could three, so the initial procedural instruction for Pueblo officers was to form four-officer teams, each with a defined area of responsibility to make that initial entry.

Intense training included noise and light generating devices, simulated gunfire and explosive detonations. Actors from local community theater groups portrayed victims, suspects, and persons fleeing the scene in panic. It was found that rigidly formed teams quickly disintegrated as hazards were encountered during the hunt for the perpetrators. The initial procedures and training protocols were therefore quickly modified.

Statistics indicated that in almost every actual active shooter situation, the random shooting and killing of innocents ceased once the shooter(s) was confronted with deadly force directed against them. The aim became one of confronting the perpetrator with directed gunfire as quickly as possible. Thus, the four-person team concept was all but eliminated and the procedure morphed into having the first officer on scene, or any one officer, such as a school resource officer already on scene, proceed immediately on a hunt— search—and confront mission. As additional officers arrived, they could make entry on their own or form teams to back up the initial officer as circumstances dictated. The procedure has worked very well in training sessions. Fortunately, it has not been necessary to test it in an actual crisis-killing situation locally.

Shortly after taking office in October 1998, Chief Billings began exploring innovative ways of addressing chronic criminal activity that for years had plagued the more vulnerable areas of the city. Working with the U.S. Department of Housing and Urban Development (HUD), the chief organized a program utilizing federal funds that became known as POSH, or Pueblo Operation Safe House. A companion operation would become the first in Pueblo's history to use a fully commissioned recruit police officer to work in a deep undercover role to infiltrate Pueblo's criminal underground.

The objective was to recover stolen property, seize contraband, identify career criminals, gather information about ongoing criminal activity and aggressively address violent crime occurring in and near Pueblo's assisted housing developments.

The centerpiece of the operation was to be a covert "repossession business" to run out of a storefront in South Pueblo. It took some time to identify the right recruit—one with a law enforcement background in another agency far from Pueblo with the right "look" to play the part of a crooked "repo man." It wasn't until September 1999 that a promising candidate surfaced.

Operation Repo Man

About a week before newly-hired police officer Jeffrey Maize was to begin initial training in the police academy, he was approached by two of the department's deputy chiefs (Charlene Graham—commander of Investigations, and me—commander of Tactical Services) and recruited to work in the top-secret undercover capacity. Upon accepting the job, his name disappeared from all department rosters, and those who asked were told he had declined the police position.

With the knowledge of only the very top command staff and selected support personnel, he was secretly sent to

Pueblo Police Officer Jeffrey Maize worked undercover for almost a year in a police sting operation from a "repo shop" on South Prairie Avenue. Operation Repo Man netted the department scores of stolen vehicles and other illicit property and contraband and resulted in numerous arrests.

a training center in Canada for some intensive schooling in undercover operations and tactics, then deployed to operate the repo business.

His repossession business was established in a vacant storefront in a strip mall on Prairie Avenue near what most Puebloans called "the Projects." Informants were surreptitiously given information about the criminally run repossession business that doubled as a front for the purchase of stolen property, other contraband and illicit drugs. As planned, that information was quickly relayed to the criminal element that had infiltrated the housing projects.

All property transactions were secretly filmed by hidden cameras in the repo shop and recorded by officers stationed in a back room as security for officer Maize who played the part of the crooked business entrepreneur. Several layers of sandbags were placed below the counter of the business, and heavily armed tactical officers secretly covered all business transactions from behind two-way mirrors.

The wildly successful venture lasted for almost a year and resulted in the recovery of scores of stolen vehicles and other illicit property and contraband with numerous arrests. It was only terminated when crucial evidence from a murder case in a neighboring jurisdiction was brought to the storefront, and the magnitude of that development trumped the other cases being pursued by Operation Repo Man.

Recognizing that working in concert with other law enforcement organizations was the best way to combat crime that impacts Pueblo and neighboring jurisdictions, Chief Billings further established alliances with regional law enforcement agencies. La Junta, Colorado, is a smaller community about 65 miles east of Pueblo. When La Junta Police developed a major narcotics case and needed assistance in executing simultaneous search warrants at multiple locations in their city, they called upon the Pueblo department. Chief Billings sent me along with 22 SWAT officers to assist. All La Junta warrants were served without incident. Similarly, when the small community of Las Animas needed help serving a search warrant against a local criminal enterprise that had been violently threatening the entire community, I took a dozen SWAT officers there to deal with the problem.

Chief Billings also assigned several additional officers to federal task forces working specialized crime problems that crossed many jurisdictional lines. The DEA (Drug Enforcement Administration) Southern Colorado Task Force was and continues to be particularly successful in combating narcotics related crimes that plague the entire Front Range of Colorado and New Mexico. Many Pueblo officers have been assigned to that effort and many of them have worked in extremely dangerous undercover assignments, resulting in seizures of large amounts of illegal drugs and illicit funds. Chief Billings also assigned officers to the FBI's Joint Terrorism Task Force, the FBI Fugitive Task Force, and the BATF (Federal Bureau of Alcohol, Tobacco, and Firearms) clandestine firearms task force.

Jim Billings was a very innovative administrator who was not afraid to try new, and in some cases, unorthodox or controversial methods. Among the many programs and projects introduced during his tenure, were the "take-home car policy" and the four-year degree requirement for new hires. The take-home car policy was very popular among individual department employees as it provided a marked police vehicle to every patrol and traffic officer. Participating officers could use the vehicle as they would their own, but had to agree to certain rules, including the requirement to respond if close to a critical incident and to assist in any way possible if contacted by a citizen needing help—whether the officer was on or off duty. A requirement of participation in the take-home-car policy was that the officer had to live in the city of Pueblo or within a few minutes of the city. Most of the officers were very enthusiastic about it. Those who lived further away were not as enamored with the program.

Though viewed by some as an expensive and unnecessary "perk" for department members, the benefit of the program was an omnipresence of police throughout the community which resulted in a huge reduction in response times to urgent calls and an increase in the public's sense of safety. The program worked well but only lasted a few years until city budget constraints could not sustain it.

The requirement of a four-year college degree for all police candidates was also met with mixed enthusiasm in the community. Many thought it meant the department would be recruiting and hiring better educated and more sophisticated officers while others thought it would severely limit opportunities for less affluent and minority candidates. The program was implemented incrementally and when the chief retired in 2011, over half of the working officers held four-year degrees or higher. When Chief Billings called it quits the program was abandoned by a new chief who was less enthusiastic about the degree requirement.

Serious Active Felon Enforcement

One very successful program initiated by Chief Billings was the SAFE Unit. SAFE was an acronym for Serious Active Felon Enforcement. It was started after a series of thefts of metal products from homes under construction and businesses dealing in metal products. Incredibly, thieves were tearing out copper piping from new homes, doing many thousands of dollars in damage in the process. The bounty reaped by those thefts would get the thieves only a few hundred dollars or so at one of many scrap metal dealers in Pueblo County or beyond. One such theft had resulted in a spectacular car chase punctuated by gunfire directed against police officers.

Right at 11:30 p.m. on Saturday, October 9, 2004, Officers Vince Petkosek and Michael Sincerbox answered a burglary in progress call to the alley behind 324 South Union Avenue. The reporting party had said two men were putting metal products and equipment from the back of a business into a car. The men also appeared to be hiding some of their bounty behind a tree at that location.

As the officers turned onto C Street near the alley, they heard a radio broadcast from other officers saying a vehicle was recklessly speeding away from the scene. Officer Corey Purvis pursued the vehicle emerging from the opposite end of the alley with its lights off. It turned to the north on Union Avenue and accelerated. The chase was on.

The pursuit went north on Union Avenue, turned onto Main Street then on to westbound 4th Street toward the south side of Pueblo. Shortly after crossing the West 4th Street bridge, one of the vehicle's occupants leaned out the passenger side door window and fired several rounds at the pursuing police vehicles. One of those rounds struck the emergency light bar atop Sergeant Danny Ingraham's car.

The chase continued for several blocks to the campus of Pueblo Community College where the suspects crashed into a large chain link gate and came to a stop. Though both suspects fled on foot, they were quickly apprehended in the neighborhood adjacent to the college campus. One of them fired at officers during the foot chase and was himself slightly injured by return gunfire.

During an interview with the two suspects, it was learned that rumors had been circulating among several unorganized groups of metal thieves active in the city. One of those rumors or assumptions was "if the cops start to chase you and you shoot at them, they'll back off and abandon the chase."

Nothing, of course, could be further from the truth. But those apprehended following the chase had acted as though that assumption was correct. They had come close to injuring or killing police officers with gunfire and had led officers on a wild chase through both business and residential neighborhoods, thus putting untold numbers of citizens at risk. Chief Billings was rightfully concerned, and he asked me to organize a special team to track down the source of the dangerous rumors and reinforce for the criminal element that they could not deter police intervention in their activities by firing shots at officers.

I chose a team of smart, aggressive and innovative officers to man a unit we would call SAFE—initially an acronym for Special Active Felon Enforcement. Chief Billings did not like the word "special" as he felt it would insinuate the team was somehow superior to the patrol division officers with whom it was supposed to work. I changed the name to Serious Active Felon Enforcement, thus maintaining the acronym SAFE. The chief liked the modified acronym.

I chose two highly successful Narcotics Section officers, Detective Mark Thalhamer, who had experience with the DEA Task Force, the SWAT Team, the Narcotics Section, as well as the Vice and Violent Crime Unit of the previous administration and Ron Gravatt Jr. Gravatt is the son of retired Deputy Chief Ron Gravatt, and he had similar experience in specialized units as did Thalhamer. I also pulled a detective from the Crimes Against Property Section, Chad Jeffries, as he had accumulated most of the cases involving metal thefts and had SWAT experience. Officer Jeremy Mathews, an aggressive patrol officer, rounded out the initial SAFE investigative team. I also recruited Sergeant Danny Ingraham as the team supervisor because he had direct involvement with the metal thieves and had been shot at during the aforementioned car chase.

Initial members of the SAFE Unit

Left: *Detective Corporal Mark W. Thalhamer. He was chosen as one of the original members of the SWAT Team in 1989 and subsequently participated in every team deployment during the team's first five years of operation. He was a "super-cop" with extensive experience as a narcotics officer, a gang officer, a tactical officer and in other specialized assignments. He retired in 2015 and tragically passed away in 2020 during the early months of the COVID pandemic.*

Right: *Sergeant Danny Ingraham, the first supervisor of the SAFE Unit. He was fired upon during the car chase that resulted in the creation of the SAFE Unit.*

Above left: Detective Ron Gravatt Jr. He had served in virtually the same units as had Thalhamer, often as his partner.

Above right: Detective Chad Jeffries was a tenacious property crimes detective.

Bottom right: Police Officer Jeremy Mathews who had distinguished himself as a gang unit and patrol officer.

SAFE would be a non-divisional element of the department, meaning it would not be assigned to any formally organized division. SAFE officers would report directly to me, and their hours would be flexible to accommodate the expected duties of their assignments which included conducting investigations, engaging in undercover work, selective patrol assignments, known-perpetrator surveillance and other orthodox and unorthodox investigative or tactical activity deemed necessary to resolve the problem of metal thieves or other local criminals who were willing to engage officers in gunfire. It was anticipated the SAFE assignment would be temporary in nature, disbanding when the metal theft problem and other emerging crime problems were resolved.

In the six months following the creation of the SAFE Unit, the team made over 90 arrests of criminals who had engaged in a multitude of crimes, including simple thefts, burglaries (including those resulting in metal thefts), strong arm robberies (robberies from the person or presence of another without a weapon) and armed robberies. In most of those cases, illegal drugs had been the catalyst for the criminal activity. So impressed was Chief Billings by the success of the SAFE Unit, he made it a permanent operational element of the department. It remained so, as a very successful operation throughout the Billings administration, being disbanded only when a new chief, Lou Velez, assumed command of the department in 2011.

School Resource Officer Program

The issuance of laptop computers to every officer, which resulted in "paperless" reports and a much more rapid distribution of information, was one of the more successful and enduring programs initiated by Chief Billings, as was the expansion of the highly successful School Resource Officer Program into every middle school and high school in the city.

Chief Jim Billings could also foresee the increase in violence directed against school children, and the benefit of having an armed officer available on school campuses to deter those wishing to harm students or faculty members and act as a first line of defense should a school come under attack. Though initially frowned upon by school officials, the school resource officers were issued long guns (rifles and shotguns) to enhance their abilities to confront heavily armed assailants.

The Billings administration also oversaw the investigation of two of the most senseless murders of the 1990s. The first one was an unnecessary crime that was captured, nearly in full, by a surveillance camera. The perpetrator was identified and arrested in less than 24 hours by a particularly aggressive crimes against persons detective named Mark Bravo—with the help of one of my youthful police interns.

Annette Martinez Murder

Annette Martinez was enjoying the evening with her family. She and her children had been decorating their Christmas tree on Friday evening, December 9, 2005, when Annette announced she had to get ready for work. "We can finish tomorrow night," she told her three young boys.

Annette normally worked a day shift as a clerk at the 7-11 Convenience Store at 4th and Glendale on Pueblo's east side. This day, however, she agreed to substitute for a friend on the midnight shift. Though aware that the midnight shift could be dangerous— at least more dangerous than the earlier shifts at the store, she was not too worried. The store was well lit, and customers came and went frequently. She knew many of the regular customers— even those who were out and about well into the early morning hours. And she knew Pueblo Police officers drove through the parking lot regularly to check on the on-duty clerk.

However, she did not know the stocky little man in the Oakland Raiders jacket who entered the store just before 2:30 the next morning. It was just a couple of hours after the beginning of her shift when the man walked in and looked around. "Can I help you?" she asked with a smile. The man said he needed to use the restroom. Annette reached under the counter, got the keys to the small unisex bathroom at the rear of the store, and accompanied the man to the back to unlock the restroom door. She did not want to just hand over the keys.

Bathrooms at all local 7-11 stores had been locked in past years to prevent thieves from secreting merchandise on their persons and using the restrooms for other inappropriate purposes. Customers needing the restroom would be allowed to do so at the discretion of the on-duty clerks, one of whom was required to unlock the bathroom door personally while the other watched the counter. But Annette Martinez was working alone this shift.

The in-store security camera was operating that morning, and it captured the interaction of Annette and the man in the Raiders jacket, up to the point the two went back toward the restroom. That area was out of the camera's view. The camera's audio function, however, captured what happened next.

The sounds of Annette's screams could be plainly heard on the recording as the man stabbed her repeatedly with a large hunting knife. It would later be determined that she suffered 13 deep stab wounds to the neck alone. The killer, now on camera again, went to the cash register but found he could not open it. He made off with three cartons of cigarettes.

Shortly thereafter, customers entering the store found the bloody crime scene and called police. As with all homicide scenes, detectives from the crimes against persons section responded along with patrol officers. One of those detectives was a clever and tenacious investigator, Mark Bravo. Bravo immediately had the store manager, who had been summoned to the scene, pull the digital recording of the activity leading up to the stabbing of Annette Martinez in the store. He and other detectives who viewed the recording were shocked by what they saw. The case-hardened detectives were also sickened by what they heard as Annette begged to no avail for her life and screamed pitifully as she was stabbed unmercifully—over and over—in that small back room.

Bravo took that recording to police headquarters and had identification officers isolate and print the best photos of the perpetrator. As other businesses near the 7-11 Store were closed by the time the investigation began, Bravo spent all night going through arrest records and photos of previous offenders. He came up with nothing. When morning dawned, he took the photos of the killer from the surveillance system and began showing them to his many informants in the hope someone would recognize the man. Again, nothing came from his efforts.

As the bars, restaurants, and other businesses on the East 4th Street began opening for business, Bravo began contacting businesspeople in the area, particularly bartenders and liquor store owners. He hypothesized that the killer had visited one of the bars at some time prior to the crime, and he felt the black and white Raider's jacket worn by the man in the photos would have been noticed. He hoped someone could provide a name to go with that jacket.

He continued through the day visiting the businesses near the 7-11 store, and by late afternoon he hit pay dirt. One of the customers who frequented the East Side Tavern just a block from the scene of the crime said they knew the name of the man in the photograph. The man was Freddy Delariva.

Bravo then went to work to identify Freddy Delariva. His efforts led to family members who said Freddy had gone to Pueblo West, a separate community just west of Pueblo, where he had a girlfriend. The address of the girlfriend and a description of the car Freddy was driving were obtained and Detective Bravo, accompanied by Detective Cody Wager, another bright, aggressive and upwardly mobile officer, were on their way to Pueblo West.

It was just getting dark as the detectives headed west on Highway 50 toward an anticipated encounter with their quarry. Though traffic was heavy, the detectives observed the Delariva vehicle as it passed them, heading back toward Pueblo. They turned around at their first opportunity and raced to catch up with their suspect who was quickly approaching Interstate 25.

A 17-year-old police intern named Brian Laut and I were just finishing our dinners at a restaurant in downtown Pueblo when my portable police radio came to life with a broadcast of a chase in progress. It was Detective Bravo radioing that he and Wager were in pursuit of the Martinez murder suspect. When we heard Bravo say the chase was entering Pueblo on Highway 50 West, we jumped up and headed to the counter to pay our restaurant bill. I looked at Brian and asked, "Do you want to catch a killer?" "Yes," Brian replied, a grin on his face.

As we left the restaurant, we heard Bravo report that the chase was progressing southbound on Interstate 25 from

Highway 50. It was headed directly toward us.

Bravo then reported that the suspect vehicle had turned onto the Belmont off ramp toward the east side of town. Brian and I were by then headed east on 4th street. Numerous other police vehicles were converging on the east side as Bravo continued broadcasting the chase. "East on Bypass 50, south on Hudson, east on 13th street." We could hear sirens coming from every direction as I steered my unmarked vehicle east then north toward the last location Bravo had given.

When Bravo radioed that the vehicle had suddenly stopped in the 1100 block of East 13th Street and the suspect had bailed and ran between houses in that block, I turned north on Kingston Avenue to get ahead of the suspect. At the intersection of 12th and Kingston, I saw Detective Bravo on foot in the middle of the intersection. I stopped. Bravo pointed to the west and said, "He has to be in this block somewhere—I got down to this intersection too quickly for him to have crossed into the next block." He further said Detective Wager was in foot pursuit.

I killed the headlights of my car and drove slowly through the block indicated by Bravo. As I neared the intersection of 12th and Joplin, Brian, who had been scanning the north side of that block said, "There he is." I looked and saw the suspect duck back into an alcove of the corner house at that location. I threw the beam of my spotlight on the alcove, told Brian to stay in the car and jumped out of the vehicle—pistol in hand. I ran to the fence that surrounded the house and yelled very loudly, "Show me your hands and get down on the ground." The suspect complied.

Hearing my commands, several officers who had been searching for Delariva in the backyards of homes in that block converged on our location and took the suspect into custody. He appeared to be wearing the Raider's jacket the surveillance camera had shown him wearing the night before.

The suspect, who identified himself as Freddy Delariva, had a bloody laceration on his forehead. Officers traced his path from his abandoned vehicle and found that he had run straight into a metal post in the darkness and cracked his head open.

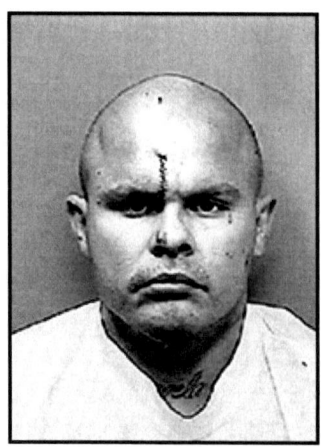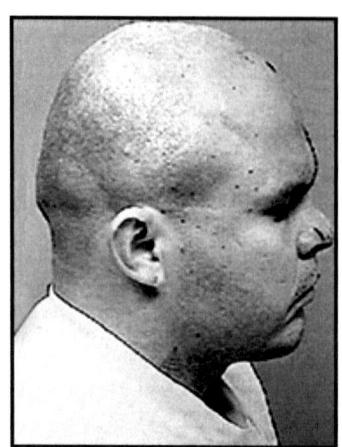

Detective Wager, several inches taller than Delariva, had run into some wires connected to the post and been knocked down. When he was able to get on his feet, his prey had disappeared in the darkness, leaving a blood smear on the unyielding metal post. Though frequently described as a clothesline and clothesline pole in news stories, the wire and pole contraption that had cracked open Delariva's head and taken Detective Wager out of the foot pursuit in the darkness was actually a set of wires designed by the homeowner at that location for hanging meat out to dry to make jerky and other dried meat products.

I looked at Brian and said, "Brian, you haven't yet become a full-fledged police officer, but you've already caught your first murder suspect." Brian smiled from ear-to-ear.

Delariva was taken to police headquarters and detained for further investigation. A text message was sent to the chief letting him know a suspect was in custody. Chief Billings immediately called me by phone and asked, "Did you get that latest text? They have a murder suspect in custody; do you know who it is and how that happened so fast?"

I was standing next to the suspect in the Investigations Division hallway, so I merely looked over at him and asked, "What's your name?" "Freddy Delariva" was his reply. I turned back to the phone but before I could answer the chief he said, "I heard—you're busy, I'll talk to you later—good job—bye." The praise was all for Detective Mark Bravo who had done such a great job in quickly identifying and tracking down the killer.

When the Raider's jacket he had been wearing when he was captured was checked in the lab, it was found that Delariva's girlfriend had washed it, erasing most, but not all the visible traces of blood. Annette Martinez's blood had also been found soaked into the inside pockets and the dark sleeves of the jacket which were made of a different material than its slick exterior. The physical evidence, along with the surveillance photos of Delariva at the scene of the crime, was conclusive evidence of his guilt in the horrible and unnecessary murder of Annette Martinez.

Under questioning, Delariva admitted to killing Annette Martinez. He said he initially intended to merely rob the store to get some money. (Technically, a person cannot "rob" a store. Robbery, in Colorado law, is a crime against a person—not against property. Many people will inaccurately say their house or business was robbed when they correctly mean burglarized. Delariva would have been correct had he said he initially meant to rob Annette—not rob the store.) Martinez, he said, had resisted and put up a fight, so he stabbed her. The district attorney's office announced it would seek the death penalty because of the especially heinous way the crime was committed. Likely because of the surety of conviction and the specter of the death penalty hanging over him, Delariva and his attorney negotiated a plea agreement in which he would plead guilty in return for a life sentence without the possibility of parole. His plea was accepted, and he was sentenced appropriately. As of September 2023, he remains confined in the Colorado State Penitentiary.

Two years later, Chief Billings oversaw the investigations of two homicides that occurred within hours of one another on

Halloween Eve, 2007. The first involved a mentally unstable man who killed his own mother while suffering a psychotic episode, and the second was the especially brutal murder of a local cab driver.

Halloween Horror

Shortly after 1:20 a.m. on the cool morning of October 30, 2007, Halloween eve, a woman who lived in the 1500 block of East 11th Street in east Pueblo heard what she described as "a loud noise, like an M-80 firecracker exploding." She wasn't too concerned—after all, it was Halloween week. When she looked out her front window, she saw a taxicab pulled partially into the driveway of the house directly across the street from her home. She said there was another car in the street behind the cab. That car quickly drove away going westbound on 11th Street. She also saw two figures running to the east toward the intersection of 11th and Ogden. The cab did not move. Though she expected to observe some sort of Halloween prank, she did think the activity was suspicious and she determined to keep an eye on the cab.

Hearing a car engine a few minutes later, she looked out her front window a second time to see the same vehicle she had seen earlier again parked in the street behind the cab. Feeling something was just not right, she called the police.

Simultaneously, the man who lived at 1523 East 11th was on the line with the 911 operator reporting a taxicab was parked in his driveway and "a couple of people appeared to be looking for something inside the cab." He also saw the car in the street behind the cab and he too thought the activity was highly suspicious. Neither caller could see if the cab driver was behind the wheel. A police unit was immediately dispatched to investigate.

Officer Daniel Pratt arrived on scene a few minutes later to find the cab with its lights on and the right rear door open. The suspicious car reported as having been in the street behind the cab was no longer there and Pratt had not seen a vehicle leave that block of East 11th as he approached. Pratt cautiously made his way to the cab to find what appeared to be the driver slumped over into the front seat. He was obviously dead, his head blown apart by what appeared to have been a shotgun blast fired from the cab's back seat. Officer Pratt called for detectives and all the proper people.

The investigation began with interviews with people living in the 1500 block of East 11th, and with the City Cab company dispatcher. It was soon revealed that the cab driver had earlier been sent to an apartment in the 4000 block of O'Neal on Pueblo's south side to pick up two fares and take them to 1523 East 11th.

In checking the O'Neal address, a large multi-building apartment complex, detectives were told a party had taken place there the previous evening. The renter of the apartment at that location reported that four or five young men had crashed the party but had only stayed a few minutes when a taxi had picked a couple of them up, and the others had left the parking lot in a car. The car appeared to be following the cab. A complete description of the car and of the five men was obtained by detectives.

The cab driver, 51-year-old David Chance, had worked for the City Cab company for four years. He was originally from Michigan, having moved to Pueblo six or seven years earlier. An autopsy revealed he had been shot in the back of the head from the rear seat of the cab. A shotgun, likely a sawed-off weapon, had delivered the fatal shot. Chance had died instantly. He left behind a wife, three children and two grandchildren.

The investigation initially yielded little information about the identity of the suspects, but detectives had gathered several items of evidence and were optimistic the case would be solved with some continued hard work. A cellphone found discarded near the scene of the horrendous crime was used to summon the cab to the apartments at the O'Neal address. It also turned out to be the telephone stolen the prior evening during a strong-arm robbery of a 24-year-old man in an alley near East 4th Street and Fountain Avenue—about a mile and a quarter from the shooting scene. The weapon used in the crime had not been found by Halloween evening.

On Thursday, November 1st, a meeting was held in the chief's office to review the evidence and discuss strategies for the continuing investigation. I attended that meeting along with Chief Billings, District Attorney Bill Thiebaut, Thiebaut's Chief Investigator John Koncilja, Detective Captain John Barger, and several detectives from the Crimes Against Persons Section of the police department.

Chief Billings asked for a complete rundown concerning the evidence so far collected, and the descriptions of the suspects believed involved. When Detective Don Litton reported the description of a young man believed to be with those who had followed the cab from the O'Neal address, DA Investigator Koncilja lowered his head into his hands. "Can you go over the description of that young man again?" he asked. "Is there anything else known about him?" Investigator Koncilja was a retired and very savvy police sergeant and experienced detective who had worked countless narcotics and organized crime assignments.

Litton reviewed his notes, then went over the description again, including a description of the young man's clothing. When he reported that people at the O'Neal party said they thought the young man was a bit slow and likely gay, Koncilja spoke up. "That description perfectly matches my grandson," he said, obviously shaken by the disclosure.

His revelation, however, led to a new focus of investigative activity. Within days, detectives would elicit a confession from young Matthew Koncilja. They were also able to obtain a list of others involved in the crime. The leader of the conspiracy to rob the cab driver to obtain money to buy drugs was a 23-year-old Fort Carson soldier named Olin Ferrier. Ferrier reportedly recruited co-conspirators Maximo Ramos, 20, Raymond Terrones, 17, David Montoya, 18, and

25-year-old Koncilja. It was allegedly Ferrier who had fired the fatal shot when Chance balked at turning over the night's receipts. Montoya and Koncilja reached plea agreements with prosecutors for leniency in return for their testimony against the others.

Pueblo District Attorney Thiebaut withdrew his office from the case due to defendant Matthew Koncilja's familial relationship with Thiebaut's chief investigator. The El Paso County district attorney's office, headquartered in Colorado Springs, about 45 miles north of Pueblo, accordingly, handled the prosecution.

Ferrier was ultimately convicted of first degree murder and sentenced to life in prison. Others involved in the case received lesser but still severe sentences.

I knew Sergeant John Koncilja very well and worked closely with him on several cases over the years. He and I had traveled to Spain in 1986 to attend an FBI National Academy retraining session at the Spanish National Police School in the town of Avila, about 70 miles from Madrid. We got to know each other well during that trip, and the camaraderie we experienced there only intensified the respect we felt for each other.

Koncilja was a no-nonsense "super-cop" who could quickly recognize wrong-doing and would always do whatever was right to expose and deal with it. He was both feared and respected by criminals throughout the state due to his past involvement with the Colorado Organized Crime Task Force. I was very impressed by the rapidity with which he recognized, from a tenuous description given by witnesses, his beloved grandson as being one of those involved in the horrendous murder of the cab driver. I felt bad for him knowing how much it hurt him to bring his suspicions to the attention of the others in that strategy meeting. At that moment, I felt very proud of him, and very proud of my department. John Koncilja Jr. retired from the Pueblo Police Department in 1997. He passed away in 2021.

Officer Nick Heine Tragedy

It was a sweltering summer evening and the bars in the downtown area were packed with revelers, some of them quite intoxicated. Police presence was also high, particularly in the Union Avenue Historic District where the many music and drinking venues always presented a problem for officers around the 2 a.m. closing time as tavern owners and bouncers began ushering people out of the various establishments. The resulting surge of so many people onto the sidewalks and into the streets frequently meant fights, minor instances of property damage, public drinking and urination and loud and boisterous disturbances.

This Friday night, which had become an early Saturday morning, June 21, 2008, kept the team of officers assigned to patrol duties in the downtown area exceptionally busy. Officer Nicholas Heine, a seven-year veteran of the department, was one of those officers. An energetic and resourceful patrol officer who had displayed unique prowess at conducting complex initial investigations, 30-year-old Nick was on the fast track to becoming a detective. He was proud to be following in the footsteps of his mother, Corporal Pat Heine, a well-known police officer and crime prevention specialist who served as a detective with the Special Victims Section of the department.

It was just past 2 a.m. and Nick, along with several of his teammates, was bouncing from disturbance to disturbance in the area of C Street and Union Avenue, where hundreds of drunk and boisterous patrons from three of the more popular night clubs in the area were gathering. "It was one fight after another," one of the officers later said, "we could hardly keep up with it." In an effort to avoid physical arrests for the more minor skirmishes, which would take at least one officer off the street for an extended period of time, the officers were merely breaking up the minor fights and sending the combatants on their way.

Suddenly, a call was aired about a major disturbance involving multiple parties in the 300 block of Victoria Avenue, a little over a block away. Nick and several other officers began running in that direction, hoping to quell the fighting before anyone got injured. As the officers neared the intersection of C Street and Victoria, Nick slowed and staggered a bit. His teammates immediately recognized that he was in some distress, and as he began to fall, they grabbed him and eased him to the pavement. It was apparent that Nick was not breathing, and officers began performing CPR as they simultaneously radioed for a Fire Rescue response.

Nick was quickly rushed to Parkview Medical Center where emergency department personnel began frantically working to save his life. Police Chief Jim Billings was awakened, and he rushed to Parkview along with numerous on and off duty officers and firefighters—all concerned for the welfare of their friend and colleague. Nick's mother, Pat,

Police Officer Nicholas K. Heine

quickly arrived and was ushered to a private room with the chief to await a report from emergency department personnel. Minutes seemed like hours for those waiting there. Officers who had gathered outside the trauma room waited in hushed silence casting tear-filled glances at each other as it became increasingly evident that the ordeal was not going to end well.

Officer Nicholas Karl Heine was pronounced dead a little before 3 a.m. He was the 13th Pueblo Police Officer to die in the line of duty. The autopsy, conducted the next day, revealed that Nick had a congenital heart defect that put his heart in a fatally irregular rhythm. It was a condition no one knew he had, and the coroner reported that it could have happened "10 years prior, or 25 years in the future." Nick left behind his wife of seven years, Melissa, and daughters, Nichole, then age 7, and Rebecca, then age 4.

Police Chief Jim Billings never quite got over the death of Nick Heine. He later lamented that he had hoped and prayed that he would get through his term as chief without losing an officer to a line-of-duty death. He shook his head and whispered, "It didn't happen."

During his tenure, however, Billings did preside over numerous endeavors that brought widespread attention to the department. One was the acquisition of state accreditation for the agency, a feat that paved the way for national accreditation a few years later. Another was the hosting of the International Crime Stoppers Conference in 2001 which brought hundreds of law enforcement personnel from around the world to Pueblo.

Attendees of the Crime Stoppers Conference were treated to demonstrations of expertise from several of the department's specialized units. The Mounted Unit gave a demonstration of horseback assisted arrest, crowd control, escort maneuvers, and other skills, while the K-9 Unit gave a demonstration of contraband searches, obedience skills and armed confrontation. The Pueblo Police SWAT Team provided a program highlighting deployment tactics from an armored vehicle and the utilization of explosives to breach an entry into a barricaded structure. Conference goers also enjoyed a ranch rodeo and western style barbecue, along with a posh dinner at the Pueblo Convention Center.

The keynote speaker at the conference was John Walsh, host of popular television programs America's Most Wanted and America Fights Back. In the summer of 1981, Walsh's 6-year-old son, Adam, was abducted and later found murdered. Following the tragic event, Walsh and his wife Revé, turned their unbearable grief into positive energy to help missing and exploited children nationwide. Their untiring work eventually led to the passage of the Missing Children's Act of 1982, and the Missing Children's Assistance Act of 1984. The latter bill founded the National Center for Missing and Exploited Children, which maintains a hotline number for reporting a missing child, or the sighting of one.

Michael Gordon-Gibson, a sergeant with the London, England, Metropolitan Police who served four terms as President of Crime Stoppers International and headed the Crime Stoppers Unit at Scotland Yard, attended the Pueblo conference with a colleague from his agency, Detective Constable Daryl Gaudin. Following the conference, both officers publicly lauded the hospitality of Chief Billings and the Pueblo Police Department. Sergeant Gibson, who has subsequently visited numerous American cities and other cities throughout the world as part of his International Crime Stoppers responsibilities, recently told me that when he thinks of the United States, it's Pueblo that he visualizes because of the outstanding reception he and his colleague had received during their first visit to the USA.

Ether Man

Nathan Pruce was one of the biggest, strongest, and toughest officers employed by the Pueblo Police Department. He was also one of the sharpest and most intuitive. Like many Pueblo city employees, he chose to live in one of the city's quieter and more countrified suburbs rather than in the older and busier city limits. Nathan and his wife and son lived in Pueblo West, a few miles west of the larger city.

On October 6, 2009, Nathan, who worked the night shift in the Patrol Division, arose early. He dressed, had a light breakfast, then headed out to attend court. He had two subpoenas that day—one that morning for a minor licensing violation, the other in the early afternoon for a trial of a man named Robert H. Bruce whom Pruce had arrested a few months earlier. Bruce had been charged with being a Peeping Tom, a misdemeanor under Colorado law.

As he left his house and headed for his car which was parked in front of his home because his garage was full of furniture stored there while some interior decorating work was taking place, he noticed something strange in front of his garage. It appeared to be a propane tank.

"That's odd," he thought. He cautiously approached the tank and saw that a valve on top of the tank was turned on, and a hose had been fed from the tank under the garage door and into the garage. He could also smell the unmistakable and very strong odor of propane emanating from the garage. He immediately realized the danger of an explosion should someone cause a spark by entering the garage or starting a vehicle if one were inside. He instinctively knew someone had set a trap designed to kill him and perhaps his whole family. He immediately evacuated his wife and son from the home and called 911. He also called the Pueblo police dispatch center.

Within minutes the Pueblo West Fire Department was on scene, followed by Sheriff Kirk Taylor and several Pueblo County deputies. Pueblo police officers were not far behind. The fire crew cautiously dismantled the makeshift bomb, aired out the garage, and confirmed that even the slightest spark—even a static electrical spark—could have leveled at least a portion of the structure and killed or severely injured anyone inside. The Sheriff's Office began an attempted murder investigation.

Pruce's intuition immediately kicked in. He would later say, "I just knew Robert H. Bruce was the one who laid the deadly trap—he wanted to kill me before I could testify against him." He relayed his feelings to Sheriff Taylor and to the city officers present at the scene. As Chief Billings was out of town that morning, I was acting chief. After consulting with Sheriff Taylor, he and I decided our departments would conduct a dual investigation, utilizing the talents and resources of both departments.

Robert Bruce was the only suspect to emerge early in the inquiry, but everyone at the scene had the same question—"Why would a man charged with a relatively minor misdemeanor as peeping into windows risk killing a police officer to escape conviction?" It just didn't seem logical. But we all knew we were not dealing with a logical mind. I assigned Detective Mark Bravo to the case with instructions to check the morning's movements of Robert Howard Bruce.

Robert Howard Bruce— the elusive Ether Man serial rapist.

It was quickly discovered that Bruce, who came to Pueblo from Albuquerque, New Mexico, had no criminal history in Pueblo or Albuquerque, but he had failed to appear that morning for his court hearing on the Peeping Tom charge. A bench warrant was issued for his arrest and information was relayed to all law enforcement units to be on the lookout for him. At about 8 p.m. that evening he was found passed out in his car parked on a service road behind the north side Kmart store. He was extremely incapacitated by alcohol consumption and after being treated on scene by the Pueblo Fire Department, was rushed to Parkview Hospital.

Officers at the scene noted a large, depressed ring on the fabric of his car's back seat that indicated something round and heavy had recently rested there. It was found that the size of the ring corresponded exactly with the size of the base of the propane tank used in the Pruce case. Robert Howard Bruce was arrested for his failure to appear in court and, following his recovery from his alcohol binge, was questioned about the attempted murder of Officer Nathan Pruce and the Pruce family. His car was towed to the police station and a warrant was obtained to search it. Several items of evidence found in the vehicle convinced the officers their suspicions about the homicide attempt were correct.

Though he denied involvement in the attempted murder, his answers to questions regarding his morning movements and items of interest found in his vehicle gave officers probable cause to charge him with the more serious crime of attempted murder. At a meeting with the District Attorney's office, Detective Mark Bravo requested permission to go to Albuquerque to further pursue information about Bruce. Prosecutors indicated that would not be necessary as they had developed enough information to likely prevail in court on the charge of attempted murder.

Bravo was not satisfied—he believed there was much more to the case than an attempt to evade a conviction for a relatively minor Peeping Tom charge. He theorized Bruce likely feared having his DNA entered into a law enforcement database which would automatically be done should he be convicted of a sexually motivated crime like window peeping. Bravo was given permission by his brother, Sergeant Eric Bravo, who was supervisor of the police department's crimes against persons section, to make the trip to Albuquerque. Chief Billings, who had by then returned to town, approved Sgt. Eric Bravo's approval of the trip and soon a contingent of officers from the police department and the sheriff's office was on the way to the New Mexico city.

After consultation with Albuquerque investigators, the Pueblo team contacted Bruce's ex-wife who still resided in that city. The interview with her at first revealed nothing of particular interest until Bravo mentioned that she appeared to be afraid of Bruce, and asked why that was. Her reply gave the officers the break they needed. She said she was afraid of her ex-husband because she suspected him for a number of reasons, of being the "Ether Man." "Who is the Ether Man?" Bravo asked. She said the Ether Man was an unknown serial rapist who had terrorized the Albuquerque area for months. It all started to make sense. Bravo immediately recontacted detectives with the Albuquerque Police Department and inquired about the Ether Man. He discovered the Ether Man was a name the local press had given to an unknown serial rapist who had attacked several women over a period of several years in the Albuquerque area.

Bravo provided Albuquerque detectives the information gleaned from Bruce's wife. Albuquerque officers provided Bravo with the information needed to obtain a warrant for Bruce's DNA and the Pueblo officers returned home. Once back in Pueblo, Bravo obtained a search warrant and had a blood sample drawn from Bruce and forwarded to Bravo's New Mexico counterparts. A few days later Albuquerque officers called the Pueblo Police Department and asked if Pueblo was still holding Bruce. When told Bruce was still in custody, they could barely conceal their excitement. "Well, keep him, he's our guy—we'll be right up to Pueblo.

It turned out Bruce's DNA matched DNA found at several of Albuquerque's crime scenes. Bravo was informed that the method of operation of the elusive Ether Man was to approach women in the dark or from behind so they could never positively identify him. The victim was then rendered unconscious by having a chemically soaked rag held tightly over their mouths and noses. They were then brutally raped. It was never positively determined that the chemical substance was ether, but the ether story was close enough for the New Mexico press to run with it. It also sparked some additional investigation in Pueblo because two recent unsolved attacks of woman in Pueblo were committed by the use of chemical-soaked rags to render them unconscious before they were assaulted. In one of those attacks the chemical used was so caustic it caused a severe chemical burn around the lower part of the victim's face. That substance was never identified. As cases in the Albuquerque area progressed it was speculated that ether may have been used in some, but chloroform was likely used in other attacks.

As the Robert Bruce investigation continued, other states began showing interest. Both Oklahoma and Texas reported a series of sexual assaults perpetrated after an assailant rendered victims unconscious by use of chemical substances prior to the assaults. Time after time, Bruce's DNA gave authorities in those states the key to solving their cases.

Bruce was eventually tried and convicted of the attempted murder of Corporal Nathan Pruce, and in 2011 was sentenced to 64 years in prison. As there was limited direct evidence in the two local assaults, prosecution was declined until he could be tried in New Mexico. His numerous sexual assaults in three states, other than Colorado, earned him an additional 333 years in prison—156 years in New Mexico alone. It is extremely unlikely that he will ever be released to prey upon others.

In February 2011, Albuquerque officers returned to Pueblo to present the Pueblo Police Department with a plaque recognizing the hard work by Detective Mark Bravo and the Pueblo Police Detective Bureau in pursuing an airtight case that allowed the successful closure of sexual assault cases in four states. Bruce is now serving his sentence in an undisclosed federal penitentiary in another state.

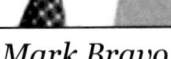

Mark Bravo   *Eric Bravo*

Mark Bravo has since retired. His brother, Eric was promoted to captain and assumed command of the Crimes Against Persons Section, which he held for several years. Sadly, he passed away after a courageous fight against leukemia in 2023. Both the "Bravo Boys" had incredible careers with the Pueblo Police Department that earned them each the reputation as "Super cops," or extraordinary crimefighters.

New, modern police station

Arguably, the most significant accomplishment of the Billings administration was the long-awaited and much anticipated new police building. The need for a modern new facility had been bantered about for several years but did not receive the support from the city administration necessary for it to become a reality. Budgetary concerns were frequently given as reasons for stalling or derailing serious efforts to approve construction of a multimillion-dollar building. It was not until 2008, with the backing of a forward-thinking local citizens' group, that serious plans for such a structure were forged.

Following numerous public meetings, planning sessions and an aggressive public information campaign, Chief Billings was able to garner the community support necessary for the new building project to move forward.

Once approved by the city council, work progressed quickly and within two years the new building, housing both police and municipal courts, was opened in the 200 block of South Main Street. Guided tours for the general public and representatives of the press were very positive.

The new Municipal Justice Center opened to great excitement in the community in 2010.

Chief Billings announced his retirement in February 2011. He had served honorably for almost 13 years and had guided the department through some demanding times that required the strength and compassion of a true leader. The appointment of a new chief later that year heralded controversy and some tumultuous times for the Pueblo PD.

RECENT YEARS

Following the retirement of Chief Billings in early 2011, a new chief, Luis Velez, was appointed to the position. Velez's appointment came almost five years after he retired from the same position with the Colorado Springs Police Department following what the *Colorado Springs Gazette* newspaper called "a scandal involving the revelation that more than 20,000 pieces of evidence in nearly 10,000 cases had been improperly disposed."

A vote of no-confidence in their chief by Colorado Springs officers followed disclosure of the scandal which placed thousands of criminal cases in jeopardy. Many are still being worked through the court system; so, it is unknown exactly how many cases may be dismissed because of the lack of evidence. Though not directly involved in the improper destruction or improper release of evidence, Velez was criticized for a lack of leadership in overseeing the department's property and evidence unit. Only he knows whether the scandal unfolding at that time had any bearing on his decision to retire from the CSPD.

In defending Velez's appointment to the top cop position in Pueblo, City Council President Ray Aguilera said the Colorado Springs scandal did not factor into Pueblo's decision to hire him. Aguilera was quoted by the *Pueblo Chieftain* as saying, "We think he's the right guy for Pueblo."

Chief Luis Velez

In Velez's six years as Pueblo's chief, he strove to improve officer training, and he succeeded in acquiring new and improved equipment and vehicles. But he faced criticism for reducing the number of officers assigned to the Gang Unit, and for an internally unpopular restructuring of the Patrol Division. He was also criticized for not living in Pueblo.

In January 2016, Pueblo's police union, Local 537 of the International Brotherhood of Police Officers, conducted a survey of employee satisfaction with department leadership. Of the 99 officers who completed the survey, 94 indicated they had "no confidence" in the chief.

An open letter released by the police union after the survey results were published in the *Chieftain*, laid out numerous complaints about the chief's management of the department. It reported, "Chief Velez has been here now for nearly five years. We admit that he has done some positive things, but crime is up, morale is down, and we have fewer officers now than when he started." The letter concluded by saying the union board appreciated the fact that Velez had been looking forward to his "not too distant retirement," and that the employees of the City of Pueblo, specifically the police union, can only say, "Godspeed, and the sooner the better."

Chief Velez announced his retirement from the Pueblo department in July 2017. He had been plagued with some minor health problems during the latter years of his tenure, but he would later tell the *Chieftain* that he came to the decision to retire not because of health concerns but because he felt the department was in a "good place," and it was the "right time to step away." He further said his health factored into his decision to retire but only as a secondary issue.

Perhaps the biggest achievement of Velez's administration, and the one of which he said he was most proud, was the acquisition of National Accreditation for the Department. Accreditation is awarded to agencies that demonstrate compliance with a plethora of national standards promulgated by an organization called the National Commission on Accreditation for Law Enforcement Agencies (CALEA). The number of standards varies by agency depending on several factors, including the number of officers employed, the mission of the agency, the population of the community served and the types of assets employed by the agency.

CALEA was created in 1979 through the joint efforts of the country's major law enforcement executive associations as a credentialing authority for public safety agencies. CALEA accreditation demonstrates to the public that the agency has met those standards of professional excellence. Accreditation can also protect an agency from liability exposure when those standards are followed. Accreditation status must be reevaluated periodically to assure continued compliance.

Chief Velez praised the hard work of every member of the agency over a four-year period to make accreditation possible and told the local press that "of over 18,000 law enforcement agencies in the country, only five percent are nationally accredited. We've joined an elite group, and I'm very proud of that," he said. Pueblo Police Captain Kenny Rider, acting under Chief Velez's direction, had the arduous task of managing the department's successful efforts to attain accredited status.

The other accomplishment of which Velez was proud was the acquisition of body cameras for every officer. Body cameras are designed to record an officer's view of situations involving their interaction with members of the public. The cameras can disclose wrongdoing by the officer, but can also prevent groundless complaints against the police.

Velez said the biggest challenge that he faced as chief was the manpower issue. "The manpower situation when I got here was not optimal to begin with, but for the next four years it went downhill," he told the *Chieftain*. "Those were dark hours for us. We were having to force our officers to work overtime. We were doing that on a wholesale basis. It was just a horrific situation. Luckily, we were able to get through it because the employees didn't riot."

Appointment of Chief Davenport

Following Chief Velez's retirement in 2017, the city elevated Deputy Chief Troy Davenport to the top position. Davenport began his career with the Pueblo County Sheriff's Office in 1989. He was hired by the Pueblo Police Department in 1994, and he served time in virtually every division of the department until 2011 when he was promoted to Deputy Chief following my retirement.

Police Chief Troy Davenport

Upon assuming the top position, Chief Davenport established a list of what he wanted to accomplish as soon as possible. At the top of the list was to strengthen the Investigations Bureau so major crimes and suspected criminal activity could be properly addressed. He appointed Sgt. Eric Bravo to head a task force of the department's sharpest detectives to resolve problematic cases left over from the previous administration. He recognized that to be successful in bringing those cases to closure, the Crimes Against Persons Section, as well as the narcotics and gang components, which had been weakened during the previous administration, would need more resources. He vowed to do all he could to get those resources restored.

Chief Davenport knew that Chief Velez had tried hard, to no avail, to convince city administration that full staffing was needed in those specialty units as well as in patrol operations. Velez had been stymied by a lack of funds in the city budget. Davenport therefore approached the city council with a request to establish a special sales tax to fund enhanced public safety efforts. Astonishingly, likely because of his persistence and the support of prominent citizens, a tax initiative passed a vote of the people and additional money was made available to address the critical needs he had pointed out.

Accordingly, the department was able to increase participation in the FBI Safe Streets Task Force, which resulted in record numbers of felony arrests and seizures of large amounts of contraband and illicit funds during the first two years under Davenport's leadership. The chief had also strengthened community-oriented policing practices by allowing individual officers to participate in the planning process. Patrol officers were encouraged to identify crime problems specific to their individual areas of responsibility, and then suggest solutions.

Davenport recently told me he was proud that the innovative community-oriented policing philosophy was enthusiastically embraced by almost every department member. He noted that portions of the city experienced a noticeable reduction in crime and disorder due to the aggressive participation of officers in strategies they helped to develop.

Another interesting and wildly successful project initiated by Chief Davenport during the first year of his administration was the deployment of drones to assist with various police operations. Drones are ground controlled aircraft equipped with video or photographic capabilities designed to provide quicker and safer observational resources for officers engaged in potentially dangerous field operations. Pueblo police drones have been used to find crime suspects who have fled from police and to search for missing persons. Drones provide officers with an overhead view of accident and crime scenes they otherwise would not have. Drones can also greatly assist tactical officers in managing critical incidents involving hostage taking, barricaded suspects or other life-threatening situations.

Chief Davenport recently told me the biggest advantage of deploying a drone in a police operation is the officer safety factor. A drone can quickly and safely locate an armed suspect and prevent the necessity of officers exposing themselves to danger by searching for suspects blindly on foot. Several officers have been trained to operate or pilot the drones, and others are in training.

Troy Davenport served only four years as department chief. He was successful in establishing policies that allowed officers working with federal authorities to remove increased numbers of violent criminals from Pueblo's streets. He also established a criminal intelligence section to focus on gang activity, which had increased since the years of the Billings administration. Traffic fatalities had been on the rise before Davenport was appointed chief; he strengthened traffic enforcement activities, especially DUI enforcement, which decreased the number of fatal and critical injury traffic crashes. Fatalities had been on the rise before he was appointed chief.

Chief Davenport's retirement came as a surprise to many in the community following his mere four years in the position. He had regained the trust of the department following a period of uncertainty. He was well liked by the community as well as by the department members.

Chris Noeller Becomes Chief

Chief Davenport retired in 2021 and Deputy Chief Stephen "Chris" Noeller was appointed to the top position after a nationwide search for the best candidate for the job. Noeller was a sharp and aggressive officer who had distinguished himself in the many positions he held with the agency since he was hired in 1996. He had served as a patrol officer, a detective, a member of the DEA Southern Colorado drug task force and a member of the SWAT Team. He had been an outspoken proponent of increased training opportunities for officers and better equipment for specialized units.

Noeller's appointment, however, was not devoid of controversy. During his tenure as deputy chief, he had been the subject of two investigations stemming from complaints by fellow officers. Those complaints involved allegations of bullying, intimidation, cursing at subordinates and favoritism. It was also alleged that Noeller had engaged in discrimination against officers of Hispanic heritage, but no specific instances of discriminatory actions were found to exist.

Though Noeller's temper and intensity was a consistent theme in the complaints against him, no adverse employment action caused by his conduct was found. The *Pueblo Chieftain* reported that Mayor Nick Gradisar said Noeller would not have been appointed if any of the comprehensive investigations into his conduct had found anything to be disqualifying. The mayor said he was confident Noeller's overly intense leadership style and perceived bullying attitude would soften as he began his duties in the chief's office. Mayor Gradisar further pointed out that Noeller's education and extensive training in management and leadership practices, as well as his exposure to virtually every aspect of the department, would likely make him an excellent chief.

In talking with individual police officers following Chief Noeller's appointment, I found a few did not care for him but the majority accepted him as a fair and conscientious administrator with whom they are proud to serve.

The Future

The world has gotten a lot smaller during the past decades. Incidents that occur in cities a thousand miles or more away can influence public confidence in local institutions as surely as can incidents occurring next door. When a school shooting occurs in Uvalde, Texas, active shooter protocols of departments all over the country are called into question. When a serial killer escapes justice for more than a few days on the East Coast, local police are questioned about their readiness to handle a similar situation. And when an incident of police brutality or racial discrimination is reported hundreds of miles from home, local officers are placed under intense scrutiny.

The easing of penalties for criminal conduct and the refusal of radical prosecutors in major cities to aggressively prosecute perpetrators of egregious crimes has made the job of police officer more difficult and frustrating by the day. When I competed for a position with the Pueblo Police Department in late 1969, there were over 400 candidates for six available jobs. Today there are less than 200 applicants for thirty or more jobs. It seems like fewer people want to be cops anymore.

But I am an optimist. I feel the pendulum will swing the other way as citizens tire of being victims of crime and business owners can no longer endure the onslaught of criminal activity that makes it difficult or impossible to turn a profit. I am proud of the men and women of the Pueblo Police Department, and I salute those who have stuck with the agency through good times and bad.

With technological advances occurring at a rapid pace, and with forward thinking and innovative people in charge, I am confident the future of the Pueblo Police Department is secure. Time will march on, philosophies will evolve, police tactics will change, officers will come and go, and community standards will fluctuate, but the department will continue to grow and to keep pace with the changing times as it has for the past 150 years.

John P. Ercul

Born September 19, 1947
Pueblo, Colorado

End of Watch
October 13, 2024
Pueblo, Colorado